For Microsoft Windows® 95
and Windows NT® Operating Systems

Microsoft®
by Publisher 97
Design

Luisa Simone

PUBLISHED BY
Microsoft Press
A Division of Microsoft Corporation
One Microsoft Way
Redmond, Washington 98052-6399

Library of Congress Cataloging-in-Publication Data
Simone, Luisa, 1955-
    Microsoft Publisher 97 by design / Luisa Simone. -- 4th ed.
       p.   cm.
    Rev. ed. of: Microsoft Publisher by design. 1996.
    Includes index.
    ISBN 1-57231-355-2
    1. Microsoft Publisher. 2. Desktop publishing. I. Simone,
Luisa, 1955- Microsoft Publisher by design. II. Title.
Z253.532.M53S58   1997
686.2'2544536--dc21

                                        96-45662
                                         CIP

Printed and bound in the United States of America.

1 2 3 4 5 6 7 8 9 QEQE 2 1 0 9 8 7

Distributed to the book trade in Canada by Macmillan of Canada, a division of Canada Publishing Corporation.

A CIP catalogue record for this book is available from the British Library.

Microsoft Press books are available through booksellers and distributors worldwide. For further information about international editions, contact your local Microsoft Corporation office. Or contact Microsoft Press International directly at fax (206) 936-7329.

Macintosh and TrueType are registered trademarks of Apple Computer, Inc. Microsoft, Windows, and Windows NT are registered trademarks and MSN is a trademark of Microsoft Corporation. Other product and company names mentioned herein may be the trademarks of their respective owners.

Acquisitions Editor: Kimberlea Fryer
Project Editor: Patricia Draher
Technical Editor: Linda Rose Ebenstein

To J.V.S.—otherwise known as Mom

Contents

Part 2   Design Projects

Acknowledgments

Publishing is a collaborative art, and so, no book is complete until the author thanks all the people who contributed their time and talent to it.

Thanks to my editor, Patricia Draher, and technical editor, Linda Rose Ebenstein, for the attention they lavished on this project. The thousands (okay, hundreds) of decisions they made improved the accuracy and language of the book.

Thanks also to Amy Peppler Adams of designLab and Bill Teel, who took an already great-looking design and made it better.

Finally, for her invaluable help with the design projects, including writing imaginative copy, generating preliminary layouts, and acquiescing to the changes I made to her work, a special thank you goes to my good friend Robbin Juris.

Introduction

Preferred by over 1 million people, Microsoft Publisher has proven that a desktop publishing program can be powerful *and* easy to use. Microsoft Publisher 97 doesn't fix what ain't broken, so you'll find many familiar tools in this version of the program. You can create sophisticated designs using the automated help offered by PageWizard design assistants, the instant effects generated with WordArt, and the preformatted objects found in the Design Gallery. Publisher can handle just about any design task, thanks to its robust and flexible layout tools, such as special page impositions for books and posters, user-defined text styles, movable guides, and custom rotation. Producing the final printed version of a document is still blissfully simple regardless of whether you are printing to a standard desktop printer, setting up a document for a remote color digital printer, preparing a file for high-resolution black-and-white output, or generating two-color separations for a commercial printing press.

What's New in Microsoft Publisher 97

Though many of its key features remain unchanged, Publisher 97 boasts several enhancements. You can now create custom BorderArt patterns simply by importing an image into the BorderArt dialog box. And radically expanded collections of clip art (over 5200 images) and fonts (over 150 fonts) give you more design choices than ever before. But without a doubt, the most significant improvements to Publisher 97 are its new abilities to generate mail merge documents and Web publications.

Publisher 97 and the World Wide Web

When you choose the Web Page layout, Publisher modifies its tool set and provides functions you need to create electronic—rather than traditional paper-based—documents. For example, the hyperlink function lets you add interactive controls to your Web publications. Using hyperlinks, your readers can move to different pages within the current Web site, surf to other sites, send you email, and even download specified files.

Behind the scenes, Publisher automatically produces HTML-format Web documents that are geared to perform (read "download") as efficiently as possible. For example, when creating a design, you can insert images in any of the file formats that Publisher normally supports, including resolution-independent vector clip art and high-resolution bitmapped pictures. When Publisher generates the final Web document, it converts the artwork to a VGA-resolution GIF picture, the format supported by all graphical Web browsers.

Powerful Mail Merge Functions

Publisher 97 takes the drudgery out of addressing large—or small—mailings. The new mail merge feature can take advantage of internally generated address lists as well as data sources created in other applications, such as Microsoft Access, Word, and Excel. The mail merge feature lets you insert a placeholder, called a field code, for information such as a name or address. At print time, the field codes are replaced by names and addresses from your data source. Because you can customize fields in an address list and filter and sort the entries, you have the power to store, retrieve, and massage all sorts of information. For a personal touch, you can automatically insert the first name of the addressee in the salutation of a marketing piece. In addition, you can use selection criteria to send a mailing to only a subset of your customers. You can even print your mailings in zip code order to receive discounts on postal costs.

Why This Book Is Easy to Use

This book is not a manual, but it does contain valuable reference material. The first part of the book, "Publisher 97 Fundamentals," provides a guide to the features and tools that Publisher offers. Each chapter in this section focuses on a related group of tools. For example, Chapter 4, "Layout Tools," discusses the functions needed to build a cohesive page design, such as object positioning, grouping, alignment, and rotation. Whenever appropriate, these chapters also include technical information to help you understand how Publisher functions within the context of other computer-based graphics applications. For example, Chapter 11, "Creating Documents for the World Wide Web," explains why and how Publisher's wide range of formatting options must be restricted to produce well-behaved HTML documents for the Web.

The second part of the book, "Design Projects," illustrates essential desktop publishing concepts, teaches fundamental skills, and elucidates the elements of good design. In this edition, the design projects have been revamped and expanded. If there is a faster or smarter way to accomplish a task in Publisher 97, the design projects take advantage of it. Projects have been added to the book to showcase Publisher's new mail merge and Web publishing tools. Small businesses, families, nonprofit organizations, and individuals will find all of these projects inspiring—whether used as step-by-step blueprints or as the starting point for original designs.

The projects give you the opportunity to put design theory into practice. To show you how content drives design, each project contains text and pictures that reflect real-life business and personal situations. The tutorials illustrate, in a way that no description can, the synergy among Publisher's various functions.

Desktop publishing terms are defined in the glossary. The concepts described by these terms will become familiar to you as you develop your own publications.

A Graphical Approach to Explaining Application Features and Design Concepts

Even a cursory inspection will reveal that *Microsoft Publisher 97 by Design* is chock-full of illustrations. This visual presentation of information not only is aesthetically appealing but also stresses the procedural nature of much of the book. For example, instead of simply telling you how to use a dialog box, this format *shows* you how to use a dialog box by annotating an illustration of the computer screen with numbered steps.

Much of the ancillary information appears in a separate Tip column in the left-hand margin of the page. This arrangement allows the step-by-step instructions to proceed uninterrupted and lets you more easily find certain types of information by looking for these icons:

Power Tips give you the inside scoop on advanced functions or shortcuts in the program. Within the project chapters, Power Tips offer design advice.

Troubleshooting Tips answer frequently asked questions and warn you about potential problems.

Cross-references point you toward more information on a given topic.

Keyboard Shortcuts provide the keystroke equivalents for frequently used commands.

If I've done my job, you should be able to use this book in three ways:

@ As a step-by-step instructional guide to Publisher's tools and functions

@ As a reference book that explains computer graphics concepts and technology

@ As a design tutorial for a wide variety of publications

What You Need to Begin Using Publisher 97

To use Microsoft Publisher 97, you need to be running Microsoft Windows 95 or Microsoft Windows NT version 3.51 or later. The absolute minimum hardware requirements include the following:

@ 386DX processor

@ 6 MB of memory (12 MB for NT)

@ Hard disk with 9.5 MB of free disk space

- VGA monitor

- Mouse

- A CD-ROM drive or a 3.5-inch floppy disk drive, depending on whether you purchase the CD-ROM version or the disk version of the software

If you plan to create large documents, or if you want Publisher to perform quickly, you'll need more processing power. That translates to a 486 or Pentium processor, 8 MB of memory (preferably more), a 256-color or 24-bit color monitor and video adapter, and *lots* of hard-disk space. (At least 116 MB is highly recommended for the CD-ROM version of the software, and at least 73 MB is highly recommended for the disk version.) Depending on your input and output needs, you might also require a graphics-capable printer and a TWAIN-compliant scanner.

A Desire to Experiment

I've said it before, and it's still true: to become a competent designer, you need a little something more than hardware and software—you need the willingness to experiment. You can rely on PageWizards, the Design Gallery, and special effects such as BorderArt and WordArt to jump-start the design process and to serve as a source of visual inspiration, but Publisher's powerful tools ultimately let you develop your own design ideas. Luckily, the tools are so easy to use that the experimentation often feels more like play than work.

This book encourages you to exercise your creativity and develop confidence in your own aesthetic judgments. By the time you've finished reading this book, you'll look at the publications that surround you with new eyes—as designs that you too can create.

PART 1

Publisher 97 Fundamentals

Windows 95 supports long, descriptive filenames.

The Format toolbar makes Publisher look and feel like Microsoft Office applications.

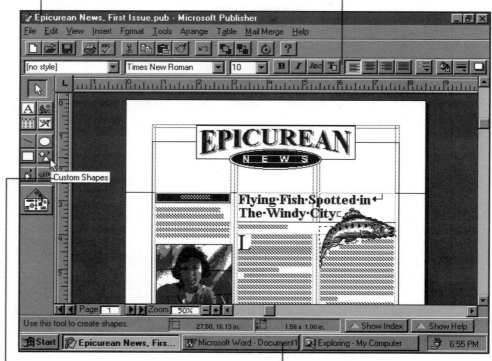

ToolTips appear whenever the mouse pointer is positioned over a button.

The Windows 95 taskbar provides instant access to other applications.

Microsoft Publisher 97 and the Windows 95 Interface

Can I run Publisher 97 with Windows 3.1? No. If you want to run Publisher 97 (or Publisher version 3), you must upgrade to Windows 95. Publisher 97 won't work with earlier versions of Windows.

Microsoft Publisher 97 is designed to run with Microsoft Windows 95. The synergy between Publisher and Windows 95 allows you to work efficiently when creating documents.

As you can see in the illustration on the facing page, many key features are right on the surface—in the user interface of the program. This chapter acquaints you with Publisher's interface and the enhancements offered by Windows 95.

Moving Around the Screen: Working with a Mouse

Like the computer keyboard, a mouse is an input device. While you use a keyboard to type information, you move the mouse to point at an object on the screen and you click a mouse button to select that object. Most mice have two buttons, although a few have three.

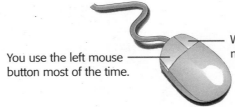

You use the left mouse button most of the time.

Windows 95 takes advantage of the right mouse button to display shortcut menus.

The mouse pointer moves in response to the motion of your mouse. Although the pointer usually appears on screen as an outlined arrow, it can, and frequently does, change shape, depending on the current tool you are using or operation you are performing, as the following illustration shows.

 Use standard Windows 95 pointers instead of Publisher's helpful pointers. The pointers shown on this page constitute a unique set of context-sensitive and self-explanatory pointers provided by Publisher. You can disable these pointers and use standard Windows 95 pointers instead by turning off the Use Helpful Pointers check box on the General tab in the Options dialog box. (Choose Options on the Tools menu.)

Standard pointer: lets you select tools or objects

Move pointer: lets you move objects

I-beam pointer: lets you select text and position the pointer to insert text

Crossbar pointer: lets you draw frames for your objects

Resize pointers: let you change the size of objects

Crop pointer: lets you trim pictures

You'll need to learn four mouse operations before you can work efficiently: click, drag, double-click, and right-click.

Four Ways to Use the Mouse		
Action	**Description**	**Primary Purpose**
Click	Clicking is the most basic mouse action in Publisher. Position the mouse pointer over an element and then lightly press and release the left mouse button. Unless otherwise noted, always click the left mouse button.	Selecting an object, a menu command, or another element.
Drag	Press and hold the left button without releasing it. Move the mouse to a new location. Release the mouse button.	Moving the object beneath the mouse pointer. Drawing frames.

Action	Description	Primary Purpose
Double-Click	Click the left mouse button twice with hardly a pause between clicks and without moving the mouse.	Opening an application, a window, or another element.
Right-Click	Click the right mouse button and release it.	Opening a shortcut menu that pertains to the clicked element. The menu commands vary depending on the type of object you select.

Starting Publisher

Now that you understand how to use a mouse, you can start Publisher. Windows 95 gives you several options at startup time. You can double-click the program icon found in the Microsoft Publisher folder. You can even create shortcut icons in order to start Publisher directly from the desktop. But the Start button is the simplest way to load Publisher.

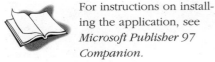

For instructions on installing the application, see *Microsoft Publisher 97 Companion*.

Open the Microsoft Publisher Application

1 Install Microsoft Publisher on your hard disk.

2 Click the Start button and open the Programs menu.

3 Click the icon for Microsoft Publisher. After you complete the Introduction To Publisher, Publisher's Startup dialog box appears, providing you with four tabbed options.

For more information about PageWizard design assistants, see Chapter 13.

Why can't I find a Templates tab in my Startup dialog box? Publisher doesn't create a Template folder or a Templates tab during the installation process. The first time you save a publication as a template, however, Publisher will automatically create a Template folder and a Templates tab. If you are upgrading from a previous version of Publisher, and have templates stored on your hard disk, Publisher will preserve the Template folder and Templates tab.

Open the Microsoft Publisher Application *(continued)*

This option starts you off with a blank page and lets you build your original design from the ground up.

This option retrieves a file that you previously stored on disk.

This option lets you select a template to use as the starting point for a new publication.

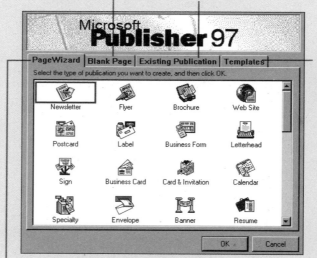

PageWizard design assistants create formatted documents for you.

 Select a tab to choose an option.

Start smarter with shortcuts. Shortcuts let you start Publisher directly from the Windows 95 desktop. You can work more efficiently by creating multiple shortcuts to Publisher and renaming each shortcut to reflect the nature of a different project. For example, if one of your projects is a newsletter, you could name its shortcut *Newsletter*. After renaming the shortcuts, assign a different working folder and a different shortcut key to each duplicate icon.

Customize the Startup Process

1 Open the folder that contains the Publisher software. The folder is typically named Microsoft Publisher and is located in the Program Files folder, but it may have a different name and location if you changed the defaults during installation.

2 Drag a copy of the Microsoft Publisher icon labeled Mspub.exe from the Microsoft Publisher folder to the Windows 95 desktop.

3 Right-click the shortcut icon.

4 Select Properties.

5 Select the Shortcut tab.

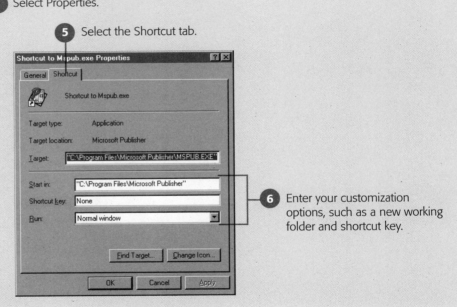

6 Enter your customization options, such as a new working folder and shortcut key.

Communicating with Publisher: Menus and Commands

Most applications running under Microsoft Windows 95, including Publisher, display a menu bar at the top of the window that enables you to perform tasks.

A triangle next to a command indicates that this command is actually the title of another menu, called a cascading menu, which contains more choices. The second menu cascades from the first. Highlighting such a command, by positioning the mouse cursor over it without clicking it, automatically displays the cascading menu.

When you click a menu title, a drop-down list of commands appears.

Think of the menu bar as the top level of an outline, with related items (or commands) appearing under each title.

 What if I open a menu by mistake? To close the menu without issuing a command, press the Esc key or click anywhere else on the screen.

 The keyboard is faster than the mouse. You can also operate Publisher using the keyboard. Keyboard equivalents are shown to the right of the command names on the menus that drop down from the menu bar. Keystrokes are often faster than the mouse if your hands are already on the keyboard, or if you must perform repetitive tasks. For example, you can quickly save a file by holding down the Ctrl key and typing *s* (Ctrl-S).

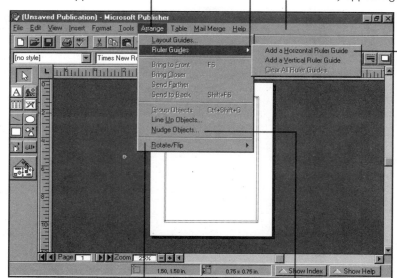

A command is executed when you click it.

A check mark (not shown) placed next to a command on a menu signifies that the command is currently active. Click the command to remove the check mark and deactivate the command. This type of command, which you can click on and off, is called a toggle.

A command followed by an ellipsis (three dots) signals that Publisher will open a dialog box when you choose the command. The dialog box opens because Publisher needs more information before it can execute your command.

Providing Requested Information: Dialog Box Options

Whenever Microsoft Publisher needs information from you to complete a command, it presents you with a window called a dialog box. Within a dialog box, use the mouse to select options and to set the insertion point for typing text.

List boxes and drop-down list boxes present you with all of the available choices for a given function. Open a drop-down list box by clicking the arrow. Then select (highlight) the item you need from the list by clicking it.

Command buttons allow you to select a command, cancel an operation, or call up additional options. The most important command button in a dialog box is the OK button; none of the choices you make will take effect until you click OK. In some dialog boxes, a Close button serves the same function as OK.

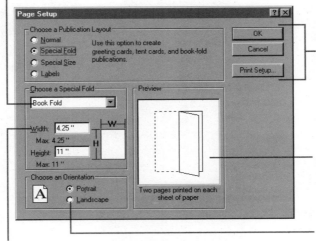

Preview areas let you see how the current settings will affect your publication.

Text boxes require that you type in information. The text box must be selected before you type. When a text box is selected, the characters in it are highlighted, or the insertion point appears in it. To select a text box, click anywhere within it. A single click places the insertion point in the text box. A double click highlights some or all of the characters in the text box.

Option buttons and check boxes (not shown) are toggles that can be clicked on or off with a mouse.

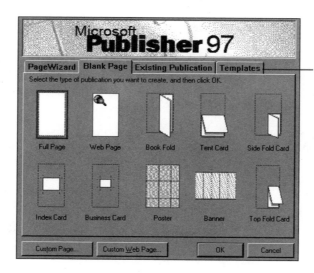

The options you want might be in distinct but related dialog boxes. Windows 95 organizes these dialog boxes with tabs. Select a tab to bring it to the front of the stack and to reveal a new set of options.

Design Alternatives: Toolbars and Tools

A toolbar works in much the same way as a menu, but uses icons instead of words to represent the various functions. The main toolbar, located along the left-hand side of the screen, provides the tools to create and select objects.

 Keeping tools active. Normally after you select a tool and create an object, Publisher automatically reverts to the Pointer tool. This can be inconvenient when you want to draw a series of text objects, picture objects, or geometric shapes. To keep a tool active while you create several objects, hold down the Ctrl key when you select the tool. To return to normal working mode, click the Pointer tool.

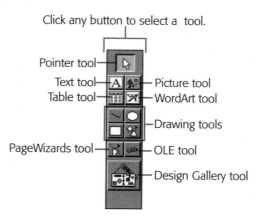

Click any button to select a tool.

Pointer tool
Text tool — Picture tool
Table tool — WordArt tool
— Drawing tools
PageWizards tool — OLE tool
— Design Gallery tool

Use the toolbar to identify the currently selected object. Sometimes when you are working with a publication—especially one based on a template or generated with a PageWizard design assistant—you may have trouble determining whether an object is a text frame, a picture frame, or a WordArt frame. The Format toolbar can help you correctly identify the currently selected object. For example, text formatting options only appear when a text frame is selected.

Publisher also has toolbars that appear along the top of the window under the menu bar. The Standard toolbar makes Publisher look and behave like other Microsoft Office applications, such as Microsoft Word and Microsoft Excel. This toolbar contains frequently used functions, such as starting and saving a file.

Other toolbars are task specific and change depending on which tool or object is active.

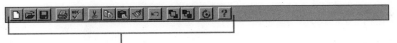

The Standard toolbar contains frequently used functions.

Tools to change text attributes are available when the Text tool or Table tool is active (or when a text or table object is selected).

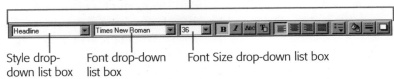

Style drop-down list box   Font drop-down list box   Font Size drop-down list box

Formatting options for picture frames are available when the Picture tool is active or when a picture frame is selected.

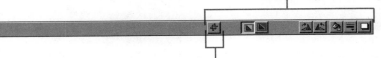

The Crop Picture tool is added when a picture object, OLE object, or WordArt frame is selected.

Text transformation tools are available when you are creating or editing WordArt content (not the WordArt frame).

Formatting options for arrow heads, line weight, and shadow are available when you select the Line tool.

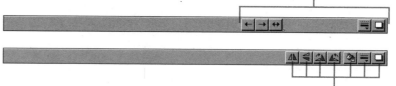

Formatting options include flip, rotate, color, line weight, and shadow when you create a geometric object (oval, box, or custom shape).

Getting the Right Answers: Publisher's Help System

Publisher offers several different kinds of help to meet the needs of both experienced and novice designers. Your document and the help tools can all be on screen simultaneously, so you can get answers to your questions without interrupting your work session.

The Question Mark icon identifies the Help button and gives you quick access to the help system. Within dialog boxes, you can use a special question mark cursor to click an item for context-sensitive help.

Hold the pointer over a tool or screen element for a few seconds to bring up a ToolTip for the item.

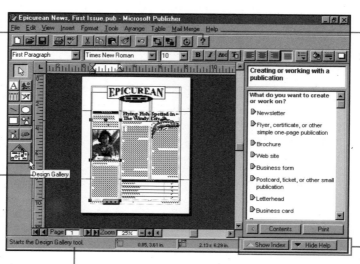

The Help menu lets you access the full range of Publisher's help system, including Quick Demos and the Print Trouble-shooter.

Buttons at the bottom of the screen let you quickly show and hide the help windows.

For more information about the status line, see Chapter 4.

The status line always reports on the current tool or activity.

Moving Through Help

Publisher's help system is divided into two windows—one for an index and one for detailed information.

Type a word to quickly search for help on a specific topic.

Click the How To tab to display step-by-step instructions.

The help topic description window gives you a brief synopsis of the topic.

The help index is organized as an outline.

Click an item to display more specific information in the second help window. A selected item remains highlighted.

Click the plus sign to open additional topics under this outline heading.

Click the minus sign to collapse the displayed topics under this outline heading.

Use the scroll bars to move up, down, or sideways within the index.

Click the More Info tab to display background information.

Click a square button to display an answer or definition box.

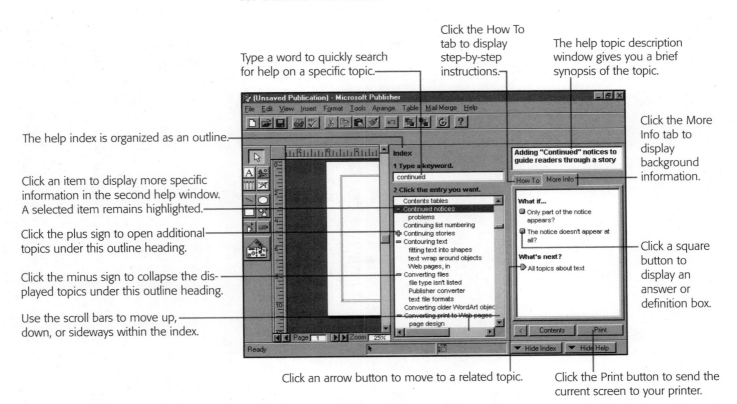

Click an arrow button to move to a related topic.

Click the Print button to send the current screen to your printer.

On-Screen Tutorials: Introduction To Publisher and Quick Demos

You can think of Publisher's tutorials as a form of first-time help. The Introduction To Publisher pops up when you first run the application, and the Quick Demos appear on screen automatically the first time you use any of fourteen different tools or functions. These demos teach you basic skills and concepts.

In the dialog box it presents to you, Publisher always gives you the option of viewing or skipping these demonstrations. You can view a Quick Demo at any time by opening the Help menu and clicking Quick Demos.

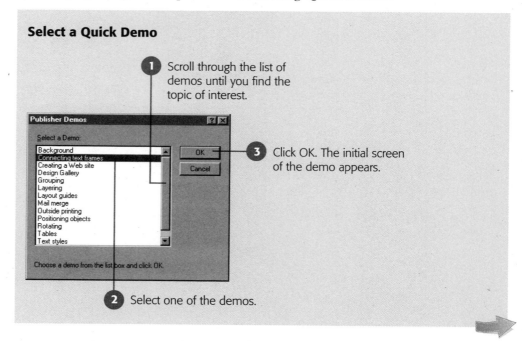

Select a Quick Demo

1 Scroll through the list of demos until you find the topic of interest.

3 Click OK. The initial screen of the demo appears.

2 Select one of the demos.

Select a Quick Demo *(continued)*

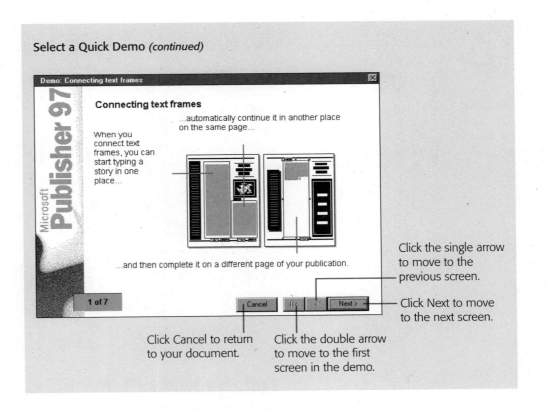

When You Know Your Way Around: Turn Off Quick Demos

1 Open the Tools menu and choose Options.

2 At the top of the Options dialog box, select the Editing And User Assistance tab.

What if I've forgotten how to use some Publisher features? If you want a short refresher course in Publisher, you can reset Quick Demos so that they pop up as if you were using Publisher for the first time. Click the Reset All button on the Editing And User Assistance tab in the Options dialog box.

When You Know Your Way Around: Turn Off Quick Demos *(continued)*

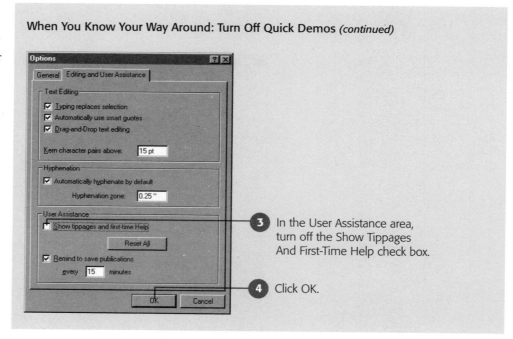

3 In the User Assistance area, turn off the Show Tippages And First-Time Help check box.

4 Click OK.

Helpful Hints: Reminders, Tippages, and Alert Boxes

Reminders, tippages, and alert boxes are message boxes that pop up in response to specific situations.

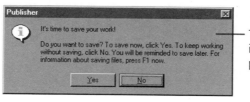

This reminder appears after a specified interval has passed. Publisher can periodically remind you to save your file.

Why can't I get rid of the alert box? Reminders and alert boxes are true dialog boxes, which means that you must respond to them before you can return to your document. In some cases, the help boxes require only that you click OK to acknowledge that you've read the dialog box. In other cases, Publisher can carry out a command from the dialog box.

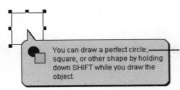

You can draw a perfect circle, square, or other shape by holding down SHIFT while you draw the object.

A tippage (pronounced "tip page") pops up when Publisher suspects that you are having trouble using a tool. For example, drawing a *nearly* perfect square will display this tip.

An alert box appears if you attempt to do something illogical or something Publisher can't do. For example, if you try to type into a rectangle that isn't truly a text frame, Publisher will remind you that you can insert text only into a text or table frame.

Words can be stretched, turned, and transformed with artistic effects.

The Flavor Workshop!

This month Epicurean Delights is pleased to showcase Lucinda Marino, Executive Chef at the Bellagio Spa in northern California. Chef Marino has spent the last six years perfecting a low-calorie menu that leaves guests feeling not only satisfied but indulged.

Chef Marino is making headlines in the food industry because she is

(Continued on page 2)

Stories can jump from page to page.

(Continued from page 1)
ready to reveal her secret techniques to the public. Marino explained her decision, "I realized that two weeks at a spa eating balanced, low-calorie meals may get you fit, but it won't keep you fit if you return to bad eating habits. People need the skills to help them prepare healthy meals at home."

Toward that end, Chef Marino is offering a unique cooking class to the guests at the Bellagio spa. Over the course of two weeks guests

Field trips to local producers and to the farmer's market serve for both entertainment and education. A morning walk through a field of sunflowers and pumpkins, is followed by an afternoon of cooking pumpkin soup garnished with sunflower seeds.

can attend workshops where they will learn how to replace the fat and salt in their food with flavor. Participants will have the opportunity to experiment with ethnic cuisines where herbs and spices flavor the dish in lieu of salt. Chef Marino will also share the recipes she developed for low-fat salsas and reduction sauces. The northern California location ensures that absolutely fresh ingredients are always available to the class. In fact, Chef Marino actually conducts shopping trips to a local farmer's market to teach her students how to choose the best produce. And proximity to some of the finest vineyards in the country guarantees that each meal prepared in class will be accompanied by an appropriate—often exquisite— wine.

EPICUREAN DELIGHTS

Participants in the class will visit several local wineries, known for exceptional Merlots and Cabernets. An understanding of the wine-making process—from the vine to the bottle to the table—will help students choose wines for both cooking and quaffing.

Decorative elements such as rules and logos can add visual excitement.

Elements can appear side by side or overlapped.

Becoming Familiar with Microsoft Publisher 97

Microsoft Publisher 97 is easy to use. When you master a few basic concepts and skills, you can create sophisticated and professional-looking publications. Taking a few minutes now to familiarize yourself with Publisher's approach to document creation and design will save you valuable time later and enable you to turn out products with a minimum of confusion and frustration.

What Is Desktop Publishing?

Microsoft Publisher is a desktop publishing application—not a word processing application. Although Publisher provides some word processing features (including a spelling checker and a find-and-replace feature), it is not intended to function as a true word processing application.

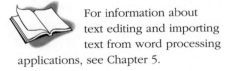

For information about text editing and importing text from word processing applications, see Chapter 5.

Word processing documents are linear: one character leads to the next, lines of text are sequential, and pages follow each other in a predictable order. Desktop publishing documents are nonlinear. You use text and pictures as building blocks to construct a page design in any order you wish.

The Building Blocks of Documents: Text, Pictures, Drawn Elements, and Other Objects

Publisher treats words, pictures, and everything else in a document as objects. A document is simply a collection of different kinds of objects. Understanding object attributes and how objects behave and interact with one another is the key to working with Publisher. A Publisher document can contain four basic kinds of objects, as shown in the following table.

Types of Objects in Microsoft Publisher		
Object Type	**Content**	**Description**
Text	Words	Text that you type directly in a Publisher document or that you import from a word processing file
Picture	Any visual material imported from an external source	Scanned photographs, technical diagrams, clip-art images, pie charts, and other graphics
Drawn	Visual elements that you create in Publisher	Lines, arrows, decorative borders, and geometric shapes such as boxes, ovals, and polygons
OLE	Objects that are created by other programs	Any kind of computer-based data such as cells from a spreadsheet, text from a word processor, pictures from a drawing application, and fields from a database

Components of Objects

In a Publisher document, each object consists of the content, the frame, and the formatting attributes. Attributes are the qualities that determine an object's appearance.

Content

You can think of the content of an object as its meaning. For example, the content of a picture object is the picture itself, and the content of a text object is the words. You can change characteristics such as the size, shape, position, or color of an object without altering its content.

Frames

Publisher's frames function much like the picture frames you use at home. In the same way that picture frames contain pieces of art and allow you to position that art on the wall anywhere you please, Publisher's frames contain words, pictures, drawn elements, or other objects and allow you to size and position those objects on the publication page. You can design an entire publication with empty frames and then fill the frames with text and pictures imported from external sources. The composition of frames on the page is called a layout.

Formatting Attributes

We often define objects by describing their properties or attributes. For example, a balloon can be red or blue, a chair can be straight-backed or cushioned, and a person can be tall or short. All objects in Publisher also have attributes, and you can alter the appearance of objects by changing their attributes. This alteration process is called formatting. The following illustration shows how attributes affect the way that objects and object frames appear.

Is a border the same as a frame? No. These two terms should not be used interchangeably. A frame is the rectangle that defines an object's boundary. A border is a formatting attribute, such as a 1-point black line, that can be applied to a frame.

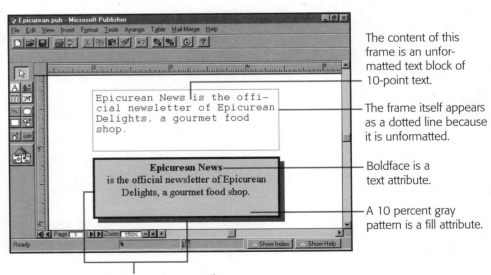

The content of this frame is an unformatted text block of 10-point text.

The frame itself appears as a dotted line because it is unformatted.

Boldface is a text attribute.

A 10 percent gray pattern is a fill attribute.

A border and a shadow are frame attributes.

Why can't I see object boundaries on screen? In all likelihood, you have hidden the object boundaries. To display them, open the View menu and choose the Show Boundaries And Guides command, or use the keyboard shortcut Ctrl-Shift-O.

Instant frames. You can create a frame—or any Publisher object—by simply activating the appropriate tool and then clicking in the workspace. If you can't access this function, select Options on the Tools menu. Turn on the Single-Click Object Creation check box, located on the General tab of the Options dialog box that appears. One word of warning: the frames you create in this way appear on the page in a standard size. You must then resize each frame.

Drawing in any direction. You can create and size frames starting from any corner. This is useful when you want to align a frame with other elements or guides on the page.

Positioning Objects Using Object Boundaries

As your designs increase in complexity, the number of objects on the page will also increase. Publisher helps you see where one object ends and another object begins by displaying a dotted line around each text, picture, or other object.

This dotted line represents an object boundary. Although you can see object boundaries on screen, they never print.

Creating a Frame

Before you can type text, import a picture, design WordArt, or insert an OLE element, you must draw the appropriate frame for that type of object.

Draw a Frame

1 Activate the toolbar tool that will create the kind of object you want. The pointer changes into the Crossbar pointer.

2 Position the Crossbar pointer on the page.

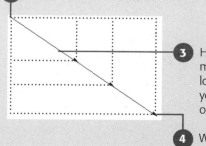

3 Holding down the left mouse button, drag the mouse diagonally. The frame boundary will look like a square or a rectangle. Essentially, you are drawing from one corner to the opposite corner of the object.

4 When the shape and size of the frame are to your liking, release the mouse button.

Preparing to Work with an Object

To modify or format any object, first you must select it. You can tell that an object has been selected because selection handles appear on the frame surrounding the object.

— Selection handles

Mix and match selection tools. You can work more efficiently by using the various selection tools in combination. For example, if you want to select every element on a page but one, use the Select All command and then use the Shift key to deselect a single object.

Learn the difference between a multiple selection and a group. A multiple selection is a temporary group that is created when you select more than one object at a time. As soon as you deselect the elements, they are once again treated as individual objects. Publisher allows you to convert a multiple selection to a permanent group of objects that are "glued" together until you ungroup them. Grouped objects offer you flexibility because you can treat them like a single object while you design your publication.

For more information about working with grouped objects, see Chapter 4.

Select and Deselect an Object

1 If the pointer is not the standard pointer, click the Pointer tool on the toolbar.

2 Using the pointer, click an object. The object remains selected until you click another object or any blank area of the screen.

3 Click away from the selected object to deselect it.

Multiple Selections

Sometimes it is efficient to work with more than one object at a time, particularly when you want to move or delete them. Publisher lets you select several objects simultaneously in what is known as a multiple selection. Every currently selected object in a multiple selection is displayed with gray (rather than the usual black) selection handles.

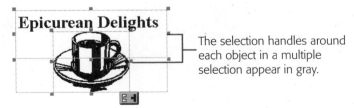

The selection handles around each object in a multiple selection appear in gray.

You can select more than one object in several ways, as explained in the table on the following page.

Methods of Creating a Multiple Selection

Selection Method	Directions for Use	Recommendations
Select All	Choose the Select All command on the Edit menu.	Selects every object on the page.
Shift key	Hold down the Shift key and click a series of objects. Each time you click a new element, it is added to the current selection. If you Shift-click an object that is already part of a multiple selection, Publisher removes that object from the multiple selection—that is, it deselects it.	Ideal for selecting objects that are not close to each other on the page or for excluding objects from a multiple selection.
Pointer tool	Draw a special boundary, or selection box, around objects by starting outside the farthest object and dragging the standard pointer diagonally, being sure to completely surround all the objects you want to select. When you release the mouse button, all the objects within the selection box are selected.	Good for selecting objects that are adjacent to one another on the page.

Why is the Undo command grayed out? If Publisher can't undo something, it will let you know by displaying the Undo command as gray (rather than black) text. Undo reverses only the last action Publisher performed, so you must issue the Undo command before executing any other command.

Quickly undoing a command. Click the Undo button on the Standard toolbar to reverse the last action you performed.

To undo the last action, press Ctrl-Z.

Reversing a Mistake: The Undo Command

Publisher can usually undo the last action you performed. If you don't like a modification you made to your design—if you accidentally deleted an object, or inadvertently changed an object's size or shape—you can open the Edit menu and select Undo.

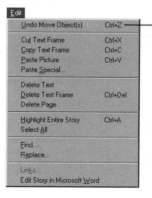

The Undo command tells you exactly what it will undo—in this case, a move.

Previewing Your Layout Using the WYSIWYG Screen

To toggle the display of special characters, press Ctrl-Shift-Y. Press Ctrl-Shift-O to toggle the display of boundaries and guides.

For more information about layout tools, see Chapter 4.

You can preview your printed document using Publisher's WYSIWYG, or What You See Is What You Get, display. Publisher attempts to show you how the final printed page will look, regardless of whether you are using a desktop laser printer or a high-resolution output device at a service bureau. You can enhance the appearance of the screen preview by hiding layout guides and nonprinting characters (such as paragraph marks).

Preview Your Document

1 Open the View menu.

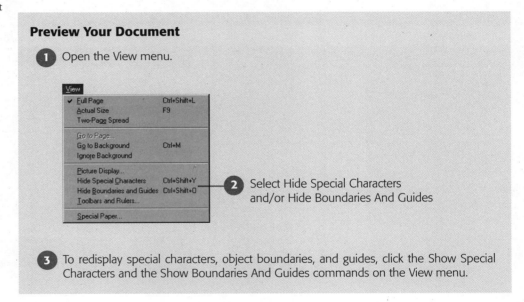

2 Select Hide Special Characters and/or Hide Boundaries And Guides

3 To redisplay special characters, object boundaries, and guides, click the Show Special Characters and the Show Boundaries And Guides commands on the View menu.

Publisher mimics the look of paper pages on a desktop.

The Standard toolbar lets you quickly create, open, and save publications.

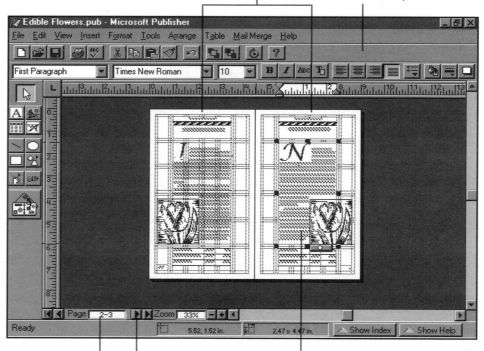

Publisher keeps track of page numbers automatically.

Move through a document with electronic page controls.

You might need to enlarge the pages to see the actual text.

Beginning Work
on a Publication

Microsoft Publisher 97 simulates paper publications in many ways. For example, a Publisher file contains pages—albeit electronic ones—in the same way that a paper document contains pages. Instead of stacking and shuffling sheets of paper, however, you use Publisher's commands to manage and move around in your electronic document.

Circumvent the Startup dialog box. You can choose to bypass the Startup dialog box when you open Microsoft Publisher. Choose Options on the Tools menu. In the Options dialog box that appears, turn off the check box labeled Use Startup Dialog Box and then click OK.

To start a new publication, press Ctrl-N.

For more information about these and other page layout options, see Chapter 4.

Starting a Publication from Scratch

The Startup dialog box appears whenever you open Microsoft Publisher or choose the Create New Publication command from the File menu.

Begin Designing a New Publication

The new Web Page option produces screen-based publications.

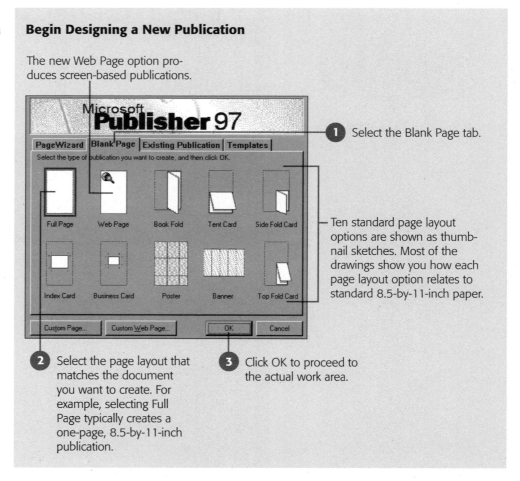

1 Select the Blank Page tab.

Ten standard page layout options are shown as thumbnail sketches. Most of the drawings show you how each page layout option relates to standard 8.5-by-11-inch paper.

2 Select the page layout that matches the document you want to create. For example, selecting Full Page typically creates a one-page, 8.5-by-11-inch publication.

3 Click OK to proceed to the actual work area.

To open an existing file, press Ctrl-O and select the file in the Open Publication dialog box that appears.

Opening an Existing Publication

The Startup dialog box appears whenever you choose the Open Existing Publication command from the File menu.

Open a Recently Used File

Like the File menu, this list box displays the filenames (and paths) of the last four files you worked on.

1 Select the Existing Publication tab.

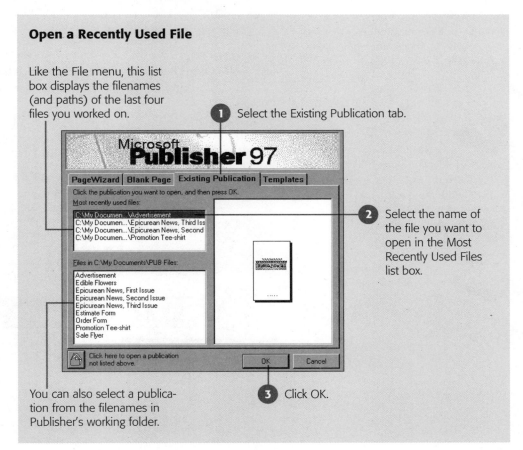

Microsoft **Publisher** 97

PageWizard | Blank Page | **Existing Publication** | Templates

Click the publication you want to open, and then press OK.

Most recently used files:

C:\My Documen...\Advertisement
C:\My Documen...\Epicurean News, Third Iss
C:\My Documen...\Epicurean News, Second
C:\My Documen...\Promotion Tee-shirt

Files in C:\My Documents\PUB Files:

Advertisement
Edible Flowers
Epicurean News, First Issue
Epicurean News, Second Issue
Epicurean News, Third Issue
Estimate Form
Order Form
Promotion Tee-shirt
Sale Flyer

Click here to open a publication not listed above.

OK | Cancel

2 Select the name of the file you want to open in the Most Recently Used Files list box.

You can also select a publication from the filenames in Publisher's working folder.

3 Click OK.

Open a publication directly from the File menu. At the bottom of the File menu you'll find a list of the last four publications you worked on. Clicking on a filename, or typing the number that precedes the filename, circumvents the Startup dialog box and opens the file immediately.

Organizing files. By default, Publisher stores your documents in the Microsoft Publisher folder (or in the folder where you installed the Publisher application). You can work more efficiently by storing all of the related files for each design project in a separate folder.

For instructions on creating new folders, refer to the Windows 95 online help.

Searching for a Filename

If you don't see the name of the publication you want to open, Publisher lets you search for the file in two ways:

- Using the Look In drop-down list box and the files list box in the Open Publication dialog box.

- Using the Find File command on the File menu or the Find File button in the Open Publication dialog box. The Find File feature allows you to specify search criteria when you don't remember a filename or a file location.

Open an Older File Using the Look In Drop-Down List Box and the Files List Box

1 Select the Files icon (shown here, found at the bottom of the Startup dialog box). The Open Publication dialog box appears.

2 In the Open Publication dialog box, use the Look In drop-down list box and the files list box to locate the file you want.

If the Preview File check box is turned on, Publisher displays a thumbnail sketch to help you identify the file visually.

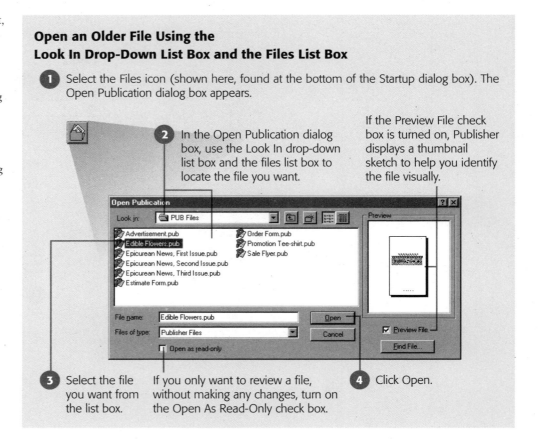

3 Select the file you want from the list box.

If you only want to review a file, without making any changes, turn on the Open As Read-Only check box.

4 Click Open.

Wildcard symbols. In the Find This File text box, you can use the standard wildcard symbols—the asterisk (*) and the question mark (?).

Open an Older File Using the Find File Command

1 Click the Find File button in the Open Publication dialog box, or choose the Find File command on the File menu. The Find File dialog box appears.

2 Select the type of file you want to find. For example, *.pub locates only Publisher files.

6 Select the name of the file you want to open.

3 Alternatively, specify the particular filename after selecting the Find This File option.

4 Specify the drive that you want Publisher to search.

5 When you have entered all the search information, click the Start Search button. The results of your search appear in the Files Found list box.

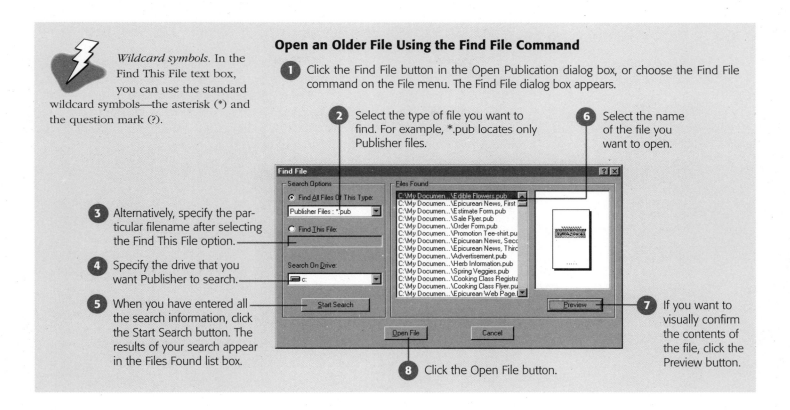

7 If you want to visually confirm the contents of the file, click the Preview button.

8 Click the Open File button.

Setting Up the Publication Page

You choose a paper size in the Print Setup dialog box, which is described in Chapter 14.

The page layout determines the general size and orientation of your publication and affects how the pages will be arranged at print time. The key to setting up a publication properly is understanding that page size and paper size are not the same thing. Page size refers to the dimensions of your publication. Paper size refers to the physical dimensions of the paper in your printer. Minimum and maximum paper sizes are determined by the capabilities of your printer.

In Publisher, the size of a page can be smaller or larger than the paper size. Most desktop printers use a standard 8.5-by-11-inch sheet of paper. In Publisher, the smallest allowable page size is 0.25 by 0.25 inch, and the largest is 240 by 240 inches (which is 20 by 20 feet).

When you begin a new publication with a blank page, Publisher takes the guesswork out of creating page layouts by providing a number of predefined choices in the Startup dialog box. For more advanced options, such as customizing a page size, you can access the Page Setup dialog box by choosing the Page Setup command on the File menu or by clicking the Custom Page button on the Blank Page tab in the Startup dialog box.

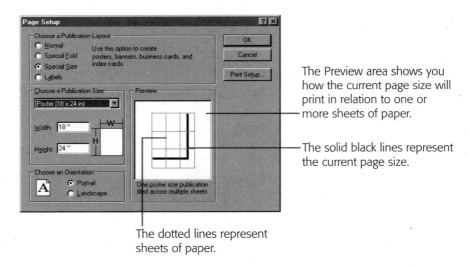

The Preview area shows you how the current page size will print in relation to one or more sheets of paper.

The solid black lines represent the current page size.

The dotted lines represent sheets of paper.

Publisher assumes four possible relationships between page size and paper size:

@ The page size can equal the paper size.

@ The page size can be smaller than the paper size. In this case, the page size is the trim size of your document.

@ Two or more pages can fit on a single sheet of paper. Publisher can arrange the pages so that they can be folded to become a card or a book.

@ A single page can be larger than a single sheet of paper. Publisher can print the page across several sheets of paper, as in a banner.

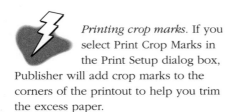

Printing crop marks. If you select Print Crop Marks in the Print Setup dialog box, Publisher will add crop marks to the corners of the printout to help you trim the excess paper.

Creating a Publication Page Equal to the Paper Size

You will often want to create 8.5-by-11-inch pages on 8.5-by-11-inch sheets of paper, which is the standard size of paper used for business correspondence in the United States.

Is the Normal setting synonymous with letter-sized paper? No. When you choose the Normal option, Publisher assumes that the page size and paper size are equal. If you choose a paper size other than 8.5 by 11 inches in the Print Setup dialog box, such as legal size (8.5 by 14 inches) or ledger size (11 by 17 inches), the Normal option in the Page Setup dialog box reflects the size of the chosen paper.

For more information about Print Setup options, see Chapter 14.

Create a Page Size That Matches the Size of Your Paper

1 Choose Page Setup on the File menu, or click the Custom Page button on the Blank Page tab in the Startup dialog box. The Page Setup dialog box appears.

2 Select Normal.

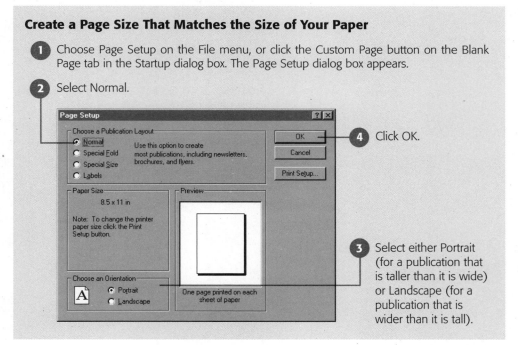

4 Click OK.

3 Select either Portrait (for a publication that is taller than it is wide) or Landscape (for a publication that is wider than it is tall).

Creating a Publication Page Not Equal to the Paper Size

Publisher allows you to create document pages that are larger or smaller than the paper installed in your printer. Publisher can crop down to small pages, tile the paper together to create large pages, and arrange pages into book form.

Whether you are creating small documents, such as index cards and business cards, or oversized documents, such as banners and posters, Publisher always figures out the best way to position the page on the paper. For small documents, Publisher centers the page on the paper. For oversized documents, Publisher prints your design across several sheets of paper.

When planning a design for a special-sized publication, think carefully about how you want the publication to look before choosing Portrait or Landscape orientation. For example, changing the orientation of a banner has a dramatic effect: in Portrait mode, the banner is 11 inches tall, but in Landscape mode, the banner is only 8.5 inches tall.

Folded Documents

Folded publications include books and cards. Although a folded document may seem simple to create, some pages might need to be printed out of order—or upside down—for the publication to be ordered and oriented correctly after the paper is folded. The following illustration shows you the four predefined ways Publisher can arrange the individual pages on each sheet of paper. Each arrangement is called an imposition (the technical term for how multiple pages are placed on a single sheet of paper).

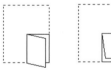

The Book Fold prints two pages at a time. You can create an entire book by starting with the first and last outside pages and working toward the center spread.

The Tent Card prints two pages on one side of the paper, which is then folded in half, as for a place card at a dinner. The interior of the card is blank.

The Side Fold and Top Fold Cards print four pages on one side of the paper, which is then folded in half twice, as for a greeting card. All four pages of the card can contain words and pictures, but the interior of the folded card (the side of the paper you can't see) is left blank.

Indicating the unit of measurement. Don't worry about indicating the unit of measurement when you type new values in the Width and Height text boxes. Publisher assumes you mean inches.

Will my printer be able to print the folded layouts? The Book Fold layout requires that pages be printed on both sides of the paper (duplex printing). If your printer can't do this, photocopy the pages back to back, and then fold, collate, and staple the pages into your book.

The Top Fold and Side Fold Card layout options require that two of the four pages be printed upside down, and the Tent Card option requires that the second page be printed upside down. Some older laser printers or dot matrix printers might have difficulty printing inverted text. To solve this problem, use Publisher's WordArt tool to create and rotate text.

Create a Folded Document

1 Choose Page Setup on the File menu, or click the Custom Page button on the Blank Page tab in the Startup dialog box. The Page Setup dialog box appears.

2 Select the Special Fold option.

3 Open the Choose A Special Fold drop-down list box, and select one of the predefined layouts. Publisher computes the maximum page size and displays the values in the Width and Height text boxes.

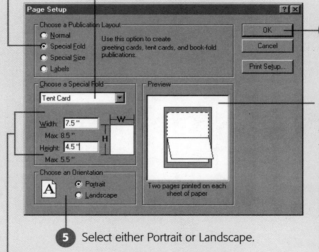

6 Click OK.

Notice that the Preview area changes to reflect your choices. If you decide to create smaller pages, Publisher will show you approximately how much paper will be trimmed (indicated by a gray tint). If you change the width or height, click another active area in the dialog box to change the preview before you click OK.

5 Select either Portrait or Landscape.

4 To change the page size, type smaller values in the Width and Height text boxes.

Fit multiple copies on a single page. If you are working with a small publication, such as a label or a business card, you can save paper and printing time by printing multiple copies on a single sheet of paper and then cutting them apart. Publisher lets you accomplish this automatically in two ways:

- From the Startup dialog box, access one of the PageWizard design assistants. You can use PageWizards to print multiple copies of small publications—such as labels, business cards, and postcards—on a single page.

- Select the Labels option in the Page Setup dialog box. You can choose from 69 predefined layouts that match the Avery label product line.

For other small publications, such as Rolodex cards, adjust the layout manually using the row and column guides—or even the Table tool. Then create multiple instances of the design by using Publisher's standard Copy and Paste functions.

Create a Document Larger or Smaller Than the Paper Size

1 Choose Page Setup on the File menu, or click the Custom Page button on the Blank Page tab in the Startup dialog box. The Page Setup dialog box appears.

2 Select the Special Size option.

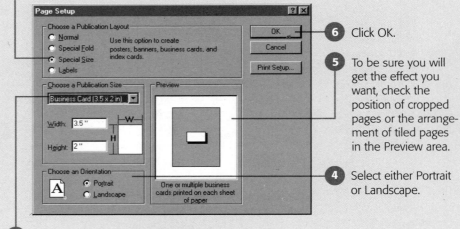

6 Click OK.

5 To be sure you will get the effect you want, check the position of cropped pages or the arrangement of tiled pages in the Preview area.

4 Select either Portrait or Landscape.

3 Open the Choose A Publication Size drop-down list box, and select one of the predefined options:

- Printer Sheet Size
- Index Card (5 x 3 in)
- Business Card (3.5 x 2 in)
- Poster (18 x 24 in)
- Poster (24 x 36 in)
- Custom
- Banner (5 ft)
- Banner (10 ft)
- Banner (15 ft)
- Custom Banner

When you choose a predefined publication size, Publisher displays the dimensions in the Width and Height text boxes. You can change these measurements only if you choose one of the custom options. Publisher suggests widths and heights for Custom and Custom Banner publications, but you can type any new values from 0.25 inch through 20 feet.

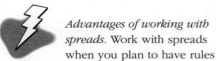

Advantages of working with spreads. Work with spreads when you plan to have rules or other elements print across facing pages, or when you want an overview of your design.

Viewing a Single Page or a Spread

You can view the pages in your document singly or by spreads. A spread consists of facing pages; the left-hand page is always an even-numbered page, and the right-hand page is always an odd-numbered page. Publisher's screen view of a two-page spread mimics the layout of a book or magazine that is lying open in front of you.

Look at Your Design on Facing Pages

1 Open the View menu.

2 Choose Two-Page Spread. Now every time you turn a page, you will see the two facing pages in the work area.

3 To return to single-page view, choose Single Page from the View menu.

Inserting and Deleting Pages

You can add pages to your publication at any time during the design process.

 How do I insert pages into a spread? If you already have more than one page in your document and are working with a two-page spread, Microsoft Publisher modifies the Insert Page dialog box slightly, allowing you to insert pages before the left page, after the right page, or between the pages of the spread. If you indicate that you want to insert an odd number of pages in the middle of a spread, Publisher asks, with an alert box, whether you want to change the way the pages are paired.

Add Pages to Your Document

1 Move to the page that falls just before or just after where you want to insert the new page.

2 Choose Page on the Insert menu. The Insert Page dialog box appears.

3 Type the number of pages you want to add to the publication.

4 Indicate the location of the new pages.

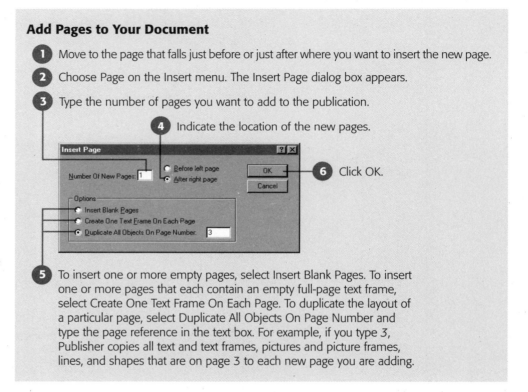

6 Click OK.

5 To insert one or more empty pages, select Insert Blank Pages. To insert one or more pages that each contain an empty full-page text frame, select Create One Text Frame On Each Page. To duplicate the layout of a particular page, select Duplicate All Objects On Page Number and type the page reference in the text box. For example, if you type 3, Publisher copies all text and text frames, pictures and picture frames, lines, and shapes that are on page 3 to each new page you are adding.

What happens to my text and pictures when I delete a page? When you delete a page, you also delete all the pictures and text frames on that page. The text itself will be deleted if the text frames are not linked to other frames. If links do exist, the text will reflow to other pages in the document.

For more information about linking text frames, see pages 89 through 90 in Chapter 5.

Move to a specific page. To jump to a specific page, you can choose Go To Page from the View menu.

Although you can use one operation to add as many pages as you need, you can delete only one page or one spread at a time.

Delete Pages from Your Document

1 Check to make sure that the page you want to delete is the current one.

2 Choose Delete Page on the Edit menu. If you are working in single-page view, Publisher deletes the page and renumbers the remaining pages.

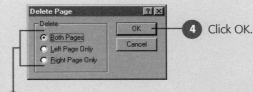

4 Click OK.

3 If you are working with a two-page spread, the Delete Page dialog box appears. Publisher allows you to delete both pages, the left page only, or the right page only. Select the appropriate option.

Moving from Page to Page

You can move forward or backward through the pages of your document with the set of page controls at the bottom of the work area, as shown here.

To move to the next page (or spread), click this arrow, the Next Page button.

To move to the first page, click this arrow, the First Page button.

To move to the last page, click this arrow, the Last Page button.

To move to the previous page (or spread), click this arrow, the Previous Page button.

To jump to a specific page in your publication, click the Page Indicator box. In the Go To Page dialog box that appears, type your destination page number in the text box and then click OK.

Find the best magnification level for the design task. The various zoom levels are suited for specific design tasks. Actual Size shows you the page at the printed size. A zoom factor of 400 percent is ideal for precision work, whereas 10 percent magnification gives you an overview of large posters or banners. Working in a 50 percent or 66 percent view is ideal for positioning elements on the page, but you'll need at least 75 percent magnification (or larger) for text editing.

Other methods of accessing magnification levels. Full Page and Actual Size magnification are also available from the View menu.

Toggle between Actual Size and the current magnification level by pressing the F9 key.

Changing the Magnification of a Page

To see your document page more clearly, you can switch among magnification levels. The Zoom controls, which appear at the bottom of the work area, are shown in the illustration below.

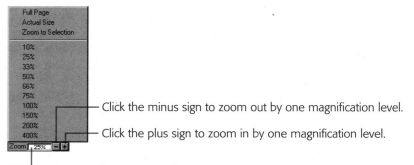

Click the minus sign to zoom out by one magnification level.

Click the plus sign to zoom in by one magnification level.

Click the Zoom Indicator box to display Publisher's 13 magnification choices.

Magnify a Particular Element

1 Select an object or a block of text.

2 Select any magnification level using the Zoom controls. Publisher always keeps the selected object in the center of your window. (Choosing Zoom To Selection will automatically enlarge the object to the edges of the window.)

Identifying the Background and the Foreground

Whenever you start a new design, Publisher automatically creates a blank background for your document. Because all the pages or spreads in a single publication share the same background, the background is the ideal place on which to position elements that should appear on every page of the document. In contrast, the foreground contains text and design elements that are specific to an individual page. You work on the background and foreground separately, but when you look at a page on the screen or print it, Publisher combines the two into a complete layout.

The repetitive text and graphics that you place on the background, such as rules or a logo, show through the foreground overlay and appear on every page in your publication.

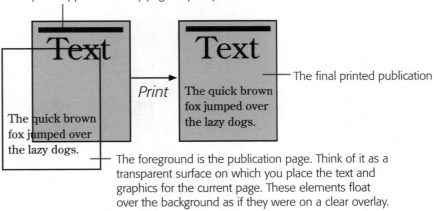

Print

The final printed publication

The foreground is the publication page. Think of it as a transparent surface on which you place the text and graphics for the current page. These elements float over the background as if they were on a clear overlay.

At times you might find it difficult to distinguish the background from the foreground. When they are empty, they look identical. Publisher identifies the background by replacing the page controls located at the lower left-hand corner of the window with a symbol that represents the background. When you have different backgrounds for the right-hand and left-hand pages, Publisher displays two background indicators, as the next illustration shows.

You work with the background and foreground in exactly the same way. You must draw text frames to add words and picture frames to add art. But you can't work on the background and foreground *simultaneously*. For example, when you are on the foreground, you can't select background objects. You can

To switch between the background and the foreground, press Ctrl-M.

switch between the background and the foreground at any time using commands on the View menu.

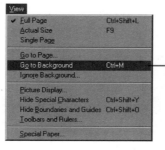

Choose Go To Background to bring the background to the front. The View menu will change to reflect that you are currently working on the background. When you open the menu again, the command will be Go To Foreground.

Adding Page Numbers

You insert automatic page numbers on the background. Publisher then adjusts the page numbering whenever you add or delete pages.

For more information about the Text tool, text selection, and text attributes, see Chapter 5.

Insert Automatic Page Numbers

1 If you are not already on the background, choose Go To Background on the View menu.

2 Select the Text tool on the main toolbar. Draw a text frame, and position it where you want the page number to appear on the page.

3 Select Page Numbers on the Insert menu. A small number sign (#) appears in your newly created text frame.

4 With the text frame still selected, click the Zoom Indicator box and then choose Actual Size.

5 Highlight the number sign.

6 Using tools on the Format toolbar, or commands on the Format menu, set the text attributes (such as font and point size) for the page number.

7 Choose Go To Foreground on the View menu. Publisher replaces the number sign with the correct page number on each page.

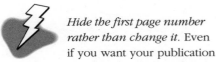

Hide the first page number rather than change it. Even if you want your publication to print without a number on the first page, the first page is still considered to be page 1. Don't change the starting page number unless you want Publisher to begin counting with a completely different number, such as 35. Instead, on the first page, choose Ignore Background from the View menu to turn off the background and hide the page number.

If you want to hide the page number—but not other elements on the background—use this trick: on the foreground, create a box formatted with a solid white fill and no border. Position the box over the page number. The box will act like electronic correction tape, concealing the page number on the background.

Changing the Starting Page Number

You might want to begin your publication with a page number other than 1. For example, your document might be a section of a long report or a chapter of a book.

Specify the Starting Page Number

1 Select Options on the Tools menu.

2 In the Start With Page text box, type the number you want to assign to the first page of your document. The starting page number must be between 1 and 16,766.

Creating Different Backgrounds for Left-Hand and Right-Hand Pages

A publication might need similar but slightly different backgrounds for its left-hand and right-hand pages. You can create completely different designs for the left-hand and right-hand backgrounds manually, but Publisher also offers mirrored guides so that the left-hand page background is a reflection of the right-hand page background.

Mirrored guides allow you to place page numbers on the outside edges of facing pages, where they are easier to find. Mirrored guides also let you adjust the interior margins (called the gutters) for stapled or spiral-bound books.

Use Mirrored Layout Guides

1 Open a new, one-page document.

2 Choose Go To Background on the View menu.

3 Design the single background as the right-hand page. Position those elements you want to appear on *both* pages of a spread, such as the page number.

Follow page numbering conventions. If you plan to bind your publication as a book, remember to design it so that right-hand pages are always odd and left-hand pages are always even. This rule is easy to remember: the very first page of a book, which is always a right-hand page, must be page 1. Traditionally, book page numbers are positioned on the outside edges of facing pages. Left-hand page numbers are usually placed in the lower left corner of the page, and right-hand page numbers in the lower right corner.

For more information about layout guides, see Chapter 4.

What happens when I turn off the background? When you turn off the background, all of the elements positioned on the background disappear from the current page. They have not been deleted; they are hidden from view and will not print. The background elements will continue to appear on all other pages in the document, including any new pages that you insert.

Use Mirrored Layout Guides *(continued)*

4 Choose Layout Guides on the Arrange menu. The Layout Guides dialog box appears.

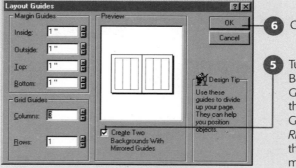

6 Click OK.

5 Turn on the Create Two Backgrounds With Mirrored Guides check box. Notice that the names for the Margin Guides change from *Left* and *Right* to *Inside* and *Outside*—the appropriate labels for a mirrored layout.

Accommodating Unique Pages in a Multipage Document

No matter how hard you strive for consistency, every publication contains a few unique pages. For example, title pages rarely contain page numbers or running heads. You can accommodate these pages by turning off the background.

Turn Off the Background

1 Be sure that you are on the foreground.

2 Go to the page whose background you want to suppress. If your view includes a spread, go to the spread that contains that page.

3 Choose Ignore Background on the View menu.

4 If you are on a spread, the Ignore Background dialog box appears. Specify the left or right page, and then click OK.

Saving a Document

Save files faster. You can decrease the amount of time it takes to save a file to disk by turning off the Backup and Save Preview check boxes in the Save As dialog box.

After you have created or changed a document, you must save it on a disk if you want to use it again. The way you save your document depends on whether you are working on a new document or on one that has been saved before. A new document is untitled. When you save the file, you must give it a name.

Microsoft Windows 95 lets you type a long, descriptive filename. You don't need to type the file extension; *.pub* will be added automatically. Even though the file extension is normally hidden in folder listings, Windows 95 uses it internally to identify the file as a Publisher document.

For more information about saving and using templates, see Chapter 13. For more information about Publisher's ability to import and export word processing formats, see Chapter 5.

Save a New Document

1 Choose either Save or Save As on the File menu. In either case, the Save As dialog box appears.

2 Select a location for the file. Use the Save In drop-down list box and the files list box to select a drive and to move up and down in the folder tree.

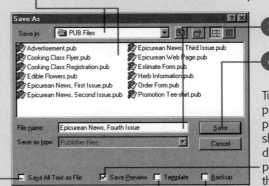

3 Type the title of the document in the File Name text box.

4 Click Save.

Turning on Save All Text As File lets you export all the text in your document in a standard word processing format, such as that for Microsoft Word. Select your desired text format from the Save As Type drop-down list box. (If you have highlighted some of the text in your document, the check box will be labeled Save Selection As File, allowing you to export only the selected text.)

Turning on Save Preview creates a preview of the first page of your publication. The preview will be shown in the Open Publication dialog box when you select the publication, allowing you to check that you are opening the correct file.

Turning on Template saves the current document as a template that you can use to create similar publications. Publisher saves the file in the subfolder called Template, without affecting any previously saved copies of the document.

Turning on Backup creates an extra copy of your document. Each time you save the document, the backup file is updated with the previous copy. If your original file is lost or corrupted, you can use the backup file to recover the last saved version of the document. The backup file for *XXX.pub* appears in the file list as *Backup of XXX.pub*.

To save your document, press Ctrl-S.

What is the difference between the Save and the Save As commands? The Save command simply stores the current file on disk, using the filename and the file options you selected when you first saved the document. The Save As command opens a dialog box that allows you to type a new filename and to choose options that increase your productivity or help you recover lost or corrupted files. You can also use the Save As command to save a copy of an existing publication with a new filename or a new location.

How often should I save my publication? You should save your publication periodically while you are working on it to safeguard your work from a power outage or a system failure. Most people find that issuing the Save command (Ctrl-S) every 10 to 15 minutes guarantees that they have the most current version of the publication saved on disk. If you work more quickly, save more often. If you work more slowly—or dislike interruptions—save less frequently. But be warned: the longer you delay saving a file, the more work you will lose in the event your system fails. It is also wise to create backups for your files.

Save an Existing Document

1 Open the File menu.

2 Choose the Save command. Publisher saves the file under the current name by overwriting the previous version of the file stored on disk.

Discarding Changes Made to a Document

Publisher also lets you close your publication without saving your edits. Use this feature if you want to revert to the most recently saved version of your publication. This method is particularly useful if you make changes to your publication and then decide you don't like the result.

Close a Document Without Saving Changes

1 Open the File menu, and choose Close Publication.

2 When asked whether you want to save the changes, click No.

Using Autosave as a Reminder

The Autosave feature can remind you at predetermined intervals to save your publication.

Use Autosave as a Reminder

1 Open the Tools menu and choose Options.

2 Select the Editing And User Assistance tab.

3 Make sure the Remind To Save Publications check box is turned on.

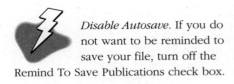

Disable Autosave. If you do not want to be reminded to save your file, turn off the Remind To Save Publications check box.

Use Autosave as a Reminder *(continued)*

4 In the text box, enter a value between 1 and 999 minutes.

5 Click OK.

When the Autosave alert box appears on your screen, you have two options: click Yes to save the current version of your publication, or click No to return to the current document without saving the changes made since you last saved.

Rulers can be moved to any
position on screen, allowing
you to align objects.

The Pasteboard serves as
a storage area for graphics
or text that you've cut.

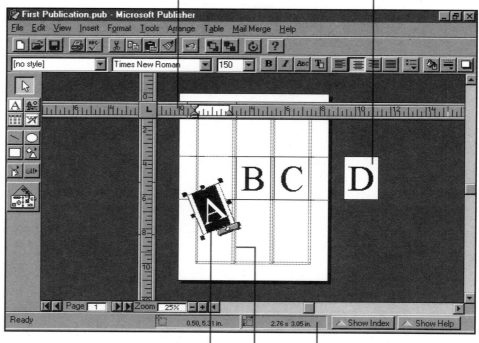

Objects can be rotated
or restacked easily.

The status line reports on the
size and position of objects.

Layout guides
structure the page.

Layout Tools

Look at the drafting table of any professional art director or designer, and you'll find a collection of layout tools, such as rulers, T-squares, rubber cement, and X-Acto knives, within easy reach. Microsoft Publisher provides these same layout tools in an electronic form that makes them easy to access and easy to use. The illustration on the facing page shows many of the tools you'll find in Publisher.

Customization Options: Modifying Publisher's Working Environment

Each time you open Microsoft Publisher 97, the application reverts to the original settings (called defaults) for layout options such as the display of rulers, units of measurement, and column and row guides. You can customize the way Publisher works by changing those default settings. The new settings will then be used for all of the publications you create from scratch.

Change the Default Settings

1 Open a new blank publication.

2 Change the settings for any of the customizable layout tools described in this chapter. For example, you can change the margin settings and the number of columns by using the Layout Guides command on the Arrange menu.

3 Save the document as a template with the name Normal.pub.

4 Close the publication.

Increase the size of the work area. If you want to increase the size of the work area, you can remove the Standard toolbar, the rulers, and the status line. To do so, open the View menu and select Toolbars And Rulers.

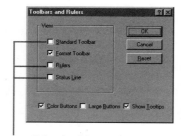

Turn off the check boxes for the Standard toolbar, the rulers, and the status line.

Right-clicking any portion of the work area displays a shortcut menu from which you can access the Toolbars And Rulers dialog box.

New publications will automatically reflect the changes you have made to the layout tools. You can change your new default settings at any time by opening Normal.pub and repeating steps 2 through 4.

Rulers

Publisher's rulers lie along the left and top sides of the work area. You use these rulers to measure where you are placing text and objects in relation to each other and in relation to the edges of your publication page.

The zero points on the rulers align with the upper left corner of your document's page, not with the corner of the work area.

The ruler displays finer increments as you zoom in on the page.

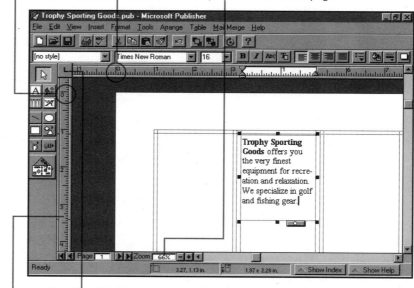

Double-click this box to return the zero points to their original settings.

The rulers always display tick marks with which you can measure the width and height of the currently selected object.

Setting Ruler Increments

Publisher can display and work in whichever unit of measurement you're most comfortable with—inches, centimeters, picas, or points.

Why don't my rulers display points? If you choose points, Publisher shows inches on the rulers because points are too small to be displayed clearly. The status line at the bottom of the work area does use points as the unit of measurement to report the size and position of objects.

Change the Default Unit of Measurement

1 Choose Options on the Tools menu. The Options dialog box appears.

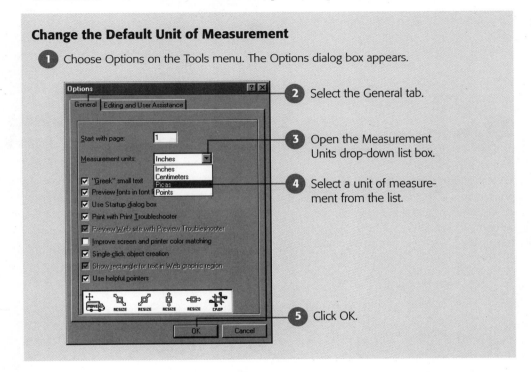

2 Select the General tab.

3 Open the Measurement Units drop-down list box.

4 Select a unit of measurement from the list.

5 Click OK.

Sometimes you'll want to use different units of measurement within a single publication. For example, margins are typically specified in inches, and paragraph indents are typically measured in picas. You can override the default unit of measurement in any of Publisher's dialog boxes by typing the numeric value followed by the abbreviation for your preferred unit of measurement. For example, to create a paragraph indent of 1 pica, you would type *1 pi* into the Indents And Lists dialog box (available on the Format menu when a text or table object is selected). You use the following abbreviations for units of measurement:

- *in* or a double quote (") for inches

- *cm* for centimeters

- *pi* for picas

- *pt* for points

Publisher will automatically convert your entry to the default unit of measurement. If you enter *1 in,* for example, and the default unit of measurement is centimeters, Publisher will display *2.54 cm.*

Sizing and Aligning Objects Using the Rulers and the Snap To Ruler Marks Command

You can move and position objects by eye, using Publisher's rulers as a visual guide, but you'll produce tighter layouts if you take advantage of the Snap To Ruler Marks command. If you use this command, any object you draw, move, or resize will align with the closest ruler mark and cling to that alignment in much the same way that an iron filing clings to a magnet. Objects already placed on a page will not move, but new objects you add will align along the nearest ruler mark.

Snap To Ruler Marks is a toggle command. A check mark appears next to the command on the menu when Snap To Ruler Marks is turned on.

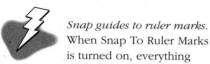

Snap guides to ruler marks. When Snap To Ruler Marks is turned on, everything you move—including ruler guides and layout guides—will snap into precise alignment with the tick marks on the ruler. This can help you create accurate layouts.

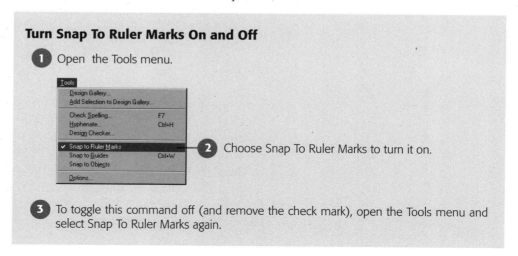

Turn Snap To Ruler Marks On and Off

1 Open the Tools menu.

2 Choose Snap To Ruler Marks to turn it on.

3 To toggle this command off (and remove the check mark), open the Tools menu and select Snap To Ruler Marks again.

Indents and tabs ruler.
Whenever you select a text object, an indents and tabs ruler appears, showing a zero point that aligns with the left corner of the selected text object. You can use this ruler to set indents and tabs for the words in the text object and to measure the width of the text object. If you want to measure the height of a text object, however, you'll have to use standard ruler functions, such as resetting the vertical zero point.

For more information about Publisher's indents and tabs ruler, see Chapter 5.

Setting the Ruler Zero Points

When you begin a new document, the zero points on the vertical and horizontal rulers are aligned with the upper left corner of your document page.

You can use the rulers to measure objects and the distances between objects by aligning the zero points with the edges of an object.

Set Both Zero Points

1 Position the pointer in the box where the rulers intersect at the upper left corner of the work area. The pointer changes to a double-headed arrow.

2 Hold down the Shift key, use the right mouse button, and drag the pointer to the new position on the document page—next to the object you want to measure. The zero points on the rulers reflect this new location.

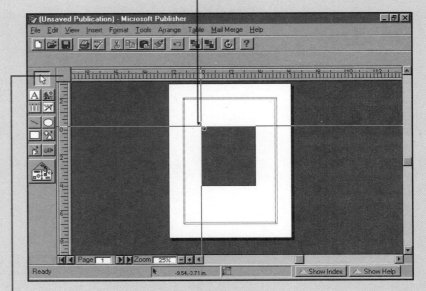

3 To return the zero points to their original positions, double-click the left mouse button on the box at the intersection of the vertical and horizontal rulers.

Set One Zero Point

1 Position the pointer on the ruler that contains the zero point you want to move. Make sure that the pointer is positioned at the exact location where you want the zero point to appear. The pointer changes to a double-headed arrow.

2 Hold down the Shift key, and click the right mouse button.

3 Release the mouse button. The zero point moves to the new position.

4 To return the zero point to its original location, double-click the left mouse button on the box at the intersection of the vertical and horizontal rulers.

Moving the Rulers

Sometimes it's easier to measure accurately if you can move one or both rulers next to an object.

Reposition One or Both Rulers

1 To reposition a single ruler, place the pointer on the vertical or the horizontal ruler. To reposition both rulers, place the pointer in the box where the two rulers intersect. The pointer changes to a double-headed arrow.

2 Using the left mouse button, drag the ruler to the new location. The ruler remains in its new position until you drag it back to its original location. The next illustration shows both rulers in a new position.

Zoom in before moving the rulers. If you move the rulers and then zoom in on a portion of the page, you'll find that Publisher can't reposition the rulers automatically. If you want to keep the rulers and the object you are measuring in sync, first zoom in on the object and then move the rulers.

For more information about Publisher's magnification tools, see Chapter 3.

Reposition the Rulers and Zero Points Simultaneously

1 Place the pointer in the box where the two rulers intersect. The pointer changes to a double-headed arrow.

2 Hold down the Ctrl key, and using the left mouse button, drag the rulers to the new location.

Notice that the zero points now indicate the upper left corner of an object, not of the page.

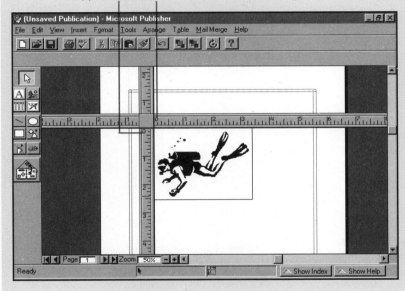

Hiding ruler guides. You can temporarily hide ruler guides by selecting the Hide Boundaries And Guides command on the View menu.

To toggle the display of ruler guides on or off, press Ctrl-Shift-O.

Why don't objects snap to the ruler guides when Snap To Ruler Marks is turned on? Ruler guides are pulled down from the rulers. But once created, they function like layout guides. In order to have ruler guides exert a magnetic pull, turn on the Snap To Guides command on the Tools menu.

Why can't I see the ruler guides when I move to another page? Ruler guides are part of the page on which they are created. Normally, you create ruler guides for each page in a publication. If you want identical ruler guides to appear on all the pages in your publication, you have two choices: you can create ruler guides on the background page, or you can use layout guides.

Ruler Guides

Instead of moving the rulers themselves, you can create ruler guides, which are more flexible than the rulers. You can create ruler guides by using the Shift key or by selecting menu options. Ruler guides can be positioned anywhere on the page, and you can adjust their position as you work.

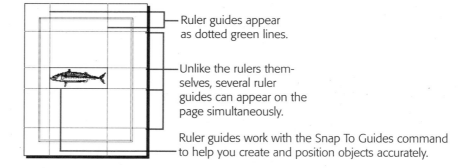

Ruler guides appear as dotted green lines.

Unlike the rulers themselves, several ruler guides can appear on the page simultaneously.

Ruler guides work with the Snap To Guides command to help you create and position objects accurately.

Create a Ruler Guide Using the Shift Key

1 Holding down the Shift key, position the pointer over the horizontal or the vertical ruler. The pointer changes to the Adjust pointer.

2 Press the left mouse button and drag a ruler guide to any position on the page.

Create a Ruler Guide Using Menu Commands

1 Open the Arrange menu and select Ruler Guides.

2 On the cascading menu, select either Add A Horizontal Ruler Guide or Add A Vertical Ruler Guide. A single ruler guide will appear on the page.

3 Holding down the Shift key, position the pointer over the ruler guide. The pointer changes to the Adjust pointer.

4 Drag the ruler guide to the desired location.

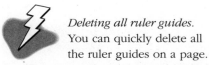

Deleting all ruler guides. You can quickly delete all the ruler guides on a page. On the Arrange menu, choose the Ruler Guides command. On the cascading menu, select Clear All Ruler Guides.

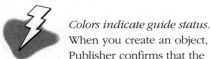

Colors indicate guide status. When you create an object, Publisher confirms that the pointer has correctly snapped to the guide by displaying the overlap between the guide and the object boundary in reverse video. That means the pink margin guides turn bright green, the light blue layout guides turn orange, and the green ruler guides turn pink.

Why can't I find my layout guides? Layout guides (and ruler guides) are obscured by opaque objects, such as a text or picture object with a solid or tinted background. If you want to see the layout guides at all times, you must make any opaque objects transparent. Select each object and then press Ctrl-T.

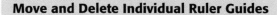

Move and Delete Individual Ruler Guides

1 Holding down the Shift key, position the pointer over the ruler guide you want to move or delete. The pointer changes to the Adjust pointer.

2 Drag the ruler guide to a new location on the page, or delete it by dragging it off the page entirely or back to the ruler with which it is parallel.

Layout Guides

Layout guides are visual guidelines that appear on every page of your electronic document but never on the printed output. They function purely as an internal tool that helps you position objects accurately and maintain a consistent look from page to page.

Layout guides let you divide a page into columns and rows.

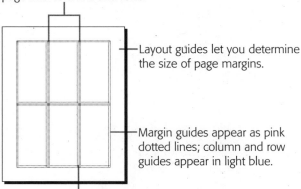

Layout guides let you determine the size of page margins.

Margin guides appear as pink dotted lines; column and row guides appear in light blue.

Notice that columns and rows are separated from one another with white space. This internal margin is called a gutter.

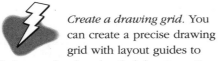

Create a drawing grid. You can create a precise drawing grid with layout guides to help you develop detailed drawings. For example, you could create the electronic equivalent of 0.25-inch graph paper by dividing an 8.5-by-11-inch sheet of paper into 34 columns and 44 rows, without margins.

Create Margins, Columns, and Rows on Every Page

1 Choose Layout Guides on the Arrange menu.

2 Set the margin guides by entering values in these text boxes.

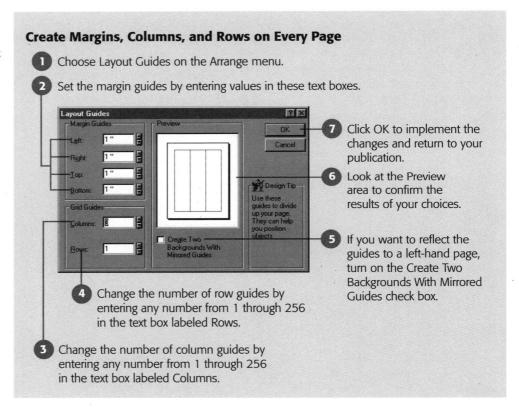

7 Click OK to implement the changes and return to your publication.

6 Look at the Preview area to confirm the results of your choices.

5 If you want to reflect the guides to a left-hand page, turn on the Create Two Backgrounds With Mirrored Guides check box.

4 Change the number of row guides by entering any number from 1 through 256 in the text box labeled Rows.

3 Change the number of column guides by entering any number from 1 through 256 in the text box labeled Columns.

Customizing the Position of Layout Guides

When you first create layout guides, Publisher divides the page into columns of equal width and rows of equal height. Your page design, however, might require irregularly sized columns and rows.

The background is discussed in more detail in Chapter 3.

Return column and row guides to standard positions. After you have created custom positions for column and row guides, you can easily return to a standard layout with evenly spaced columns and rows. Select Layout Guides on the Arrange menu to open the Layout Guides dialog box. Turn on one or both of the Reset Even Spacing check boxes. These check boxes only appear when you have moved the column or row guides, or both, to custom positions. When you click OK, Publisher will reposition the column and row guides to standard positions.

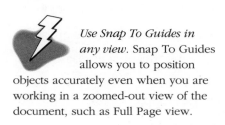

Use Snap To Guides in any view. Snap To Guides allows you to position objects accurately even when you are working in a zoomed-out view of the document, such as Full Page view.

Move Column and Row Guides to New Custom Positions

1 Create the appropriate number of column and row guides by following the procedure on the facing page.

2 Go to the background. The background will display the column and row guides.

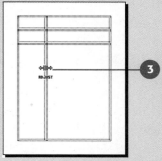

3 Holding down the Shift key, position the pointer over the column or row guide you want to move. The pointer changes to the Adjust pointer.

4 Drag the column or row guide to a new location.

5 Go to the foreground. The new custom arrangement of columns and rows will appear on every page.

Sizing and Aligning Objects Using the Snap To Guides Feature

After you've established the layout guides, you can use them to size and align the various elements of your design with great precision by working in the Snap To Guides mode. When you turn on Snap To Guides, objects you create or move will jump into alignment with the nearest guide. The pointer will also snap to the guides as you move it around the publication page.

Snap To Guides is a toggle command. A check mark next to the command signifies that Snap To Guides is on.

To toggle Snap To Guides on or off, press Ctrl-W.

Why are my objects snapping around the page even though the guides are not displayed? Even though you have turned off the display of guides, the guides still exist and will continue to exert a magnet-like pull on objects if Snap To Guides is turned on.

Showing and Hiding Guides

Layout guides, although helpful, are sometimes distracting. Turning off the display of ruler guides, layout guides, and object boundaries gives you an accurate screen preview of the printed page.

To clear up the clutter on your screen and hide the guides, choose Hide Boundaries And Guides on the View menu. To display guides and object boundaries, choose Show Boundaries And Guides from the View menu.

To switch between hiding and showing boundaries and guides, press Ctrl-Shift-O.

Object Groups

Every time you select two or more objects, you automatically create a temporary group, called a multiple selection. Publisher always gives you the option of converting a multiple selection into a permanent group. You can think of a group as a collection of objects that are "glued" together. A true group gives you a lot of layout and design flexibility because you can do the following:

For more information about linking text frames, see pages 89 through 90 in Chapter 5. For more information about multiple selections, see Chapter 2.

- Copy, move, rotate, resize, or delete a group as though it were a single object.

- Subselect any element within the group to change its formatting attributes.

- Select all the elements in a group to apply new formatting attributes to all elements equally.

- Type or import text into text objects within the group, and link text frames.

- Group groups. Each group can contain 16 subgroups.

- Even when you deselect a group, the elements remain together until you ungroup them.

In a multiple selection, selection handles (in gray instead of black) surround each object.

A Group button appears at the bottom right of any selection box containing two or more objects. Click the Group button to "lock" the two parts of the icon together, and to change the multiple selection to a group.

You can also choose Group Objects or Ungroup Objects on the Arrange menu.

To group or ungroup objects, press Ctrl-Shift-G.

A single set of selection handles surrounds the whole group. Individual object boundaries, however, are maintained.

You can subselect objects within a group. A subselected object within a group is indicated by a pink outline (or another color if the background is colored).

Clicking the locked Group button will ungroup the objects and change them back to a multiple selection.

Positioning Objects

To find the perfect arrangement of elements within a design, you'll want to move objects around until they are visually balanced. Publisher makes it easy to move individual objects, a multiple selection, or a group of objects on the same page or from page to page.

Why did my object change size when I tried to move it? You inadvertently positioned the pointer over a handle when you were moving the object. Use the Undo command (on the Edit menu) to restore the object to its original size. Reposition the pointer along the object's edge but away from a selection handle.

Move objects in a perfectly straight line. You can move an object, a multiple selection, or a group in a perfectly straight line by holding down the Shift key as you drag the mouse. Your movement will be constrained in a vertical or horizontal direction.

Why can't I move more than one object at a time? You can move all the objects in a multiple selection or a group at the same time. But you must be sure to position the Move pointer over one of the objects. If you click on the background (even if the area seems to be included in the multiple selection or group box), you will deselect the objects instead of moving them.

Move a Single Object, a Multiple Selection, or a Group

1 Select the object or objects you want to move.

2 Position the pointer along the edge of the object. The pointer changes to the Move pointer.

3 Drag the object or objects to the new position, and release the mouse button.

— As you move the object, Publisher displays its outline. When you release the mouse button, the entire object is redrawn in its new location.

As you move a grouped object (or a multiple selection), Publisher displays the outline of each individual object. This can help you to position both multiple selections and grouped objects more precisely in relation to other objects on the page.

What happens to objects in the scratch area? If you leave objects in the scratch area, they will be saved along with the publication file. They will not print, however, because they fall outside the page boundaries.

Move Objects from Page to Page

1 Select the object or objects you want to move.

The scratch area, or Pasteboard, refers to the gray area outside the page. This is a temporary holding area for objects.

2 Drag the selected object completely off the page onto the scratch area.

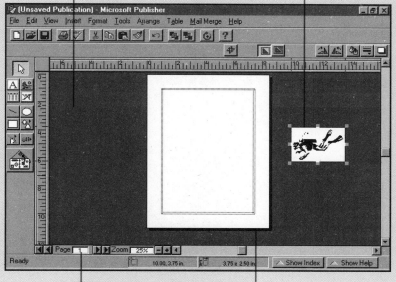

3 Use the page controls to turn to any other page in your document.

Page boundaries are indicated with a solid black border and a drop shadow. Objects outside of this area do not print.

4 Drag the object from the scratch area onto the current page.

Why does the pointer turn into a circle with a diagonal line as I drag an object? If you drag an object to an area of the screen where it cannot be moved or copied, Windows 95 displays the Unavailable pointer (shown below).

If you release the mouse button while the Unavailable pointer is showing, the move or copy operation is aborted. Release the mouse button only when the Drop pointer (shown below) is displayed.

Moving or Copying Objects Between Publications

You can easily move objects between two different Publisher documents, thanks to the drag-and-drop capabilities of Windows 95.

Although Publisher doesn't allow you to have more than one publication open at the same time, you can simultaneously run two copies of the Publisher application in order to display two publications side by side.

Run Two Copies of Publisher Simultaneously to Move or Copy an Object from One Publication to Another

1 Run Publisher, and open the document from which you want to move or copy an object.

2 Run Publisher a second time, and open (or create) the document to which you want to move or copy an object.

3 Select the object you want to move or copy.

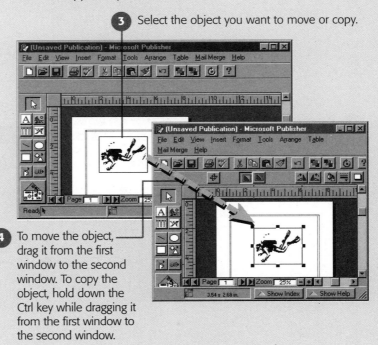

4 To move the object, drag it from the first window to the second window. To copy the object, hold down the Ctrl key while dragging it from the first window to the second window.

What if I can't see where the object has moved because of screen clutter? You might need to move the Nudge Objects dialog box out of your way to judge the effects of your nudging. Drag the box by its title bar to a new location on your screen.

To move the selected object 1 pixel at a time (or whatever amount you specified in the Nudge By text box), hold down the Alt key and press any of the direction keys on your keyboard.

What is the smallest amount that I can nudge an object? If you turn off the Nudge By text box, Publisher will move an object by 1 pixel increments. But be warned: a pixel represents a different distance depending on the resolution of your screen and the current magnification level. For the smallest possible nudge, zoom in to 100 percent view or higher.

Nudging Objects

Dragging is the easiest way to move an object, but it isn't the most accurate, especially if the object is already positioned in almost—but not quite—the right spot. You can nudge objects up and down or left and right in very small increments, 1 pixel at a time, by using the Nudge Objects command.

Nudge an Object into Place

1 Select the object you want to move.

2 On the Arrange menu, choose Nudge Objects. The Nudge Objects dialog box appears.

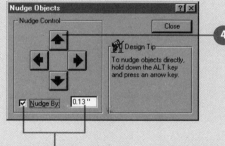

4 Click the appropriate Nudge Control arrow to move the selected object up, down, left, or right. If you did not specify a value in the Nudge By text box, Publisher will move the object 1 pixel at a time.

3 If you want to specify the increments by which the object will move, turn on the Nudge By check box and either accept the value Publisher suggests or type a new value from 0 through 2 inches in the text box.

Resize an object from its center. Holding down the Ctrl key as you move a selection handle enlarges or reduces an object from its center. This can help you to keep objects in a complex layout properly aligned.

Resize pictures with precision. If you are working with a picture, a WordArt object, or an OLE object (but not text objects, tables, or drawn shapes), you can use the Scale Picture or the Scale Object command on the Format menu to specify the exact size of the object.

For more information about the Scale Picture dialog box, see Chapter 9.

Resizing Objects

Often you must reduce or enlarge the size of individual elements to create a balanced, visually pleasing layout. You can resize only the height, only the width, or both the height and the width simultaneously. When you resize an object, it is often important to maintain the object's proportions, as the following example shows.

The relationship between an object's width and its height is called the aspect ratio.

If you don't maintain an object's aspect ratio, the object will be distorted when you resize it.

Holding down the Shift key as you resize an object with one of the corner selection handles changes an object's width and height by the same percentage. This maintains the aspect ratio, or original proportions.

Resize an Object

1 Select the object.

Grab a selection handle on either side of an object to change only its width.

Grab a selection handle at the top or bottom of an object to change only its height.

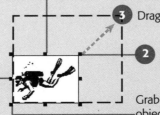

3 Drag the handle until the object is the size you want.

2 Position the pointer on a selection handle. The pointer changes to the Resize pointer.

Grab a selection handle at one of the four corners of an object to change its height and width simultaneously.

Layering Objects

In a complex design, objects frequently overlap. Think of overlapping objects as pieces of paper stacked on top of one another. In fact, the order in which objects overlap is called the stacking order. By default, Publisher always stacks objects in the order you create them.

Can I change the stacking order of objects even if they are on the background?

Yes and no. You can change the stacking order of objects provided that they are all on the background or all on the foreground. You can't change the stacking order if objects on the background are obscured by objects on the foreground.

The picture frame was drawn first and is positioned at the bottom of the stack.

The circle was drawn next and is positioned in the middle of the stack.

Trophy Sporting Goods

The text frame was drawn last and is at the top of the stack.

Selecting and Seeing Stacked Objects

The following illustrations explain how to select objects in a stack.

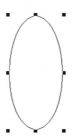 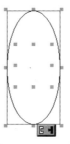 

A large opaque object hides any smaller objects and guides layered beneath it in the stack. Clicking selects only the topmost object.

You can select all of the objects in the stack by drawing a selection box around the elements. Then Shift-select the topmost object to deselect it.

To see and select only the objects lower in the stack, you can make the topmost object transparent by selecting it and using the Ctrl-T keyboard shortcut.

Rearranging the Stacking Order Using the Arrange Menu

You can rearrange the stacking order by selecting an individual object, a multiple selection, or a group, and choosing one of four commands from the Arrange menu.

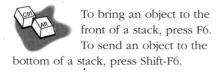

To bring an object to the front of a stack, press F6. To send an object to the bottom of a stack, press Shift-F6.

Bring Closer: moves the object up one layer in the stack

Send To Back: moves the object to the bottom of the stack

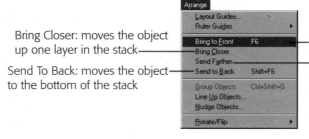

Bring To Front: moves the object to the top of the stack

Send Farther: moves the object back one layer in the stack

Can I change the stacking order of grouped objects? You can change the stacking order of grouped objects only in relation to other objects on the page. Publisher moves the whole group of objects up or down in the stacking order. But within the group, the objects maintain their order relative to one another. If you want to change the stacking order within a group, you must ungroup the objects.

Rearranging the Stacking Order Using the Standard Toolbar

Although it doesn't provide as many options as the Arrange menu, the Standard toolbar does give you two quick ways of changing the stacking order of objects.

Click here to send the currently selected object to the bottom of the stack.

Click here to bring the currently selected object to the top of the stack.

Rotating Objects

You can add visual interest to a page design, or simply make elements fit together better, by rotating objects. As you'd expect, Publisher can rotate standard objects such as text frames, picture frames, and geometric shapes. But Publisher can also rotate WordArt frames, table frames, and OLE objects.

Rotating Objects Manually

You can change the orientation of an object by dragging it. Use this option when you want to experiment with the angle of rotation.

Rotate an Object Without Specifying Degrees

1 Select the object you want to rotate.

2 Holding down the Alt key, position the pointer over a selection handle. The pointer changes to the Rotate pointer.

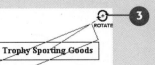

3 Continue to press the Alt key, and drag the pointer in a circular path to rotate the object.

Rotating and Flipping Objects by a Standard Amount

Although Publisher can rotate an object by any amount, two rotation options are used frequently. Publisher offers you quick methods for turning an object by 90 degrees or flipping an object to create a mirror image.

Why are the Flip Vertically and Flip Horizontally commands unavailable?
Publisher only flips drawn objects. Publisher cannot create a mirror image of text, picture, or WordArt objects.

Rotate an Object by 90 Degrees or Flip an Object to Create a Mirror Image

1. Select the object you want to rotate or flip.

2. Open the Arrange menu, and select the Rotate/Flip command.

3. On the cascading menu, choose one of the following commands:

   - Rotate Left turns an object counterclockwise by 90 degrees.

   - Rotate Right turns an object clockwise by 90 degrees.

   - Flip Vertically inverts an object, top to bottom. It creates an up-down mirror image and is not the same as rotating an object by 180 degrees.

   - Flip Horizontally inverts an object left to right. It creates a left-right mirror image and is not the same as rotating an object by 180 degrees.

Publisher's Format toolbar also gives you quick access to standard degrees of rotation.

Click here to flip an object vertically (top to bottom).

Click here to flip an object horizontally (left to right).

Click here to rotate an object 90 degrees to the left (counterclockwise).

Click here to rotate an object 90 degrees to the right (clockwise).

Rotate in 15-degree increments. You can rotate objects in 15-degree increments by holding down the Shift and Alt keys as you rotate an object manually.

To rotate objects clockwise in 5-degree increments, press Ctrl-Alt-right arrow key. To rotate objects counterclockwise in 5-degree increments, press Ctrl-Alt-left arrow key.

Quickest access to rotation. The fastest way to display the Rotate Objects dialog box is to click the Rotate icon located on the Standard toolbar.

Rotating Objects by a Specified Number of Degrees

If you know the angle of rotation you need for your page layout, you can specify it in the Rotate Objects dialog box.

Specify the Rotation Angle

1 Select the object you want to rotate.

2 Open the Arrange menu, and select the Rotate/Flip command.

3 From the cascading menu, select the Custom Rotate command. The Rotate Objects dialog box appears.

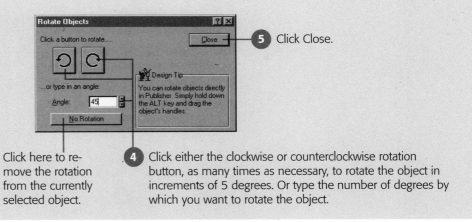

5 Click Close.

Click here to remove the rotation from the currently selected object.

4 Click either the clockwise or counterclockwise rotation button, as many times as necessary, to rotate the object in increments of 5 degrees. Or type the number of degrees by which you want to rotate the object.

Center an object on the page.
The Line Up Objects dialog box doesn't contain a command to center an object on the page, but you can center objects. Choose the Centers option for both the Left To Right and the Top To Bottom alignments, and then select Align Along Margins. Making these three selections for a group of objects stacks the objects concentrically in the middle of the page.

Aligning Objects

To align objects with each other or with the page margins, use the Line Up Objects command.

Align Objects

1 Select the objects you want to align by drawing a selection box around them or by Shift-selecting each object.

2 Choose Line Up Objects on the Arrange menu. The Line Up Objects dialog box appears.

3 Select the options you want for Left To Right alignment and Top To Bottom alignment. Publisher aligns the selected objects in the direction that you choose.

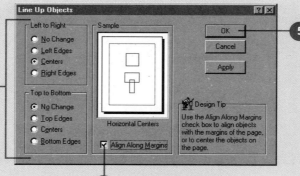

5 When the Sample area displays the arrangement you want (such as the horizontally centered option shown here), click OK.

4 Turn on this check box if you want to align the objects along the margin guides you specified for your publication.

Why won't objects align with each other even when I have Snap To Objects turned on?

Snap To Objects might not work as you expect for two reasons:

- You didn't move the objects close enough to one another. Remember, the objects must be within 0.125 (⅛) inch of each other for Snap To Objects to work properly.

- You've turned on Snap To Ruler Marks or Snap To Guides. These snap modes can interfere with Snap To Objects. It's best to toggle them off before using Snap To Objects.

Refer to the Size box to draw with accuracy. You can draw shapes, lines, and frames with great precision by referring to the Size box on the status line. The Size box shows the object's exact size as you create or resize it. If you are drawing or resizing a line, the Size box shows the length and angle of the line.

Sizing and Aligning Objects to Other Objects Using the Snap To Objects Command

In addition to snapping objects to ruler marks, ruler guides, and layout guides, Publisher lets you snap objects to other objects. When Snap To Objects is active, elements that you create, move, or resize will align with the top, bottom, left, or right side of the closest object. When the object you create or move is within 0.125 (⅛) inch of another object, the boundaries will touch or coincide. This is particularly useful when you are using the drawing tools or creating a very tight layout—as in a logo design.

Snap To Objects is a toggle command. A check mark appears next to the command on the menu when Snap To Objects is turned on. To turn on Snap To Objects, open the Tools menu and choose Snap To Objects (if it is not already checked). To toggle this command off (and remove the check mark), open the Tools menu and select Snap To Objects again.

The Status Line

The status line runs along the bottom of the screen. The right side of the status line tells the size and location of a selected object.

| 2.16, 3.03 in. | 4.00 x 4.00 in. |

The Size box reports on the size of a selected object (width by height). When no object is selected, no values are displayed.

The Position box gives the location of a selected object's upper left corner by displaying its horizontal and vertical position relative to the zero points. When no object is selected, this box shows the position of the mouse pointer on the screen relative to the zero points.

The Clipboard

On the Windows 95 Clipboard, you can temporarily store text, numbers, and pictures until you need them. You can then paste any of these elements within the same publication, into different publications, or into different Windows-based applications.

How do I save items from the Clipboard? Because the Clipboard is for temporary storage, it holds only the last item moved to it. Each time you cut or copy an object to the Clipboard, you overwrite the previous Clipboard contents. To save the contents of the Clipboard permanently, either paste the contents into another application or use the Save As command on the Clipboard Viewer's File menu to save the contents to disk. The Clipboard Viewer is accessed by clicking the Windows 95 Start button, selecting Programs, and then choosing Accessories from the cascading menu.

 Quick access to Clipboard commands. You can quickly cut, copy, and paste objects by clicking the appropriate icons on the Standard toolbar.

Alternatively, you can right-click on an object. The shortcut menu that pops up contains all the Clipboard commands.

 All Clipboard operations have keyboard shortcuts:

- Ctrl-C copies objects.
- Ctrl-X cuts objects.
- Ctrl-V pastes objects.

The tasks you can perform depend on the kind of object you have selected. Publisher modifies the Clipboard commands to identify the currently selected type of object.

If you select a picture object, Publisher cuts, copies, or pastes the entire picture frame *and* its contents.

If you use the text insertion pointer to highlight specific words or paragraphs, however, Publisher cuts, copies, and pastes only the highlighted text.

If you select a group, the Edit menu offers group commands.

Copy, Cut, Paste, and Delete Operations in Publisher		
Command	**Directions for Use**	**Results**
Copy text or objects to the Clipboard	Highlight the text or select the object that you want to copy, then choose the Copy command on the Edit menu.	A copy of the text or object is placed on the Clipboard. The original text or object remains in the publication.
Cut text or objects to the Clipboard	Highlight the text or select the object that you want to cut, then choose the Cut command on the Edit menu.	The text or object is removed from the current publication and placed on the Clipboard.

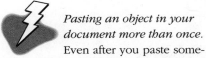

Pasting an object in your document more than once. Even after you paste something into your Publisher document, a copy remains on the Clipboard until you cut or copy something else, so you can paste it into your publication as many times and to as many places as you like.

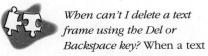

When can't I delete a text frame using the Del or Backspace key? When a text frame contains text, the Del or Backspace key deletes the text only—not the text frame. If you want to delete the text frame containing text, use Ctrl-Del or Ctrl-Backspace on the keyboard, or choose Delete Text Frame on the Edit menu. If the text frame is empty, however, the Del or Backspace key will delete the frame.

For more information about deleting text, see page 91 in Chapter 5.

Command	Directions for Use	Results
Paste objects from the Clipboard	Choose Paste Object(s) on the Edit menu.	Depending on the magnification level, Publisher places the object on the new page either in approximately the original position or in the center of the window.
Paste text from the Clipboard	Select a text frame and click to set the insertion point. Choose Paste Text on the Edit menu.	Publisher flows the text into the text frame at the insertion point.
Delete text or objects	Highlight the text or select the object that you want to delete. Press Del or Backspace, or choose the Delete command on the Edit menu.	The text or object is removed completely. No copy is placed on the Clipboard. You can't retrieve objects that you delete unless you choose Undo Delete Object(s) on the Edit menu immediately. Deleting text or objects is a good option when you want to remove an object and still preserve the current contents of the Clipboard.

The Design Checker

To check the final document for layout problems before you print it, use the Design Checker.

Check Your Design for Errors

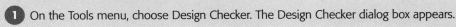

① On the Tools menu, choose Design Checker. The Design Checker dialog box appears.

Make a mock-up. The best way to proof your design is to print it on paper. A sample printout created for proofing purposes is referred to as a dummy, or mock-up. Seeing the publication trimmed to the final size is the only way to determine whether the design really works and to spot errors or omissions.

For information about the background and foreground, see Chapter 3.

Check Your Design for Errors *(continued)*

2 To check every page in your publication, select All. To check a specified range of pages, select Pages and type the starting and ending pages in the From and To text boxes.

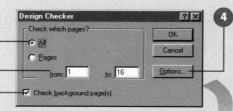

4 Click Options to display a dialog box where you can choose to have Publisher look for all possible problems in a document or for one or more of nine specific errors.

3 To check the background as well as the foreground, turn on the check box at the bottom of the dialog box.

5 Click OK to close each dialog box. Publisher begins checking the layout.

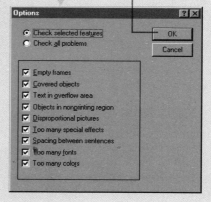

The power of modeless dialog boxes. The Design Checker uses a special kind of window called a modeless dialog box. That means you don't need to close the Design Checker dialog box while you work on your document. Simply move it out of your way by dragging the title bar.

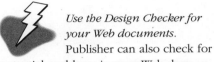

Use the Design Checker for your Web documents. Publisher can also check for potential problems in your Web documents. Instead of searching for potential printing problems, however, Publisher searches for problems specific to publishing documents on the Internet. For example, Publisher looks for Web pages that can't be reached by hyperlink and for images that will take a long time to download.

For information about creating Web documents, see Chapter 11.

For more information about Publisher's help system, see Chapter 2.

Check Your Design for Errors *(continued)*

6 If Publisher finds a problem, it describes it in a dialog box and suggests ways to fix it. As shown here, the Design Checker has found an empty text frame and suggests deleting it. Click the button that corresponds to the action you want to take.

  ❧ You can take Publisher's suggestions and fix each problem before you continue with the design check. Publisher also allows you to ignore the current instance or all instances of the problem.

  ❧ If you don't understand how to fix the problem, click the Explain button. Publisher's Help system is activated to assist you in analyzing and fixing the problem.

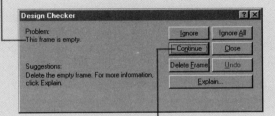

8 When Publisher finishes checking the layout (or if it finds no problems), it displays an alert box advising you that the design check is complete.

7 Click Continue to proceed with checking your document.

Embellish text with fancy first letters, bullets, or indents.

Change the appearance of words and paragraphs with formatting attributes.

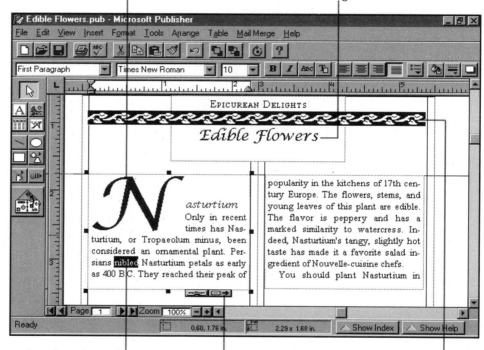

Tools such as the spelling checker help you to manage the content of your document.

Text frames include tools to flow text from column to column or page to page.

Add decorative borders to your designs.

Text Tools

The words in your publication function on two different, yet complementary, levels. On the most basic level, readers respond to what your words actually say—that is, to the content. On a more subtle level, readers respond to the way your words look—to the fonts and formatting attributes that you apply to your text. The way that content and form reinforce one another determines the power of your design.

Text Frames

One of the most basic rules in Microsoft Publisher 97 is that you cannot type or manipulate text unless the text is inside a frame. Text frames allow you to position blocks of text on the page. Publisher distinguishes between the content of a frame and the frame itself, so you can format them independently. For example, when you resize a text frame, the actual text it contains does not change size, as the following examples illustrate.

For information about creating text frames, see page 22 in Chapter 2. For more information about resizing frames, see Chapter 4.

Keeping the Text tool active. To keep the Text tool selected, press and hold the Ctrl key as you click the tool with the left mouse button. The Text tool will remain active, allowing you to draw a series of text frames until you select another tool.

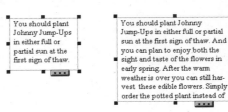

Enlarging or shrinking a text frame changes how much text can fit into it.

Changing the shape of a text frame (short and wide versus tall and skinny) affects how the text flows within the frame.

Text Overflow Mode

For more information about text flow and connecting text frames, see pages 89 through 91.

When a text frame is too small to display all of the text in a story, Publisher preserves the entire text file; the text you can't see is stored in the overflow area. To display text held in the overflow area, either enlarge the text frame or connect it to an empty text frame.

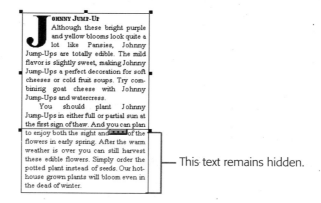

This text remains hidden.

Text Frame Margins

For more information about selecting the default unit of measurement by using the Options dialog box, see page 51 in Chapter 4.

Publisher defines margins for all four sides of a text frame using whatever unit of measurement you selected in the Options dialog box. If you selected inches as the unit of measurement, the default text frame margin is 0.04 inches.

The text frame margin is the space between the actual type and the text frame.

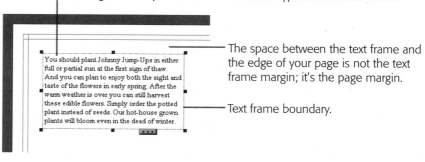

The space between the text frame and the edge of your page is not the text frame margin; it's the page margin.

Text frame boundary.

Text frame margins affect how text wraps around artwork. The text frame margins you create affect how text appears next to the art in your publication. If you create narrow margins—or none at all—in your text frames, the body copy prints very close to the picture frame.

If you create wide margins in your text frames, your layout is more open because the text will give the pictures a wide berth.

Change the Text Frame Margins

1 Select the text frame whose margins you want to set.

2 On the Format menu, choose Text Frame Properties. The Text Frame Properties dialog box appears.

3 Enter any value from 0 through 16 inches into the Left, Right, Top, and Bottom text boxes.

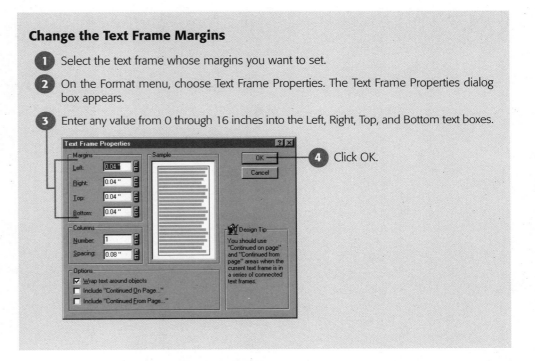

4 Click OK.

Multiple Columns Within a Text Frame

In addition to margins, the Text Frame Properties dialog box lets you set up your text in columns. Columns automatically adjust the alignment and flow of your text.

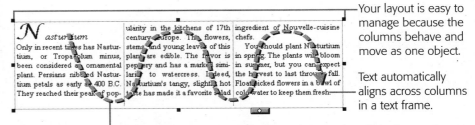

Your layout is easy to manage because the columns behave and move as one object.

Text automatically aligns across columns in a text frame.

Text you type or import will flow from column to column, left to right, within the text frame.

Press Ctrl-Enter to force a column break if you want type to appear in the next column even if it has not yet filled the current column.

What is the difference between Highlight Entire Story and Select All on the Edit menu? The Highlight Entire Story command on the Edit menu selects all the text in a story without selecting the text *frames*. The Select All command on the Edit menu selects all the *objects* on the current page or spread, which means that it selects the text frames as well as the text they contain. Use the Highlight Entire Story command when you want to reformat or delete all of the text in a story, even if the copy flows through linked text frames, runs across several pages in a document, or is hidden in the text overflow area.

Ctrl-A highlights all of the text in a story.

Format the Text Frame as Two or More Columns

1 Select the text frame.

2 On the Format menu, choose Text Frame Properties.

3 Enter any value from 1 through 63 to indicate the number of columns you want for your text.

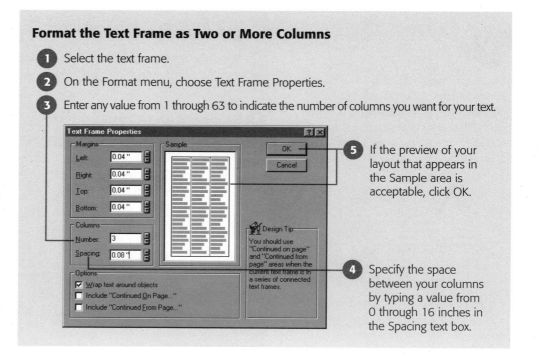

5 If the preview of your layout that appears in the Sample area is acceptable, click OK.

4 Specify the space between your columns by typing a value from 0 through 16 inches in the Spacing text box.

Typing and Editing Text

When you create or select a text frame, you can begin typing immediately because the current text frame always contains an active insertion point. You can enter text using one of two typing modes:

@ Insertion mode is like straightforward typing—you add words or characters to the text already in your frame.

@ Replacement mode replaces highlighted text with new text you type, saving you the step of deleting the selected text first.

You enable insertion or replacement mode with the Typing Replaces Selection check box on the Editing And User Assistance tab in the Options dialog box, available on the Tools menu.

For more information about the Windows 95 Clipboard functions, such as Cut, Copy, and Paste, see Chapter 4.

Why doesn't Drag-And-Drop text editing work in my document? You must enable Drag-And-Drop text editing on the Editing And User Assistance tab in the Options dialog box, available from the Tools menu.

What does the Unavailable pointer mean? If you try to drop text outside a text frame, Publisher displays the Unavailable pointer (shown below) to indicate that you cannot place text there.

Moving and Copying Text

To move or copy text to another page in your document, to another publication, or to a different application, you can use the Cut Text, Copy Text, and Paste Text commands on the Edit menu. To move or copy highlighted text quickly, you can use the Drag-And-Drop text editing functions.

Move or Copy Text Using Drag-And-Drop Editing

1 Position the pointer over the highlighted text until you see the Drag pointer.

2 Press and hold the left mouse button to change the Drag pointer to the Move pointer, and then drag the highlighted text to a new location. Holding down the Ctrl key as you hold the left mouse button will change the pointer to the Copy pointer instead of the Move pointer.

Finding and Replacing Text

By using the Find command, you can locate specific words or phrases anywhere in your document. With the Replace command, you can simultaneously find text and change it. The Replace command is particularly helpful when you edit long documents. For example, if you discover that you misspelled a client's name in your marketing materials, you can search for each occurrence of the incorrect spelling and replace it with the correct spelling.

Find Text

1 Click the I-beam pointer anywhere in a text frame to set the insertion point. It's best to start at the beginning or the end of a story.

2 On the Edit menu, choose Find. The Find dialog box appears.

Searching for partial words. Publisher can search for a word even if you're not sure of the spelling. Simply substitute a question mark character (?) for each letter you are unsure of. For example, you could type *h?tch* to search for *hatch* or *hitch*.

Find Text *(continued)*

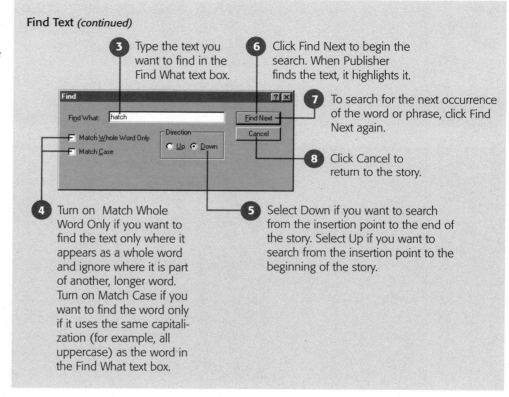

3 Type the text you want to find in the Find What text box.

6 Click Find Next to begin the search. When Publisher finds the text, it highlights it.

7 To search for the next occurrence of the word or phrase, click Find Next again.

8 Click Cancel to return to the story.

4 Turn on Match Whole Word Only if you want to find the text only where it appears as a whole word and ignore where it is part of another, longer word. Turn on Match Case if you want to find the word only if it uses the same capitalization (for example, all uppercase) as the word in the Find What text box.

5 Select Down if you want to search from the insertion point to the end of the story. Select Up if you want to search from the insertion point to the beginning of the story.

Replace Text

1 Click the I-beam at the beginning or end of a text frame to set the insertion point.

2 On the Edit menu, choose Replace. The Replace dialog box appears.

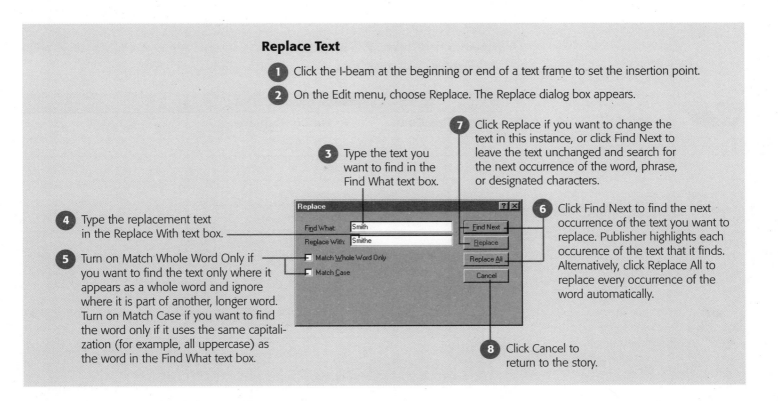

3 Type the text you want to find in the Find What text box.

7 Click Replace if you want to change the text in this instance, or click Find Next to leave the text unchanged and search for the next occurrence of the word, phrase, or designated characters.

4 Type the replacement text in the Replace With text box.

6 Click Find Next to find the next occurrence of the text you want to replace. Publisher highlights each occurence of the text that it finds. Alternatively, click Replace All to replace every occurrence of the word automatically.

5 Turn on Match Whole Word Only if you want to find the text only where it appears as a whole word and ignore where it is part of another, longer word. Turn on Match Case if you want to find the word only if it uses the same capitalization (for example, all uppercase) as the word in the Find What text box.

8 Click Cancel to return to the story.

Finding and Replacing Special Characters

In addition to searching for standard letters and punctuation marks, you can use the Find command to search for special characters such as tabs and spaces. You can use the Replace command to insert such characters in your text. For example, you might import a long text file into Publisher and decide to delete extra spaces between sentences. Two spaces after a period is good typing style, but the spaces will look too wide when the document is typeset. Instead of manually scrolling through a long document to remove extra spaces, you can use the Replace command to search for and delete them.

The codes in the following table show some of the most common special characters you'll want to find or replace. You type the codes in the Find What and Replace With text boxes, just as you would normal text.

Viewing special characters on screen. Publisher can display special characters as part of a text block. This is purely a convenience feature that can help you keep track of the special characters, such as tabs and end-of-paragraph markers. To display special characters, select Show Special Characters on the View menu. To preview your text as it will print, select Hide Special Characters on the View menu.

To toggle the display of special characters on and off, press Ctrl-Shift-Y.

Commonly Used Special Character Codes	
Type This Code	**To Find or Replace…**
Spacebar	A space.
^	A caret.
^?	A question mark.
^-	An optional hyphen.
^~	A nonbreaking hyphen.
^m	The contents of the Find What text box plus the contents of the Replace With text box. For example, if the Find What text box contains the word *leap* and the Replace With text box contains the text ^*ming*, Publisher creates the word *leaping* every time it finds *leap*.
^n	A line break.
^p	The end of a paragraph.
^s	A nonbreaking space.
^t	A tab.
^w	Any white space between characters, including spaces and tabs.

Importing Text

When you work with small amounts of text, such as headlines and captions, the most efficient way to add or change the copy is to type it directly into the text frame. When you want to compose longer blocks of text, such as stories, articles, or reports, create the copy in your word processing application and then import

Can I import a Microsoft WordPad file into a text object? Yes. Because WordPad is compatible with Microsoft Write, you can choose Microsoft Write when you import the file.

Importing text via the Clipboard. To avoid the whole issue of compatibility, copy the text you want to import to the Windows 95 Clipboard and then paste the file into a selected text frame. The Clipboard uses a standard text file format that all Windows-based applications support. Windows 95 even allows you to cut and paste text between Windows-based and DOS-based applications.

Publisher and Word work together. You can choose to use Word as your text editor from within a Publisher document. Even if you have created a nonlinear design in Publisher, where text flows through linked frames and appears on noncontiguous pages, within Word the story will appear in a straightforward linear fashion—making it easier to edit. To activate Word, simply right-click on a text frame and click Edit Story In Microsoft Word. To take advantage of this feature, you must be using Publisher 97 and Word 6 or later.

the files into your publication. Word processing applications are designed to accommodate the editing and formatting requirements of lengthier, more complicated text projects. The ability to import text files also lets you accept contributions from multiple authors easily.

Publisher's Compatibility with Word Processing Applications

Publisher can import and read text files from many word processing applications:

- Microsoft Word versions 2, 6, and 7
- Microsoft Works versions 3 and 4
- WordPerfect versions 5 and 6
- Microsoft Write
- Microsoft Publisher, all versions

When you import a file from one of these applications, Publisher usually retains any text formatting you've used, such as font and point size, italics and boldface, paragraph indents, customized line spacing, and defined text styles.

Using Plain Text or the Rich Text Format

If your word processing application is not directly compatible with Publisher, you can still import text into Publisher by using a standard file format. First open your word processor and save your file as a plain text or as a Rich Text Format (RTF) file. Publisher preserves the formatting information contained in an RTF file. As for plain text files, Publisher accepts two types: Plain Text and Plain Text (DOS). Upon importing plain text files, Publisher applies its default No Style format.

Import a Text File Created in a Word Processing Application

1 Select the frame into which you want to import text.

2 On the Insert menu, choose Text File. The Insert Text File dialog box appears.

Sharing import filters with other Microsoft products. Publisher can use text import filters that other Microsoft products might have installed on your computer system. For example, some applications include a filter for Excel worksheet files. Publisher can take full advantage of this filter, allowing you to select individual worksheets within the spreadsheet file or individual named ranges within the worksheet. Provided that you've structured the spreadsheet properly, this feature allows you to extract only the data you need from a larger Excel file. Although you select an empty text frame to import an Excel worksheet, Publisher always creates a new table containing the data.

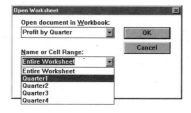

Import a Text File Created in a Word Processing Application *(continued)*

4 Locate and select the file you want to import.

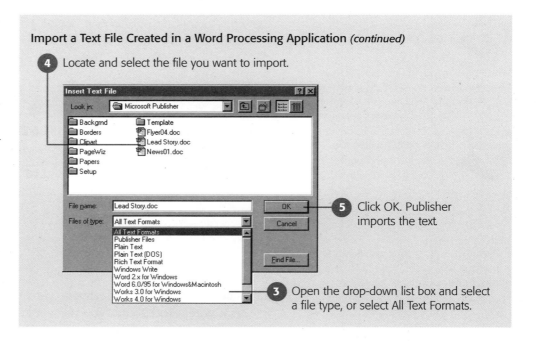

5 Click OK. Publisher imports the text.

3 Open the drop-down list box and select a file type, or select All Text Formats.

How Imported Text Behaves

How the text will look and behave in the text frame depends on a number of factors, explained in the following table.

Changes to Formatting of Imported Text	
If the text file...	**Then Publisher...**
Is too long to fit into the selected text frame	Asks whether you want text to flow to other frames.
Does not contain formatting information	Assigns the default No Style format: Times New Roman, 10 points, left-aligned.
Contains formatting information	Tries to duplicate the formatting.

Text Flow in Text Frames

You can control the way the stories flow in your publications by connecting, disconnecting, and deleting text frames, or by using the Autoflow option. You can connect frames that are adjacent to each other on the same page, or that fall on different pages. The text frame buttons and pointers described in the table below simplify your work on long, complex stories.

Why can't I see all of the text flow buttons on a text frame? Like the I-beam and the insertion point, the Connect and Frame Jump buttons appear only when the text frame is selected.

Text Frame Buttons and Pointers

Button or Pointer	Location	Function
	Lower right of last text frame	Assures you that the end of the story appears within the text frame. Clicking this button allows you to connect the frame to another text frame.
	Lower right of last text frame	Indicates that text is in the overflow area. Although overflow text is not visible, it is still part of your story. Clicking this button allows you to connect the frame to another text frame.
	Lower right of text frame	Indicates that the current frame is connected to another text frame. Clicking this button disconnects text frames.
	Lower right of text frame	Clicking this button takes you to the next frame in a chain of connected frames.
	Upper left of text frame	Clicking this button takes you to the previous frame in the chain.
	Appears when you begin to connect two text frames	Indicates that the pointer is not positioned over a text frame and that Publisher cannot flow text.
	Appears when you are connecting two text frames	Indicates that the pointer is over a text frame. Click to flow text into the frame. If the frame already contains text, an alert box appears stating that the text frame must be empty before Publisher can flow text into it.

Connecting text frames on noncontiguous pages. If you need to connect a text frame on another page, position the pointer over the page controls; the Pitcher pointer becomes the standard pointer. Go to the page that contains the next text frame to be added to the chain. When you move the pointer over the text frame, the tilted pitcher will reappear.

Connect Text Frames

1 Using the Text tool, create any number of text frames on the same page or on different pages in your publication.

2 Select a text frame that will be the first in the chain. This frame can be empty, or it can contain text.

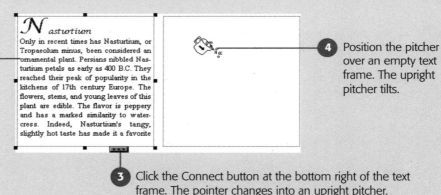

4 Position the pitcher over an empty text frame. The upright pitcher tilts.

3 Click the Connect button at the bottom right of the text frame. The pointer changes into an upright pitcher.

5 Click the empty text frame to connect the two frames. If the overflow area of the first frame contains any text, the overflow text will flow into the newly connected text frame. If all of the overflow text does not fit into the newly created text frame, continue to add more text frames to the chain.

Disconnect a Text Frame

1 Select the text frame that immediately precedes the point at which you want to break a chain of text frames.

2 Click the Connect button with the chain on it. The text from the disconnected text frame and all subsequent frames in the chain flows into the overflow area for the currently selected frame.

To delete a frame, select the frame and press Ctrl-Del.

What happens to the text when I delete a text frame from a chain of frames? You delete only the frame. The text itself flows into the remaining text frames in the chain or into the overflow area for the previous text frame.

What happens when I delete text frames along with a page? If you delete a page that contains *unconnected* text frames, Publisher deletes the frames and their text along with the page. If you delete a page that contains *connected* text frames, however, Publisher deletes only the text frames with the page. The text itself flows into the remaining connected frames in the chain or into the overflow area for the previous text frame.

Delete a Text Frame from a Chain

1 Select the frame you want to delete.

2 Choose Delete Text Frame from the Edit menu.

Use Autoflow to Flow Text Automatically When an Imported Text File Is Too Long for the Selected Text Frame or Text Frame Chain

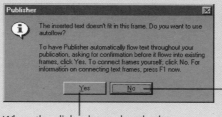

Choose No to place text in the overflow area.

When the dialog box asks whether you want to use the Autoflow feature, choose Yes if you want text to flow into frames that already exist in your publication.

Click Yes if you want Publisher to automatically connect a frame during the autoflow process, or click No if you want Publisher to skip to the next frame. If you still have text remaining, Publisher prompts you to create new text frames.

For each preexisting text frame, Publisher asks whether you want to autoflow text into it or skip it, regardless of whether these frames are connected.

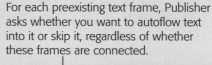

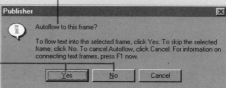

Click Yes if you want Publisher to create new pages and new connected text frames to accommodate the entire text file. The formatting will match that of the text frame you started with. If the original text frame has two columns, for example, the new text frames Publisher creates will also have two columns.

Automated Continued Notices

A good text layout makes it easy for the reader to follow a story from page to page, in part by including features such as Continued notices. You can add Continued notices easily by using Publisher's flexible, automated Continued notices feature, which allows you to modify the style of the text.

Changing the text style of all Continued notices in a document. When Publisher creates Continued notices, it also defines two separate text styles, called Continued-From Text and Continued-On Text. You can change the formatting of all the Continued notices in your document by editing these text styles.

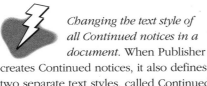

For more information about editing text styles, see pages 111 through 114.

Can I change the contents of the Continued notices? Yes, but you must edit each Continued notice individually using Publisher's standard text editing features—there is no way to change the wording globally.

Why are words missing from my new Continued notice? A Continued notice can occupy only one line. Any text that wraps beyond the first line will not appear in your text frame.

Insert a Continued Notice

1 Select the text frame in which you want to add a Continued notice.

2 On the Format menu, choose Text Frame Properties.

3 Turn on the check boxes you prefer and click OK. Publisher automatically applies a standard format to Continued notices, as shown below.

Note that both the Include "Continued On Page" and Include "Continued From Page" check boxes are available. Depending on where your text frame is located within the story, you can choose to include one or both Continued notices.

Continued notices are set as 8-point italic Times New Roman.

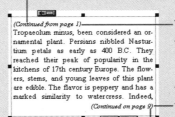

The Continued From Page notice appears at the upper left corner of the text frame.

The Continued On Page notice appears at the lower right corner of the text frame.

Publisher adds the appropriate page numbers.

Why doesn't the formatting change for words I've already typed? To make changes to a few words in a block of copy, you must first highlight the words. If you change the formatting attributes without highlighting the text, you will change only the attributes of the next text you type.

Suppress previews in the font drop-down list. You can display a simple list of font names, rather than an actual preview of each font, in the Font drop-down list on the Format toolbar. Doing so enables you to fit more font names into the drop-down list box. To disable the preview, choose Options from the Tools menu. On the General tab, turn off the Preview Fonts In Fonts List check box.

Character Formatting

In order to format characters within a block of text, you must first highlight them. At that point you can use any of several methods to reformat the selected copy: choose a feature from the Format toolbar, choose options in the Character dialog box, or use Publisher's additional formatting options.

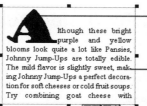

Character-level formats, such as a fancy first letter, can be applied to selected letters within a larger block of text.

You can combine paragraph-level and character-level formats. Here, the majority of the paragraph is formatted with a legible font (times New Roman).

Basic Text Formatting Options: The Format Toolbar

Whenever you create or select a text frame, tools for formatting text appear on the Format toolbar. This toolbar is often the fastest way to apply formatting to text. Although it provides access to only a portion of Publisher's text formatting options, it does include the most frequently used attributes.

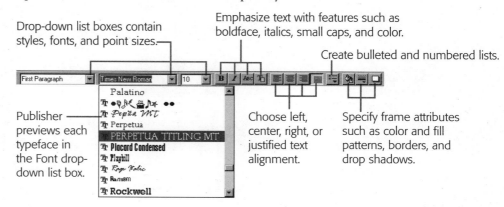

Drop-down list boxes contain styles, fonts, and point sizes.

Emphasize text with features such as boldface, italics, small caps, and color.

Create bulleted and numbered lists.

Publisher previews each typeface in the Font drop-down list box.

Choose left, center, right, or justified text alignment.

Specify frame attributes such as color and fill patterns, borders, and drop shadows.

Why can't I see my changes after clicking the Apply button? The Character dialog box may be covering your text frame. Drag the dialog box by the title bar to a different part of the screen.

Format Text Using the Format Toolbar

1 Highlight the text you want to format.

2 Select an option from a drop-down list box or click a formatting button.

The Character Dialog Box

A wider range of text formatting options is available from the Character command on the Format menu.

Change the Character Formatting of Text

1 Select a text frame. If the frame contains text, highlight the text you want to format.

2 On the Format menu, choose Character. The Character dialog box appears.

3 Select the options you want.

To change the point size, open the Size drop-down list box. Scroll through the list of available sizes and click to select a new size, or type any value between 0.5 and 999.5 in the Size text box. You can specify type size in 0.5-point increments, such as 22.5 points.

To change the font, open the Font drop-down list box. Use the scroll bar to move through the list of available fonts, and click the desired font name.

To change the emphasis of your text, open the Font Style drop-down list box and choose Regular, Italic, Bold, or Bold Italic.

To change the color of your text, open the Color drop-down list box and click one of the available colors.

Turn on one or more check boxes to add effects to your text.

4 To accept your changes and return to your document, click OK. Click Cancel to return to your publication without changing the formatting, even if you clicked Apply.

Preview your changes in the Sample box, or click the Apply button to see how the new formatting affects the selected text in your document.

To position text above or below the baseline, select Superscript or Subscript.

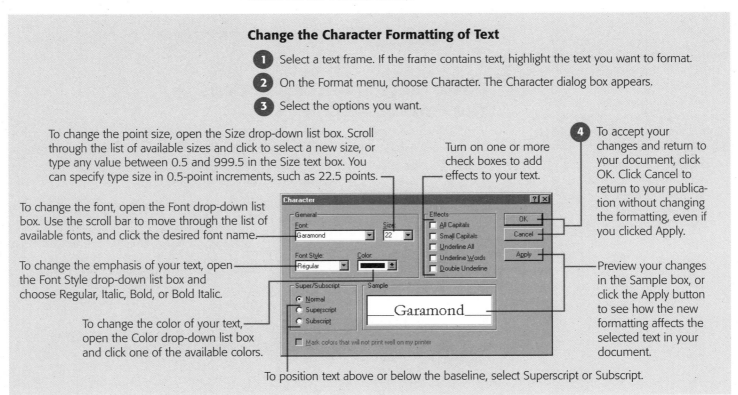

Why are some font attributes missing from a drop-down list box? Depending on the font, some formatting attributes might not be available. Only the applicable options will appear in the list box.

Either/or text effects. Some check boxes in the Effects area are mutually exclusive. For example, only one of the underline check boxes can be active at a time.

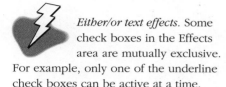

Overriding or maintaining existing text formats. You might select a text block that contains conflicting formatting attributes. For example, a paragraph in the Times New Roman font might contain some italicized words. When you highlight words or text blocks that contain characters with multiple formats, the corresponding drop-down list boxes, check boxes, options, and Sample area in the Character dialog box are empty or not available.

You can take advantage of this feature to change one formatting attribute without overriding the settings for other attributes. For example, you can change the font for the entire paragraph but leave any italicized words italic by leaving the drop-down list box for Font Style blank. Of course, you can also choose to override conflicting formatting attributes. Select the formatting you want and apply it to the entire block of selected text.

Formatting Shortcuts

You can use keyboard shortcuts to quickly change the format of the characters that you are *about* to type. For example, if you type Ctrl-I, all of the subsequent text you type will be in italics. You can also use keyboard shortcuts to reformat highlighted text. The same keyboard shortcuts allow you to remove formatting attributes as well. For example, if you highlight a boldface word and press Ctrl-B, the text will return to the normal (or roman) weight. The following table summarizes the most frequently used formatting shortcuts.

Text Formatting Shortcuts	
Keyboard Shortcut	**Attribute**
Ctrl-B	Boldface
Ctrl-I	Italic
Ctrl-Shift-K	Small caps
Ctrl-=	Subscript
Ctrl-Shift-=	Superscript
Ctrl-Spacebar	Removes character formats
Ctrl-Q	Removes paragraph formats

Character Spacing

You can adjust the spacing between characters to fine-tune the legibility of text (especially critical at very small or very large point sizes) and to turn plain text into dramatic graphic elements.

Control the Spacing Between Characters

1 Highlight the text you want to change.

Set spacing for an entire paragraph. If you select the Entire Paragraph option in the Spacing Between Characters dialog box, you can quickly change the spacing for large blocks of text—a function known as tracking. You must choose between five different levels of tracking:

- Normal
- Very Tight
- Tight
- Loose
- Very Loose

Ctrl-Shift-[decreases the space between highlighted letters in 0.25-point increments. Ctrl-Shift-] increases the space between highlighted letters in 0.25-point increments.

Control the Spacing Between Characters *(continued)*

2 On the Format menu, choose Spacing Between Characters. The Spacing Between Characters dialog box appears.

3 Choose Selected Characters Only.

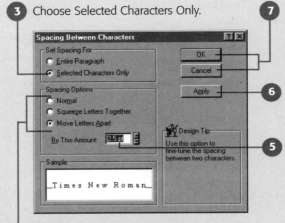

7 To accept your changes and return to your document, click OK. To return to your document without implementing the new spacing, click Cancel.

6 To see how the new character spacing looks in your document, click Apply.

5 Enter the number of points you want to subtract or add between letters. You can enter any value from 0 through 500 points in 0.25-point increments.

4 Choose one of the spacing options.

Automatic Kerning

Some letter combinations, such as *TO* and *AV,* always appear a little too loose. Whereas standard spacing for these and other troublesome letter pairs is often acceptable at small point sizes, the awkward intercharacter spaces are much too noticeable at larger point sizes.

The apparent gap is an optical illusion caused by the shape of the letters.

You can compensate with automatic kerning—a process that moves letter pairs closer together.

Automatic kerning can be customized. By default, Publisher applies kerning to letter pairs when the type size is 15 points or greater. You can specify that Publisher should begin kerning above a different point size.

Specifying the kerning point size to speed up performance. Publisher will kern letter pairs at point sizes greater than or equal to any point size you specify. Typing a point size greater than the largest point size you intend to use in your publication effectively disables kerning and speeds up Publisher's performance. Typing a size smaller than 15 points can seriously degrade Publisher's performance.

Customize the Kerning Options

1 Choose Options on the Tools menu.

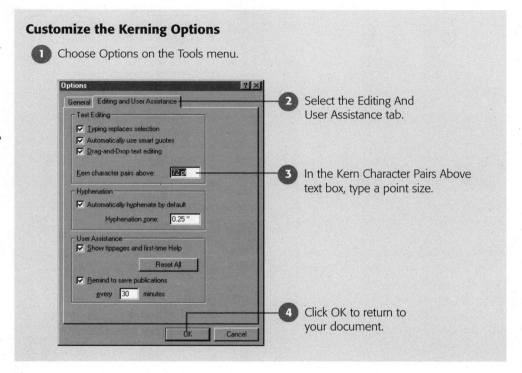

2 Select the Editing And User Assistance tab.

3 In the Kern Character Pairs Above text box, type a point size.

4 Click OK to return to your document.

Fancy First Letters

Fancy first letters are a common design device, often used to indicate the beginning of a new text unit, such as a chapter. Publisher provides a host of preformatted fancy first letters. You can also create your own fancy first letters and apply their custom formatting attributes to multiple letters or an entire word.

First letters that hang below the first line of text are called drop caps.

Only in recent times has Nasturtium, or Tropaeolum minus, been considered an ornamental plant. Persians nibbled Nasturtium petals as early as 400 B.C. They reached their peak of popularity in the kitchens of 17th century Europe. The flowers, stems, and young leaves of this plant are edible. The flavor is peppery and has a marked similarity to watercress. Indeed, Nasturtium's tangy, slightly hot taste has made it a favorite salad ingredient of Nouvelle-cuisine chefs.

O nly in recent times has Nasturtium, or Tropaeolum minus, been considered an ornamental plant. Persians nibbled Nasturtium petals as early as 400 B.C. They reached their peak of popularity in the kitchens of 17th century Europe. The flowers, stems, and young leaves of this plant are edible. The flavor is peppery and has a marked similarity to watercress. Indeed, Nasturtium's tangy, slightly hot taste has made it a favorite salad

First letters that share a baseline with the first line of text are called initial caps.

Can I change or remove fancy first letters? Yes. Select the paragraph, then open the Fancy First Letter dialog box. Choose a different preformatted style, select custom options, or return the fancy first letter to normal by clicking the first style in the gallery (or by clicking the Remove button). You can even use Publisher's Character command (available on the Format menu) to change many—but not all—text formatting attributes, such as font, font style, and color. You can't use the Character command or Publisher's normal text editing tools to change the size of or remove the fancy first letter. These changes can only be accomplished via the Fancy First Letter dialog box.

Insert a Preformatted Fancy First Letter

1 Select the paragraph where you want to add a fancy first letter.

2 On the Format menu, choose Fancy First Letter.

3 Select the Fancy First Letter tab.

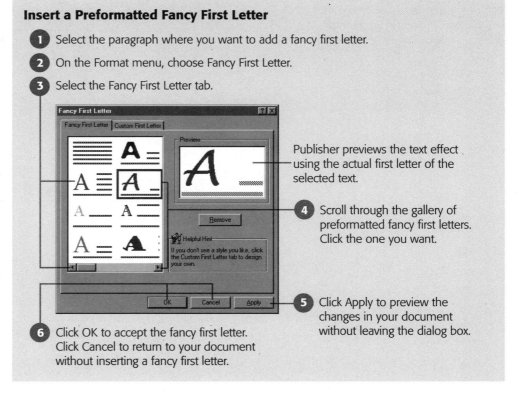

Publisher previews the text effect using the actual first letter of the selected text.

4 Scroll through the gallery of preformatted fancy first letters. Click the one you want.

5 Click Apply to preview the changes in your document without leaving the dialog box.

6 Click OK to accept the fancy first letter. Click Cancel to return to your document without inserting a fancy first letter.

Create a Custom Fancy First Letter or a Fancy First Word

1 Select the paragraph where you want to add a fancy first letter or fancy first word.

2 On the Format menu, choose Fancy First Letter.

3 Select the Custom First Letter tab.

4 Choose a dropped cap, an up (initial) cap, or a custom position. If you choose the custom position, you must enter a value from 0 through 2.

5 Open the Font drop-down list box and choose a typeface.

6 Enter a value from 2 through 254 in the Size text box. The size of a fancy first letter is always relative to the height of the remaining text in the paragraph. For example, a size of 4 will produce a fancy first letter 4 lines tall.

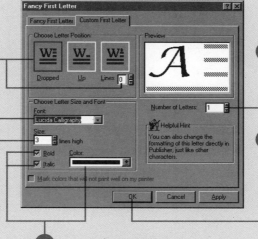

7 Format the text with boldface, italics, or a color.

8 If you want to apply the effect to multiple letters or an entire word, enter a value between 1 and 15 in the Number Of Letters text box.

9 If you are happy with the fancy first letter shown in the Preview area, click OK. Publisher includes your customized fancy first letter in the design gallery. It will be available in this and all future publications that you create.

Special Typographic Characters

You can enhance the professional look of your publications by using true typographic characters instead of typewriter-style characters. Publisher makes it easy to insert special characters such as the ones below.

Disable the Smart Quotes feature. If you use straight typewriter-style quotation marks and single hyphens more frequently than typographic curly quotation marks and em-dashes, you can turn off the Smart Quotes feature. On the Tools menu, choose Options. Select the Editing And User Assistance tab, and turn off Automatically Use Smart Quotes. You can still insert curly opening and closing quotation marks and em-dashes in your text, but you'll have to do it manually using the Insert Symbol dialog box.

If you must type a straight double quotation mark (to designate inches, for example) while Automatically Use Smart Quotes is turned on for the rest of your publication, hold down the Ctrl and Shift keys and press the quotation mark key. To type a straight single quotation mark, hold down the Ctrl key and press the quotation mark key.

Comparison of Typographic and Typewriter-Style Characters			
Typographic Character Name	**Typographic Example**	**Typewriter-Style Character Name**	**Typewriter-Style Example**
Curly quotes	" "	Straight quotes	" "
Em dash	—	Double hyphen	--
Copyright and trademark symbols	© ™	Normal text	(c) (tm)
Diacritical marks	øüñàé	Not normally available	

Smart Quotes and Symbols

You can rely on Publisher's Smart Quotes feature to insert basic typographic characters automatically. This feature is available on the Editing And User Assistance tab in the Options dialog box. If you turn on Automatically Use Smart Quotes, Publisher will substitute opening and closing curly quotation marks whenever you type a single or double quotation mark. In addition, Publisher will substitute an em dash whenever you type double hyphens.

The Insert Symbol dialog box allows you to insert in your document all of the available letters and symbols that don't appear on your keyboard.

Why are there typewriter-style characters in my imported text? The Smart Quotes feature only works for new text that you type. Imported text must be edited to convert typewriter-style characters to typographic characters. Use Publisher's Replace function to make the changes quickly.

To enter the codes for curly quotation marks and em dashes in the Replace With dialog box (in the Replace dialog box), use the Windows 95 Character Map to copy the character to the Clipboard. (Click the Windows 95 Start button, choose Programs, then Accessories, then Character Map.) Use the Ctrl-V keyboard shortcut to paste the character in the Replace With text box. Publisher might display a thin black rectangle in the Replace With text box instead of the special character, but the character you've specified will be correctly inserted in your text.

Insert a Symbol

1 Click to position the insertion point where you want to insert the symbol.

2 On the Insert menu, choose Symbol.

3 Open the Show Symbols From drop-down list box and choose a font.

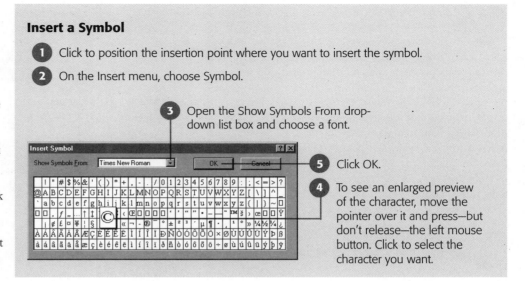

5 Click OK.

4 To see an enlarged preview of the character, move the pointer over it and press—but don't release—the left mouse button. Click to select the character you want.

Paragraph Formatting

Publisher defines a paragraph as any amount of text followed by a carriage return. Therefore the formatting applied to paragraphs in Publisher can be as short as one character or as long as the whole publication.

When you select settings for paragraph indents and alignment, you determine the shape and density of a block of text. You can choose from numerous preset options to create the most commonly used paragraph formats (shown in the following illustration). Alternatively, you can create new paragraph styles.

Use the indents and tabs ruler as a shortcut to setting indents. When you create or select a text object, the indents and tabs ruler appears on the horizontal ruler. The indents and tabs ruler, which is exactly the same width as the text object, displays the current indent settings, represented with triangles that you can move with the mouse. Any change you make on this ruler is reflected in the Indents And Lists dialog box the next time you open it.

For information about using the ruler to set indents and tabs, see page 110.

Although these bright purple and yellow blooms look quite a lot like Pansies, Johnny Jump-Ups are totally edible. The mild flavor is slightly sweet, making Johnny Jump-Ups a perfect decoration for soft cheeses or cold fruit soups. Try combining goat cheese with Johnny Jump-Ups and

This is a flush left paragraph with no indent. Blank lines usually separate individual paragraphs. This is a typical format for business correspondence. Notice that the right margin is irregular—or ragged.

Although these bright purple and yellow blooms look quite a lot like Pansies, Johnny Jump-Ups are totally edible. The mild flavor is slightly sweet, making Johnny Jump-Ups a perfect decoration for soft cheeses or cold fruit soups. Try combining goat cheese with Johnny Jump-Ups and wa-

Newspapers and magazines typically have indented first lines of second and subsequent paragraphs. The paragraph is justified so that text is flush with both the left and right margins.

1. These bright purple and yellow blooms look quite a lot like Pansies.
2. Johnny Jump-Ups are totally edible.
3. The mild flavor is slightly sweet, making Johnny Jump-Ups a perfect decoration for soft cheeses or cold fruit soups.
4. Try combining goat cheese with Johnny Jump-Ups and watercress.

Publisher considers each of these numbered items to be a new paragraph because each is followed by a carriage return. Numbered lists often use a hanging indent to offset the numeral from the rest of the text.

Regardless of the paragraph format you choose or create, you should pay special attention to the values in the Left and First Line text boxes in the Indents And Lists dialog box. These values are added to one another to produce the final indented effect for the paragraph.

Although these bright purple and yellow blooms look quite a lot like Pansies, Johnny Jump-Ups are totally edible. The mild flavor is slightly sweet, making Johnny Jump-Ups a perfect decoration for soft cheeses or cold fruit soups. Try combining goat cheese with Johnny Jump-Ups and watercress.

Although these bright purple and yellow blooms look quite a lot like Pansies, Johnny Jump-Ups are totally edible. The mild flavor is slightly sweet, making Johnny Jump-Ups a perfect decoration for soft cheeses or cold fruit soups. Try combining goat cheese with Johnny Jump-Ups and watercress.

If you choose a standard paragraph indent with the left indent set at 0.5 inch, typing a value of 0.5 in the First Line text box creates a cumulative effect: the first line indent now measures 1 inch from the margin.

To create a hanging indent, set the left indent at 0.5 inch and the first line indent at –0.25. The first line of text then hangs to the left of the remaining text lines by 0.25 inch.

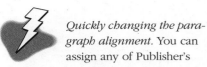

Quickly changing the paragraph alignment. You can assign any of Publisher's standard alignment options to the currently selected paragraph or paragraphs by clicking the Left, Right, Center, or Justified buttons on the Format toolbar.

Choose a Preset Indent

1 Click in the paragraph you want to format. To format more than one paragraph at a time, highlight them all.

2 Choose Indents And Lists on the Format menu. The Indents And Lists dialog box appears.

3 Select the Normal option.

4 Open the Preset drop-down list box to choose one of six options:

- Original: makes no changes to the existing indents
- Flush Left: aligns all text with the left margins
- 1st Line Indent: creates a 0.25-inch indent for the first line only
- Hanging Indent: indents every line *after* the first by 0.25 inch
- Quotation: indents text by 0.5 inch on both the left and right
- Custom: allows you to create your own paragraph formats

5 Click OK.

Customize the Paragraph Indents

1 Click in the paragraph you want to format. To format more than one paragraph at a time, highlight them all.

2 Choose Indents And Lists on the Format menu. The Indents And Lists dialog box appears.

Controlling line breaks. By inserting nonprinting characters, you can control the word spacing and the line breaks in a paragraph. In this way you can improve the rag—the pattern formed by the ends of text lines. To force a line break without starting a new paragraph, press Shift-Enter. To prevent a line break between two words, insert a nonbreaking space by pressing Ctrl-Shift-Space.

Customize the Paragraph Indents *(continued)*

4 The Left and Right text boxes specify the distance between the left and right edges of the text and the frame margins. Enter a value from 0 through 20 inches.

3 Select the Normal option.

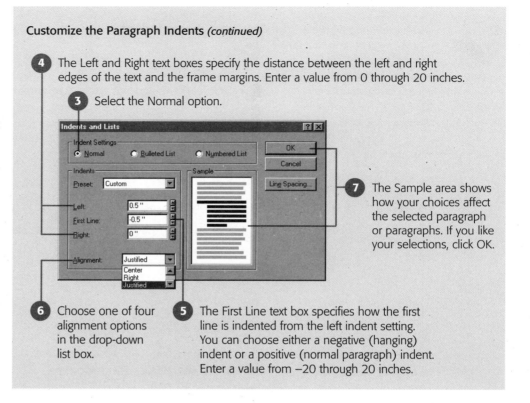

7 The Sample area shows how your choices affect the selected paragraph or paragraphs. If you like your selections, click OK.

6 Choose one of four alignment options in the drop-down list box.

5 The First Line text box specifies how the first line is indented from the left indent setting. You can choose either a negative (hanging) indent or a positive (normal paragraph) indent. Enter a value from −20 through 20 inches.

The New Bullet dialog box is identical to the Insert Symbol dialog box. See page 101 for more information.

Better bullets. You can insert decorative bullets into your text by choosing a font such as Wingdings in the New Bullet dialog box.

Accurate previews. Although the Sample area shows only broad shaded lines for text (referred to as greeked text), the preview of a bulleted list is accurate. Use it to make sure that the carryover lines align under the first character of the first line. For this to occur, the indent you specify in the Indent List By text box must be equal to the amount of space required for the bullet plus the white space between the bullet and the text.

Bulleted Lists

Bulleted lists draw attention to the important points in your publication and create visual interest by breaking up dense blocks of text. You can add bullets to your text manually, but it's faster to have Publisher create a bulleted list for you.

Format Several Paragraphs as a Bulleted List

1. Select the paragraphs you want to include in the bulleted list. Remember that a paragraph can consist of a character, a single word, or a sentence.

2. Choose Indents And Lists on the Format menu. The Indents And Lists dialog box appears.

3. Choose Bulleted List. The Bullet Type area appears.

4. Either choose one of the six bullets displayed, or click New Bullet to bring up the New Bullet dialog box. In the New Bullet dialog box, you can select the font used for the bullet. If you select a new bullet character from the New Bullet dialog box and click OK, the new bullet will appear as one of the six bullet choices in the Bullet Type area.

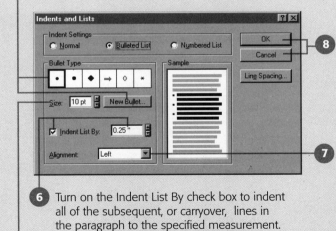

8. Click OK to accept your choices, or click Cancel to return to your document without implementing any of the bulleted list settings.

7. Open the Alignment drop-down list box and choose one of the four options for text alignment: Left, Center, Right, or Justified.

6. Turn on the Indent List By check box to indent all of the subsequent, or carryover, lines in the paragraph to the specified measurement. Enter a value from –20 through 20 inches.

5. Change the bullet size by typing any value from 0.5 and 999.5 points in the Size text box.

Change the appearance of numbered lists. You can create distinctive formats for your lists by choosing among the options in the Format and Separator drop-down list boxes. For example, instead of using ascending numerals, you can organize a list with ascending letters.

The Format drop-down list box offers you three choices:

- Arabic numerals
- Lowercase letters
- Uppercase letters

The Separator drop-down list box gives you eight options:

- None (a small white space)
- A period
- A single closing parenthesis after the number
- A single closing bracket after the number
- A colon
- Parentheses around the number
- Brackets around the number
- Hyphens around the number

Numbered Lists

Numbered lists enumerate series of items, give sequential instructions, or create outlines. When you use the numbered list format, every new paragraph automatically begins with the next higher number or letter in the series.

Set Up a Numbered List

1 Select the paragraphs you want to include in the numbered list.

2 Choose Indents And Lists on the Format menu. The Indents And Lists dialog box appears.

3 Choose the Numbered List option. The Number area appears.

4 Open the Format drop-down list box and choose one of three options (see the adjacent Power Tip).

5 To specify how you want the numbers separated from the text, open the Separator drop-down list box and choose one of eight options.

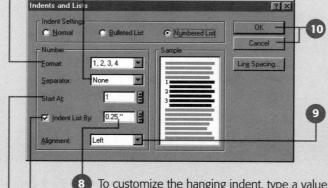

10 Click OK to accept your choices, or click Cancel to return to your document without implementing the numbered list settings.

9 Open the Alignment drop-down list box and choose Left, Center, Right, or Justified.

8 To customize the hanging indent, type a value from –20 through 20 inches in the Indent List By text box.

7 If you want to remove the indent for the text, turn off the Indent List By check box. You don't need to set the value in the Indent List By text box to 0. The text will wrap to the left margin for all lines.

6 If you are formatting paragraphs that are part of a larger, interrupted sequence, type the number or letter that should begin the current sequence.

The line spacing changes automatically according to the text point size. Publisher's default single spacing (1 sp) is set at 120 percent of point size. As an example, for 10-point type, the 1 sp setting inserts 12 points from baseline to baseline. The advantage of this arrangement is that the line spacing changes automatically when the point size changes. For example, if you decide to format your text at 12 instead of 10 points, the line spacing of 1 space automatically increases to 14.4 points.

Why did my text disappear? If your text disappears when you change the line spacing, you probably accidentally entered a very large value in the Between Lines text box. Either you typed in the wrong numbers, or you forgot to add the *pt* abbreviation to indicate that you want to use points as the unit of measurement.

Line Spacing

Publisher uses the measurement called line spacing, or leading, to determine the amount of space between the bottom, or baseline, of the characters in one line of text and the baseline of the next line, as illustrated below. To give you even more control over the appearance of your text, you can add extra spacing before and after paragraphs, independent of the leading.

Although these bright purple and yellow blooms look quite a lot like Pansies, Johnny Jump-Ups are totally edible. The mild flavor is slightly sweet, making Johnny Jump-Ups a perfect decoration for soft cheeses or cold fruit soups. Try combining goat cheese with Johnny Jump-Ups and watercress.

Increasing the leading of a text block can improve legibility or create a special effect.

Although these bright purple and yellow blooms look quite a lot like Pansies, Johnny Jump-Ups are totally edible. The mild flavor is slightly sweet, making Johnny Jump-Ups a perfect decoration for soft cheeses or cold fruit soups. Try combining goat cheese with Johnny Jump-Ups and watercress.

Decreasing the leading, even by a small increment such as 0.5 point—which is only 0.0069 ($^1/_{144}$) inch—can help you to fit more text on a page.

Change the Line Spacing from the Default of 1 Space

1 Click anywhere in the paragraph, or select the paragraphs you want to reformat.

2 On the Format menu, choose Line Spacing.

3 Enter a new value from 0.25 through 124 spaces (sp) in increments of 0.01 line space.

4 Click OK to accept the new line spacing and return to your document, or click Cancel to return to your document without changing the line spacing.

Using points as the unit of measurement. By default, Publisher uses a relative unit of measurement (line spaces) to add spaces between lines of text. You have much more control over line spacing if you use an absolute unit of measure such as inches, centimeters, picas, or points. Because points are the smallest unit of measurement, specifying points gives you the most control over the look of your design.

To change the line spacing using points, enter a value from 3 through 1488 points in 0.05-point increments in the Between Lines text box (in the Line Spacing dialog box). Remember to add the *pt* abbreviation to specify points.

Add the appropriate spacing between paragraphs. Pressing Enter to add space between paragraphs creates a full blank line space, which can disrupt the text flow. Use the Line Spacing dialog box to add small amounts of white space before or after paragraphs to separate them without disrupting text flow.

Specify Extra Leading Before and After Paragraphs

1. Click anywhere in the paragraph, or select the paragraphs you want to reformat.

2. On the Format menu, choose Line Spacing.

3. Enter any value from 0 through 1440 points (pt) or from 0 through 120 spaces (sp) in the Before Paragraphs and After Paragraphs text boxes.

4. Click OK if you like the effect as shown in the Sample area, or click Cancel to return to your document without changing the line spacing.

Tabs

Tabs are useful if you want to align several items in column-and-row format or space several words evenly across a wide column. By default, Publisher places tab stops at 0.5-inch intervals. Use the Tabs dialog box to alter those settings.

Set and Delete Tabs in the Tabs Dialog Box

1. Click in any paragraph or select the paragraphs for which you want to set tabs.

2. On the Format menu, choose Tabs. The Tabs dialog box appears.

When not to use tabs. You should *never* use the Tabs command to indent the first line of a paragraph. If you subsequently modify your design, you'll have to manually edit each paragraph. Use the Indents And Lists dialog box instead. It lets you modify indents globally.

Consider using the Table tool to format rows and columns. The Table tool, which can format text into rows and columns, is often easier to use than the Tabs command. Adding or deleting text from a table does not alter the row and column alignment. However, adding or deleting tabbed text can misalign text elements.

For more information about Publisher's Table tool, see Chapter 7.

Set and Delete Tabs in the Tabs Dialog Box *(continued)*

3 To add a tab stop, type the measurement of the distance between the left margin of the text frame and the alignment position of the tab, and then click the Set button. The new tab setting is included in the Tab Positions list box.

5 Select one of the four alignment options.

- Left: aligns the left edge of the text and is ideal for row headings and table text.
- Center: centers the text on the tab and works well for column titles.
- Right: aligns the right edge of the text after the tab and works well for numerical data.
- Decimal: aligns the decimal point within the text at the tab stop. It is used almost exclusively for numerical data, although it will work with any text containing a period.

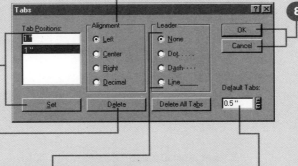

8 Click OK to create the tabs. Click Cancel to return to your document without changing the current tab settings. Now each time you press the Tab key, Publisher moves the insertion point (and any text to the right of the insertion point) to the next tab stop.

6 To select a leader character (which fills the space between the point at which you press the Tab key and the tab stop) select one of these options.

7 Change the default tab setting for the current text frame by entering a value in the Default Tabs text box. For example, if you enter a value of *1"*, Publisher places tab stops at 1-inch intervals.

4 To delete a tab stop, select the tab from the Tab Positions list box, and then click Delete. Click Delete All Tabs to remove all the tabs that have been set for the selected paragraphs.

Indents and Tabs Ruler

Every time you create or select a text object, the indents and tabs ruler appears on the horizontal ruler. You can set or modify indent and tab positions by clicking and dragging icons that appear on this ruler.

Set Indents on the Indents and Tabs Ruler

1 Click in the paragraph, or select the paragraphs for which you want to adjust indents. The indents and tabs ruler appears.

2 Drag any of the triangles to a new position on the ruler.

The upper left triangle controls the First Line indent.

The right triangle controls the Right indent.

The lower left triangle controls the Left indent.

Identify tab markers. Publisher always identifies the alignment associated with a tab marker.

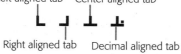

Left aligned tab   Center aligned tab

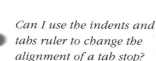

Right aligned tab   Decimal aligned tab

Can I use the indents and tabs ruler to change the alignment of a tab stop? You can use the indents and tabs ruler to access the Tabs dialog box quickly. Double-click the tab marker whose alignment you want to change. The Tabs dialog box, in which you can specify alignment and a leader character, will appear.

Set and Delete Tabs on the Ruler

1 Click in the paragraph, or select the paragraphs for which you want to set tab stops.

2 Click the indents and tabs ruler where you want to place the tab stop. A tab marker, which looks like a bent line, appears on the ruler.

The default tab is left aligned and appears as a bent line.

To move a tab stop, drag the tab marker to a new location on the ruler.

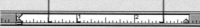

3 To remove a tab stop, drag the tab marker off the ruler.

Can I use a text style on one word in my document? You can't apply a text style to single words in a sentence or to particular characters within a text string. Using the Text Styles command always changes the entire paragraph.

Naming your text styles. You can use up to 32 characters for the text style name, so make the name as descriptive as possible. For example, *Headline 32pt* tells you a lot more than *Heading01*.

Text Styles

When you want to apply the same formatting options to many paragraphs in your document, you can save a lot of time by creating a text style. A text style is a combination of formats that you name, save, and reuse. A style can include character-level formats (such as font, point size, boldface, italics, and color) and paragraph-level formats (such as indents, alignment, line spacing, tabs, and bullets).

The benefits of using text styles include the following:

- You can apply formatting commands for characters, indents, line spacing, character spacing, lists, and tabs with a single mouse click.

- You can guarantee consistency throughout a long document.

- You can make global formatting changes to a document by editing the text style.

- You can apply text styles you've created for one publication to other publications.

You can create text styles in one of two ways:

- By example. If you aren't sure how to format a particular paragraph, experiment with sample text. After you've created a good-looking paragraph, you can create a text style based on it.

- From scratch. If you know how to define the features of your paragraph, you can create a text style from scratch in the Text Styles dialog box. You don't need to select a paragraph before you start.

Create a Text Style by Example

1. Format the paragraph.
2. Click inside the paragraph.
3. Highlight the contents of the Style drop-down text box, located on the left end of the Format toolbar.

Copy formatting from one object to another. Publisher gives you four ways to copy styles from one text object to another.

- Format Painter. Select the text block whose style you want to copy. Click the Format Painter icon on the Standard toolbar, then highlight the text you want to reformat. Alternatively, click a blank area in the text frame to reformat all the text in the frame.

- The text object shortcut menu. Right-click any text object to display its shortcut menu, where two commands—Pick Up Formatting and Apply Formatting—let you quickly copy a text style from one selected text block to another. The Pick Up Formatting and Apply Formatting commands can also be found on the Format menu.

- Right drag. You can simply use the right mouse button to drag one text object over another text object. Then click the Apply Formatting Here command on the shortcut menu.

- Keyboard shortcuts. To copy formats, press Ctrl-Shift-C. To paste formats, press Ctrl-Shift-V.

Create a Text Style by Example _(continued)_

4 Replace the existing style name by typing a new style name, and then press Enter. The Create Style By Example dialog box appears.

5 In the Create Style By Example dialog box, click OK to create the new text style, or click Cancel to return to your document without saving the new style.

Create a Text Style from Scratch

1 On the Format menu, choose Text Style. The Text Styles dialog box appears.

2 In the Click To area, choose Create A New Style. The Create New Style dialog box appears.

3 In the Enter New Style Name text box, type a new name.

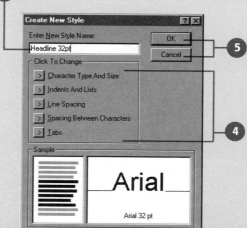

5 When you have changed the text formatting options to your liking, click OK to create the style. Click Cancel to return to your document without creating the style.

4 Click one of these five buttons. Publisher presents you with the standard text and paragraph formatting dialog boxes.

6 Click Close in the Text Styles dialog box.

Apply Text Styles

1 Click in the paragraph, or highlight the paragraphs to which you want the style to apply.

2 Open the Style drop-down list box on the Format toolbar and select a style name.

Modify Existing Text Styles

Even after you have created a style and applied it to your text, you can still modify it. When you modify an existing text style, you make global formatting changes to all paragraphs associated with that style. You can modify an existing style by example or by using the Text Styles dialog box.

Can I return a paragraph to the previously defined text style? Yes. After you select the paragraph and change its formatting, open the Style drop-down list box and click the name of the style you want to reapply. In the Change Or Apply Style dialog box that appears, select Return The Selection To The Original Formatting Of The Style? Click OK.

Modify Existing Text Styles by Example

1 Select the paragraphs whose style you want to change.

2 Change the formatting to your satisfaction.

3 Open the Style drop-down list box. Click the style you want to change. The Change Or Apply Style dialog box appears.

4 Select the first option to modify the style based on the currently selected paragraph.

5 Click OK. Publisher reformats all paragraphs that use this style.

Managing text styles. The Text Styles dialog box lets you organize text styles for greater efficiency. You can do the following:

@ Delete styles you no longer use.

@ Rename styles so that related styles are grouped together on the Style drop-down list box. Because Publisher arranges style names alphabetically, styles such as Table Text and Table Titles would appear next to each other.

Modify Existing Text Styles Using the Text Styles Dialog Box

1 On the Format menu, choose Text Style. The Text Styles dialog box appears.

2 In the Choose A Style list box, select the name of the style you want to modify.

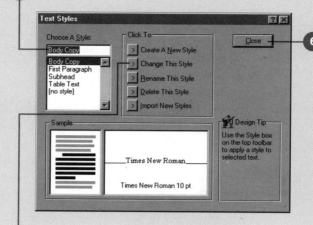

6 Click Close in the Text Styles dialog box.

3 Select Change This Style. The Change Style dialog box appears.

4 Use the option buttons—Character Type And Size, Indents And Lists, Line Spacing, Spacing Between Characters, and Tabs—to access the standard text formatting dialog boxes.

5 When you have modified the text formatting options to your satisfaction, click OK to accept the changes, or click Cancel to return to the previous dialog box.

Import styles from a word processing file to reconcile duplicate text style names. If you insert text from a word processing file, Publisher does its best to maintain the actual text formatting but often reassigns the style name. This is a particularly frustrating problem if your word processing file and the Publisher document contain duplicate style names. The solution is simple. Before you insert the text itself, use the Import New Styles button to bring the style names from the word processing document into your Publisher document and to automatically reconcile duplicate style names.

Importing Text Styles from Other Documents

You can get more value from the text styles you've created for one Publisher document by using them in other Publisher documents. You can also import and use styles you've created in your word processing application if Publisher can read the word processing format in its native form.

Import a Text Style

1 On the Format menu, choose Text Style.

2 Choose Import New Styles. The Import Styles dialog box appears.

4 Use the Look In drop-down list box and the Files list box to locate the file.

5 Select the file that contains the styles you want to import.

3 Open the Files Of Type drop-down list box and select any file type. The default is Publisher's format.

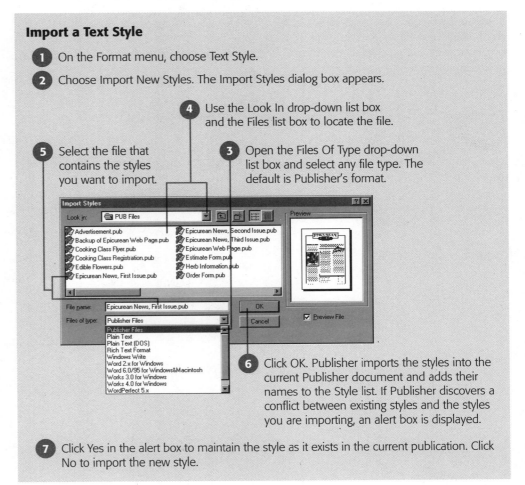

6 Click OK. Publisher imports the styles into the current Publisher document and adds their names to the Style list. If Publisher discovers a conflict between existing styles and the styles you are importing, an alert box is displayed.

7 Click Yes in the alert box to maintain the style as it exists in the current publication. Click No to import the new style.

Automatically format long documents. If you change the default text frame properties *before* you import a long text document, you can take full advantage of Publisher's Autoflow feature. Each new text frame that Publisher creates as part of the Autoflow process will contain the new customized formatting attributes.

To learn how to save defaults for use with all future publications, see page 49 in Chapter 4.

Changing the Default Text Style via Text Frames

You can increase your efficiency by changing the default attributes associated with the Text tool. When you do so, every text frame will be created with the formatting attributes you specify. These defaults will remain in effect until you change them again, or until you open a new document.

Change the Default Text Frame Attributes

1 Select the Text tool, but don't draw a text frame.

2 Change the default formatting attributes by using the Format toolbar, commands on the Format menu, or keyboard shortcuts. You can set new defaults for the following attributes:

- Text frame borders
- Fill colors, patterns, and shading
- Drop shadows
- Text frame margins and columns
- Text frame options such as Continued notices
- Character styles
- Paragraph alignment
- Indents and lists
- Line spacing
- Tabs
- Spacing between characters

Checking Spelling

Publisher's robust spelling checker catches misspellings in your documents. If you use unusual or technical words, you can add them to the dictionary.

Checking the spelling of specific words or phrases.
You can check the spelling of a single word or a selected text block by highlighting it before you choose the Check Spelling command. If Publisher does not find the word in its dictionary, it presents the usual Check Spelling dialog box. When Publisher finishes checking the spelling of the word you highlighted, it offers you the opportunity to check the spelling in the rest of the story.

Check the Spelling in a Publication

1 Select a text frame and choose Check Spelling on the Tools menu. One of three things will happen:

- If Publisher finds no questionable words, it returns you to the document.

- If your document contains more stories and the Check All Stories check box is turned off, Publisher asks whether you want to check the rest of your publication. (Clicking Yes will automatically turn on Check All Stories.)

- If Publisher finds a word not in its dictionary or a word with a capitalization error, it displays the Check Spelling dialog box.

Publisher shows the misspelled word in the Not In Dictionary text box and also highlights it in your publication.

If the word has a capitalization error, Publisher displays it in the Error In Capitalization text box, which replaces the Not In Dictionary text box.

Click Ignore to leave the word alone.

Click Ignore All to ignore every instance of the word throughout the story.

2 If Publisher's best guess for the correct spelling or capitalization (in the Change To text box) is not the word you intended, select one of the words from the Suggestions list or type the correct spelling directly into the Change To text box.

3 If you agree with Publisher's spelling of the word, or if you selected or typed the correct word, click the Change button to replace the incorrect spelling with the correct spelling in the document. If you click the Change All button, Publisher will search for and replace every instance of the misspelled word.

Click Add to permanently add the word to Publisher's dictionary.

To check all of the stories in your document, turn on Check All Stories.

To ignore acronyms or other words that are usually set in all capital letters, turn on this check box.

Check Spelling dialog box

Not in dictionary: `patial`

Change To: `Patel`
Suggestions: Patel / partial

Ignore   Ignore All
Change   Change All
Add   Close

☐ Ignore Words In UPPERCASE
☐ Check All Stories

Hyphenation Options

You can smooth ragged margins by using hyphens to break words that fall at the ends of lines. Publisher offers several different hyphenation options:

- Automatically hyphenate every story in your publication.

- Customize hyphenation for a single story. Use automatic hyphenation, approve each of Publisher's suggested hyphens, or completely turn off hyphenation.

- Manually insert optional hyphens.

- Insert nonbreaking hyphens for words that are always hyphenated and that you do not want to break between two lines. Use these hyphens to avoid bad breaks in compound words, for example.

When automatic hyphenation is active, Publisher breaks words based on the size of the hyphenation zone. The hyphenation zone, located along the right text margin, defines a region in which Publisher looks for words to hyphenate.

Controlling automatic hyphenation with text frames. The size of the text frame can make a difference in how words break at the end of a line and therefore how many hyphens appear: a narrow text frame produces shorter lines and more hyphens; a wider text frame produces longer lines and fewer hyphens.

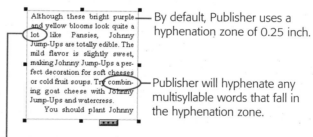

Although these bright purple and yellow blooms look quite a lot like Pansies, Johnny Jump-Ups are totally edible. The mild flavor is slightly sweet, making Johnny Jump-Ups a perfect decoration for soft cheeses or cold fruit soups. Try combining goat cheese with Johnny Jump-Ups and watercress.
You should plant Johnny

By default, Publisher uses a hyphenation zone of 0.25 inch.

Publisher will hyphenate any multisyllable words that fall in the hyphenation zone.

One-syllable words that are too long to fit are pushed to the next line.

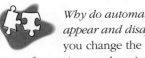

Controlling the number of hyphens in your story. Increase the hyphenation zone to hyphenate fewer words. If the text you're hyphenating is left aligned, increasing the hyphenation zone will create a more irregular, or ragged, right margin. Decrease the hyphenation zone to hyphenate more words and create a more regular right margin.

Why do automatic hyphens appear and disappear? As you change the text by editing, reformatting, or changing the layout, different words fall in the hyphenation zone and are hyphenated to accommodate the changes. Words formerly hyphenated that move out of the hyphenation zone are closed up again.

Hyphenation in justified text. If the text you're hyphenating is justified (aligned on both the left and right margins), increasing the hyphenation zone will leave more spaces between words, which can create unpleasant gaps between the words in your text. Decrease the hyphenation zone setting to hyphenate more words and give your text a smoother appearance.

Automatically Hyphenate Every Story in Your Publication

1 Choose Options on the Tools menu, and then select the Editing And User Assistance tab.

2 Choose Automatically Hyphenate By Default.

3 Enter a value from 0 through 10 inches in the Hyphenation Zone text box.

4 Click OK to accept the hyphenation settings.

Customize Hyphenation for a Single Story

1 Select the text object that contains the story whose hyphenation you want to modify.

2 Choose Hyphenate on the Tools menu.

3 Select the appropriate option.

Click here to turn off automatic hyphenation for this story.

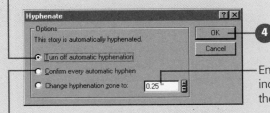

4 Return to your document by clicking OK.

Enter a value from 0 through 10 inches in 0.01-inch increments in the Hyphenation Zone text box.

To review, and if necessary edit, the hyphens that Publisher suggests, click here. If you click OK, a dialog box containing Publisher's suggested hyphenation appears, allowing you to move the hyphenation point to a different syllable. Click Yes to accept the suggestion, or click No to leave the word unbroken.

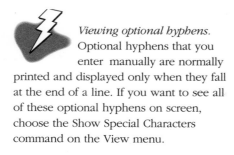

Viewing optional hyphens. Optional hyphens that you enter manually are normally printed and displayed only when they fall at the end of a line. If you want to see all of these optional hyphens on screen, choose the Show Special Characters command on the View menu.

Manually Insert Optional Hyphens

1 Position the insertion point between the two characters where you want Publisher to break the word.

2 Press Ctrl-hyphen.

water⌐cress

If Show Special Characters is turned on, Publisher displays a modified hyphen that looks bent.

Insert Nonbreaking Hyphens

1 Position the insertion point between two characters or between two words if you are creating a compound word.

2 Delete all spaces between the words.

3 Press Ctrl-Alt-hyphen.

Johnny·Jump⌐Ups·

If Show Special Characters is turned on, a nonbreaking hyphen is displayed as a larger-than-standard hyphen.

Give individual letters a shadow.

Create wavy banners with text.

Wrap text around a circle.

Twist text into unusual shapes that look like pictures.

Display Type.pub - Microsoft Publisher

File   Edit   View   Insert   Format   Tools   Arrange   Table   Mail Merge   Help

EPICUREAN DELIGHTS

EPICUREAN DELIGHTS

Epicurean Delights
Epicurean Delights

EPICUREAN DELIGHTS

DELIGHTS

Epicurean Delights

EPICUREAN DELIGHTS

EPICUREAN DELIGHTS

Page 1   Zoom 66%

Ready

Show Index   Show Help

Deflate and inflate text.

Turn WordArt text on a slant.

Fill text with color and a pattern.

WordArt Tool

With Microsoft Publisher 97's WordArt tool, you can enhance the appearance of text by creating special effects that are not available when you work with ordinary text objects. You can combine and control these effects to create a wide variety of display type designs ranging from sophisticated logos to whimsical headlines.

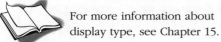

For more information about display type, see Chapter 15.

WordArt Frames

WordArt frames are similar—but not identical—to Publisher's normal text frames. One difference is that you must draw a WordArt frame and then use a special dialog box to enter text.

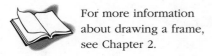

For more information about drawing a frame, see Chapter 2.

Enter Text into a WordArt Frame

1 Click the WordArt tool, shown in the following illustration, and draw a frame. The WordArt toolbar and dialog box appear.

Why do the commands for importing, copying, and pasting text that normally appear on the Edit and the Insert menus disappear when I'm working on a WordArt element? You cannot import text into WordArt, nor can you use standard Clipboard functions to copy and paste text directly into a WordArt frame. You must use the Enter Your Text Here dialog box for entering your text.

Formatting WordArt frames is explained on page 134.

Enter Text into a WordArt Frame *(continued)*

3 If you want to add a special character to the text, choose the font you want to use from the WordArt toolbar before choosing the symbol.

2 Type your display copy here. When you type multiple words and short phrases into the text box, you must manually break the lines by pressing the Enter key.

8 After you have completed the WordArt design to your satisfaction, click anywhere outside the WordArt frame to return to your publication.

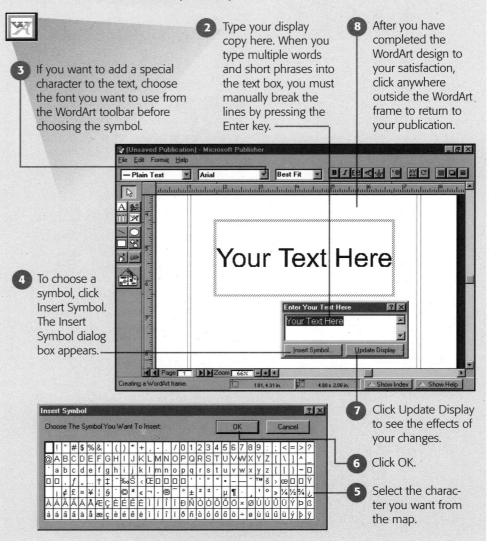

4 To choose a symbol, click Insert Symbol. The Insert Symbol dialog box appears.

7 Click Update Display to see the effects of your changes.

6 Click OK.

5 Select the character you want from the map.

WordArt Fonts

A font is more than a complete set of characters. Each font has a unique style, or look. As you can see in the following examples, each font projects a different mood.

Goudy Old Style — A restrained, conventional-looking font is appropriate for business or formal designs.

Comic Sans MS — A font that looks like it's straight out of a comic book would be a good choice for an informal party invitation.

Publisher automatically installs numerous TrueType fonts on your computer system, any of which you can select. TrueType fonts that other software applications have installed on your computer are also available to you. All TrueType fonts are listed in the Font drop-down list box.

Why can't I see all of the fonts installed on my system when I open the Font drop-down list box? WordArt uses only TrueType fonts, so only TrueType fonts appear in WordArt's Font drop-down list box. Fixed-size fonts or PostScript fonts cannot be accessed in WordArt.

For more information about the differences between TrueType, fixed-size, and PostScript fonts, see Chapter 14.

Select a Font for WordArt Text

1. If the WordArt toolbar and the Enter Your Text Here dialog box are not active, double-click the WordArt object to display them.

2. Open the Font drop-down list box on the WordArt toolbar.

3. Select a font name. You can apply only one font to all of the text in each WordArt frame. If you need to use a second font, create a second WordArt frame for the text.

Why does Publisher try to resize the WordArt frame when I specify a large point size for my text? If you choose a point size that is too large for the current dimensions of the WordArt frame, Publisher displays an alert box asking if you want to enlarge the WordArt frame. Click Yes to enlarge the frame. If you click No, you must either make the text smaller by choosing a smaller point size or resize the WordArt frame manually.

 Copy WordArt formatting to another WordArt object. You can quickly assign a whole range of formatting attributes to a WordArt object by copying them from an existing WordArt object. Simply select the WordArt object whose format you want to copy. Click the Format Painter on the Standard toolbar and move the pointer over the WordArt object you want to reformat. The pointer changes to the Format Painter pointer.

Now click the WordArt object to reformat it. You can also copy formatting from one WordArt object to another by using the right mouse button in either of two ways. Right-click a WordArt object and use the shortcut menu that appears, or drag one WordArt object over another with the right mouse button.

Changing the Size of WordArt Text

You can assign a specific point size to WordArt text to control its size, or you can use WordArt's powerful Best Fit option, which generates the best type size to fit your frame.

Size Text Manually

1 If the WordArt toolbar and the Enter Your Text Here dialog box are not active, double-click the WordArt object to display them.

2 Open the Font Size drop-down list box.

3 Select a numeric value from the list. Alternatively, type any point size from 6 through 500 in the text box and press Enter.

Size Text Automatically: The Best Fit Option

1 If the WordArt toolbar and the Enter Your Text Here dialog box are not active, double-click the WordArt object to display them.

2 Open the Font Size drop-down list box.

 **3** Select Best Fit. Now the WordArt frame functions like a picture frame. The text shrinks or grows to fit the frame, even if you resize the frame.

Shape and edit WordArt text to fit your design. To create successful WordArt designs, you must choose the most appropriate shape for your text—or edit your text so that it works with a particular shape. For example, to make a successful design for the button shown below, you must enter the words out of order (Epicurean, Cafe, Delights) and then separate them with a hard return.

Some WordArt shapes don't work well with long phrases. In the next example, the Inflate shape distorts the letters of Epicurean Delights Cafe. Shortening the phrase to a single word, Epicurean, avoids a cramped look.

Text Shaping Options

The single most powerful aspect of WordArt is its ability to manipulate the outlines of a font. The following illustrations demonstrate a few of the shapes you can create with WordArt.

EPICUREAN DELIGHTS—Align text along wavy lines.

Create arched or circular text.

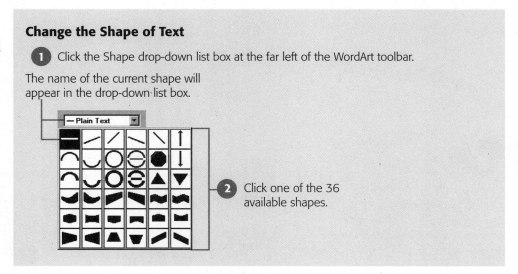

Change the Shape of Text

1 Click the Shape drop-down list box at the far left of the WordArt toolbar.

The name of the current shape will appear in the drop-down list box.

— Plain Text

2 Click one of the 36 available shapes.

Customizing the Text Shape with Special Effects

You can fine-tune any of the WordArt shapes by clicking the Special Effects button on the WordArt toolbar and changing the settings in the Special Effects dialog box. It presents you with different effects depending on the shape you chose for your

How is the rotation effect in WordArt different from Publisher's object rotation feature? When you use the WordArt rotation effect, text is rotated *within* the frame. In addition, the WordArt rotation effect can simulate 3-dimensional rotations for certain shapes, such as the Wave 1 shape shown here.

Publisher's object rotation feature, on the other hand, rotates an entire object—frame and all—and always rotates an object in 2-dimensional space.

WordArt enables you to print special effects on older printers. If you own a dot matrix printer or an older laser printer, you might experience problems when attempting to print a standard text object that has been rotated. To avoid this printing problem, use WordArt. WordArt prints text as a graphic and, in effect, bypasses the limitations of older printers.

text. For example, if your WordArt text follows a straight line or fills a shape, a dialog box offering rotation and slider effects appears. If your WordArt text follows an arc or a circle, a dialog box offering effects for rotation, arc angle, and letter-height reduction appears.

Special Effects button

Change the Rotation and Angle of a Shape

1 Enter a value from -360 through 360 degrees in the Rotation text box.

The slider effect decreases or increases the intensity of a shape effect. Changing the value will make the angles of individual letters more or less acute or will flatten or exaggerate the arc of a curve.

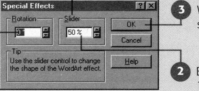

3 When you are satisfied with the special effect changes, click OK.

2 Enter a value from 0 through 100 percent in the Slider text box.

Change the Rotation and Curve of Arced or Circular WordArt Text

1 Enter a new value in the Arc Angle text box. Arc-shaped text can be modified to have a value from 0 through 180 degrees. Text in a circle can be modified to have a value from 0 through 360 degrees.

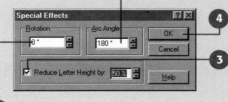

4 When you are satisfied with the special effect changes, click OK.

3 To change the size of the effect, turn on the Reduce Letter Height By check box. Enter a value from 0 through 100 percent in the text box.

2 Enter a value in the Rotation text box from -360 through 360 degrees.

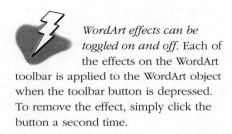

WordArt effects can be toggled on and off. Each of the effects on the WordArt toolbar is applied to the WordArt object when the toolbar button is depressed. To remove the effect, simply click the button a second time.

Formatting Options: Toolbar Button Effects

When the WordArt toolbar is displayed, you can change the overall appearance of your text by simply clicking the appropriate toolbar button. The effects range from standard formats to extravagant transformations, as illustrated below.

Epicurean Delights

Boldface adds emphasis.

Epicurean Delights

The Even Height button creates zany text effects.

Click the Italic button to italicize characters.

Click the Bold button to boldface characters.

Click the Stack Letters button to display text vertically (top to bottom).

Click the Even Height button to make upper-case and lowercase letters the same height.

Click the Stretch button to stretch characters both vertically and horizontally to the boundaries of the WordArt frame.

Letterspacing and Alignment Controls

There are times when the success of a special effect depends entirely on small details such as letterspacing and alignment. Publisher gives you two controls to fine-tune them.

Changing the Spacing Between Letters

Letterspacing is especially crucial when you are wrapping text around a circle or an arc. Increasing the letterspacing can avoid crashing letters. Decreasing the letterspacing can help you add artistic effects, as the following samples illustrate.

DECREASING

Very Tight Tracking

INCREASING

Very Loose Tracking

Can I apply formatting changes to individual letters within a word? No. WordArt formats, which include standard attributes such as font and point size as well as the various special effects, apply to the entire phrase you type into the WordArt text entry box. You can apply different formats to the individual letters of a word or to the individual words of a sentence only by creating each letter or word in a separate WordArt frame.

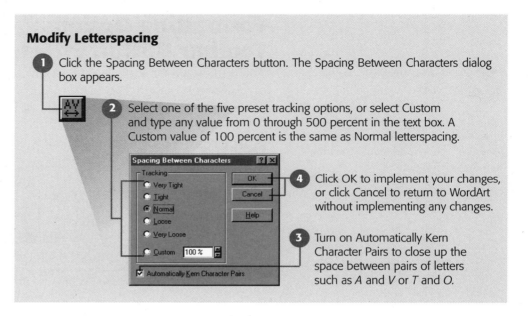

Modify Letterspacing

1 Click the Spacing Between Characters button. The Spacing Between Characters dialog box appears.

2 Select one of the five preset tracking options, or select Custom and type any value from 0 through 500 percent in the text box. A Custom value of 100 percent is the same as Normal letterspacing.

4 Click OK to implement your changes, or click Cancel to return to WordArt without implementing any changes.

3 Turn on Automatically Kern Character Pairs to close up the space between pairs of letters such as *A* and *V* or *T* and *O*.

Aligning Letters in a WordArt Frame

Clicking the Alignment button opens a drop-down list box of six options. The Center, Left, Right, and Word Justify options within WordArt correspond to alignment options for normal text.

Unique to WordArt are Stretch Justify and Letter Justify. These options help you create special effects and align words horizontally with great precision.

Epicurean

Stretch Justify

E p i c u r e a n

Letter Justify

Stretch Justify widens the letters themselves to fill the width of the WordArt frame. Unlike the Stretch button, the Stretch Justify option stretches letters only horizontally.

Letter Justify adds space evenly between letters of a word to align the text against both the left and right margins of the WordArt frame.

Word Justify is identical to the Justified option for normal text; it adds extra space evenly between words to align the text against both the left and right margins of the WordArt frame.

Color, Fill Pattern, Shadow, and Letter Outline Options

Why does my WordArt type take so long to print? If you have an older printer, you may find that WordArt takes a long time to print, especially if it is formatted with a pattern instead of a solid color.

You can create dramatic and playful WordArt text designs using color, fill pattern, shadow, and letter outline options. You might find these WordArt options especially useful for short text displays. If you don't have a color printer, experiment with different combinations on screen.

You can assign colors and fill patterns to WordArt text.

You can alter the color and thickness of each letter's outline (border) without affecting its fill color.

You can apply 3-dimensional shadows to all letters in the WordArt frame.

Why can't I see a fill pattern?
To see a fill pattern, you must choose different colors for the foreground and background. Although the terminology is identical, the foreground and background colors you choose in the Shading dialog box are not in any way related to the foreground and background of your document.

Fill a WordArt object with a custom color, tint, or shade.
Normally you can fill a WordArt object with one of 35 standard colors. To fill a WordArt object with a customized color, tint, or shade, you must exit WordArt (by clicking outside the WordArt frame), select the WordArt frame, and then choose the Recolor Object command on the Format menu.

The WordArt Object will appear in the new color in the Publisher document on screen and at print time. However, if you double-click the WordArt object in order to edit it, the screen display will revert to the original (incorrect) color until you exit WordArt again.

The Recolor Object command is explained on page 206 in Chapter 9. For more information about tints and shades, see Chapter 8.

Shade WordArt Text by Choosing a Color and Fill Pattern

1 Click the Shading button. The Shading dialog box appears.

2 Select one of 24 different fill patterns. The first option is the null sign, which produces transparent letters.

5 Click OK to implement the effects. Click Cancel to return to WordArt without implementing any changes.

4 Click Apply to see the effect of your choices in your publication without closing the dialog box.

3 In the Color area, open one or both of the drop-down list boxes. Then choose a foreground or background color, or both, from Publisher's standard palette of colors.

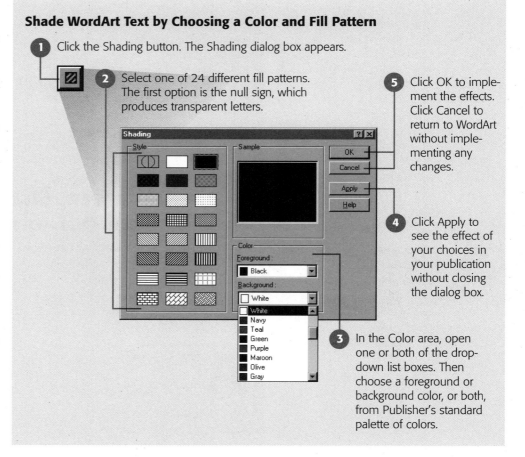

Use WordArt's formatting options to bypass the limitations of normal text.

WordArt is a useful feature, even if you don't want to twist headlines and logos into fanciful shapes. WordArt's less dramatic formatting options allow you to create conservative (but still inventive) text designs that would not be possible using the standard text tools. As you can see in the following illustration, WordArt's formatting options include the ability to assign colors to a letter's outline or to make a letter itself transparent.

Change the Letter Outlines

1 Click the Border button. The Border dialog box appears.

2 Select None to delete the outline from the letters, or select one of the six preset line weights.

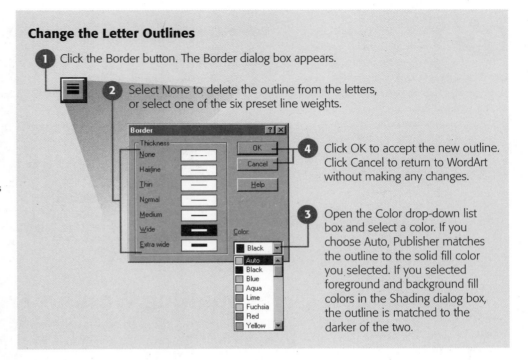

4 Click OK to accept the new outline. Click Cancel to return to WordArt without making any changes.

3 Open the Color drop-down list box and select a color. If you choose Auto, Publisher matches the outline to the solid fill color you selected. If you selected foreground and background fill colors in the Shading dialog box, the outline is matched to the darker of the two.

Why does the shadow appear around the WordArt frame instead of the individual letters? You have selected the WordArt frame by single-clicking the object. Double-click to invoke WordArt. You can then edit the text and apply shadows to individual letters.

Create a Shadow

1 Click the Shadow button. The Shadow dialog box appears.

The No Shadow option on the far left removes shadows from the WordArt text.

2 Choose a shadow option.

4 Click OK to accept the shadow. Click Cancel to return to WordArt without making any changes.

3 Open the Shadow Color drop-down list box and select a color.

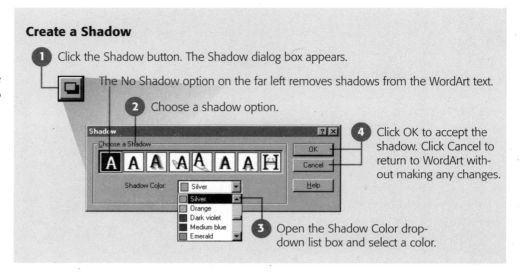

Formatting WordArt Frames

Publisher treats the text within a WordArt frame differently than it treats the frame itself. To produce the initial WordArt text, you must create a WordArt object. To edit WordArt text, you must double-click a WordArt object. To alter the appearance of the WordArt frame itself, you must single-click the object (after closing WordArt by clicking outside the object). Standard frame formatting options then appear on the Format toolbar as shown below:

For more information about using the Text Wrap tools, see Chapter 9. For more information about adding color, shading, borders, or shadows to a WordArt frame, see Chapter 8.

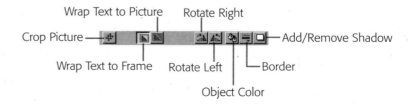

Crop Picture — Wrap Text to Picture — Rotate Right — Add/Remove Shadow

Wrap Text to Frame — Rotate Left — Object Color — Border

For more information about PageWizard design assistants, see Chapter 12.

Running WordArt in a separate window. If you choose Microsoft WordArt 3.0 Object from the Edit menu and then select Open on the cascading menu, the WordArt functions will appear in a separate window instead of on a toolbar. Which method you choose is purely a matter of preference and has no impact on performance.

Can I edit objects created with WordArt 1.0? Yes, you can transform WordArt 1.0 objects to WordArt 3.0 objects by opening the Edit menu and choosing Convert on the Microsoft WordArt 1.0 Object command's cascading menu. The older WordArt 1.0 fonts will be converted to the closest matching TrueType fonts. The substitution ensures compatibility with Publisher and produces better printouts. But the new fonts won't match the old fonts exactly.

Editing Options

Whether you create a WordArt object yourself or use a PageWizard design assistant, chances are that at some point you'll want to edit the text or change the special effects.

Edit Text and Formatting

1 Select a WordArt frame.

2 Open the Edit menu and select Microsoft WordArt 3.0 Object.

3 Choose Edit on the cascading menu. The Enter Your Text Here dialog box and the WordArt toolbar appear. The toolbar displays the current formatting attributes for the selected object.

4 Type new text and/or choose new formatting options.

5 Click anywhere outside the WordArt frame to accept the changes and return to your publication.

A table is a collection of individual items called table cells, which are arranged horizontally and vertically in a matrix of rows and columns. Table cells contain text.

A row is composed of a horizontal line of cells, and a column (highlighted here) is composed of a vertical line of cells.

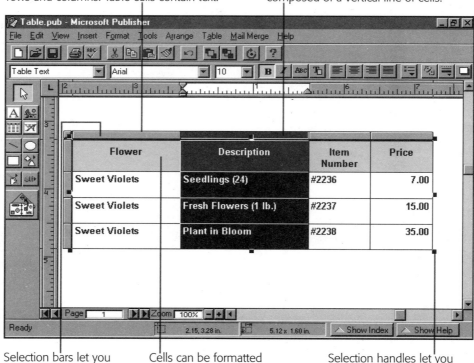

Flower	Description	Item Number	Price
Sweet Violets	Seedlings (24)	#2236	7.00
Sweet Violets	Fresh Flowers (1 lb.)	#2237	15.00
Sweet Violets	Plant in Bloom	#2238	35.00

Selection bars let you highlight all the cells in a row or column.

Cells can be formatted with rules and tints.

Selection handles let you resize the entire table.

Table Tool

When you are dealing with lots of small, interrelated pieces of information, a table is often the best way to organize your text. Using Microsoft Publisher 97, you can create the following with the Table tool:

- Price sheets
- Tables of contents
- Comparison charts
- Indexes
- Schedules
- Business forms

Table Components: Rows, Columns, and Cells

A single table can contain as many as 128 rows, 128 columns, and thousands of individual cells. You can control the table structure with functions built into the table's borders, and with commands on the Table menu. You can move the table and table components, resize them, and change their appearance by assigning text formatting, borders, shadows, color, and shading.

To help you manage all of these objects, Publisher displays row and column buttons in addition to the standard selection handles whenever you select a table.

How can I tell where one cell ends and another cell begins?
A table normally displays gridlines showing the boundaries between the individual cells. The gridlines appear on screen to help you arrange elements, but they never print. If the gridlines don't appear on screen, choose Show Boundaries And Guides on the View menu. If you want to print lines between the rows and columns in a table, you must assign borders to the gridlines.

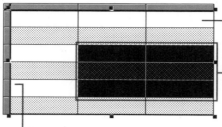

When you want to move or change a table element or an entire table, you must first select the table by clicking anywhere within its boundaries.

To select any rectangular combination of adjacent cells, columns, or rows, first select a single cell. Drag the pointer over adjacent cells to select them, or Shift-click another cell to automatically select everything between it and the originally selected cell.

To select an empty cell, click inside it. The insertion point appears. Drag the I-beam pointer to select all or part of the contents of a cell.

Quick ways of selecting cells and cell contents.
The Highlight Entire Table command (on the Table menu) highlights all the cells in a table. The Highlight Text command (on the Edit menu) selects all text in the current cell.

To select the contents of the entire table, click the table selector in the upper left corner of the frame.

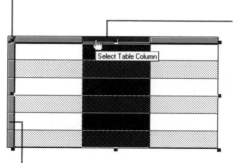

Select Table Column

To select an entire column in a table, position the pointer over the gray column selector at the top of the column. Click when the pointer changes to the Hand pointer.

To select an entire row in a table, position the pointer over the gray row selector directly to the left of the row. Click when the pointer changes to the Hand pointer.

For more information
about creating frames,
see Chapter 2.

Create a Table

1 Click the Table tool and draw a table frame. The Create Table dialog box appears.

2 Enter a value from 1 through 128 in the Number Of Rows text box.

3 Enter a value from 1 through 128 in the Number Of Columns text box.

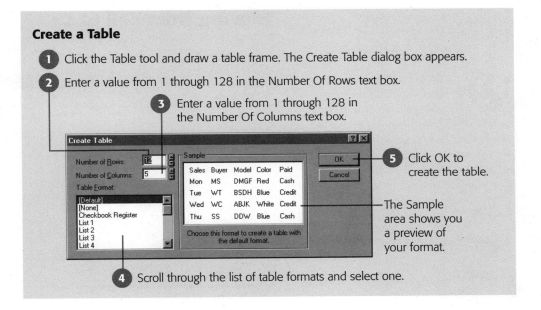

5 Click OK to create the table.

The Sample area shows you a preview of your format.

4 Scroll through the list of table formats and select one.

Entering Text in a Table

When you first create a table, the upper left cell contains the insertion point, indicating that the cell is active. Text can be entered only in the active cell, but you can make any cell active by clicking it with the I-beam pointer. You can use any of the text editing commands, as if you were working in a normal text object, to perform these tasks:

For more information about
Publisher's text editing
features, see Chapter 5.

- Import text from an external word processing file into the current cell.

- Cut, copy, and paste text via the Windows 95 Clipboard.

- Move and copy text from the current cell using the Drag-And-Drop feature.

- Fine-tune your copy with the Check Spelling, Find, and Replace commands.

- You can also use special table commands to copy text into every cell in a selected range.

Moving from Cell to Cell

Key combinations let you move from cell to cell in a table, as explained below:

How to Move Between and Within Table Cells	
To move ...	Press ...
To the next cell in a table	Tab
To the preceding cell	Shift-Tab
Forward one character (or to the next cell if there is no more text)	Right arrow key
Backward one character (or to the previous cell if there is no more text)	Left arrow key
Up one line or cell	Up arrow key
Down one line or cell	Down arrow key

Controlling How Text Behaves in Table Cells

Cells within a table automatically expand vertically to accommodate the text you type. To maintain alignment, Publisher increases the height (but not the width) of every cell in the current row.

To lock the table size and prevent Publisher from increasing row height, disable the Grow To Fit Text command (on the Table menu). Any text that doesn't fit into the current cell is placed in the invisible overflow area. If you have locked the table size, make text in the overflow area visible again with any of these techniques:

@ Reduce the point size to fit more text into the current cell.

@ Edit the text to shorten your copy.

@ Resize the table, making the cell larger.

@ Unlock the table size by turning on the Grow To Fit Text command.

If pressing Tab moves me from cell to cell inside a table, how do I insert an actual tab stop in a single cell? Use the Tabs dialog box (accessible from the Format menu) or the indents and tabs ruler to set tab stops. To move to a tab stop within a cell, press Ctrl-Tab.

For more information about tabs, see Chapter 5.

For more information about table sizing, see pages 144 through 147.

When should I lock the table size? If the table *must* fit into a tight layout, turn off the Grow To Fit Text command to guarantee that the table won't interfere with other elements on the page. Be warned: unlike text frames, table cells do not alert you when the overflow area contains text. Therefore, you should lock a table's size only when you are satisfied with the content and formatting. Otherwise, you could inadvertently print a publication that contains hidden table text in the overflow area.

Why does Publisher insert all of my imported text into a single table cell? When you use the Text File command on the Insert menu to import text into a table, Publisher places the entire file into the current cell. In most cases, this isn't useful. If you want to preserve tabular material, don't use the Text File command—use the Clipboard as explained in the procedures on the next page.

What happened to my original table data when I imported new cells? Publisher imports data into the cell you've selected as well as into as many adjacent cells as necessary to maintain the original row and column structure. Publisher overwrites the contents of these cells rather than inserting new cells. To avoid losing important information by inadvertently pasting new data over old, be sure you've added the correct number of empty rows and columns to your table. If your table does not contain enough cells to hold the new data, Publisher offers you the option of expanding the table to accommodate all the items. Click Yes to add sufficient rows or columns.

Convert tabbed text into tables. Select a table before pasting tabbed text into a Publisher document. Each tabbed item will be pasted into a separate cell.

Inserting Identical Text in Cells

You can add the same piece of information to every cell in a selected range, which is useful when you need to repeat an identifying code or part number, as in tables for catalogs or price sheets.

Repeat Text in a Range of Cells

Flower	Description	Item Number	Price
Sweet Violets	Seedlings (24)	#22	7.00
Sweet Violets	Fresh Flowers (1 lb.)		15.00
Sweet Violets	Plant in Bloom		35.00

1 Type the text you want to repeat in a cell.

2 Highlight the cell that contains the text as well as the cells where you want to repeat the text.

3 Open the Table menu. Choose Fill Down to repeat the text in the selected area below the original cell, or choose Fill Right to repeat the text in the selected area to the right of the original cell.

Importing a Table or Part of a Table from an External Source

Taking advantage of the Clipboard allows you to import a table or part of a table that you've created in another application, such as Microsoft Excel, Microsoft Word, or Microsoft Works. You can either add the external table to an existing Publisher table, or you can create a completely new Publisher table from the external data. Publisher maintains the row and column structure by placing each individual table item in its own cell.

Why does the text I just imported into my table look so strange? When you import an external table or part of an external table, Publisher preserves its original formatting, which may be inconsistent with your existing table design. Use Publisher's text formatting features to reformat the inconsistent cells.

Import Excel worksheets. If you own a Microsoft product that installed the Excel Worksheet file filter, Publisher can directly import a table in the Excel Worksheet format. Select a text or table frame, and then choose Text File from the Insert menu. Select Microsoft Excel Worksheet from the Files Of Type drop-down list box. When you select an Excel worksheet file (with the XLS extension) and click OK, the Open Worksheet dialog box appears.

You can choose a worksheet within the file, or a named range within a worksheet. When you click OK, Publisher does not import the data into the existing text or table object you selected. Instead, Publisher creates a new table object.

Import a Table or Part of a Table into an Existing Publisher Table

1 Open the application and then the file that contains the table you want to import.

2 Highlight the cells you want to copy.

3 Choose Copy on the Edit menu (or press Ctrl-C) to place the cells on the Clipboard.

4 Open the Publisher document that contains the table you want to edit.

5 Select the table and then select the first cell in which you want to insert information.

6 Choose Paste Cells on the Edit menu (or press Ctrl-V) to add the external data to your Publisher table.

Create a New Publisher Table from an External Table

1 Open the application and then the file that contains the table you want to import.

2 Highlight the cells you want to copy.

3 Choose Copy on the Edit menu (or press Ctrl-C) to place the cells on the Clipboard.

4 Open your Publisher document.

5 Open the Edit menu and choose Paste or Paste Special. If you choose Paste, you are done. If you choose Paste Special, the following dialog box appears.

6 Select Paste.

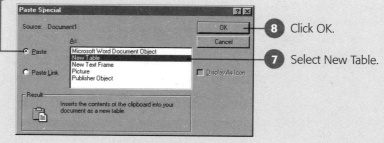

8 Click OK.

7 Select New Table.

9 Publisher pastes the table into your publication, preserving any formatting.

Moving Tables and Table Text

Publisher allows you to move an entire table to a new position on the page just as you would move any other object. You can also reorganize the contents of a table and change its layout by selecting only portions of the table.

Move an Entire Table

1 Select the table.

Flower	Description	Item Number	Price
Sweet Violets	Seedlings (24)	#2236	7.00
Sweet Violets	Fresh Flowers (1 lb.)	#2237	15.00
Sweet Violets	Plant in Bloom	#2238	35.00

3 Drag the table to its new location.

2 Move the pointer to the edge of the table until you see the Move pointer.

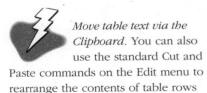

Why don't I see the Drag pointer? If you have turned off the Drag-And-Drop text editing feature, you need to turn it back on to be able to use the Drag pointer. Choose Options on the Tools menu, select the Editing And User Assistance tab, and turn on the Drag-And-Drop Text Editing check box.

Move table text via the Clipboard. You can also use the standard Cut and Paste commands on the Edit menu to rearrange the contents of table rows and columns.

Move the Contents of a Cell or of a Block of Cells

1 Select the table.

Flower	Description	Item Number	Price
Sweet Violets	Seedlings (24)	#2236	7.00
Sweet Violets	Fresh Flowers (1 lb.)	#2237	15.00
Sweet Violets	Plant in Bloom	#2238	35.00

2 Use the I-beam pointer to highlight the rows or columns containing the text you want to move.

3 Position the pointer over the selected cells until it changes to the Drag pointer.

4 Press the left mouse button to change the Drag pointer to the Move pointer. Drag the selected cells to the new location. Alternatively, hold down the Ctrl key as you press the left mouse button to change the Drag pointer to the Copy pointer. Drag a copy of the selected cells to the new location.

Resizing Tables and Table Components

Publisher offers you several ways to change the size of a table. You can resize an entire table, resize individual rows and columns, and insert or delete rows and columns. You can even merge or split cells to accommodate information such as a table heading.

Rows and columns can be increased to the size of your page, but rows and columns cannot be smaller than the text they contain.

When you resize an entire table, the dimensions of all the rows and columns are changed equally. To change the height of a row or the width of a column (without affecting the other rows and columns), use the Adjust pointer.

 For more information about resizing objects in Publisher, see Chapter 4.

Resize an Entire Table

1 Select the table you want to resize.

2 Position the pointer over one of the selection handles until the Resize pointer appears.

Flower	Description	Item Number	Price
Sweet Violets	Seedlings (24)	#2236	7.00
Sweet Violets	Fresh Flowers (1 lb.)	#2237	15.00
Sweet Violets	Plant in Bloom	#2238	35.00

RESIZE

3 Drag the handle to a new location, either inside the table to decrease its size or outside the table to increase its size.

Change row or column size while maintaining the overall size of a table. Using the Adjust pointer to resize rows and columns increases or decreases the size of the entire table. To resize a row or a column without changing the overall size of the table, hold down the Shift key as you drag the Adjust pointer. Notice that, if you increase the size of a row or column, the adjacent row or column decreases by the same amount. If you decrease a row or column, the adjacent row or column increases by the same amount.

Resize Individual Rows and Columns

1 Select the table.

3 Position the pointer on the gridline between two row or column selectors. The pointer changes to the Adjust pointer.

2 If you want to resize more than one row or column simultaneously, highlight the rows or columns by Shift-clicking the row or column selectors or by dragging the pointer across the row or column selectors.

4 Drag the Adjust pointer to a new position.

Flower	Description	Item Number	Price
Sweet Violets	Seedlings (24)	#2236	7.00
Sweet Violets	Fresh Flowers (1 lb.)	#2237	15.00
Sweet Violets	Plant in Bloom	#2238	35.00

Notice that Publisher always shows you the new sizes of the rows or columns by displaying dotted lines. In this illustration, one column is being resized.

Insert Rows or Columns

1 Select the table, and click a cell adjacent to where you want a new row or column to appear.

2 Open the Table menu, and choose Insert Rows Or Columns. The Insert dialog box appears.

Insertion limits for table rows and columns. The number of rows and columns you can insert on a given page depends on the size of the cells in the row or column that contains the insertion point. The smaller the cells, the more rows or columns you can insert.

Insert rows quickly. The fastest way to insert rows into a table is to press the Tab key when you reach the last cell in the table. Publisher adds a new row and also advances the insertion point.

Insert Rows or Columns *(continued)*

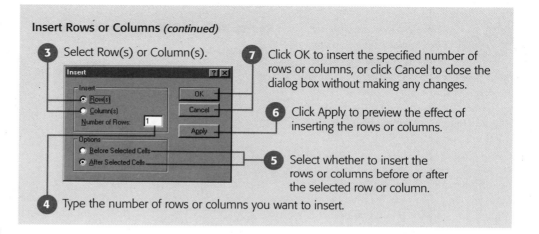

3 Select Row(s) or Column(s).

4 Type the number of rows or columns you want to insert.

5 Select whether to insert the rows or columns before or after the selected row or column.

6 Click Apply to preview the effect of inserting the rows or columns.

7 Click OK to insert the specified number of rows or columns, or click Cancel to close the dialog box without making any changes.

Delete Rows or Columns

1 Select the table.

2 Select the rows or columns you want to delete. Alternatively, select one or more cells in the rows or columns you want to delete.

3 On the Table menu, choose Delete Rows Or Delete Columns. The Delete dialog box appears.

4 Select Current Row(s) or Current Column(s).

5 Click Apply to preview the effect of deleting the rows or columns.

6 Click OK to delete the current rows or columns, or click Cancel to close the dialog box without making any changes.

Can I merge cells vertically? No. Publisher can merge two or more cells in a single row, but it cannot merge cells in a column.

Create more than one merged cell at a time. If you select a rectangular block of cells with more than one row and more than one column and then choose Merge Cells, Publisher will create a merged cell in each row that you selected.

Merge Cells in a Row

1 Select the table, and then select the cells you want to merge.

Ordering Information			
Flower	Description	Item Number	Price
Sweet Violets	Seedlings (24)	#2236	7.00
Sweet Violets	Fresh Flowers (1 lb.)	#2237	15.00
Sweet Violets	Plant in Bloom	#2238	35.00

Ordering Information			
Flower	Description	Item Number	Price
Sweet Violets	Seedlings (24)	#2236	7.00
Sweet Violets	Fresh Flowers (1 lb.)	#2237	15.00
Sweet Violets	Plant in Bloom	#2238	35.00

2 Open the Table menu and choose Merge Cells. One long horizontal cell is created.

Split a Merged Cell

1 Select the merged cell.

2 Open the Table menu and choose Split Cells. The long horizontal cell is split according to the existing column structure.

Formatting Tables and Table Components

You can change the appearance of a table by assigning formatting attributes. All of Publisher's formatting attributes can be applied to the entire table. Except for BorderArt and Shadow, all formatting attributes can also be applied to selected rows and columns or to individually selected cells. There are several ways to format the different table elements, as the following table describes.

Methods of Formatting Tables		
Table Element	**Formatting Method**	**Description**
All table components	AutoFormat command on the Table menu	AutoFormat provides a collection of predefined table styles that include attributes such as borders; fill colors, tints, and shades; patterns; and text alignment. Except for the Default option, you cannot redefine the AutoFormat table styles. Nor can you create your own table formats and save them as AutoFormat options. But you can choose to apply only certain attributes contained in an AutoFormat table style.
Table text	Format toolbar, which is presented at the top of the work area when you select a table, and commands on the Format menu	Table text is identical to the text in regular text frames. You can apply both character-level and paragraph-level formatting attributes, as well as define special text styles. You can format text in the entire table or in selected rows, columns, or cells.
Cell margin (the amount of space between the text and the boundaries of each cell)	Table Cell Properties command on the Format menu	The Table Cell Properties command allows you to specify left, right, top, and bottom margins.
Borders	Border button on the Format toolbar, or Border command on the Format menu	You can choose a predefined border or create a customized border for an entire table or for selected cells. If you want to modify the perimeter of the entire table, you can add a decorative border by selecting the BorderArt tab in the BorderArt dialog box.
Shadow	Shadow button on the Format toolbar, or Shadow command on the Format menu	A shadow can be added to the perimeter of the table.

Table Element	Formatting Method	Description
Entire table, rows, columns, range of selected cells, individual cell	Object Color button on the Format toolbar or Fill Color and Fill Patterns And Shading command on the Format menu	You can fill cells with colors, tints, shades, patterns, and gradients to emphasize certain information.

Why doesn't the typeface change when I use Auto-Format? AutoFormat changes font styles, such as boldface and italics, but does not change the typeface used in a table. You must change the typeface using the buttons on the Format toolbar or the Character command on the Format menu.

Copy a table's formatting. You can quickly copy formatting attributes to other tables by using the Format Painter on the Standard toolbar. Select the table containing the formatting you want to copy. Click the Format Painter icon, and then click the table to which you want to copy the formatting.

Select a Predefined Table Format

1 Select the table.

2 Open the Table menu and choose AutoFormat. The Auto Format dialog box appears.

3 Select one of the 23 table formats.

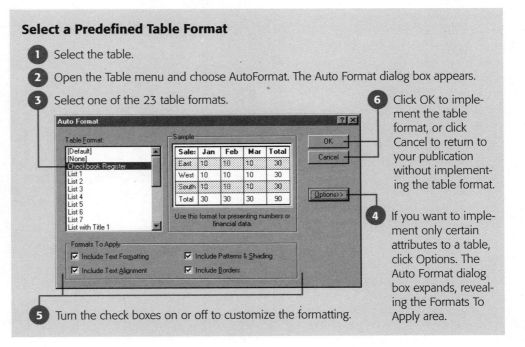

6 Click OK to implement the table format, or click Cancel to return to your publication without implementing the table format.

4 If you want to implement only certain attributes to a table, click Options. The Auto Format dialog box expands, revealing the Formats To Apply area.

5 Turn the check boxes on or off to customize the formatting.

Customize the Table Tool

1 Select the Table tool, but don't create a table.

2 Select the new default formatting attributes you want, such as typeface, point size, border, and fill color.

Save the new default settings for the Table tool. Publisher automatically applies the new default attributes you've set for the Table tool to any tables you subsequently create within the current work session. These settings also consitute the new default table style within the Auto Format dialog box for the current work session. However, the next time you open Publisher, the default format will revert to the original settings. You can save the new default settings as described below:

@ To save the new default settings for the current document only, save the file to disk. The tables you create whenever you are working on this particular document will be formatted with the new attributes.

@ To save the new default settings for all your documents, save the file as a template named Normal.pub. The tables in all new documents you subsequently create will be formatted with the new attributes.

For more information about changing Publisher's default tool settings, see Chapter 4.

Customize the Table Tool *(continued)*

3 Click anywhere in the workspace, and then choose Default in the Create Table dialog box that appears.

4 Click OK to create a table with the new default format, or click Cancel to set the new default format without creating a table.

Adjust Cell Margins

1 Select all or some of the cells in the table.

2 On the Format menu, choose Table Cell Properties. The Table Cell Properties dialog box appears.

3 Enter any value from 0 through 16 inches for the Left, Right, Top, and Bottom margins.

4 Click OK to implement the new margin settings, or click Cancel to return to the table without making any changes.

Add Predefined Borders to a Table, Row, Column, Range of Cells, or Individual Cell

1 Select the element that will have a border: the entire table, a row, a column, a range of cells, or an individual cell.

2 Click the Border button on the Format toolbar.

3 Choose one of four predefined line weights: hairline, 1 point, 2 points, or 4 points.

Why are colored borders printing poorly? Thin borders formatted with colors or tints may not print well. You should apply a color or tint only to borders with weights of 4 points or more.

See an accurate preview of your table. The Select A Side preview area shows you all the borders you've created for the selected cells.

Use BorderArt instead of line borders. Click the BorderArt tab in the BorderArt dialog box to add one of more than 150 decorative borders to the perimeter of a table (but not to the interior gridlines within the table).

For more information about BorderArt, see Chapter 8.

Customize Borders of a Table, Row, Column, Range of Cells, or Individual Cell

1 Select the element whose border you want to customize: the entire table, a row, a column, a range of cells, or an individual cell.

2 Click the Border button on the Format toolbar and choose More on the flyout menu, or open the Format menu and choose Border. The BorderArt dialog box appears.

3 Select the Line Border tab.

4 Select the border options you want.

Select one of the predefined line weights, or enter any value from 0 through 127 points in 0.25-point increments.

Publisher indicates which sides are selected by displaying triangles at either end of each selected line.

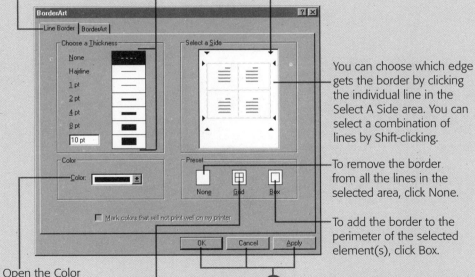

You can choose which edge gets the border by clicking the individual line in the Select A Side area. You can select a combination of lines by Shift-clicking.

To remove the border from all the lines in the selected area, click None.

To add the border to the perimeter of the selected element(s), click Box.

Open the Color drop-down list box to select one of the available colors, tints or shades.

To add the border to *all* the lines in the selected area— all four sides plus row and column divisions—click Grid.

5 Click Apply to preview the table with the border options you've selected. Click OK to implement your choices, or Click Cancel to return to the table without implementing your choices.

Add a Shadow to a Table

1 Select the table.

2 Click the Shadow button on the Format toolbar, or choose the Shadow command on the Format menu.

Fill a Table, Row, Column, Range of Cells, or Individual Cell with a Color

1 Select the element you want to fill: the entire table, a row, a column, a range of cells, or an individual cell.

2 Click the Object Color button on the Format toolbar, or choose the Fill Color command on the Format menu.

3 Choose one of the available colors.

4 Click Apply to preview your selection. Click OK to implement your selection, or click Cancel to return to your table without implementing any changes.

5 If you want to further modify the fill, click the Object Color button on the Format toolbar, and then click the Patterns & Shading button in the pop-up box that appears. Alternatively, choose the Fill Patterns And Shading command on the Format menu.

6 Choose one of the tint, shade, pattern, or gradient options.

7 Click OK to implement your changes.

For more information about Publisher's color capabilities, see Chapter 14. For more information about Publisher's tints, shades, patterns, and gradients, see pages 168 through 172 in Chapter 8.

With Publisher's drawing tools, you can create a wide variety of shapes.

Draw lines and format them with arrowheads.

With BorderArt, transform a plain box or frame.

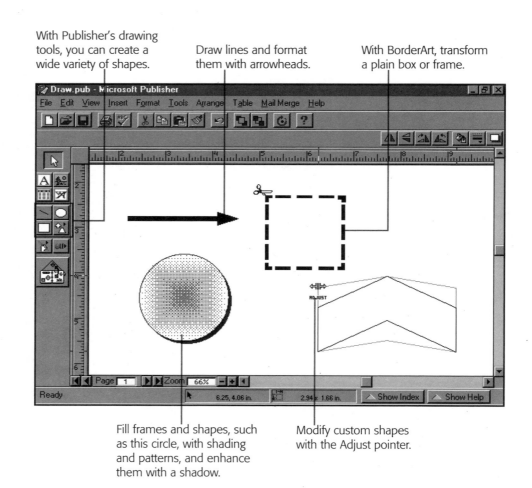

Fill frames and shapes, such as this circle, with shading and patterns, and enhance them with a shadow.

Modify custom shapes with the Adjust pointer.

Drawing Tools

You can draw a wide variety of shapes with Microsoft Publisher 97's four drawing tools. These tools are not intended for complex illustrations, but you can create schematic drawings such as flow charts and symbols, or decorative elements such as shaded backgrounds and borders quite effectively.

Lines, Boxes, Circles, and Custom Shapes

The drawing tools are located on the main toolbar. They are all easy to use: once a tool is activated, all you have to do is click and drag the Crossbar pointer in the workspace to create shapes.

You can increase the accuracy of your drawings by pressing certain keys as you create shapes. The Shift key enables you to draw horizontal, vertical, and 45-degree lines as well as perfect squares and circles.

For more information about creating objects, see pages 20 through 22 in Chapter 2.

When you draw an object or a frame, you typically begin at the upper left corner, but you can also draw an object from its center out using the Ctrl key. This method is especially useful when you want to draw multiple objects with a common center.

Draw a Shape

1 Click the Line, Box, Oval, or Custom Shapes tool.

2 If you clicked the Custom Shapes tool, select one of the 36 choices from the flyout menu.

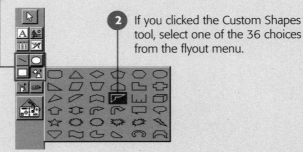

3 Position the Crossbar pointer where you want the first corner of the object to begin.

4 Click and drag the pointer until you are satisfied with the size and shape of the object. Release the left mouse button. When drawing a line, you can drag the pointer horizontally, vertically, or at any angle. For a 2-dimensional shape, such as a circle or a rectangle, you must drag the pointer diagonally.

Create a Straight Line, Perfect Square, True Circle, or Proportional Shape Using the Shift Key

1 Click the drawing tool you want to use.

2 Hold down the Shift key.

3 Click and drag the Crossbar pointer to draw the object. Because you are holding down the Shift key, the tools perform in the following ways:

- The Line tool draws perfectly horizontal, vertical, or 45-degree diagonal lines.
- The Box tool draws perfect squares.
- The Oval tool draws perfect circles.
- The Custom Shapes tool draws the selected object with its original proportions.

4 Release the mouse button before you release the Shift key.

The power of the Shift and Ctrl keys. You can use the Shift and Ctrl keys alone or in combination when you create, resize, or move text frames, picture frames, WordArt frames, and drawn shapes.

Use the Shift key to make any of the frames you draw of equal width and height, and use the Ctrl key to begin drawing any frame from its center.

You can also use the Shift key to constrain the movement of an object to the horizontal or vertical axis. That is, if you want to realign an object in only one direction, press Shift and you can move the object either up and down or from side to side.

Center an Object Using the Ctrl Key

1 Click the tool you want to use.

2 Hold down the Ctrl key.

3 Position the Crossbar pointer where you want the object's center to be. Click and drag the pointer to draw the object.

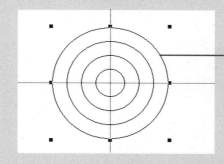

A series of circles drawn while holding down the Ctrl and Shift keys simultaneously are perfectly round and concentric, provided you start each circle from the same center (same coordinates).

Changing the Shape of Drawn Objects

You can alter the shape of many of the objects created with the Custom Shapes tool.

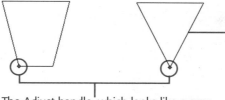

You can change the shape of arrows, create segments of a pie, and (as shown here) turn trapezoids into triangles.

The Adjust handle, which looks like a gray diamond, appears at a vertex when you draw or select certain custom shapes.

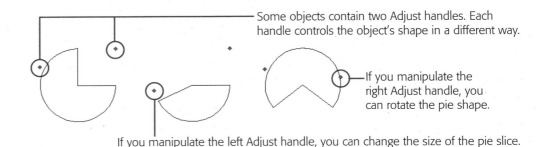

Some objects contain two Adjust handles. Each handle controls the object's shape in a different way.

If you manipulate the right Adjust handle, you can rotate the pie shape.

If you manipulate the left Adjust handle, you can change the size of the pie slice.

Can I create a free-form shape from a drawn shape?
No. Unlike a drawing application, Publisher (a desktop publishing application) does not let you erase portions of drawn shapes to create free-form shapes. When you draw a box, you can resize it or change it from a rectangle into a square, but you can't alter its boxlike nature. If you want to draw a free-form shape, you must use Microsoft Draw or another drawing application.

For more information about Microsoft Draw, see pages 172 through 176.

For more information about Publisher's layout tools, such as stacking, grouping, rotating, and aligning, see Chapter 4.

Alter the Outline of a Shape

1 Position the pointer over the Adjust handle. The Adjust pointer appears.

2 Drag the Adjust handle to change the shape of the object.

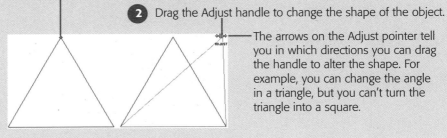

The arrows on the Adjust pointer tell you in which directions you can drag the handle to alter the shape. For example, you can change the angle in a triangle, but you can't turn the triangle into a square.

Combining Drawn Objects

To create more complex shapes, you can draw several simple objects and combine them in a variety of ways by using the layout tools. For example, you can do the following:

- Control how objects overlap by using Publisher's stacking order commands.
- Group separate objects together.
- Rotate and flip objects.
- Align multiple objects automatically using the Line Up Objects command on the Arrange menu.

This international cancellation sign was created by grouping two objects: a line and a circle.

This simple airplane shape is composed of three shapes: an oval, a chevron, and a triangle. Notice how the shapes have been rotated to add a sense of movement to the plane.

The benefits of formatting frames. You can dramatically change the appearance of objects in a Publisher document, including drawn objects, text frames, picture frames, table frames, and WordArt frames, by using the formatting options discussed in this chapter. By applying formatting directly to text, picture, table, or WordArt frames, you make the formats integral to the object, which in turn makes the combination easy to manage. When you move a text frame that has a BorderArt format, for example, the decorative border moves with the text automatically.

Formatting Objects

Playing with formatting can dramatically change the appearance of objects. Publisher's formatting options fall into five general categories, each with a range of capabilities.

Borders and lines can range in width from 0.25 through 127 points.

Drop shadows can be added to any shape or frame to create a 3-dimensional effect.

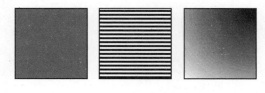

Fill options include 35 basic colors, a virtually unlimited choice of custom colors, 21 predefined tints and shades, 18 patterns, and 44 gradients. You can make objects transparent by using the Clear option, which reveals objects placed lower in the stacking order.

BorderArt designs come in over 150 patterns, from simple dots to zany cartoons. BorderArt can range in width from 4 through 250 points.

Arrowheads of 10 different types can be added to a line.

Formatting Lines

You can change the appearance of lines by specifying thickness and color. Formatting lines is very similar to formatting the borders of frames and drawn objects. However, you can also format a line by adding arrrowheads to the right end, the left end, or both ends. Arrowheads are ideal whenever you want to point to a particular object or show direction in a flow chart.

Alternate access to choices for line thickness. You can also open the Format menu and choose the Line command to access additional line thickness options.

For more information about color choices, see Chapter 14.

Lines with a light color or tint should be thick to print well. Thin lines that have been formatted with a light color or tint may not print well. Use a light color or tint only with a line thickness of 4 points or more.

Format Lines

1 Draw or select a line to format.

2 Click the Border button on the Format toolbar. A flyout menu appears, containing four preformatted choices: Hairline (0.25 point), 1 point, 2 points, or 4 points.

3 Select one of these four options, or, to access additional options, open the Line dialog box by selecting More on the flyout menu.

4 Select one of the six preset line weights, or type a value from 0.25 through 127 points in the text box.

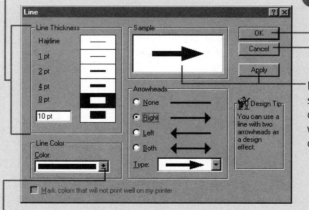

6 If you like the current effect, click OK. Click Cancel to return to your publication without making any changes.

Preview the current line settings in the Sample area, or preview the actual line within your publication by clicking the Apply button.

5 Open the Color drop-down list box and do one of the following:
- Select one of the predefined colors.
- Click More Colors to create a custom color.
- Click Patterns & Shading for tint and shade options.

Control the size of the arrowhead. The size of the arrowhead is determined by the thickness of the line. To increase the size of the arrowhead, make the line thicker.

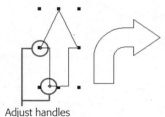

Draw arrows with the Custom Shapes tool. You can create a wide variety of arrows by choosing one of the four arrow shapes in the Custom Shapes fly-out menu. Unlike arrows created with the Line tool, these shapes include curves and can be modified using the Adjust handles.

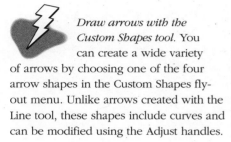

Adjust handles

Add a Default Arrowhead to a Line

1 Select the line you want to format.

2 Click one of the three arrowhead buttons on the Format toolbar. The selected arrowhead appears on the line.

Access More Arrowhead Options

1 Select the line you want to format.

2 Click the Border button on the Format toolbar.

3 Choose More to open the Line dialog box.

4 Select one of three options to specify the arrowhead's placement (Right, Left, or Both), or select None to remove arrowheads from a line.

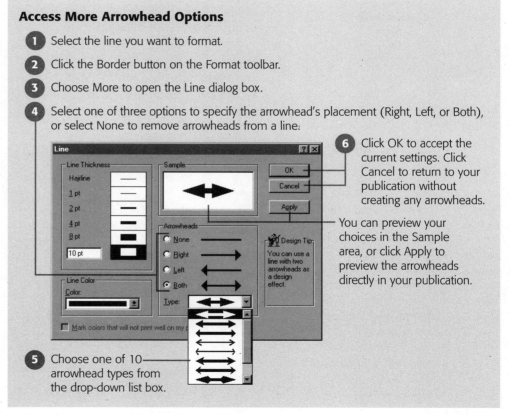

6 Click OK to accept the current settings. Click Cancel to return to your publication without creating any arrowheads.

You can preview your choices in the Sample area, or click Apply to preview the arrowheads directly in your publication.

5 Choose one of 10 arrowhead types from the drop-down list box.

Assign a different border to each side. Publisher allows you to specify a different border for each side of a box, frame, cell, or range of cells. When you are working with a simple outline, such as a box or frame, your options are limited to changing the top, bottom, left, and right borders.

When working with a table object, however, you can develop endless combinations of borders. You can format the perimeter of the table differently from the interior cell divisions.

You can even subselect ranges of cells (or a single cell) within a table and format each side of that range with distinct top, bottom, left, and right borders. The table shown here is structurally identical to the previous table, but it appears to be structured differently because of the way in which the borders have been formatted. The gridline between the two lower rows is formatted with a border of None.

Borders and BorderArt

You can add borders to a wide range of elements within a Publisher document. A rectangular border can be added to a box or to the frame surrounding a text, table, picture, or WordArt object. You can also add a border to an individual cell or range of cells in a table.

When you select a box, a frame, a cell, or a range of cells, Publisher gives you the ability to create a custom border. Each side of a custom border can be a different line thickness, color, shade, or tint.

When you select a drawn object that is not rectangular, such as a circle or a triangle, the border is applied to the irregular shape of the object.

If you want more than a simple border around an object, consider BorderArt, a collection of over 150 designs that includes geometric patterns, symbolic icons, and miniature illustrations. You can customize a BorderArt border by changing its size and color. You can even create your own BorderArt patterns based on imported clip art or other picture files.

Apply a Line Border to a Box, Frame, Cell, or Range of Cells

1 Select the box, frame, cell, or range of cells you want to format.

2 Click the Border button on the Format toolbar.

3 Select one of the four preformatted line weights (Hairline, 1 point, 2 points, or 4 points), or choose More to access additional options in the BorderArt dialog box.

Use the Format menu to access border options. You can open the Format menu and choose the Border command to access the full range of border options.

Does the frame size expand when I apply a border? Publisher draws the border inside the frame; the outside dimensions of the frame remain the same. This means that if you create a small text frame and then format it with a wide border, you might cover text within the text frame. To solve this problem, you can reduce the width of the border by entering a smaller value in the Choose A Thickness area or by enlarging the text frame.

Apply a Line Border to a Box, Frame, Cell, or Range of Cells *(continued)*

5 In the Select A Side area, choose the top, bottom, left, or right edge of the box, frame, cell, or range of cells. If two triangles point to a side, it is currently selected. You can choose any combination of sides by Shift-clicking, or you can click Box to place a border around the entire selection. In this example, four sets of triangles point to the four sides of the frame.

6 Click None if you want to remove a border.

4 Select the Line Border tab.

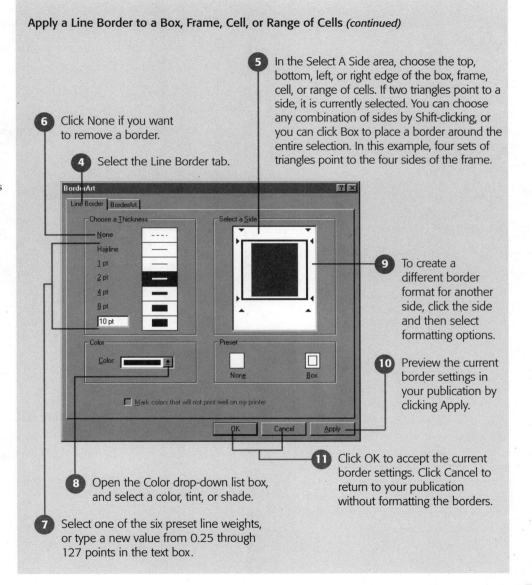

9 To create a different border format for another side, click the side and then select formatting options.

10 Preview the current border settings in your publication by clicking Apply.

11 Click OK to accept the current border settings. Click Cancel to return to your publication without formatting the borders.

8 Open the Color drop-down list box, and select a color, tint, or shade.

7 Select one of the six preset line weights, or type a new value from 0.25 through 127 points in the text box.

Can I apply a border to only a portion of an oval or a custom shape? When you select an oval or irregular shape, your Border formatting selections apply to the entire object. You can't apply different formats to individual sides of these objects. Notice that the Select A Side area is not available in the Border dialog box when you select a nonrectangular object.

Apply a Line Border to an Oval or a Custom Shape

1 Select the oval or custom shape you want to format.

2 Click the Border button on the Format toolbar.

3 Select one of the four preformatted line weights, or choose More to access additional options in the Border dialog box.

4 Select one of the preset line weights, or type a new value from 0.25 through 127 points in the text box.

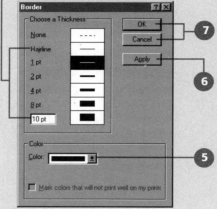

7 Click OK to accept the current settings. Click Cancel to return to your publication without adding a border.

6 This dialog box contains no preview area. Click the Apply button to preview the current choices in your publication.

5 Open the Color drop-down list box and select a color, tint, or shade.

Remove selected borders. If you have selected a box, frame, cell, or range of cells, you can remove a border from one or more selected sides. In the Select A Side area, choose the side or sides that you want to remove. Then, in the Choose A Thickness area, select None.

Removing Borders from Objects

Using the Border button's None option is the easiest way to remove the borders from a drawn object or a frame, but you can also use the Border or BorderArt dialog box.

Quickly Remove a Border

1 Select the object.

2 Click the Border button on the Format toolbar.

3 Select None on the flyout menu.

Can I apply BorderArt to an oval or custom shape, or to table cells? No. BorderArt can't follow the curved or irregular outlines of ovals and custom shapes. You can only apply standard line borders to ovals and custom shapes. You'll also find that you can't apply BorderArt to the interior cell divisions of a table. You can only apply BorderArt to the rectangular perimeter (or frame) of a table.

Remove a Border Using the Border or BorderArt Dialog Box

1 Select the object.

2 Click the Border button on the Format toolbar, and select More on the flyout menu, or choose Border on the Format menu. The Border or BorderArt dialog box appears.

3 Select the Line Border tab.

4 In the Choose A Thickness area, select None.

5 Click OK.

Add BorderArt to a Frame or a Box

1 Select the frame or box to which you want to add BorderArt.

2 Click the Border button on the Format toolbar, and select More on the flyout menu, or choose Border on the Format menu. The BorderArt dialog box appears.

3 Select the BorderArt tab.

You can view any border in the Preview area.

4 Scroll through the list of available designs and then select the BorderArt style you want.

6 Open the Color drop-down list box, and choose a color, tint, or shade to convert the BorderArt pattern into tints and shades of the chosen color.

5 Accept Publisher's recommended point size, or turn off the Use Default Size check box and type a new value from 4 through 250 points in the Border Size text box.

Turn on this check box to restore a BorderArt pattern to its original color or colors.

7 Choose Don't Stretch Pictures to maintain the proportions of the images that form the border, or choose Stretch Pictures To Fit to create a continuous BorderArt pattern in which some of the images may be distorted.

8 Click OK to accept the current settings. Click Cancel to return to your document without adding BorderArt.

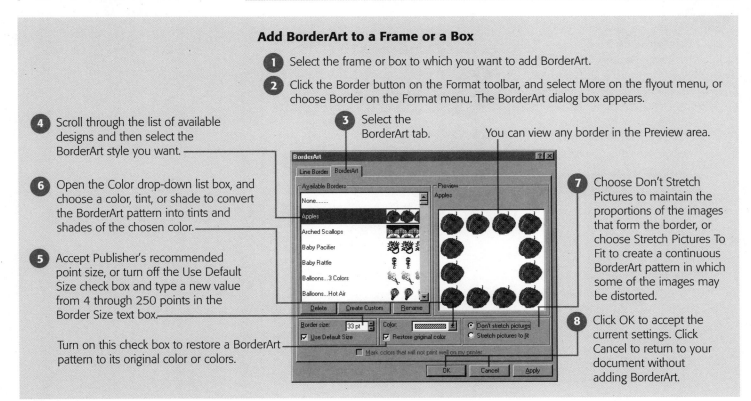

Delete BorderArt quickly. You can also choose None on the flyout menu that appears when you click the Border button on the Format toolbar. This command removes any border, whether it is a line border or BorderArt, from the currently selected object.

Create decorative lines and bullets using BorderArt. You can use BorderArt to produce decorative lines and bullets. To make a decorative line, first select a box that you have formatted with BorderArt. Then resize the box either by pulling the bottom selection handle until it overlaps the top selection handle, or by pulling the right selection handle until it overlaps the left selection handle.

To create a decorative bullet, first select a box that you have formatted with BorderArt. Then resize the box by dragging a corner selection handle until it overlaps the selection handle diagonally opposite.

Remove BorderArt

1 Select the frame or box formatted with BorderArt.

2 Click the Border button on the Format toolbar, and select More on the flyout menu, or choose Border on the Format menu.

3 Select the BorderArt tab.

4 In the Available Borders list box, select None (the first option).

5 Click OK.

Create Custom BorderArt

1 Select the frame or box to which you want to add BorderArt.

2 Click the Border button on the Format toolbar, and select More on the flyout menu, or choose Border on the Format menu. The BorderArt dialog box appears.

3 Select the BorderArt tab.

Pick a BorderArt design suitable for a bullet. When you design a BorderArt bullet, you basically collapse a box into a single corner. It's a good idea to pick a design with a stand-alone pattern (such as a string of creatures) or a strong corner motif. Here are some designs appropriate for bullets.

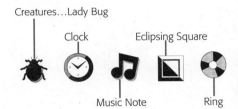

Creatures…Lady Bug

Clock   Eclipsing Square

Music Note   Ring

If you create a bullet for a text list, be sure to select a point size that matches the size of your text. If you choose a very large point size, you can create a bullet big enough to be used for clip art. For example, at 127 points, a BorderArt pattern is slightly more than 1.75 inches high.

For more information about the Microsoft Clip Gallery, see Chapter 9.

Create Custom BorderArt *(continued)*

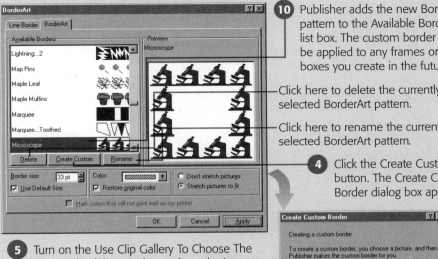

10 Publisher adds the new BorderArt pattern to the Available Borders list box. The custom border can be applied to any frames or boxes you create in the future.

Click here to delete the currently selected BorderArt pattern.

Click here to rename the currently selected BorderArt pattern.

4 Click the Create Custom button. The Create Custom Border dialog box appears.

5 Turn on the Use Clip Gallery To Choose The Picture check box to choose from the images stored in the Microsoft Clip Gallery, or turn off this check box to be able to choose any picture file that you have stored on disk.

6 Click Choose Picture to use a picture file, in any graphics file format that Publisher supports, as a BorderArt pattern. If you turned on the Use Clip Gallery To Choose The Picture check box, the Microsoft Clip Gallery 3.0 dialog box appears. Otherwise, the Insert Picture File dialog box appears.

7 In the Clip Gallery, locate the image you want to import and click Insert. In the Insert Picture File dialog box, locate the file you want to import and click OK. The Name Custom Border dialog box appears.

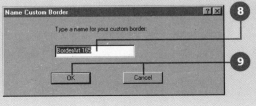

8 Replace the numerical designation with a descriptive name.

9 Click OK to add the custom border. Click Cancel to return to the BorderArt dialog box without creating a custom border.

For a complete discussion of Publisher's color options, see Chapter 14.

How does color or a fill pattern appear in a picture frame? When you fill a picture frame, the pattern or color will appear only if the picture you import into the frame has a clear background. Most clip art in the Microsoft Clip Gallery has a clear background, but scanned and bitmapped pictures have opaque backgrounds that will obscure any shading within the picture frame.

Colors, Tints, Shades, Patterns, and Gradients

You can add visual interest to a page and draw the reader's attention to important information by filling an object or a frame with tints, shades, patterns, and gradients. These fill options can be applied to any color. Your color choices, and to some extent the fill options available to you, are closely linked to the printing process you choose.

You can choose colors from one of the following palettes:

- The 7 most recently used colors

- 30 colors and 5 shades from black to white

- 72 colors and 12 shades from black to white

- The full range of computer generated colors

- A spot color palette containing 12 shades each of black, Spot Color 1, and Spot Color 2

Regardless of the specific color you choose, Publisher can mix the selected color with white to create tints or with black to create shades.

Publisher provides you with 18 patterns that run the gamut from stripes to bricks to checkerboards. You have the option of making an object transparent so that filled objects placed farther back in the stacking order show through.

A gradient fill creates a transition from one color to another. Publisher provides 44 gradient fills. In addition to standard linear gradients, Publisher provides a number of gradients with special shapes, such as radiating stars, triangles, and spirals.

 Options for accessing tints, shades, patterns, and gradients. In addition to using the Format menu, you can access the Fill Patterns And Shading dialog box in two other ways:

@ Click the Object Color button on the Format toolbar, and then click the Patterns & Shading button.

@ Right-click the object you want to fill, then select the Fill Patterns And Shadings command on the shortcut menu.

 Why aren't darker shades of my chosen color available? If you've chosen to print your publication to an outside service bureau using spot colors, Publisher restricts your choices to tints only.

In order to access tints *and* shades, you must change your print options in the Outside Print Setup dialog box.

 For information about Outside Print Setup options, see Chapter 14.

Choose a Tint or a Shade

1 Select the object you want to fill.

2 On the Format menu, choose Fill Patterns And Shading. The Fill Patterns And Shading dialog box appears.

3 Select the Tints/Shades option.

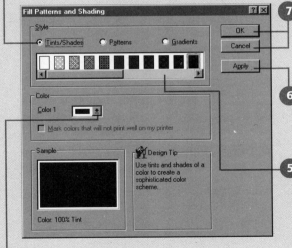

7 Click OK to accept the current settings. Click Cancel to return to the document without changing the tint or shade.

6 Preview the effect in the Sample area, or click Apply to preview the tint or shade in your publication.

5 Scroll through the tint and shade options. Click one of the 10 predefined tints to create a lighter version of the current color, or click one of the 10 predefined shades to create a darker version of the current color.

4 Open the Color drop-down list box and select colors.

Why doesn't the fill pattern get bigger when I increase the size of an object? Because Publisher's patterns aren't pictures, they can't be resized. Publisher's patterns are a type of formatting attribute—like a color or a tint. You wouldn't expect an object to change its color if you enlarged it. In the same way, no matter how large or small an object may become, the pattern that fills it will remain the same size.

Choose a Pattern

1 Select the frame or shape that you want to fill with a pattern.

2 On the Format menu, choose Fill Patterns And Shading. The Fill Patterns And Shading dialog box appears.

The first box contains a circle with a vertical line through it to indicate that it is the transparent, or clear, option. Objects or frames formatted with the clear pattern allow objects farther back in the stacking order to show through.

3 Select the Patterns option.

7 Click OK to accept the current settings. Click Cancel to return to your document without adding a pattern.

Click Apply to preview the pattern in your publication.

6 Scroll through the pattern options. Click one of the 15 patterns that combine the base color and color 2. Or click one of 2 solid colors to fill an object entirely with either the base color or with color 2.

5 Open the Color 2 drop-down list box and select a color that contrasts with the base color.

Preview the pattern in the Sample area.

4 Open the Base Color drop-down list box and select colors.

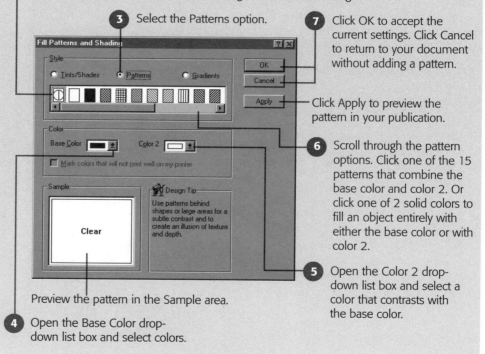

Remove tints, shades, patterns, and gradients.
If you want to remove a fill from an object, select the object and then select either a new color or the Clear option on the color palette.

If you want to change the color of an object *without* removing the fill, pick a new color from within the Fill Patterns And Shadings dialog box.

Choose a Gradient

1 Select the object you want to fill.

2 On the Format menu, choose Fill Patterns And Shading. The Fill Patterns And Shading dialog box appears.

4 Open the Base Color drop-down list box, and select one of the available colors.

3 Select the Gradients option.

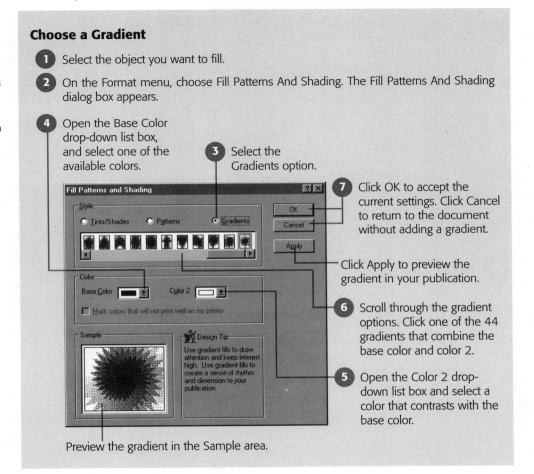

7 Click OK to accept the current settings. Click Cancel to return to the document without adding a gradient.

Click Apply to preview the gradient in your publication.

6 Scroll through the gradient options. Click one of the 44 gradients that combine the base color and color 2.

5 Open the Color 2 drop-down list box and select a color that contrasts with the base color.

Preview the gradient in the Sample area.

Create color shadows. You can create color shadows instead of gray shadows. Simply choose a color for the line border you have assigned to the object. When you subsequently assign a shadow to the object, it will appear in a tint of the border color.

This technique will even work with a BorderArt pattern, provided that you change the default colors associated with the pattern by choosing a new color from the palette within the BorderArt dialog box.

How can I apply shadows to individual letters? When you apply a shadow to a text frame, the shadow is applied to the entire frame. If you want to create a shadow effect for individual letters within a text frame, you must use WordArt to create the letters and their shadows.

Shadows

You can create the illusion of depth for frames, lines, and drawn objects by adding a drop shadow behind them.

Box and frame shadows are rectangular.

Trophy Sporting Goods

The drop shadow falls behind and to the lower right of the frame or shape.

Publisher mimics the outline of ovals and irregular shapes.

Regardless of the size of the frame or shape, the depth and placement of the shadow are always the same, and the shadow's color is always a tint of the current border color.

Add or Remove a Shadow

1 Select the frame, line, or drawn object.

2 Click the Shadow button on the Format toolbar, or choose Shadow on the Format menu.

3 Shadow is a toggle command. To remove a shadow, click the Shadow button again, or select Shadow on the Format menu again.

Microsoft Draw

Microsoft Draw is a separate drawing program that is shipped with several Microsoft applications. In many ways, its drawing functions are similar to Publisher's drawing functions, but unlike Publisher, Draw lets you change the contents of an imported picture. Specifically, you can do the following:

@ Create and edit free-form shapes.

@ Change the contents of clip-art images.

@ Change the color of individual elements within clip-art images.

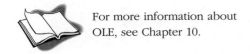

For more information about OLE, see Chapter 10.

Although Microsoft Draw is not part of Publisher, you can access it as though it were through a feature called OLE (Object Linking and Embedding). Any drawing you create in Draw is really an object embedded in a Publisher document, so Draw's File menu has no file saving options. When you save the Publisher document, you also save the embedded object as part of the document.

Open Microsoft Draw

1 Open the Insert menu and choose Object. The Insert Object dialog box appears.

Note that Create New is already selected.

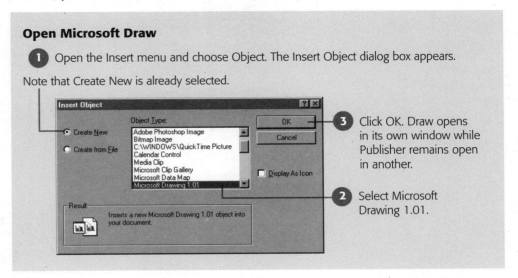

3 Click OK. Draw opens in its own window while Publisher remains open in another.

2 Select Microsoft Drawing 1.01.

Import a Clip-Art Image into Microsoft Draw

Before you can edit an existing clip-art image, you must import it into Microsoft Draw. The following instructions refer to Draw's menus and tools.

1 Open the File menu, and select Import Picture. The Open dialog box appears.

Import a Clip-Art Image into Microsoft Draw *(continued)*

2 Locate the file you want to edit.

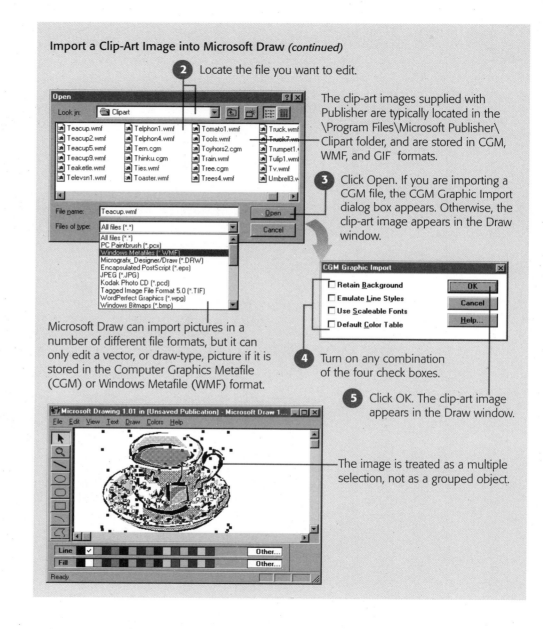

The clip-art images supplied with Publisher are typically located in the \Program Files\Microsoft Publisher\ Clipart folder, and are stored in CGM, WMF, and GIF formats.

3 Click Open. If you are importing a CGM file, the CGM Graphic Import dialog box appears. Otherwise, the clip-art image appears in the Draw window.

Microsoft Draw can import pictures in a number of different file formats, but it can only edit a vector, or draw-type, picture if it is stored in the Computer Graphics Metafile (CGM) or Windows Metafile (WMF) format.

4 Turn on any combination of the four check boxes.

5 Click OK. The clip-art image appears in the Draw window.

The image is treated as a multiple selection, not as a grouped object.

Why can't I use Publisher's Crop Picture tool to delete part of an imported picture?
You can use Publisher's Crop Picture tool to hide part of an imported picture, but you can only hide outer horizontal and vertical portions of the image, as seen below. You can't delete an element that overlaps another part of the picture without deleting the underlying element.

When you use Microsoft Draw to delete part of an imported picture, you can select and delete individual objects within the picture, as shown below. The changes you make are not limited to the straight edges of the picture. In fact, you can delete elements even when they overlap others in the picture.

For information about an alternate way to change the color of an entire clip-art image, see page 206 in Chapter 9.

Delete Part of an Imported Picture

1 Click away from the image to deselect all the individual objects.

2 Use the pointer to select one object, or Shift-click to select a number of objects.

3 On the Edit menu, choose Cut or Clear to delete the selected object or objects.

Change the Color of Individual Elements

1 Click away from the image to deselect all the individual objects.

2 Use the pointer to select one object, or Shift-click to select a number of objects.

3 In the color palettes at the bottom of the screen, do one of the following:
- Click an option in the Line palette to change the outline color.
- Click an option in the Fill palette to change the fill color.
- Click Other (at the far right of the color palettes) to display the Color dialog box.

4 Select a basic color from the palette or define a custom color.

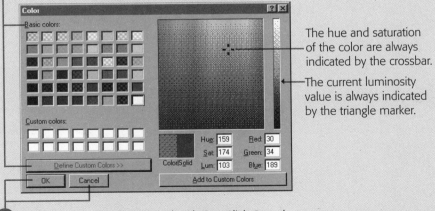

The hue and saturation of the color are always indicated by the crossbar.

The current luminosity value is always indicated by the triangle marker.

5 Click OK to accept the new color choice. Click Cancel to return to the image without changing the color.

Adding and deleting control handles. To add a new control handle, hold down the Ctrl key while you click the outline of the object. To delete an existing control handle, hold down the Shift and Ctrl keys while you click the handle.

Alter the Outline of an Object in an Imported Picture

1 Click away from the image to deselect all the individual objects.

2 Use the pointer to select one object.

3 Open the View menu and zoom to a magnification level that enables you to work with precision.

4 Open the Edit menu, and choose Edit Freeform.

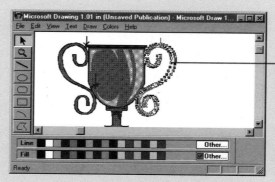

The object is now surrounded by control handles that appear at the vertex of each curve or line segment.

5 Use the pointer to grab a control handle and drag it to a new location, which changes the shape of the object.

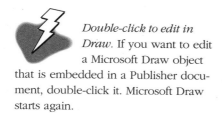

Double-click to edit in Draw. If you want to edit a Microsoft Draw object that is embedded in a Publisher document, double-click it. Microsoft Draw starts again.

Save a Microsoft Draw Drawing

1 Return to Publisher by choosing Exit And Return on the Microsoft Draw File menu. An alert box appears.

2 Do one of the following:
- Click Yes to embed the drawing in your Publisher document.
- Click No to return to your publication without creating the embedded drawing.
- Click Cancel to continue working in Draw.

3 In Publisher, open the File menu and choose Save or Save As. The embedded object is saved as part of the publication file.

Wrap text around a picture.

Recolor a picture.

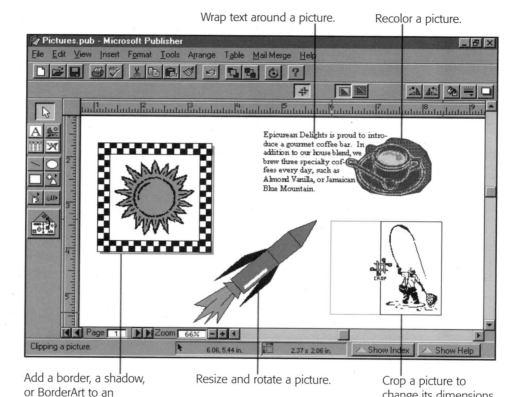

Add a border, a shadow, or BorderArt to an imported image.

Resize and rotate a picture.

Crop a picture to change its dimensions.

Picture and Clip Tools

Microsoft Publisher 97 can import a wide variety of computer-based pictures, which you can edit using the picture and clip tools. The first step toward mastering these tools is learning to distinguish between different graphics types.

Categories of Graphics

Graphics file formats can be grouped into two overall categories: bitmapped (or raster) images and vector (or draw-type) images. The following table compares the two file formats and the pros and cons of each kind of image.

Comparison of Bitmapped and Vector Images		
Image Attribute	**Bitmapped Image**	**Vector Image**
How the image data is stored and interpreted by the computer	The image data is a collection of picture elements, or pixels. The information in the image file specifies the location, or map, of each pixel. The term bitmapped image originates from the time when a screen could display only one color (white on black). A pixel could then be described by a single bit (0 or 1)—thus making the pixel map a bitmap.	The image data is a series of drawing instructions.
Overall printing quality	High, provided that the image contains the appropriate number of pixels (referred to as resolution) for your final output device, and that you do not enlarge the image in Publisher.	Always high. An image always prints at the highest resolution of the output device.
Enlargement capability	Poor. When enlarged in Publisher, the individual pixels of a bitmapped picture create a jagged staircase pattern, known as aliasing. The lines of the image do not look smooth.	High. You can scale the image or change its proportions without reducing quality.

Comparison of Bitmapped and Vector Images *(continued)*		
Image Attribute	**Bitmapped Image**	**Vector Image**
Color capability	Images contain a specific number of potential colors: 1 color (white on black), 16 colors, 256 colors or shades of gray, or 16.7 million colors.	All color information is stored as a series of instructions, which can generate white on black, gray-scale, or full-color (16.7 million) pictures.
Appropriate content	Scanned photographs and realistic illustrations.	Line drawings, illustrations, charts, and technical diagrams.
File size	As the resolution increases and as the number of potential colors increases, file size grows dramatically. Bitmapped images can require a great deal of storage space. For 16 colors, each pixel requires 4 bits of information to describe its color. For 256 colors, each pixel requires 8 bits of information to describe its color. For 16.7 million colors, each pixel requires 24 bits (or 3 bytes) to describe its color.	Drawing indications and color information are stored as a series of instructions. This results in efficient file sizes that do not require a great deal of storage space.

The following images illustrate some of the differences between bitmapped and vector images.

The computer sees this circle as a series of black-and-white dots.

Enlarging a bitmapped image also enlarges the individual dots, which creates a jagged pattern (aliasing).

The computer sees this circle as a series of drawing instructions for radius, line thickness, and fill pattern.

You can enlarge or reduce a vector image without degrading quality.

Are there other graphics formats that can contain both bitmapped and vector images? Yes, Computer Graphics Metafiles, Windows Metafiles, CorelDraw files, and Micrografx Designer files can all contain a combination of bitmapped and vector data. However, these file formats typically contain only vector information.

For information about how to send a PostScript printer file to an outside printer, see Chapter 14.

A Special Case:
The Encapsulated PostScript Format

The Encapsulated PostScript (EPS) format is a graphics format that can contain both bitmapped and vector images. The information for both image types is stored in Adobe's PostScript printer language. In fact, EPS is a subset of the commands used to control a PostScript printer.

If you are planning a publication with numerous photographs and drawings, you should consider printing to a PostScript printer for the following reasons:

- PostScript is a robust printer language. PostScript commands can create very complex vector images efficiently, and PostScript printers output bitmapped images with a broad range of gray shades.

- The same PostScript document file that you send to your 600 dots-per-inch (dpi) PostScript laser printer will print at 1200 or 2400 dpi on the typesetting machines at your service bureau. You can print proofs of your publication before you send them to a commercial printer for professional-quality reproduction.

- If you print a publication containing an EPS image to a non-PostScript printer, only the 72 dpi screen image will be printed. You will see either a low-resolution preview bitmap or a plain box in your printed document.

Title: CR
Creator:
CreationD

If no header is included, the EPS file appears as a simple box with an identifying file-name and the name of the program that created the image. The size of this box indicates the dimensions of the EPS picture.

Publisher displays a picture of an EPS file only if a bitmapped image of the picture, called a Tagged Image File Format (TIFF) header, is included in the file. The TIFF header contains a low-resolution representation of the image to help you position the picture.

Why are file extensions so important? The three-letter extension following the period identifies the picture's file format. A picture called Picture.wmf, for example, is stored in the Windows Metafile format; a file called Artwork.bmp is stored in the Windows Bitmaps format. Microsoft Windows 95 does not display extensions by default. To display file extensions, open My Computer or Windows Explorer and select Options on the View menu. On the View tab, turn off the check box labeled Hide MS-DOS File Extensions For File Types That Are Registered.

You may already have access to additional graphics file formats. Publisher can take advantage of many graphics file filters that have been installed on your system by other Microsoft products. The exact choices that appear in the Insert Picture File dialog box will vary, but here are a few formats that you might be able to access:

- Macintosh PICT (PCT)
- Enhanced Metafiles (EMF)
- Targa (TGA)
- Portable Network Graphics (PNG)
- AutoCAD Format 2-d (DXF)
- HP Graphics Language (HGL)

Importing Pictures

You can easily import many different types of pictures into your publications, which gives you a lot of design flexibility. The following table lists the many graphics file formats that Publisher can import. The Comments column provides information about each format's performance in Publisher.

Types of Graphics Files that Publisher Imports			
Format Name	**Image Type**	**Filename Extension**	**Comments**
Windows Bitmaps	Bitmapped	BMP	Best suited for white on black, 16-color, and 256-color images.
CorelDraw	Vector	CDR	Can include bitmapped data as well, but rarely does.
Computer Graphics Metafile	Vector	CGM	Many of the Microsoft Clip Gallery files are in this format.
Micrografx Designer/Draw	Vector	DRW	Can include bitmapped data as well, but rarely does.
Encapsulated PostScript	Bitmapped, vector	EPS	Can contain bitmapped and/or vector data.
CompuServe Graphics Interchange Format	Bitmapped	GIF	Best suited for white on black, 16-color, and 256-color images. A popular graphics file format for the Internet.
Joint Photographic Experts Group	Bitmapped	JPG	The highly compressed JPEG format is ideal for high-resolution images. A popular graphics format for the Internet.
Kodak Photo CD	Bitmapped	PCD	Images stored at highest resolution can be too large for Publisher to save; lower resolutions take up less disk space and print faster.

Format Name	Image Type	Filename Extension	Comments
PC Paintbrush	Bitmapped	PCX	Best suited for white on black, 16-color, and 256-color images.
Tagged Image File Format 5.0	Bitmapped	TIF	TIFF format compression options are ideal for high-resolution images.
Windows Metafile	Vector	WMF	Can include bitmapped data as well, but rarely does.
WordPerfect Graphics	Vector	WPG	Offers compatibility with WordPerfect.

Picture Import Methods

Before you import a picture into your publication, you should decide whether you need to draw a picture frame. If you want to import a picture in its original size and shape, don't draw a picture frame first. Publisher will create a picture frame to fit the image, maintaining the image's original aspect ratio—the proportional relationship between the width and height of the image—and minimizing the distortion of your image.

Alternatively, you can create a picture frame prior to importing an image. This method works best if you want to fit a picture into a predetermined layout.

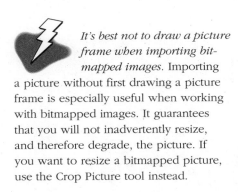

It's best not to draw a picture frame when importing bit-mapped images. Importing a picture without first drawing a picture frame is especially useful when working with bitmapped images. It guarantees that you will not inadvertently resize, and therefore degrade, the picture. If you want to resize a bitmapped picture, use the Crop Picture tool instead.

Drag and drop pictures. If your draw or paint application supports Windows 95 Drag-And-Drop functions, you can simply move a picture from its window into a Publisher document. You can also drag a picture file from Windows Explorer directly into a Publisher document.

Import a Picture into Your Publication

1 If you want Publisher to size and proportion the imported image to fit into a predetermined layout, choose the Picture tool and draw a picture frame, or select an existing picture frame. If you want to import a picture in its original size and proportions, do not draw or select any frame.

2 Open the Insert menu and choose Picture File. The Insert Picture File dialog box appears.

3 Open the Files Of Type drop-down list box, and choose the format of the file you want to import. All the files of your chosen format appear in the files list box.

What if I created my picture in an application that doesn't support a standard format? If you want to import a picture created in a Windows 95–based application that does not support any of the formats listed in the table on pages 182 through 183, copy the picture to the Windows 95 Clipboard and paste it into the publication instead of using the Picture File command on the Insert menu. The Clipboard converts files to a standard file format that all Windows 95–based applications can use.

For more information about using the Windows 95 Clipboard, see Chapter 4.

The Find File feature is described on pages 30 through 31 in Chapter 3.

For more information about aspect ratio and proportionally resizing an object, see page 199.

Shortcut for quickly accessing the Insert Picture File dialog box. You can quickly access the Insert Picture File dialog box by double-clicking a picture frame. If the image that you double-click contains a picture from the Microsoft Clip Gallery, the Microsoft Clip Gallery 3.0 dialog box is displayed.

Import a Picture into Your Publication *(continued)*

4 Locate and select the picture file you want using the Look In drop-down list box and the files list box. If you have difficulty locating the file, click Find File to search for it.

6 Click OK to import the picture into your publication. If you began this process by drawing or selecting a picture frame, Publisher displays the Import Picture dialog box, which helps you maintain the aspect ratio when you import a picture.

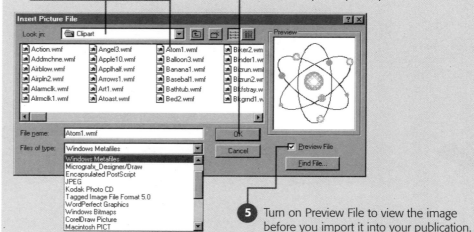

5 Turn on Preview File to view the image before you import it into your publication.

7 Do one of the following:

- To maintain the aspect ratio of the original picture, select Change The Frame To Fit The Picture. You should choose this option most of the time.

- To fit the picture into an existing frame, select Change The Picture To Fit The Frame.

8 Click OK.

Printing hidden pictures. If you choose to hide the pictures on screen to speed performance, and if you then print the document, Publisher asks whether you want to print the pictures or suppress them. Click Yes to print the pictures; click No to print the document with blank spaces where the pictures should be. Publisher prints a dotted outline to indicate where a hidden picture would normally appear on the page. Suppressing pictures can greatly decrease the time required to print a proof of your publication.

Share the Clip Gallery with other Microsoft applications. Many Microsoft products, such as Word and Excel, can take advantage of the Clip Gallery. To access the Clip Gallery from another application, select Object on the Insert menu. In the Object Type list box, select Microsoft Clip Gallery. Then use the Clip Gallery as you normally would within Publisher.

Imported Picture Display Options

You might notice performance degradation as the number of pictures in a publication increases. It takes a fair amount of processing power to update the display of graphics. You can speed Publisher's performance by reducing the quality of the picture display.

Control the Display of Pictures

1 On the View menu, choose Picture Display. The Picture Display dialog box appears.

Selecting Detailed Display might slow down Publisher's performance if the publication contains complex graphics.

Selecting Fast Resize And Zoom displays low-resolution images and speeds performance.

Selecting Hide Pictures gives Publisher the largest performance boost. All the pictures in your document (including WordArt and OLE objects) appear as crossed-out frames.

2 Select an option. The choice that you make in this dialog box only affects the display of pictures on screen. The pictures will print at the full resolution of the printer.

3 Click OK.

The Clip Gallery

The CD-ROM version of Publisher includes over 5200 clip-art images. You can store and manage these images—and any other pictures on your system—using the Microsoft Clip Gallery, as long as the file formats are ones that Publisher recognizes. You can also use the Clip Gallery to organize digital sound and video

Why don't I have thousands of clip-art choices? If you installed Publisher from 3.5-inch floppy disks, you'll have access to a smaller library of clip-art images. The floppy disk version of Publisher, however, does contain over 370 images.

 Available sound and video formats. Publisher can import any digital sound or video format supported by the Windows 95 Media Player. If the proper hardware and the necessary software drivers are installed on your computer system, you should be able to import files in these multimedia formats:

- @ WAV sound files
- @ MIDI sound files
- @ RMI sound files
- @ AVI video files

 Boost the power of the Find Clip dialog box. The Find Clip dialog box works in conjunction with keywords. You'll get much better search results if you assign descriptive information to a file when you import it into the Clip Gallery.

files for multimedia documents that you publish to the World Wide Web. Specifically, you can do the following:

- @ Search for a vector image, bitmapped image, sound file, or video file, based on criteria such as file type or keywords.

- @ Insert a vector image, bitmapped image, sound file, or video file into a Publisher document.

- @ Group vector images, bitmapped images, sound files, and video files by category.

- @ Assign a descriptive phrase to a vector image, bitmapped image, sound file, or video file.

Importing a File from the Clip Gallery

During installation, Publisher copies over 370 picture files, in both vector and bitmapped formats, to your hard disk. In addition, Publisher installs on your hard disk thumbnail sketches (miniature previews) of all the clip art contained on the CD-ROM. This means you can search and preview the entire clip-art collection of over 5200 images, even if you don't have the compact disc in the CD drive. To actually insert artwork stored on the CD into your publication, however, you must have the compact disc in the CD drive.

In many cases, you can find the image, sound, or video you want by looking through the thumbnail sketches that appear in the preview window. By default, the images are organized into general categories, such as People At Work, Sports & Leisure, and Cartoons. You can also search for a specific graphics, sound, or video file in the Clip Gallery by clicking the Find button, which opens the Find Clip dialog box. This is especially useful if you are sorting through the thousands of images that ship with Publisher, or if you have amassed a large collection of your own images, sounds, and videos.

Import a File from the Clip Gallery

1 On the Insert menu, choose Clip Art. The Microsoft Clip Gallery 3.0 dialog box appears.

2 Select the Clip Art tab to import vector images; select the Pictures tab to import bitmapped images; select the Sounds tab to import sound files; or select the Videos tab to import video files.

3 Choose one of the categories in the categories list box, or select All Categories to see all of the available files.

5 Click Insert to add the file to your publication. Click Close to return to your publication without inserting a file.

Click here to view the currently selected thumbnail sketch at an enlarged size.

4 Use the scroll bar to move through the thumbnail sketches, and select the file you want to import.

The Clip Gallery always reports the number of files in the category and the keywords associated with the currently selected file.

What's the difference between the Find button in the Clip Gallery and the Find File command on Publisher's File menu? The Find button in the Clip Gallery searches for only graphics, sound, and video files, and it looks through only the files that have been added as thumbnail sketches. In addition, you can search for files in the Clip Gallery based on keywords you assign when you add a file to the Gallery.

In contrast, the Find File command searches for document files that Publisher can open and searches any disk you specify.

Use the Find Button to Search for a Clip File to Import

1 In the Microsoft Clip Gallery 3.0 dialog box, click the Find button. The Find Clip dialog box appears.

Publisher can search for a filename with just a few letters as clues. When you use the Find button to find a file in the Clip Gallery, you don't have to type a full filename or use wildcard characters. You only need to type a few letters. Publisher searches for any file containing those letters, even if the letters fall in the middle of the word. For example, if you type *lo*, Publisher might retrieve these files: Globe.cgm, Clock1.cgm, and Lobster.wmf.

Use the Find Button to Search for a Clip File to Import *(continued)*

2 If you've assigned descriptions to your clip files and want to find all the files that match a specific keyword, type a keyword or multiple keywords separated by commas into the Keywords text box.

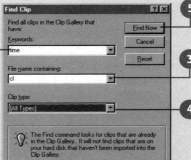

5 Click Find Now to begin the search. Publisher returns to the Microsoft Clip Gallery 3.0 dialog box.

3 To find all clip files with similar filenames, type the name (if you know it) or a few letters contained in the filename.

4 To locate a specific file type, open the Clip Type drop-down list box and choose a file format. If you leave All Types selected, the Clip Gallery will search for vector images, bitmapped images, sounds, and videos that match the search criteria.

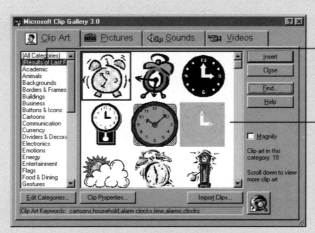

A new temporary category, which contains the results of the search, appears in the categories list box.

When Publisher returns to the Clip Gallery, you will see thumbnail sketches for only those files that match your search criteria.

6 If you selected All Types, you can select the Clip Art tab to see the vector images that match your search criteria, the Pictures tab to see the bitmapped images that match your search criteria, the Sounds tab to see the sound files that match your search criteria, or the Videos tab to see the video files that match your search criteria.

Delete unwanted Clip Gallery images. Publisher automatically copies hundreds of clip-art images to your hard disk during installation. You can conserve disk space by deleting those clip-art images that you don't use from your hard disk.

Can I delete clip files from my disk from within the Clip Gallery? No. You must delete a file by using Windows Explorer or by dragging a file icon to the Windows 95 Recycle Bin. Be sure to update the Clip Gallery after you delete files from your disk.

Maintaining the Clip Gallery

Whenever you add a vector image, bitmapped image, sound, or video to the Clip Gallery, a new thumbnail sketch is added to the already extensive collection of thumbnail sketches that Publisher created during installation. The Clip Gallery continues to show you the same thumbnail sketch even when you have moved, modified, or deleted the actual file from your disk. You'll find the Clip Gallery to be more useful if you create your own categories and assign your own keywords to your files.

You can reorganize the Clip Gallery in three ways:

- By updating the thumbnail sketches to match the current contents of your local hard disk, removable disks, and networked drives.

- By renaming or deleting existing categories, or by creating entirely new categories.

- By assigning a file to a different category or to additional categories, or by changing the descriptive search phrase associated with the file.

Update the Contents of the Clip Gallery

1. On the Insert menu, choose Clip Art.

2. Select the Clip Art tab to update vector images; select the Pictures tab to update bitmapped images; select the Sounds tab to update sound files; or select the Videos tab to update video files.

Update the Contents of the Clip Gallery *(continued)*

3 Right-click the thumbnail sketch you want to delete, or right-click any thumbnail sketch to update all the clip previews.

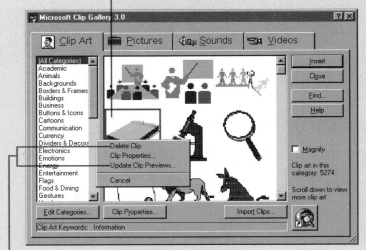

4 Choose Delete Clip to remove the selected preview from the Clip Gallery, or choose Update Clip Previews to reconcile all of the thumbnail sketches with the contents of your disks. The Update dialog box appears.

5 Turn on Network Drives to have Publisher update remote drives on a network. Turn on Removable Disks to update the contents of removable media such as floppy disks and Iomega Zip disks.

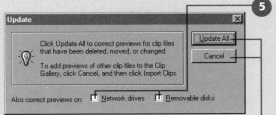

6 Click Update All to start the update process, or click Cancel to return to the Clip Gallery without updating any disks. If Publisher finds a thumbnail sketch for which it cannot find a corresponding file, it displays a second Update dialog box.

Update the Contents of the Clip Gallery *(continued)*

The full path and filename are displayed.

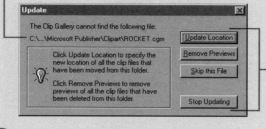

7 Click one of the four buttons:

- ✪ Update Location to allow you to browse for the file and reestablish a link between the thumbnail sketch and the file

- ✪ Remove Previews to remove from the Clip Gallery all thumbnail sketches that don't have corresponding files

- ✪ Skip This File to take no action and move on to the next thumbnail sketch for which there is no corresponding file

- ✪ Stop Updating to take no action and immediately return to the Clip Gallery

Reorganize Categories Within the Clip Gallery

1 On the Insert menu, choose Clip Art. The Microsoft Clip Gallery 3.0 dialog box appears.

2 Select the Clip Art tab to edit categories associated with vector images, the Pictures tab to edit categories associated with bitmapped images, the Sounds tab to edit categories associated with sound files, or the Videos tab to edit categories associated with video files.

3 Click the Edit Categories button. The Edit Category List dialog box appears.

Reorganize Categories Within the Clip Gallery *(continued)*

4 Select a category in the categories list box.

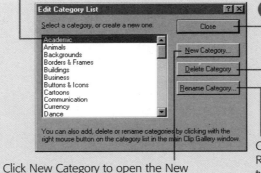

6 When you have finished reorganizing categories, click Close to return to the Clip Gallery, and then click Close in the Clip Gallery to return to your publication.

Click Delete Category, and then click Yes or No in the confirmation dialog box that appears.

Click Rename Category to open the Rename Category dialog box, and then type a new name in the New Category Name text box. Click OK to rename the category, or click Cancel to return to the Edit Category List dialog box without renaming the category.

Click New Category to open the New Category dialog box, and then type a name in the New Category Name text box. Click OK to create the category, or click Cancel to return to the Edit Category List dialog box without creating the category.

5 Create, delete, and rename categories as necessary.

Change the Information for an Individual Clip File

1 On the Insert menu, choose Clip Art. The Microsoft Clip Gallery 3.0 dialog box appears.

2 Select the Clip Art tab to modify the information for a vector image, the Pictures tab to modify the information for a bitmapped image, the Sounds tab to modify the information for a sound file, or the Videos tab to modify the information for a video file.

3 Select the thumbnail sketch for which you want to modify information.

4 Click the Clip Properties button, or right-click the thumbnail sketch and select Clip Properties on the shortcut menu. The Clip Properties dialog box appears.

A thumbnail sketch appears along with the filename, format type, and file size.

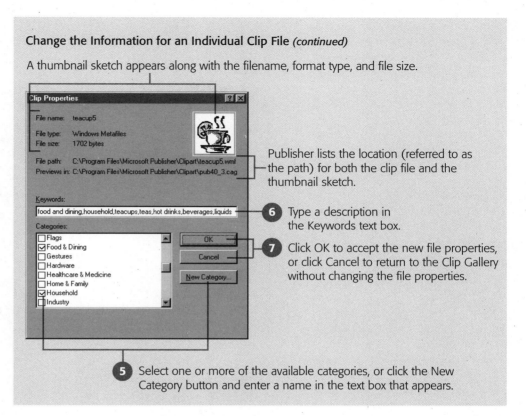

Multiple keywords. You can type several words and phrases in the Keywords text box. Separate the words and phrases with single commas and no spaces. If you search for the file in the future, you can use any of the keywords or phrases to locate it.

Play sounds and videos. When a sound or video file is selected in the Clip Gallery, the Clip Properties dialog box includes a Play button. To guarantee that you've selected the right clip, use this button to listen to the sound or to view the video.

Publisher lists the location (referred to as the path) for both the clip file and the thumbnail sketch.

6 Type a description in the Keywords text box.

7 Click OK to accept the new file properties, or click Cancel to return to the Clip Gallery without changing the file properties.

5 Select one or more of the available categories, or click the New Category button and enter a name in the text box that appears.

Building a Library of Clips

You can add vector images, bitmapped pictures, sounds, or videos to the Clip Gallery at any time. Publisher makes it easy for you to add files from a variety of sources, including your local hard disk, removable disks, and networked drives. A special version of the Clip Gallery, called Clip Gallery Live, is maintained on the World Wide Web. If you have an Internet provider, such as Microsoft Network (MSN), and browsing software, such as Microsoft Internet Explorer, you can download additional clips from Clip Gallery Live.

Add more than one file to the Clip Gallery at a time. If you install a Microsoft Clip Gallery package, you can install all the files along with keywords, categories, and previews in one step. In the Import Clips dialog box, open the Files Of Type drop-down list box, and select Clip Gallery Packages.

Even if you don't install a Microsoft Clip Gallery package, you can still add multiple files. In the files list box, Shift-click to select a group of contiguous filenames, or Ctrl-click to select nonadjacent filenames.

Why doesn't a thumbnail sketch of my new file appear in the preview area? If you've added files to the Clip Gallery, Publisher might not have updated the screen display. Close and then reopen the Clip Gallery. Your thumbnail sketches should appear in the preview area.

Sometimes Publisher can't create a preview from a file. For sound clips, Publisher substitutes an icon for the clip preview. Publisher is also unable to display an EPS file on screen unless the file has a TIFF header.

For more information about the World Wide Web and Web pages, see Chapter 11.

Add a File to the Clip Gallery

1 On the Insert menu, choose Clip Art.

2 Select the Clip Art tab to import vector images; the Pictures tab to import bitmapped images; the Sounds tab to import sound files; or the Videos tab to import video files.

3 Click the Import Clips button. The Add Clip Art To Clip Gallery dialog box that appears allows you to search local and networked drives for clip files.

4 Open the Files Of Type drop-down list box and choose either a specific file format or a general category, such as All Pictures, Sounds, or Videos, to see all the files available for import.

5 Use the Look In drop-down list box and the files list box to locate and select the file or files you want to add to the Clip Gallery.

6 Click Open. The Clip Properties dialog box appears.

7 Take any of the following actions:

    ➣ Enter descriptive phrases in the Keywords text box.

    ➣ Select one or more of the categories in the categories list box.

    ➣ Click the New Category button, and enter a name in the dialog box that appears.

    ➣ Click the Skip This Clip button to bypass the current file and proceed to the next file you selected.

8 Click OK to add the file to the Clip Gallery, or click cancel to return to the Clip Gallery without adding the file.

Use Clip Gallery Live on the World Wide Web

1 Make the connection to your Internet provider. The connection must be active before you attempt to connect to Clip Gallery Live.

2 In Publisher, choose Clip Art on the Insert menu. The Microsoft Clip Gallery 3.0 dialog box appears.

Use Clip Gallery Live on the World Wide Web *(continued)*

3 Click the Connect To Web For Additional Clips button, shown below. Publisher will load your Web browser application and locate the Clip Gallery Live Web page. (You will get an error message if Publisher doesn't recognize your Web browser. If this happens, use a different Web browser.

4 If this is the first time you are using Clip Gallery Live, read the licensing agreement and click the Accept button.

5 Click one of the four icons representing the clip types: Clip Art, Pictures, Sounds, or Videos.

6 Click Browse to view clips by category, or click Search to select clips on the basis of keyword descriptions.

Clip Gallery Live reports the number of files that are in a given category or that match your search criteria.

9 Use the scroll bar to move through the thumbnail sketches in the Preview area.

10 Click the hypertext link (which appears in blue) to select a clip file and download it to your hard disk. Be sure to select an appropriate location where you can later find the clip.

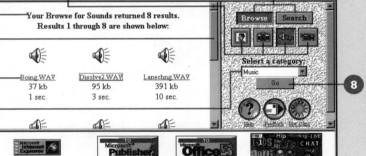

8 If you chose a category, click Go. If you entered one or more keywords, click Find.

7 If you clicked Browse, open the drop-down list box and choose a category. If you clicked Search, type in a keyword or multiple keywords separated by commas.

11 Open Windows Explorer and locate the clip file you downloaded. (The file's type will be Clip Gallery Download Package. To see the type, choose Details on the View menu.) Double-click the file's icon to import the clip into the Clip Gallery. A new category, called Downloaded Clips, will be created.

12 Disconnect from your Internet provider.

Image Acquisition Functions in Publisher

Microsoft Publisher supports the TWAIN image acquisition interface. If your hardware uses a TWAIN driver, you can directly access a scanner or digital camera from within your Publisher document. Although the TWAIN interface is an industry standard, the options you see will vary depending on your particular hardware and software setup.

Consumer-oriented digital cameras, such as the Casio QV-10a (the interface of which is shown below), generate low-resolution images at 72 dpi. This resolution is suitable for screen display and for output on a black-and-white or color desktop printer.

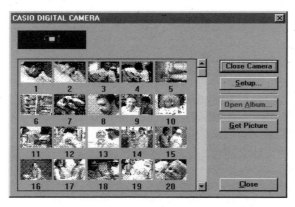

Desktop scanners can generate images at very high resolutions—typically 300 to 1200 dpi. When creating an image with a scanner, you will want to produce the smallest possible file size without degrading image quality. To accomplish this, you should scan a picture with the colors and resolution required by the final output device. For example, you shouldn't create a full-color scanned image if you will be printing to a black-and-white device. Unfortunately, there are no hard and fast rules concerning scanning parameters. The following table lists the most efficient resolutions for standard output devices.

Computing gray-scale and color photograph resolution. Photographs are reproduced using a cluster of dots called a halftone cell. Halftone resolution is measured in lines per inch (lpi). Ask your service bureau for the proper lpi setting. Scan your photographs at a dpi value of 1.5 times the lpi value. Note the following scanning recommendations:

- For 52 lpi, scan at 80 dpi.
- For 75 lpi, scan at 113 dpi.
- For 120 lpi, scan at 180 dpi.
- For 133 lpi, scan at 200 dpi.

Why doesn't the Scanner Image command appear? If the Scanner Image command does not appear, or if your scanner does not appear in the Sources list box, your scanner might not support the TWAIN interface. If that is the case, you must create the scanned photograph outside Publisher, save it in a file, and then use the Picture File command on the Insert menu to incorporate it into your publication.

Appropriate Scanning Resolutions for Standard Output Devices		
Hardware	Black-and-White Drawing	Gray-Scale or Color Photograph
Laser printer, 300 dpi	300 dpi	80 dpi
Laser printer, 600 dpi	600 dpi	113 dpi
Service bureau, Imagesetter, 1200 dpi	800 dpi	180 dpi
Service bureau, Imagesetter, 2400 dpi	800 dpi	200 dpi
Monitor, 72 dpi	72 dpi	72 dpi

Acquire a Picture While Working in Your Publication

Before you can create a scanned image, you must establish a link between Publisher and the image acquisition hardware. Unless you are switching from one device to another, you should perform this operation only once.

Link Publisher to Your Digital Camera or Scanner

1. On the Insert menu, choose Scanner Image.
2. On the cascading menu, choose Select Scanner. The Select Source dialog box appears.
3. In the Sources list box, choose the device (either a scanner or a digital camera) that you wish to use.

Acquire a Scanned Image

1. If you want Publisher to size and proportion the image to fit into a predetermined layout, click the Picture tool and draw a frame, or select an existing picture frame. If you want Publisher to automatically create a frame for the scanned image, do not draw or select any frame.

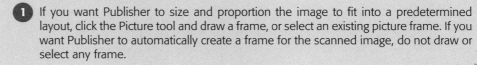

What does the Out Of Memory error message mean? Standard bitmapped file formats, such as TIFF and JPEG, use compression routines to shrink the size of a scanned image and save disk space. When Publisher incorporates a TWAIN picture (or inserts any bitmapped image into a document), it converts the picture to an uncompressed format. This uncompressed format might require more memory than your computer has available. Rescan the image at a lower resolution or with fewer colors.

Acquire a Scanned Image *(continued)*

2 Open the Insert menu and choose Scanner Image.

3 Choose Acquire Scanned Image on the cascading menu. The scanner control window appears.

4 Click Preview (or the corresponding button for your scanner) to see a low-resolution version of the image.

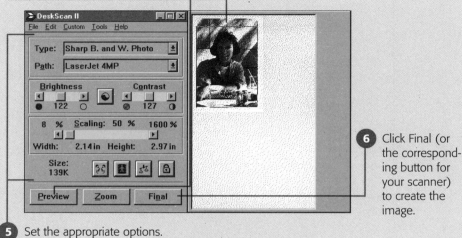

6 Click Final (or the corresponding button for your scanner) to create the image.

5 Set the appropriate options.

Modifying the Size and Appearance of Your Image

Whether you use commercial clip art, create an original drawing, or scan personal photographs, you might want to use Publisher's picture editing tools to resize, crop, or otherwise modify pictures. You can also use any of the layout tools to adjust pictures. See Chapter 4 for descriptions and procedures for using these tools.

Don't resize bitmaps.
Greatly enlarging or reducing a bitmapped image within Publisher can seriously degrade image quality. In general, you should use bitmapped images at their original size. If you must resize a bitmapped image, do it in a dedicated image editing program that can enhance the image quality by using antialiasing.

What if I want to restore the resized image to its original dimensions? If you distort an image and then want to return it to its original size, turn on the Original Size check box in the Scale Picture or Scale Object dialog box. Publisher returns the height and width to 100 percent.

Can I use the Scale Object command to resize WordArt objects? Yes. Because WordArt is inserted into a publication as an OLE object, you can use the Scale Object command to alter its size. However, because the WordArt object is generated within Publisher, the size you specify in the Scale Object dialog box becomes the "original size." You therefore cannot revert to the WordArt object's previous size by using the Original Size check box in the Scale Object dialog box.

Scaling an Imported Picture or Clip Gallery Object

The Scale Picture or Scale Object command gives you precise controls that enable you to easily maintain the aspect ratio (the original proportions) of a picture.

Resize an Image Using Scale Picture or Scale Object

1 Select the picture or Clip Gallery Object you want to resize.

2 If you are working with an imported picture, choose Scale Picture on the Format menu. The Scale Picture dialog box appears. If you are working with a Clip Gallery object, choose Scale Object. The Scale Object dialog box appears.

3 Enter equal percentage values for the height and width. For example, if you want to reduce a picture but maintain the aspect ratio, type *50* in both the Scale Height and Scale Width text boxes. The result will be a picture one-quarter the size of the original.

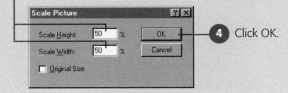

4 Click OK.

Featuring a Section of Your Image

You can hide portions of a picture by using Publisher's Crop Picture tool. Think of the picture frame as a window. Using the Crop Picture tool is like pulling the window shade up or down. Although the view doesn't change, you can see more of the landscape (or the picture) when the window shade is up and less when it is down. Cropping is not the same as resizing, which enlarges or shrinks the entire picture.

Crop a Picture

1 Select the picture you want to crop.

Crop all sides or opposite sides of your picture equally. To crop all four sides of a picture equally, hold down the Ctrl key as you drag a corner selection handle. To crop opposite sides of a picture equally, hold down Ctrl as you drag any selection handle except a corner handle.

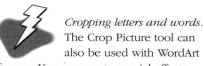

Cropping letters and words. The Crop Picture tool can also be used with WordArt frames. You can create special effects, abstract patterns, or logos by trimming portions of the letters in a WordArt frame.

Turn off text wrap. To have text overprint a picture or WordArt object, select the frame and send it to the bottom of the stack by choosing Send To Back on the Arrange menu. Make sure the text frame is transparent (by selecting it and pressing Crtl-T) so that you can see the picture or WordArt design beneath it.

Crop a Picture *(continued)*

2 Click the Crop Picture button (shown below) on the Format toolbar, or select Crop Object on the Format menu.

3 Place the pointer over any selection handle so that the pointer changes into the Crop pointer.

4 Using the Crop pointer, drag a selection handle inward until only the portion of the picture that you want to be visible is displayed. Repeat this step with as many selection handles as necessary to achieve the effect you want.

5 If you want to restore the cropped portions of the picture, use the Crop pointer to drag a selection handle outward until all of the original picture appears in the frame.

6 When you have finished trimming a picture, click the Crop Picture button on the Format toolbar again, or select the Crop Object command on the Format menu again, to deactivate the Crop Picture tool.

Text Wrapping

One of the best ways to create a cohesive design with words and objects is to wrap the text around other elements. You can wrap text around frames regardless of whether the frame contains a picture, WordArt, text, a table, or an OLE object. In addition, Publisher provides special text wrapping features that work with picture and WordArt frames. Text wrapping is affected by the stacking order of the objects. For text to wrap around an object, the object must lie on top of the text object.

Why doesn't my text wrap around a frame? In all likelihood, you have turned off the Wrap Text Around Objects check box in the Text Frame Properties dialog box (available from the Format menu). Turn the check box back on to allow the text to wrap around frames.

Wrapping text around drawn objects. You can wrap text around most of the geometric or irregular shapes created by Publisher's drawing tools. These are the restrictions:

- Text will not wrap around a transparent drawn shape. You must fill the shape with a color, tint, shade, pattern, or gradient to wrap the text.

- You can't control the shape of the irregular wrap around a drawn object. The wrap always follows the outline of the drawn shape very closely. A starburst shape, for example, will create a zig-zag wrap.

- You can't wrap text around a line or an arrow created with the Line tool. If you want to wrap text around an arrow, create the arrow using the Custom Shapes tool.

Wrap Text Around a Frame

1 Select the frame that you want to flow text around.

2 Choose Bring To Front on the Arrange menu. The text wraps around the frame.

Let's face it, Chicago is famous for stockyards, not fisheries. But times are changing. People are eating fish instead of red meat. Seafood is an important part of a heart-healthy diet because it is low in cholesterol and fat. We're proud that the freshest fish in Chicago can be found at Epicurean Delights. The arrival of aquaculture, or fish farming, as it is known among the professionals, has made trout as commonly available as beef. We found a hatchery only hours away from the heart of the city. The trout is so fresh that it tastes like the fish has jumped out of the water and onto your plate! These recipes are particularly easy to prepare because they are available as ready-to-cook dishes from the Epi-

By default, Publisher wraps text around the rectangular frame of a picture or WordArt object. You can sometimes create a more interesting and tighter text wrap by flowing the text around the outline of the image itself rather than around the rectangular frame.

Click the Edit Irregular Wrap button to alter the way text wraps around the image.

Click the Wrap Text To Frame button to wrap text around the frame.

Click the Wrap Text To Picture button to wrap text around the image.

Wrap Text Around the Outline of a Picture or WordArt Design

1 Select the picture or WordArt frame containing the image that you want to wrap text around.

2 Choose the Bring To Front command on the Arrange menu (or select the text frame and choose Send To Back) to ensure that the image lies on top of the text object.

Access text wrapping options in the Picture Frame Properties or the Object Frame Properties dialog box. You can also access text wrapping options by choosing Picture Frame Properties (if you've selected a picture frame) or Object Frame Properties (if you've selected a WordArt frame) on the Format menu:

- Select Entire Frame to wrap text around the rectangular picture or WordArt frame. Click OK.

- Select Picture Only to wrap text around the outline of the image. Click OK.

Wrap Text Around the Outline of a Picture or WordArt Design *(continued)*

3 Click the Wrap Text To Picture button on the Format toolbar. Publisher wraps text around the image outline.

Let's face it, Chicago is famous for stockyards, not fisheries. But times are changing. People are eating fish instead of red meat. Seafood is an important part of a heart-healthy diet, because it is low in cholesterol and fat. We're proud that the freshest fish in Chicago can be found at Epicurean Delights. The arrival of aquaculture, or fish farming, as it is known among the professionals, has made trout as commonly available as beef. We found a hatchery only hours away from the heart of the city. The trout is so fresh that it tastes like the fish has jumped out of the water and onto your plate! These recipes are particularly easy to prepare because they are available as ready-to-cook dishes from the Epicurean Delights kitchen. You just pop the fish into the oven, microwave, or skillet and enjoy a delicious meal ten minutes

4 If you want to change back to the default setting and wrap text around the picture frame, click the Wrap Text To Frame button.

Fine-Tuning the Text Wrap

When you wrap text around a picture or a WordArt design, Publisher maintains a nonprinting boundary between the image and the text. You can change that boundary to wrap text more tightly around the image. You can even create a special boundary shape (such as a triangle or a free-form shape) that the text will flow around.

Adjust an Irregular Text Wrapping Boundary

1 Select the image you want to fine-tune, and click the Wrap Text To Picture button on the Format toolbar.

2 Click the Edit Irregular Wrap button on the Format toolbar, or choose Edit Irregular Wrap on the Format menu.

 The Edit Irregular Wrap button appears only when the Wrap Text To Picture button is active.

Controlling text wrapping. The distance between text and the picture or WordArt design it wraps around is affected by several elements:

- The text wrapping boundary, which you can reshape using the Edit Irregular Wrap tool

- The picture frame or WordArt frame margins, which are controlled by the Picture Frame Properties dialog box, the Object Frame Properties dialog box, or the Picture Crop tool

- The margins you set in the text frame, which are controlled by the Text Frame Properties dialog box

Adjust an Irregular Text Wrapping Boundary *(continued)*

3 Position the pointer over one of the Adjust handles that appear along the dotted boundary line. The pointer changes to the Adjust pointer.

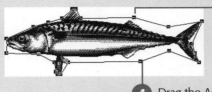

The Adjust handles are located at the vertices of the text wrapping boundary. As the shape of the boundary line becomes more complex or irregular, the number of Adjust handles increases.

4 Drag the Adjust handle to change the shape of the boundary around the image.

5 Release the mouse button. Publisher rewraps the text around the newly formed boundary.

Another way to adjust the text wrapping boundary is to add or delete Adjust handles so that you can follow the outline of an image more precisely. Deleting handles smooths the text wrap and makes the individual handle you need easier to grab.

Add and Delete Adjust Handles in an Irregular Text Wrapping Boundary

1 Select the picture or WordArt design whose text wrapping boundary you want to adjust. Click the Wrap Text To Picture button on the Format toolbar.

2 Click the Edit Irregular Wrap button.

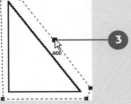

3 To add an Adjust handle, position the pointer along the text wrapping boundary where you want the new handle to appear. Hold down the Ctrl key to turn the pointer into the Add pointer, and then click the left mouse button.

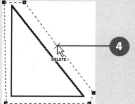

4 To delete an Adjust handle, position the Adjust pointer over a handle you don't need. Hold down the Ctrl key to turn the pointer into the Delete pointer, and then click the left mouse button.

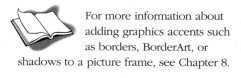

For more information about adding graphics accents such as borders, BorderArt, or shadows to a picture frame, see Chapter 8.

Adjusting Picture or WordArt Frame Margins

You can insert white space between a picture and the frame surrounding it to add a decorative touch to a picture or to allow breathing room between a picture and an elaborate border.

The picture becomes smaller if you increase the margins.

The picture becomes larger if you decrease the margins.

The margin (and background) can be filled with a color, tint, shade, pattern, or gradient.

Creating margins with the Crop Picture tool. You can create a picture or WordArt frame margin by using the Crop Picture tool. Select a handle and pull the frame out until all of the image is revealed. As you continue to pull the frame, Publisher will add white space between the image and the frame—generating a custom margin. When you use the Crop Picture tool (instead of the Picture Frame Properties or Object Frame Properties dialog box) to increase the margins, you increase the overall size of the frame without affecting the size or aspect ratio of the image itself.

Adjust Picture or WordArt Frame Margins

1 Select the picture or WordArt frame.

2 If you are working with a picture, choose Picture Frame Properties on the Format menu. The Picture Frame Properties dialog box appears. If you are working with a WordArt design, choose Object Frame Properties on the Format menu. The Object Frame Properties dialog box appears.

3 Enter values from 0 through 16 inches in the Left, Right, Top, and Bottom text boxes.

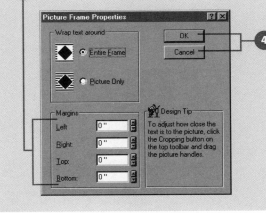

4 Click OK to implement the new margins, or click Cancel to return to your document without changing the picture frame margins.

Color Options for Imported Pictures

With a single command, Publisher allows you to change all the colors in an imported picture. You might want to adjust a color scheme for artistic reasons or for technical reasons regarding the capability of your output device. For example, you could recolor a multicolored picture to shades of gray if you are planning to output your publication to a black-and-white printer.

The Recolor Picture command works identically for draw-type and bitmapped pictures, but it has different effects, described on the following page, depending on the number of colors contained in the original picture:

For more information about color choices in Publisher, see Chapter 14.

Change the color of individual elements in a picture. To recolor individual elements in a picture, you must use a graphics application. Use a drawing program (such as Microsoft Draw) to change the color of a draw-type picture. Use a paint program (such as Microsoft Paint) to change the color of a bit-mapped picture.

For more information about Microsoft Draw, see Chapter 8.

Limitations of the Recolor Picture command. Because Publisher merely passes an Encapsulated PostScript (EPS) file to a PostScript printer, Publisher can't access the actual picture data. Therefore, you can't recolor an EPS picture. To change the colors in an EPS file, use a drawing program that can edit EPS images, such as CorelDraw or Micrografx Designer.

❷ If your original picture contains multiple colors, the Recolor Picture command replaces the different colors with varying tints of the new color you choose.

❷ If your original picture contains shades of gray, Publisher assigns a different tint of the new color you choose to each shade of gray.

❷ If your original picture is black-and-white, Publisher substitutes the new color for all black areas. White areas remain unchanged.

Recolor a Picture

1 Select the picture you want to recolor.

2 On the Format menu, choose Recolor Picture. The Recolor Picture dialog box appears.

3 Choose a color from the current palette, or click More Colors to access more options.

Confirm the effects of your choices in the Preview area.

5 Click Apply to preview the recolored picture in the actual document.

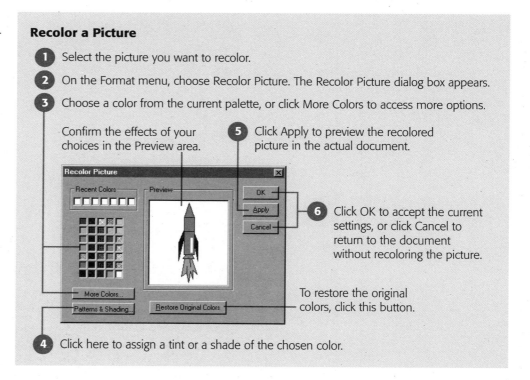

6 Click OK to accept the current settings, or click Cancel to return to the document without recoloring the picture.

To restore the original colors, click this button.

4 Click here to assign a tint or a shade of the chosen color.

OLE objects can contain any kind of data—words, numbers, or pictures. This picture was inserted via Microsoft Draw, an OLE drawing application.

Consider embedding an object in your Publisher document if no one else on your network needs access to the object. An embedded object is stored in the publication, so only you have access to it. This banner was created with WordArt, an OLE application that embeds objects in documents.

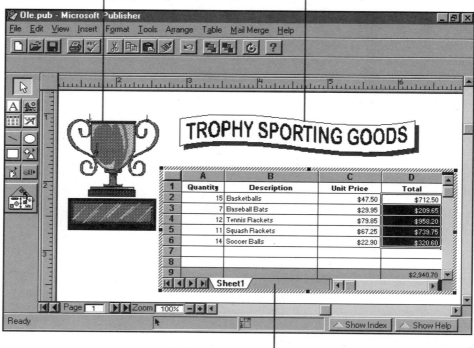

Linked objects can be updated automatically when the source file is revised, so you might consider linking the file to your Publisher document if you want to share file access. Someone in the accounting department, for example, could update this spreadsheet, and the changes would automatically appear the next time you open your document.

Working with OLE

You can easily establish connections between Microsoft Publisher 97 files and files created by other applications by using a process called Object Linking and Embedding (OLE). The OLE process allows you to link or embed objects from other applications in your Publisher documents. You can also link or embed only a portion of a file as an OLE object. For example, you might need only the summary information from a very large spreadsheet.

The two functions of OLE—linking and embedding—are related but exhibit important differences, which are described in the following table.

Functions of OLE		
	Linking Files	**Embedding Files**
Process description	You connect a file (or portion of a file) created by an external application to an OLE frame in Publisher.	You store a copy of a file (or portion of a file) in an OLE frame in Publisher. Or you create an object while working in Publisher by using another application.
Access	After you establish the link, both Publisher and the originating application have complete access to the file on disk.	Because the object is stored internally in Publisher, only Publisher has access to the object.
Advantages	You can use the same file in more than one publication. You can access files created or revised by other people on a network. Other people on a network can access the files linked to your publication.	You can easily create and edit objects within Publisher because you have direct access to all the source application's functions. No one other than you can access the OLE object embedded in your Publisher document.
Object behavior	You determine whether the links in a publication will be updated automatically or manually on a case-by-case basis. Double-clicking a linked object starts the source application.	Double-clicking an embedded object starts the source application.

When can I take advantage of OLE? You can take advantage of OLE only if the other Microsoft Windows 95–based applications on your computer support it. To see a list of the OLE-compliant programs on your system, open the Insert menu and choose Object. Scroll through the list of OLE source programs in the Insert Object dialog box.

Open Editing versus In-Place Editing. You can make changes to an OLE object with Open Editing (in a separate window) instead of In-Place Editing (which is integrated into Publisher's window). Select the OLE object, open the Edit menu, and select the command that identifies the application and the object to edit. On the cascading menu, choose the Open command.

Creating and Editing an OLE Object

You have two options when you create an OLE object: you can draw a frame yourself, or you can let Publisher size the object for you.

If you create an OLE object without first drawing a frame, Publisher creates a frame to fit the object. This method maintains the original size and aspect ratio—the proportional relationship between the width and height of the image—and minimizes the distortion of OLE objects.

Alternatively, you can draw a frame before you create an OLE object. You should draw a frame only if you want to fit an OLE object into a predetermined layout. Publisher attempts to maintain the proportions of the OLE object, but be warned: distortion can occur within very small frames. After the OLE object has been created, you can use Publisher's tools to modify the size of the object.

The current version of the OLE specification supports two editing modes, depending on the source application. When you create a new OLE object, the source application appears on screen in one of the following ways:

@ An application or utility using the Open Editing mode appears in a separate window. Microsoft Draw, which is discussed in Chapter 8, is a good example of an application that uses Open Editing.

@ An application or utility using In-Place Editing becomes part of the Publisher work area. Toolbars, menus, and dialog boxes appear for you to use. WordArt, discussed in Chapter 6, is a good example of a utility that uses In-Place Editing.

Create a New OLE Object While Working in Publisher

1 Do one of the following:

@ If you want Publisher to size and proportion the object to fit into a predetermined layout, click the OLE tool. Select an OLE object type from the flyout menu (but don't choose the More command), and draw a frame.

@ If you want Publisher to automatically size the OLE frame, open the Insert menu and choose Object. The Insert Object dialog box appears. Publisher scans your Windows 95 system and lists all the applications that support OLE as a source program.

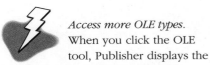

Access more OLE types. When you click the OLE tool, Publisher displays the last five types of OLE objects you created. If you want to access the Insert Object dialog box (and all the OLE object types on your computer), select the More command.

Create a New OLE Object While Working in Publisher *(continued)*

2 Choose the type of object you want to incorporate into the publication.

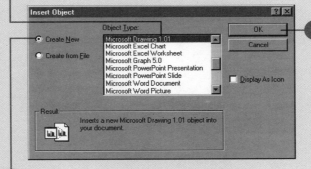

4 Click OK. The source utility or application appears.

3 Select Create New.

5 In the source application, create the object you want to embed.

6 Do one of the following:

@ If you are working within Publisher's window, click anywhere outside the OLE object to accept your changes and return to the Publisher document.

@ If you are working in a separate window, open the source application's File menu and select Exit And Return. A dialog box will appear that asks whether you want to update your publication. Click Yes to embed the object, or click No to return to your publication without creating an OLE object.

Link or Embed an Externally Stored File as an OLE Object

1 Do one of the following:

@ If you want Publisher to size and proportion the object to fit into a predetermined layout, click the OLE tool. Select an OLE object type from the flyout menu (but don't choose the More command), and draw a frame.

@ If you want Publisher to automatically size the OLE frame, click the OLE tool and select the More command on the flyout menu, or open the Insert menu and choose Object. The Insert Object dialog box appears.

Display information as an icon. The Display As Icon check box appears in both the Insert Object and Paste Special dialog boxes. This option is useful when you want easy access to information from another file but don't want the contents of the file to be displayed in your publication. You can use this option to insert an icon into your document. By double-clicking the icon, you activate the source program and display the file.

For more information about the Windows 95 Clipboard, see Chapter 4.

Link or Embed an Externally Stored File as an OLE Object *(continued)*

2 To use a file that exists on disk, select Create From File.

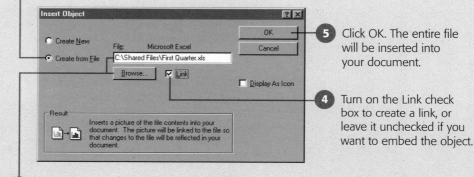

5 Click OK. The entire file will be inserted into your document.

4 Turn on the Link check box to create a link, or leave it unchecked if you want to embed the object.

3 Specify the location and name of the file. Or click Browse to search through the drives and folders on your system, and then click Insert to return to the Insert Object dialog box.

Link or Embed a Portion of a File as an OLE Object

1 Open a source application that supports OLE, such as Microsoft Word or Microsoft Excel.

2 In the source application, create or open the file you want to link. If you create a file, be sure to save it as a file on disk before you continue.

3 In the source application, select the portion of the file you want.

4 Open the Edit menu and select Copy to place the selection on the Windows 95 Clipboard.

5 Switch to Publisher.

6 Open Publisher's Edit menu and choose Paste Special. The Paste Special dialog box appears.

Why can't I access the Paste Link option in the Paste Special dialog box? Not all Windows 95–based applications support OLE in the same way. If the Paste Link option is grayed out, you cannot create a link between Publisher and the source application.

Publisher treats OLE objects like pictures. You can alter the appearance of OLE objects by using Publisher's picture editing tools:

- You can increase or decrease the size of OLE objects by dragging a selection handle or by entering sizing percentages into the Scale Object dialog box (accessed from the Format menu).

- The Recolor Object command (on the Format menu) applies varying tints of a chosen color to an OLE object.

- The Crop Picture tool lets you hide or reveal portions of an OLE object by resizing the frame without resizing the object itself.

Link or Embed Portions of a File as an OLE Object *(continued)*

7 To embed the object, choose Paste. To link the object, choose Paste Link.

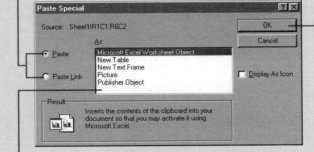

9 Click OK to return to your Publisher document.

8 In the list box, choose the appropriate format for the object. The choices in the list box vary depending on the type of data stored on the Clipboard. For example, if you have placed an Excel worksheet on the Clipboard, you can choose among Microsoft Excel Worksheet Object, New Table (which creates a Publisher table), New Text Frame, Picture, and Publisher Object.

Determining How OLE Links Behave

After you create an OLE link, you can choose whether the correspondence between the OLE object in your publication and the external file with which it is associated will be updated automatically or manually.

Select Link Options for a Particular File

1 Open the Edit menu and select Links. The Links dialog box appears.

2 Select the linked object you want to update from the file list.

Clicking versus double-clicking. A single click selects an OLE object, allowing you to then move it or edit it with Publisher's picture tools. A double click starts the source program, allowing you to change the content and internal formatting of the object.

Does clicking the Close button in the Links dialog box cancel the changes I've made? No. The Close command only returns you to your document. The functions of the Links dialog box take effect immediately when you click an option or a button. If you want to cancel the modifications you've made, you must change the options back to the previous settings.

Select Link Options for a Particular File *(continued)*

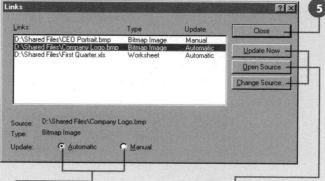

5 When you have finished modifying links and updating files, click the Close button.

3 Tell Publisher how often to update the link to the external file. If you want Publisher to check the status of the external file each time you open your document, choose Automatic. If the external file has been changed, Publisher will update the contents of the OLE frame with the latest version of the source file. If you want to control the frequency of the updates, choose Manual.

4 Optionally, take one or more of the following actions:

@ To import the latest version of the file, click Update Now.

@ To start the source application and display the contents of the OLE object, click Open Source.

@ To choose a new source file or to reestablish a link with a source file that is in a new location, click Change Source. In the Change Source dialog box that appears, locate and select the new file and then click OK.

World Wide Web documents must be viewed using a Web browser application, such as Microsoft Internet Explorer.

Publisher automatically converts imported pictures to the format required by the Internet.

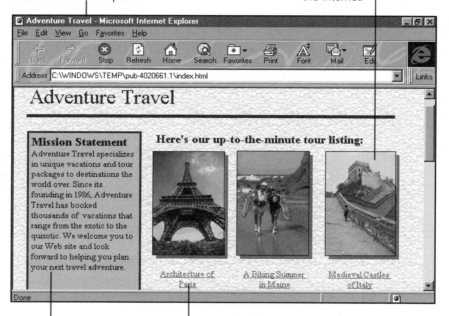

Publisher converts the text in a document to the Hypertext Markup Language specification.

Publisher can create hypertext links that perform various functions, such as allowing a reader to move to a different page in the Web document.

11

Creating Documents for the World Wide Web

How do I find an Internet Service Provider? The Internet is big business, so you'll find that most well-known on-line services, including Microsoft Network (MSN), offer Internet access. The major phone companies are also beginning to provide access. Another option is to contact a local Internet Service Provider.

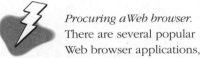

Procuring a Web browser. There are several popular Web browser applications, among them Microsoft Internet Explorer. In most cases, an Internet Service Provider (ISP) will supply you with a suite of Internet applications, including a Web browser. Once you have access to the Internet, you can download a browser directly from a vendor's Web site. This guarantees that you'll have the most current version of a browser, which is essential if you want to access the hottest features of the Web, such as on-line video, sophisticated Web page designs, and Java applets.

Microsoft Publisher 97 can generate electronic documents. In contrast to regular desktop publishing documents, which are typically printed on paper, the following is true of electronic documents:

- Web pages are intended to be read directly from the computer screen.
- Web pages can include pictures, sound files, and digital videos.
- Hyperlinks, in the form of hypertext or picture hot spots, allow you to move to other pages in an electronic publication, to other Web sites, or to other externally stored files.
- Electronic documents in the Hypertext Markup Language (HTML) format are easy to distribute via disk, network, or the Internet.

Gaining Access to the Web: Internet Service Providers and Web Browsers

In order to take full advantage of Publisher's electronic document tools, you should have access to the Internet. You can think of the Internet as a global network (actually a collection of networks) that enables computers of all sorts—PCs, Macintoshes, and Unix boxes—to communicate and exchange data. The

Load Microsoft Internet Explorer from CD. If you purchased Publisher on CD, you can install Microsoft's Web browser. On the CD, open the Netsetup folder, then open the Msie20 (Microsoft Internet Explorer version 2) subfolder, and then open the Win95 subfolder. Double-click the Msie20 file. Follow the on-screen instructions to install the application. Later you can download the most current version of Internet Explorer directly from the Web.

What do those abbreviations and acronyms for communications hardware and software mean? Computer lingo can be confusing. Here are definitions of a few key terms that you'll encounter when you hook up your computer to the Internet:

@ The device that sends and receives data over phone lines does so by MOdulating and DEModulating a signal—hence the name modem.

@ Modem speed is always measured in bits per second (bps). The speeds are typically noted in units of thousands (indicated by the letter *K*), so a 28.8K modem operates at 28,800 bits per second.

@ ISDN is an abbreviation for Integrated Services Digital Network.

@ T1 is the designation used by Bell Systems to identify a digital carrier line.

Internet provides easy access to the World Wide Web (also referred to as WWW, or simply the Web). The Web supports multimedia, which enables you to interact on line with electronic documents—complete with sound and video. In addition, hyperlinks on the Web allow you to move, or "surf," from one document to another regardless of the document's physical location. One moment you might be reading a text page stored on a network in your hometown, and the next moment you could be viewing a video stored on a computer halfway around the globe.

Before you can fully access the Web, you must have a properly configured modem, an Internet Service Provider (ISP), and appropriate Internet applications, such as email and a Web browser. The following diagram illustrates the relationship between these various elements.

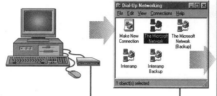

A high-speed modem physically connects your computer to a phone line. If you are using regular analog phone lines, your modem speed should be 14.4K or, better yet, 28.8K. Though it is more expensive, digital access via a 56K dedicated phone line, ISDN, or T1 connection provides much better performance.

Applications allow you to perform specific tasks on the Internet. Here a Web browser application—Microsoft Internet Explorer—allows you to read documents on line.

An ISP such as Microsoft Network (MSN), supplies communication software that connects you (via the phone line) to the Internet. You must then run separate applications to perform tasks on the Internet.

Design for the capabilities of browser software. When you design an HTML document, try to keep the capabilities of browsers in mind. It is possible for an HTML document to contain formatting instructions that a browser application can't display. For example, older browsers do not have the ability to display tables properly.

If you are designing a document for an internal network (called an intranet), or if you will supply browser software to your readers, you can take advantage of the superior functions offered by the browser program your readers will use. If, on the other hand, you are publishing your document on the Web and you have no control over which browser your readers will use, you have two choices:

- You can design for the lowest common denominator of browser software, eliminating sophisticated design elements such as frames and tables.

- You can put an alert at the top of your Web page advising readers that the document is best viewed with a particular browser.

Design Considerations: Publisher's HTML Tools

When you generate an electronic document, it must be converted from Publisher's native format (PUB) to Hypertext Markup Language (HTML), which is the standard document format used on the Web. HTML was developed to facilitate speedy transmission of documents over standard phone lines. To make HTML as efficient as possible, its designers limited the layout and formatting options available. An HTML document is therefore much more restricted in appearance than a normal Publisher document.

Whenever you create a Web page, Publisher modifies the layout options. In some cases, new commands and buttons appear on the toolbars or menus. In other cases, dialog boxes present you with only those choices that are appropriate for Web publishing. The following discussion is not meant to replace the detailed explanations of Publisher's design and layout tools in Chapters 2 through 10. Instead, it highlights the modified functions and new tools that are specific to Web design.

Beginning Work on a Web Publication

Just as with a normal Publisher document, a Web publication requires that you start a new publication and set up the page size, the background, and the layout guides.

Starting a Web Publication from Scratch

You should choose the Web Page layout to begin a Web publication. Doing so signals Publisher to make the special Web publishing tools available to you.

Begin a New Web Publication

1 Access the Startup dialog box, either by opening Publisher or by choosing the Create New Publication command on the File menu.

2 Select the Blank Page tab.

Use the Web Site PageWizard design assistant to create an electronic publication. Take advantage of the Web Site PageWizard design assistant to quickly create a sophisticated, multipage electronic document. This PageWizard helps you create a Web site for a business, a community group, or your home use. You can choose among five different designs. The PageWizard even allows you to generate multiple pages complete with hyperlinks.

For more information about using PageWizard design assistants, see Chapter 13.

Begin a New Web Publication *(continued)*

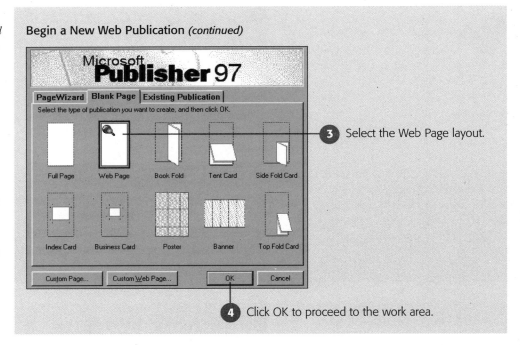

3 Select the Web Page layout.

4 Click OK to proceed to the work area.

Setting Up a Web Page

Although HTML documents are referred to as having pages, in truth they are meant to be read on screen. When you access the Page Setup dialog box (available from the File menu), Publisher gives you width options that correspond to standard VGA and SVGA screen resolutions.

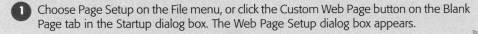

Set Up a Web Page

1 Choose Page Setup on the File menu, or click the Custom Web Page button on the Blank Page tab in the Startup dialog box. The Web Page Setup dialog box appears.

Choose a page width that matches the screen resolution used by your readers. When choosing the page width of your Web publication, remember that your readers may not have the same high-resolution monitor that you do. For example, if you choose the Wide (or SVGA) option, readers with a VGA monitor will be forced to scroll horizontally as well as vertically to read the entire page.

For more information about Publisher's standard Page Setup dialog box and the background, see Chapter 3.

Use the background to repeat elements. The background in a Web publication functions just like the background in a standard Publisher document. Place elements that you want to repeat—such as your company logo, a running head, or a page number—on the background, and Publisher automatically inserts them on every page of a document.

Set Up a Web Page *(continued)*

2 Choose one of these three options:

- Select Standard for a screen width that corresponds to the VGA resolution of 640 by 480 pixels.
- Select Wide for a screen width that corresponds to the SVGA resolution of 800 by 600 pixels.
- Select Custom to specify the width and height of your Web page.

  When you choose the Standard or Wide page formats, the width is predetermined and cannot be changed. If you want to specify a different width, choose the Custom option.

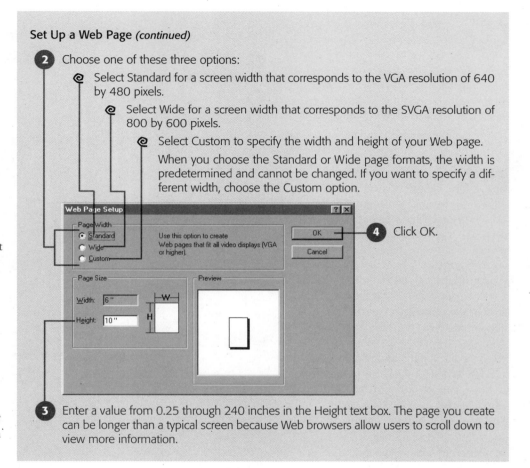

4 Click OK.

3 Enter a value from 0.25 through 240 inches in the Height text box. The page you create can be longer than a typical screen because Web browsers allow users to scroll down to view more information.

Choosing a Background

You can choose to add a color, a texture, or both to the background of a Web page layout. You can choose from 103 preformatted backgrounds, or you can create your own.

Why doesn't the Background And Text Colors command appear on the Format menu? This command only appears on the Format menu when you are working on a Web page. Open an existing Web document or create a new one to have the command appear on the Format menu.

Create an efficient custom background texture. Don't use a large bitmapped graphic as the background texture for your Web document. A picture with large dimensions, high resolution, and many colors takes a long time to download. Instead, use a small picture. You should strive for a file of 20 KB or less. For example, the picture below (the file Manhole.gif) measures only 1 by 1 inch and occupies only 9 KB of disk space. Make sure the picture is "in repeat," which means that the top, bottom, left, and right edges form a seamless match when multiple copies of the image are tiled to fill the screen. When a reader accesses your Web page, only the small original picture is transmitted. The Web browser repeats the image to form a continuous pattern.

Choose a Standard Background and Standard Text Colors

1 Open the Format menu and select Background And Text Colors. The Background And Text Colors dialog box appears.

2 Select the Standard tab.

3 Select one of the 103 preformatted combinations of background and text colors.

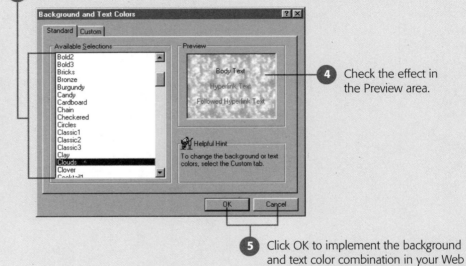

4 Check the effect in the Preview area.

5 Click OK to implement the background and text color combination in your Web document, or click Cancel to return to the document without implementing colors.

Choose a Custom Background and Custom Text Colors

1 Open the Format menu and select Background And Text Colors. The Background and Text Colors dialog box appears.

2 Select the Custom tab.

For more information about optimizing pictures for HTML documents, see the table on pages 225 through 226.

For more information about text in a Web document, see pages 228 through 232. For more information about hyperlinks, see pages 234 through 238.

table on pages 225 through 226.
pages 228 through 232. For more information about hyperlinks, see pages 234 through 238.

Choose a Custom Background and Custom Text Colors *(continued)*

3 Open the Color drop-down list box and choose one of the available colors, tints, or shades for the background. Alternatively, click the Browse button to locate a picture file to be used as a background texture.

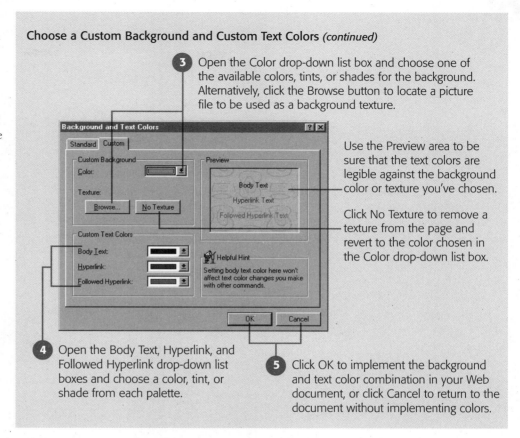

Use the Preview area to be sure that the text colors are legible against the background color or texture you've chosen.

Click No Texture to remove a texture from the page and revert to the color chosen in the Color drop-down list box.

4 Open the Body Text, Hyperlink, and Followed Hyperlink drop-down list boxes and choose a color, tint, or shade from each palette.

5 Click OK to implement the background and text color combination in your Web document, or click Cancel to return to the document without implementing colors.

Setting Up Layout Guides

For more information about graphic regions and how they are created, see page 228.

graphic regions and how they are created, see page 228.

Publisher's layout guides function normally within a Web publication and can help you design your Web page. Layout guides allow you to divide the screen into rows and columns. You should use the row and column guides to be sure that text and picture frames do not overlap. Since HTML does not support overlapping objects, Publisher automatically converts overlapping objects (even text objects) into a graphic region.

Why can't I see pictures or WordArt elements when I view a Publisher-generated Web page with my browser? Many browsers allow you to turn off the display of graphics in order to speed up performance. If you (or your readers) have turned off the display of graphics, all pictures, WordArt elements, and any text that has been converted to a graphic region will not appear on screen. To view these elements, turn on the display of graphics.

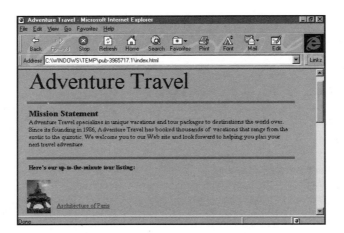

Typical Web pages rely on a simple linear layout in which text and pictures align along the left margin. This Web page can be viewed by a large number of browser applications, including older programs.

Divide the page into rows in order to create a standard (linear) Web page design.

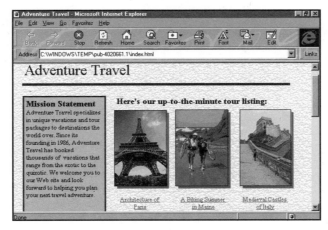

More sophisticated Web designs rely on frames to separate the screen into regions. In order to show this page properly, the browser application must be able to display frames.

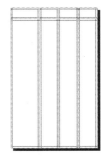

Use custom column and row guides to separate a Web page into regions.

Managing Art in a Web Document

To create efficient Web documents, you must understand how both HTML and Publisher handle picture, sound, and video files.

In-Line Graphics

For more information about bitmapped file formats, see Chapter 9.

Can I import other graphics file formats into a Web publication? Yes. You can import pictures in any format that Publisher supports into your Web publication. When you generate the HTML document, however, Publisher automatically converts the image to a GIF file.

In-line graphics are an integral part of a Web page. They appear within the browser window and are embedded in the text flow. Currently, graphical Web browsers restrict in-line graphics to two bitmapped file formats: the GIF (CompuServe Graphics Interchange Format) and JPEG (Joint Photographic Experts Group) formats. However, Publisher converts all imported graphics to the GIF format. The GIF format offers cross-platform compatibility (meaning that it can be viewed on PCs, Macintoshes, and Unix machines) and a sophisticated compression scheme. This last point is very important because bitmapped pictures can grow quite large. Your goal will be to produce the smallest, most efficient graphics files without sacrificing image quality. The following table summarizes various optimization techniques you can use when creating GIF images.

Optimizing GIF Images for Web Publications		
Feature	**Description**	**Optimization Technique**
Dimensions	The dimensions define the size at which a picture will appear on screen. Measure your graphics in pixels because monitors are measured in pixels. For example, a picture measuring 200 by 200 pixels will fill nearly 1/7 of a 640 by 480 monitor.	Create pictures that measure between 80 and 150 pixels (vertically and horizontally). Images that will be used as button icons should be even smaller—as small as 30 by 30 pixels.
Resolution	Resolution is defined as the number of dots that occur in a particular unit of measurement. Most scanning utilities measure the number of dots per inch (dpi).	It is preferable to size a picture using the actual dimensions measured in pixels (see "Dimensions" above). If your scanning utility requires you to enter a resolution, scan at 72 dpi, which is the resolution of most monitors. Because images in a Web document are always displayed at a 1:1 ratio with the screen resolution, scanning a picture at a higher resolution will not make the image appear more detailed; it will simply make it larger.

Feature	Description	Optimization Technique
	Optimizing GIF and JPEG Images for Web Publications *(continued)*	
Colors	A bitmapped graphic contains a specific number of colors. The color capability of a bitmapped file is measured by bit depth. A 4-bit file contains 16 colors, an 8-bit file contains 256 colors, and a 24-bit file contains potentially 16.7 million colors.	Use a graphics program to reduce the number of colors in a bitmapped picture. Use a full-featured graphics utility or image editing program that allows you to specify the bit depth, palette, and dither pattern. Reduce a picture to 256 colors or less, as the GIF format supports a maximum of 256 colors.
Compression	The GIF format uses a sophisticated compression routine that can dramatically reduce file size. GIF uses LZW compression, named after the two individuals who invented it (Lempel-Zir and Welch). LZW compression does not discard any picture data and typically delivers a compression ratio of 2:1. (A compressed file is approximately half the size of an uncompressed file.)	In your graphics utility or image editing program, save the image using the GIF format. The LZW compression scheme is automatically applied.
Interlacing	This encoding method keeps track of the odd-numbered and even-numbered scan lines in a picture. When the image is downloaded, all of the odd-numbered scan lines are transmitted first. The result, from the user's point of view, is that the full image, though blurry, appears on screen in half the time it would take the full image to appear. The image will come into focus as the second half of the image data (the even-numbered scan lines) are downloaded to complete the picture. Note that interlacing increases the *apparent* transmission speed of the image, not the actual speed.	To take advantage of interlacing, your graphics utility or image editing program must be able to export what are called interlaced GIF files.
Caching	Caching is not a feature of GIF images per se. Instead, it is a feature common to Web browsers. Browsers store images on the reader's local hard disk for quick retrieval.	Use the same image (such as a company logo) repeatedly in your Web documents. Because the image is cached on the reader's hard disk, it displays faster on subsequent pages.
Transparency	When displayed, one or more colors within a picture appear to be transparent. This technique is especially useful if you want to create silhouettes, the effect in which the irregular outline of a picture prints against the background of an HTML page. Instead of filling the picture with the same color or pattern as the background page, you designate the fill color as transparent.	To take advantage of transparency, your graphics utility or image editing program must be able to export version 89a of the GIF format.

How Multimedia Objects Behave in a Web Page

Using Publisher's Clip Gallery, you can easily insert multimedia objects into a Web document. Publisher allows you to import any multimedia format supported by the Windows 95 Media Player. For example, you can import sound files in the WAV format and videos in the AVI format because the drivers for these standard formats were automatically loaded when you installed the Media Player as part of Microsoft Windows 95. Other file formats, such as the MIDI and RMI formats for sound, require that you install specific drivers.

When imported into a document, multimedia files appear as static images.

Sound files are represented by an icon that includes the filename. Clicking the icon while running a Web browser plays the recording.

Video files are represented by the first frame of the movie. The filename appears at the bottom of the frame. Clicking the image while running a Web browser plays the movie.

What is the difference between helper applications and Plug-in applications?
Both helper applications and Plug-in applications work with a Web browser. MIME helper applications allow the browser to start a completely separate utility. For example, the Windows 95 Media Player functions as a helper application when it plays videos in a separate window. In contrast, a browser application (such as Microsoft Internet Explorer version 3) that supports the Netscape Plug-in specification can play multimedia files within the main browser window.

Users who wish to play the multimedia files in your Web document must have the proper hardware and software on *their* systems, including:

- A sound card to play sound files or the soundtracks associated with video files.

- A color monitor to display videos.

- The Windows 95 Media Player and appropriate sound and video drivers.

- A browser application that supports either Multipurpose Internet Mail Extension (MIME) helper applications or Netscape's Plug-in specification.

The advantages and disadvantages of graphic regions. Graphic regions have important functions—they preserve your layout. Overlapping objects, for example, will appear on screen exactly as you created them, even though HTML does not support overlapping objects. However, graphic regions do have a drawback—they can increase download times substantially.

Use graphic regions to incorporate unusual fonts in your Web documents. You can use an unusual font in your Web page for special text elements, such as headlines. But you must convert the font into a picture—or graphic region—to be sure that the typeface will be displayed properly by your reader's browser application. The easiest way to convert text to a picture is to create it using WordArt.

Why does the text in my HTML document take a long time to download? You may simply be experiencing the transmission delays that normally occur when there is a lot of traffic on the World Wide Web. However, your document may contain graphic regions rather than true text. Open the original PUB file and check for any conditions that might have forced Publisher to convert true text into a graphic region.

Graphic Regions

When you insert or create an object in a Web publication that is not supported by the HTML specification, Publisher treats the object as a picture, called a graphic region. Within an HTML document, graphic regions behave just like any other bitmapped picture. For example, they can increase download times substantially.

A full week's worth of walking tours takes you to every corner of Paris. With the help of an informed tour guide, you'll see well-known landmarks like the Eiffel Tower from a new perspective.

If you overlap frames, Publisher alerts you that it will create a graphic region by outlining the objects with a flashing red box. It does this only once—at the moment two objects overlap. The flashing red box delineates the graphic region, which is equal in size to a rectangle that encompasses all of the objects. (For a single object, the graphic region is the size of the object's frame.)

Within a Web document, Publisher creates a graphic region whenever one of the following conditions occurs:

- You overlap frames. This applies if you position a picture frame over a text frame—in order to create a text wrap—or if you overlap two text frames.
- You create a WordArt object.
- You rotate a text frame.
- You add BorderArt to a text frame.
- You fill a text frame with a pattern or gradient.

Managing Text Elements in a Web Publication

Text is the most important element in a Web document. It conveys most, if not all, of the information in your publication. Equally significant, text downloads much more quickly than a picture. Your goal as a Web publisher is twofold:

- To produce a text design that fits within the limited HTML specification.

- To avoid converting true text objects into graphic regions.

The HTML specification does not define the appearance of text. Instead, it defines the relationships among text elements. Think of this structure as a big outline. You can define the relative importance of text—for example, headings versus body copy—but you can't control the usual text formatting attributes, such as font, point size, and line spacing. You can design a document with unusual text treatments, but when Publisher converts the PUB document to an HTML document, most of your formatting will be lost. The following comparison illustrates this process.

Unusual font choices, such as Eras Bold ITC, might look correct in your Publisher document, but they will be replaced with a standard font, such as Times New Roman, if your readers do not have the same fonts installed on their computer systems.

Because HTML only supports single-spaced text, the additional line spacing in the Publisher document doesn't appear in the final Web document.

The table below summarizes formatting attributes that may prove to be troublesome when the PUB document is converted to HTML or when a reader accesses the document using a Web browser.

Text and Text Frame Formatting Guidelines for Web Publications			
Text Attribute	**In a Publisher Document**	**In an HTML Document**	**Recommended Text Formats**
Font	You can format text with any font installed on your system.	Publisher will insert a request for the font into the HTML document. However, if the reader of your Web page does not have the same font installed, a standard font will be substituted.	Format text in a Web document with the following standard fonts: Arial, Courier New, Symbol, Times New Roman, and Wingdings. You can enhance these typefaces with font styles, such as italic, bold, and bold italic.
Point size	Publisher can format text from 0.5 through 999.5 points in 0.5-point increments.	HTML supports only seven font size designations. The actual point size at which type will appear on screen is determined by the reader's browser application.	Format text ranging from 10 through 30 points. Don't use more than seven point sizes. Reserve the 10-point size for body copy.
Line spacing	Publisher allows you to set line spacing from 0.25 through 124 spaces in 0.25-space increments (or from 3 through 1488 points in 0.5-point increments).	HTML documents are displayed with single line spacing. All line-spacing attributes within the Publisher document are ignored.	Set all copy using single line spacing.
Indents	Publisher allows you to create indents for the left side, right side, and first line of a paragraph.	HTML does not allow indents. Any indents within the Publisher document will be ignored.	Distinguish the beginning of a paragraph with an extra line space.
Bulleted and numbered lists	Publisher can automatically create bulleted and numbered lists.	HTML supports both bulleted and numbered lists. Many of the advanced formatting options within Publisher (such as the ability to specify the style of bullet or change the indent) will be ignored when the publication is converted to HTML.	Create simple bulleted and numbered lists.

Text Attribute	In a Publisher Document	In an HTML Document	Recommended Text Formats
Alignment	Publisher gives you four alignment options: left, right, center, and justified.	HTML supports left, right, and center alignment only.	For maximum legibility, keep most of your text left aligned. Reserve the center alignment option for headlines and short lists.
Tabs	Publisher allows you to set four kinds of tab stops: left, right, center, and decimal.	HTML does not recognize tabs of any kind. When you insert a tab, Publisher converts it to a space.	Avoid tabs.
Hyphenation	Publisher offers both automatic and optional hyphenation.	HTML does not support automatic or optional hyphenation.	Turn off automatic hyphenation and refrain from using optional hyphens. However, you can manually insert the hyphen character or a non-breaking hyphen.
Spacing between characters	Publisher allows you to modify the spacing for an entire paragraph (called tracking) or for selected characters (called kerning).	HTML does not support tracking or kerning. All adjustments that you make in the Publisher document will be ignored.	Do not apply tracking or kerning to text in a Web document.
Underlining	Publisher allows you to choose among three underlining effects: Underline All, Underline Words, and Double Underline.	HTML displays only a single solid underline. Publisher's Underline Words and Double Underline options will be converted to a single solid underline.	In Web documents underlining is often used to signal hypertext links. You should therefore avoid underlining other types of text elements because it can confuse your readers.
Text color	Publisher lets you assign any color, tint, or shade to selected text.	The color you assign to text will be maintained in the HTML document.	Because readers may view your Web document on a 16- or 256-color monitor, you should choose text colors that contrast with the background color. On most Web pages, specific text colors are used to identify hypertext links. Do not confuse a reader by choosing the same or similar colors for normal text and hypertext links.

Text Attribute	In a Publisher Document	In an HTML Document	Recommended Text Formats
Table text	Publisher can produce true tables that are arranged like a spreadsheet, in rows and columns.	The latest version of HTML does support tables. However, some older browsers don't display tables properly.	Include tables in your Web publications if you are certain that your readers will be using the latest version of a full-featured browser.
Multiple columns	In a standard publication, you can create up to 63 columns in a text frame. In a Web publication, however, this option is unavailable.	HTML does not support multiple columns.	If you want to create multiple text columns, draw individual text frames and link them to accommodate text flow.
Object fill	Publisher lets you fill a text frame with any color, tint, shade, pattern, or gradient.	When the PUB document is converted to HTML, all text frames containing a pattern or gradient will be converted to graphic regions. In addition, older browsers may not be able to display normal fill colors in a text frame.	Avoid filling text frames with patterns and gradients. Use colors, tints, and shades in a text frame with discretion. If the reader views your Web site with an older browser, the color, tint, or shade might not be displayed. The text itself, however, will display normally.
Borders and BorderArt	Publisher allows you to assign either a line border or BorderArt to a text frame.	Older browsers might not be able to display line borders. BorderArt is not recognized by HTML. Text frames with BorderArt are converted to graphic regions.	Avoid using BorderArt on text frames. Use line borders with discretion. If the reader views your Web site with an older browser, the line border might not be displayed. The text itself, however, will display normally.
Shadow	Publisher can create a drop shadow for a text frame.	Older browsers might not be able to display shadows on text frames.	Use discretion when adding shadows on text frames. If the reader views your Web site with an older browser, the shadow might not be displayed. The text itself, however, will display normally.
Rotation	Publisher can rotate a text frame in 1-degree increments.	HTML does not support rotated text. The rotated text frame will be converted to a graphic region.	Avoid rotated text.

Are there any drawbacks to automatically converting a print publication to a Web publication? Although the Create Web Site From Current Publication command is convenient, this function should be used with caution. Many design elements commonly used in print publications (such as overlapping objects, WordArt elements, and rotated text) are not supported by HTML. If you convert a print publication to a Web publication without a careful examination of the layout and an intelligent redesign, you will produce inefficient Web documents.

Is the Design Checker only available when I convert a standard print publication to a Web publication? No, the Design Checker is always available. It is accessed from the Tools menu.

For more information about the Design Checker, see Chapter 4.

Converting a Print Publication to HTML

Publisher can create a Web document from a standard publication that has been designed for printed output.

Create a Web Publication from an Existing Publisher Document

1 Open the publication file that you wish to convert to a Web document.

2 On the File menu, choose Create Web Site From Current Publication. Publisher will display an alert box asking if you want to run the Design Checker.

3 Click Yes to activate the Design Checker in order to discover problems specific to Web pages.

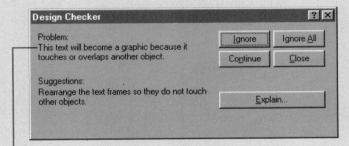

The Design Checker looks for objects that will be converted to graphic regions.

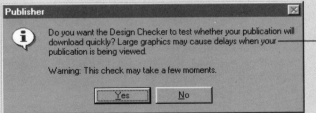

The Design Checker can also indicate large graphics that will increase the time it takes to download your Web publication.

4 When you have finished running the Design Checker and have made any necessary changes, save the publication file with a new name.

Creating and Managing Hyperlinks in a Web Document

You've probably heard the Internet described as the Information Highway. In keeping with the road map metaphor, hyperlinks are the road signs that point to specific addresses on the World Wide Web. Hyperlinks can be associated with text, in which case they are called hypertext links. Hyperlinks associated with graphics objects, such as imported pictures and drawn shapes, are called picture hot spots. The following diagram illustrates how a hyperlink works.

 For more information about URLs, see page 236.

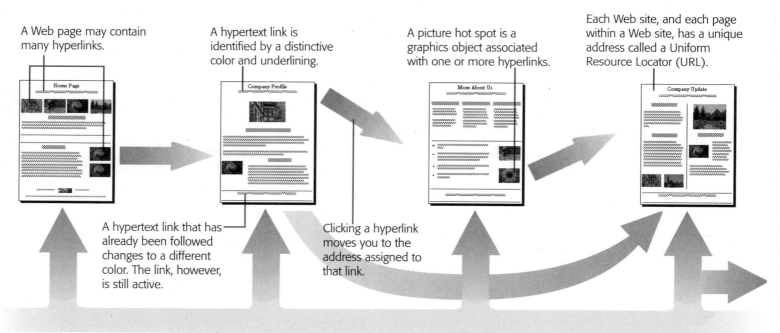

A Web page may contain many hyperlinks.

A hypertext link is identified by a distinctive color and underlining.

A picture hot spot is a graphics object associated with one or more hyperlinks.

Each Web site, and each page within a Web site, has a unique address called a Uniform Resource Locator (URL).

A hypertext link that has already been followed changes to a different color. The link, however, is still active.

Clicking a hyperlink moves you to the address assigned to that link.

Hyperlinks are not linear: they can move you forward in a document, backward in a document, or to a completely different location on the Web.

Creating Hyperlinks

A hyperlink can be assigned to a text phrase, a picture, a shape, or a picture hot spot. The Picture Hot Spot tool is especially useful when you want to add more than one hyperlink to a graphics object.

Creating a hyperlink is a two-part process. You first assign a hyperlink to a selected text phrase, picture, shape, or picture hot spot. You must then choose the appropriate function of the hyperlink. Publisher can create four types of hyperlinks, as explained in the following table.

Types of Hyperlinks		
Create this hyperlink...	**To perform this action...**	**Based on this information...**
To another page in your Web site	This is an exploring hyperlink. It will move the reader to another page in the current Web publication.	You must specify a relative or absolute page number. Relative pages (first page, previous page, and next page) are useful for generic controls, such as page turn icons, that appear on every page of a document. Absolute page numbers are useful when you are cross-referencing specific information or creating an index.
To another document already on the Web	This is an exploring hyperlink. It will move the reader to another address anywhere on the Web.	You must specify a Web address, or URL.
To an Internet email address	This is a response hyperlink. When clicked, it allows the reader to send a message to the specified address.	You must enter a valid Internet email address. If you enter your own email address, your readers can contact you or your company easily.
To a file on a Web server	This hyperlink downloads a file from your Web server (which can be your local hard disk) to the reader's hard disk.	Type the full path, including the drive designation, the folders, and the filename with its extension. If you don't know the full path, click the Browse button (in the Hyperlink dialog box) to search for the file. When you select the file and click Open, Publisher will enter the correct path information in the text box.

Entering Internet addresses correctly. If you want the hyperlinks on your Web pages to function properly, you must enter the URLs correctly. Look closely at the following sample URL, and note what each part of the address signifies.

Identifies the Hypertext Transfer Protocol, the method used on the Web to locate files.

Identifies the World Wide Web.

http://www.microsoft.com

Identifies the domain, or host, name.

Identifies the organization type. Abbreviations include *com* (commercial), *edu* (education), *gov* (government), *mil* (military), and *org* (organization).

Why is the History button grayed out? The History button in the Hyperlink dialog box is only available if you use Microsoft Internet Explorer as your browser application.

Fast access to the Hyperlink dialog box. You can activate the Hyperlink dialog box quickly in one of two ways:

- Click the Hyperlink button on the Standard toolbar.

- Right-click the object to which you want to assign a hyperlink. On the shortcut menu, choose the Hyperlink command.

Create a Hyperlink

1 Highlight text, or select a picture or a drawn shape.

2 On the Insert menu, choose Hyperlink. The Hyperlink dialog box appears.

3 Choose the type of hyperlink you want to associate with the selected object.

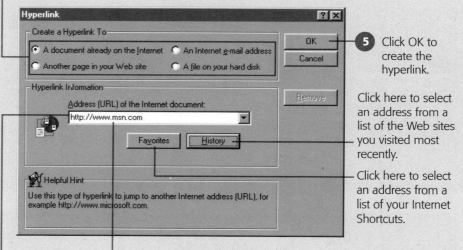

5 Click OK to create the hyperlink.

Click here to select an address from a list of the Web sites you visited most recently.

Click here to select an address from a list of your Internet Shortcuts.

The type of hyperlink you create determines what kind of information you must enter in the Hyperlink Information text box. For example, if you create a hyperlink to a document on the Web, you must enter an Internet address. If you create a hyperlink to a file on your Web server, you must enter the path to locate that file.

4 Enter the appropriate information in the Hyperlink Information text box. In this case, you must enter an Internet address.

If your selected object is a text phrase, Publisher changes the color and underlines the selected text. If your selected object is a picture or a shape, Publisher creates the hyperlink but does not change the appearance of the selected object.

Why can't I find the Picture Hot Spot tool? Publisher displays the Picture Hot Spot tool when you are working on a Web publication—and only then. If you do not see the Picture Hot Spot tool on the main toolbar, you are probably designing a standard print publication. You need to open an existing Web publication, choose the Web Site or Web Page layout in the Startup dialog box, or convert the current publication to a Web site.

Why do I have trouble selecting hot spot objects? By default, the Picture Hot Spot tool creates transparent, borderless rectangles. Like all other objects in a Publisher document, hot spots have object boundaries (which disappear when you generate an HTML document). Object boundaries are light gray dotted lines, which can be difficult to see on screen, especially when the hot spot is stacked on top of a picture. You can, however, temporarily format a hot spot object with attributes such as a line border or a fill color to make it easy to see and select.

You can also group a hot spot with a picture. When you select, move, or resize the picture, the hot spot will also be selected, moved, or resized.

Create a Picture Hot Spot

 1 Select the Picture Hot Spot tool from the main toolbar. The pointer changes to the Crossbar pointer.

2 Position the Crossbar pointer over the picture where you want to add a hot spot.

3 While holding down the mouse button, drag the mouse diagonally to create a transparent rectangle. You may create a rectangle that completely surrounds the underlying picture, or you may create a rectangle that surrounds only a portion of the underlying picture.

4 When the shape and size of the hot spot are to your liking, release the mouse button. The Hyperlink dialog box appears.

5 Choose the type of hyperlink you want to assign to the selected picture.

6 Enter the appropriate information in the Hyperlink Information text box.

7 Click OK to create the hyperlink.

Editing Hyperlinks

You can change the characteristics of a hyperlink, including its type, file path, and color. You can also delete a hyperlink from your document. The ability to edit the URL associated with a hyperlink is especially important because the World Wide Web is constantly in flux. New Web sites are created, existing Web sites are altered or abandoned, and files are moved. As a Web publisher, you have an obligation to your readers to keep the URLs up to date.

Change the Type or Destination of a Hyperlink

1 Select the text, picture, drawn shape, or picture hot spot that is your hyperlink object.

2 On the Insert menu, choose Hyperlink. The Hyperlink dialog box appears.

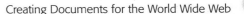

Use color consistently to identify hypertext links and body copy. In a Web document, text color has a functional as well as aesthetic purpose. Body copy, hypertext links, and followed hypertext links (hypertext links that have been clicked on the Web) appear in different, easily identified colors. Publisher helps you to use consistent colors for text by allowing you to specify colors globally in the Background And Text Colors dialog box (available from the Format menu).

For more information about the colors of hypertext and body copy, see pages 222 through 223.

One-click previews. You can use the Standard toolbar to create a preview of your Web site. Simply click the Preview Web Site button shown below.

Change the Type or Destination of a Hyperlink *(continued)*

3 Make the appropriate changes by choosing a new hyperlink type or by entering new information in the Hyperlink Information text box.

4 Click OK to implement the changes to the currently selected hyperlink, or click Cancel to return to your document without making any changes.

Remove a Hyperlink

1 Select the text, picture, drawn shape, or picture hot spot that is your hyperlink object.

2 On the Insert menu, choose Hyperlink. The Hyperlink dialog box appears.

3 Click the Remove button to delete the hyperlink associated with the currently selected object. The appearance of a picture, drawn shape, or picture hot spot will remain unchanged in the publication when the hyperlink is removed. Text color will revert to the body copy color, and the underline will disappear when the hyperlink is removed from text.

4 If necessary, use Publisher's standard tools to delete the text, picture, drawn shape, or picture hot spot.

Previewing a Web Publication

Before you actually publish your Web site on the Internet, you should preview the document on your own system. You should preview your Web publication for two important reasons:

@ A preview will reveal any formatting changes Publisher makes to accommodate the limitations of the HTML specification.

@ A preview allows you to test all the functions you've built into your Web document. For example, you can play sound and video files. You can also follow the hyperlinks to their destinations.

Test your Web site. When you preview your Web site, take the time to explore the document carefully using this checklist:

- Has any of the text changed in appearance?

- When clicked, does each multimedia object play properly?

- When clicked, does each hyperlink to another page in your Web site move to the proper page?

- When clicked, does each hyperlink that contains a URL move to the appropriate Web site?

- When clicked, does each hyperlink that allows readers to write email insert your Internet email address?

- When clicked, does each hyperlink that allows readers to download a file find the correct file on your Web server?

Turn off the Preview Troubleshooter. You can disable the Preview Troubleshooter at any time. On the Tools menu, choose Options. In the Options dialog box, turn off the Preview Web Site With Preview Troubleshooter check box on the General tab.

Preview a Web Site

1 Open the Web document you want to preview.

2 On the File menu, select Preview Web Site. Publisher displays a progress dialog box while it converts the PUB file to HTML. Publisher then activates your browser application.

3 Using the functions of your Web browser, explore the HTML document.

4 When you have finished exploring the Web document, exit from the Web browser. Publisher will reappear on screen, and the Preview Troubleshooter will be active.

Use the scroll bar to review a list of possible problems.

The Preview Troubleshooter appears in Publisher's standard help window.

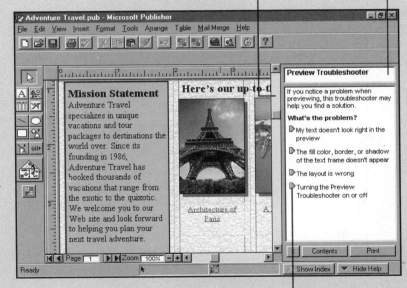

Click arrows to move through the various Preview Troubleshooter screens.

Publishing a Web Site to a Folder or to the World Wide Web

To produce the finished version of a standard publication, Publisher prints the document to paper. To produce the finished version of a Web publication, Publisher performs the following operations:

@ Converts your document to HTML. The first page of the document, or the home page, is normally saved as Index.html. Subsequent pages are normally saved as Page2.html, Page3.html, and so on.

@ Exports all pictures and graphic regions as GIF files. Each image is stored in a separate GIF file identified by a number. As an example, a Web site containing two pictures and one graphic region would contain Img0.gif, Img1.gif, and Img2.gif.

@ Copies any hyperlinked or externally stored files to the local folder or to the World Wide Web. Files that fall into this category include sound and video files and any files that the reader can download using a hyperlink.

You have two choices for the final destination of your Web publication: you can publish it locally to a folder on your hard disk or network, or you can publish it to the World Wide Web.

Publishing a Web site to your local hard disk is the simplest option, but it doesn't give other people access to the publication. Publishing a Web site to a network is slightly more complicated. You should speak to the network administrator to be sure that the following conditions are true:

@ An intranet—an internal network including a Web server—is active.

@ You have the appropriate write privileges to be able to save your Web publication on the server.

Publishing to the Web can be quite a complicated process. Microsoft provides a Web Publishing Wizard that can connect you to the Internet, determine the correct file transfer protocol (FTP), and copy the Web site to the appropriate folder on the host computer of your Internet Service Provider (ISP).

Why would I want to publish my Web document to a folder on my local hard disk? If you discover that you can't use the Web Publishing Wizard to post your Web site directly to the World Wide Web, publish your Web site to a folder instead. Then follow the instructions or use the software supplied by your Internet Service Provider to send your Web site to the Internet.

Even if you use the Web Publishing Wizard, you must still be sure that the following conditions are true:

- Your ISP supplies space on its computer where you can store your Web site. Usually 1 or 2 megabytes are provided. This service might be part of the basic subscription cost or might require an additional fee.

- You have followed your ISP's naming conventions by choosing among different naming conventions within Publisher. For example, DOS-based servers do not support a four-letter (HTML) file extension. Or you can save the Web site to a folder and rename the files as required by your ISP.

- You have direct access to an Internet server and are not accessing the Internet through a proxy server or network gateway.

- The ISP employs a standard Web server configuration (such as NCSA, HTTPD, or APACHE) that supports the file transfer protocol (FTP).

Use separate folders for each Web site. Publisher will alert you if you attempt to save a Web site to a folder that already contains a Web site. If you proceed, Publisher will overwrite existing files and destroy the Web site that already resides there. You can use this system to update an existing Web site with new information.

Publish a Web Site to a Local Folder

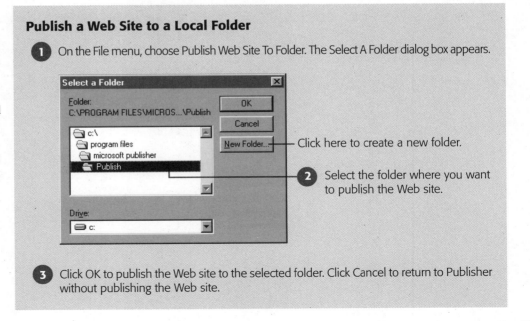

1 On the File menu, choose Publish Web Site To Folder. The Select A Folder dialog box appears.

Click here to create a new folder.

2 Select the folder where you want to publish the Web site.

3 Click OK to publish the Web site to the selected folder. Click Cancel to return to Publisher without publishing the Web site.

Why does Publisher display an alert box when I attempt to publish my Web site? You do not have the Web Publishing Wizard installed on your system. To connect to Microsoft's Web site and download the wizard, click Yes.

 How can I access the Web Publishing Wizard? You can access the Web Publishing Wizard in three ways:

- ⊜ On the Publisher File menu, choose the Publish To Web command.

- ⊜ On the Windows 95 Start menu, choose, in succession, Programs, Accessories, Internet Tools, and then Web Publishing Wizard.

- ⊜ In Windows Explorer, right-click a single filename, a group of files, or an entire folder to display the shortcut menu. Select the Send To command, and then choose the Web Publishing Wizard from the cascading menu.

Publish a Web Site to the World Wide Web

1 On the File menu, choose Publish To Web. Publisher displays a progress box while it converts the publication to HTML. The Web Publishing Wizard dialog box appears.

2 Choose a Web server profile from the drop-down list.

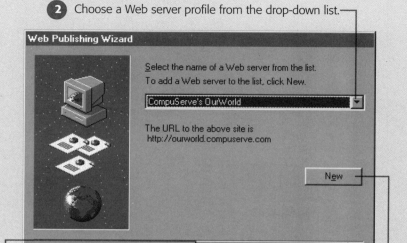

Click here to add a new Web server profile. You will be asked to type a descriptive name for the Web server, to choose an Internet Service Provider, to enter an Internet address (URL), and to configure the intranet or dial-up connection.

3 Click Next to proceed with publishing your document. The subsequent dialog boxes will differ depending on the Web server you choose. You will be asked to enter identifying information, such as your name, address, user ID, and password. When you have entered all the information, the Web Publishing Wizard will connect to your ISP and upload your Web site.

Should I change the Web site properties? Before publishing your Web site to the World Wide Web, you should contact your ISP to learn which properties are correct for its system. Some ISPs require you to change the name of the home page and the file extension. Once you have made the appropriate changes in the Web Site Properties dialog box, Publisher will automatically generate correct filenames and extensions when you publish your Web site.

Once I have published my Web site, can I update it with new information? You must return to the original PUB file in order to update your Web page. The PUB file contains standard desktop publishing objects, which can be edited. Make your changes using Publisher's tools, and then generate a new HTML file using the Publish To Web or the Publish Web Site To Folder command.

Change Web Site Properties

1 On the File menu, choose Web Site Properties. The Web Site Properties dialog box appears.

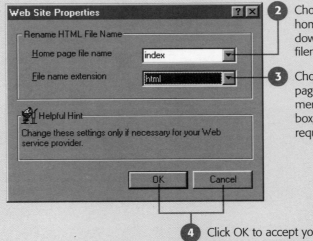

2 Choose a filename for the home page from the drop-down list box, or type the filename required by your ISP.

3 Choose a file extension for the pages in your HTML document from the drop-down list box, or type the file extension required by your ISP.

4 Click OK to accept your choices, or click Cancel to return to the document without making any changes.

Field codes refer to an address list stored in Publisher's format or in a standard word processing, spreadsheet, or database format.

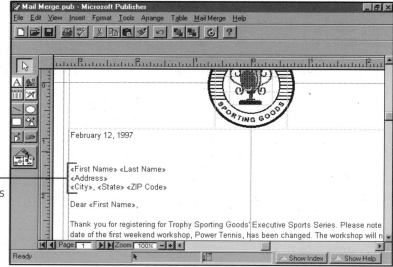

Publisher replaces field codes with entries from an address list when you preview or print your document. You can use an address list to organize information about customers, friends, and family.

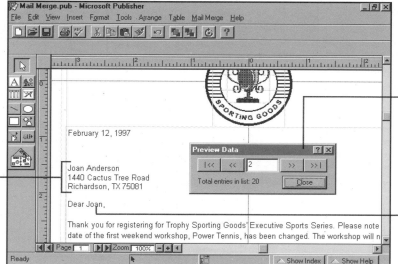

The Preview Data dialog box lets you see how the document will appear when it is merged with each entry from an address list.

To personalize mailings, you can combine field codes (in the same font used by the document) with normal text and punctuation. Here a recipient's name appears in the letter's greeting.

Working with Mailing Lists

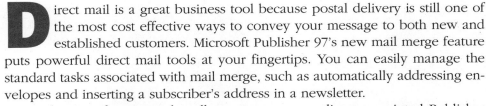

Direct mail is a great business tool because postal delivery is still one of the most cost effective ways to convey your message to both new and established customers. Microsoft Publisher 97's new mail merge feature puts powerful direct mail tools at your fingertips. You can easily manage the standard tasks associated with mail merge, such as automatically addressing envelopes and inserting a subscriber's address in a newsletter.

Mail merge functions also allow you to personalize any printed Publisher document. That sweepstakes offer that starts with the line, "You, Tom Smith, may have just won a million dollars!" is an example of a personalized document. While no one is suggesting that you start your own sweepstakes, you can use mail merge to customize a wide variety of documents, from a sale announcement postcard to a promotional brochure to a wedding invitation.

Publisher's mail merge tools are extremely flexible. You can create an address list directly within Publisher or link your publication to an address list created in another application, such as Microsoft Word or Microsoft Access. You can also use the filtering functions to access only a portion of a large address list and the sorting functions to change the order in which items will appear or print.

For more information about using an external address list with mail merge, see pages 250 through 251.

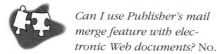 *Can I use Publisher's mail merge feature with electronic Web documents?* No. Publisher's mail merge feature works with printed publications only.

Mail Merge Fundamentals: Address Lists and Field Codes

Publisher's mail merge functions require two components:

- An address list, which you can create either in Publisher or in another application.

- Field codes, which can be thought of as placeholders in your Publisher document and which refer to the address list.

The following illustration provides an overview of the mail merge process.

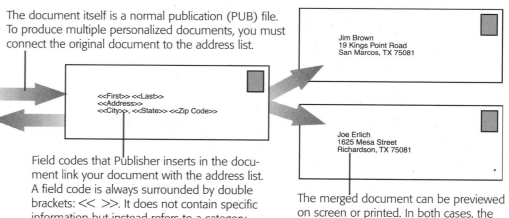

The document itself is a normal publication (PUB) file. To produce multiple personalized documents, you must connect the original document to the address list.

The address list, created in Publisher or an external application, contains names, addresses, and other information that you want to insert in your document.

Field codes that Publisher inserts in the document link your document with the address list. A field code is always surrounded by double brackets: << >>. It does not contain specific information but instead refers to a category heading (or field) within the address list.

The merged document can be previewed on screen or printed. In both cases, the field code is replaced with specific information, such as a name or address.

Creating an Address List in Publisher

An address list is simply a database of information. The data will typically be contact information, such as a name, an address, a telephone number, and perhaps an email address. You can create and modify an address list using database functions built into Publisher.

Organize data into discrete fields. When designing your address list, break the information down into small categories so that each category is a separate field. For example, split city and state information into different fields. You can then search, sort, and filter the information in the address list with much more accuracy.

Create an Address List in Publisher

1 On the Mail Merge menu, choose Create Publisher Address List. The New Address List dialog box appears.

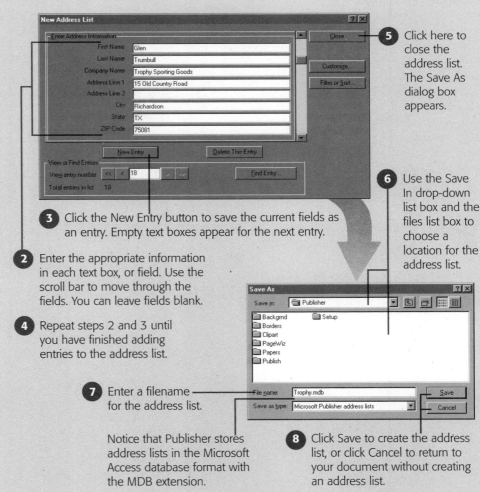

5 Click here to close the address list. The Save As dialog box appears.

3 Click the New Entry button to save the current fields as an entry. Empty text boxes appear for the next entry.

2 Enter the appropriate information in each text box, or field. Use the scroll bar to move through the fields. You can leave fields blank.

4 Repeat steps 2 and 3 until you have finished adding entries to the address list.

6 Use the Save In drop-down list box and the files list box to choose a location for the address list.

7 Enter a filename for the address list.

Notice that Publisher stores address lists in the Microsoft Access database format with the MDB extension.

8 Click Save to create the address list, or click Cancel to return to your document without creating an address list.

Can I work simultaneously on an address list and the Publisher document to which it is attached? If you have created your address list within Publisher, you can modify the list at any time. There is no need to close the current publication in order to access the address list connected to the publication. Simply choose Edit Publisher Address List on the Mail Merge menu. If, however, you are using an address list created with another program, you must close the publication file before you attempt to edit the address list connected to it.

Use the same address list for multiple publications. When you create an address list using Publisher's mail merge functions, you are prompted to save the file to disk. Doing so allows you to attach any number of publication files to the address list. This means you can create one central address list and then use it over and over for a wide range of projects.

Modify a Publisher Address List

1 On the Mail Merge menu, choose Edit Publisher Address List. The Open Address List dialog box appears.

2 Locate and select the address list you want to modify. Click Open to display the address list dialog box.

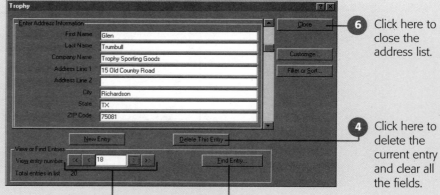

6 Click here to close the address list.

4 Click here to delete the current entry and clear all the fields.

3 Use the forward or backward arrow to move to the adjacent entry, or type an entry number in the text box and then press Enter. Use the double arrows to move to the first or last entry in the address list.

5 Click here to search for an entry by using a text phrase. In the Find Entry dialog box that appears, type up to 25 characters. Publisher ignores the capitalization of the search phrase, but spelling must be exact. You can search all fields or specify a particular field, such as Company Name.

Use Publisher's address list for nonaddress informa-tion. Publisher's address list functions just like a traditional database. By adding and modifying fields, you can customize the address list for any kind of information. You could, for example, add a field to identify large corporate customers in order to offer them special volume prices. You might want to keep a list of your customers' birthdays to offer them discounts. You could even create a catalog price list using Publisher's address list functions.

Customize the Fields in an Address List

1 On the Mail Merge menu, choose Create Publisher Address List to create a new, custom-ized address list. Alternatively, choose Edit Publisher Address List to customize an exist-ing address list.

2 If you are customizing an existing address list, the Open Address List dialog box appears. Select the file containing the address list you want to customize, and then click Open.

3 In the address list dialog box that appears, click the Customize button. The Customize Address List dialog box appears.

Click here to move the selected field up one position in the list box.

Click here to move the selected field down one position in the list box.

4 Click a field to select it.

Click here to delete the selected field.

Click here to rename the selected field.

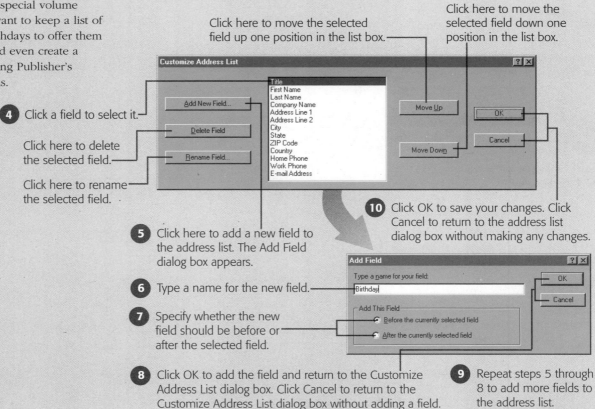

5 Click here to add a new field to the address list. The Add Field dialog box appears.

6 Type a name for the new field.

7 Specify whether the new field should be before or after the selected field.

8 Click OK to add the field and return to the Customize Address List dialog box. Click Cancel to return to the Customize Address List dialog box without adding a field.

10 Click OK to save your changes. Click Cancel to return to the address list dialog box without making any changes.

9 Repeat steps 5 through 8 to add more fields to the address list.

Publisher does not list my database or spreadsheet application in the Open Data Source dialog box. Can I use my application as an external data source? Publisher accepts external data sources if they are in a standard file format. Generate your address list in a standard file format, such as XLS or DBF.

Can I use a text file as an external data source? Yes, you can use a text file as an external data source if the information is organized properly. You must be sure to separate each field with a special character, such as a comma or tab.

Create and connect to an address list in one operation. If you choose Create An Address List In Publisher in the first Open Data Source dialog box, Publisher will display the New Address List dialog box. When you've finished entering your information, Publisher will ask if you want to merge the information from this address list into the current publication. Click Yes to connect the current publication to the address list. Click No to save the address list to disk without creating an association to the current publication.

Connecting a Publication to a Publisher Address List or Other Data Source

Before you can use an address list with a Publisher document, you must associate the document with the data source that contains the list. Only one data source can be associated with a publication at any given time. However, you can replace a data source with a new data source at any time. Publisher can access address list data stored in many different formats, as the following table summarizes.

Address List File Formats	
File Extension	**Application**
MDB	Microsoft Publisher address list
MDB	Microsoft Access
DOC	Microsoft Word tables or mail merge documents
WDB	Microsoft Works database
XLS	Microsoft Excel
DBF	dBASE III, dBASE IV, dBASE 5
DBF	Microsoft FoxPro
TXT, CSV, TAB, ASC	Text files

Connect a Publication to a Data Source

1 On the Mail Merge menu, choose Open Data Source. The Open Data Source dialog box appears.

2 Choose Merge Information From A File I Already Have. A second Open Data Source dialog box appears.

Why can't I connect my publication to an external data source? There are two possible reasons why you cannot connect to an external data source:

- The data source file might be open. Return to the application in which you created the data source and close the file.

- You might have saved the data source in an incompatible file format. Return to the application in which you created the data source and save it in a compatible file format, such as DBF.

What will happen if I open a new data source for my publication? If you have not inserted any field codes in the publication, you can proceed with the mail merge normally. However, if you have inserted field codes and they refer to fields that do not exist in the new data source, Publisher will not be able to retrieve information for those field codes. Publisher identifies such field codes by changing the text to read <<Missing mail merge field>>.

Connect a Publication to a Data Source *(continued)*

4 Use the Look In drop-down list box and the files list box to locate and select the data source.

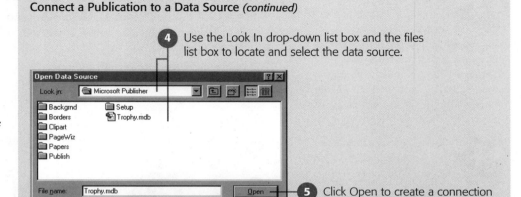

5 Click Open to create a connection between the data source and the current publication. The Insert Fields dialog box appears.

3 Open the Files Of Type drop-down list box and select the format of the file you want to locate.

6 Insert the field code or codes that you want in your document, and then click Close to return to your document. Even if you click Close without inserting any field codes, the connection between the current publication and the data source remains active, allowing you to insert field codes later in the work session.

Choose a New Data Source

1 On the Mail Merge menu, choose Open Data Source. Publisher asks you if you want to replace the currently selected data source with a new data source.

2 Click Yes to access the Open Data Source dialog box and choose a new data source. Click No to continue using the currently selected data source.

Inserting Field Codes into a Publication

A field code is a generic placeholder in your publication. It tells Publisher where to insert information from the address list. In the working view of your publication, field codes are identified by double brackets and display the name of the field to which they refer. When you preview or print the publication, the field codes are replaced by the corresponding information from the address list.

Why is the Insert Field command grayed out? You cannot insert a field code until you connect your publication to a data source. After you have used the Open Data Source command to associate the current publication with a data source, the Insert Field command will be available.

Why does the Insert Fields dialog box remain on screen after I click the Insert button? The Insert Fields dialog box remains on screen to let you add more than one field code to a publication easily. Instead of closing, the dialog box simply becomes inactive. While the Insert Fields dialog box is inactive, you can add text or punctuation to your publication.

Why can't I change the text in the field code? The field code exactly matches the field name in your address list or data source. To change a field code, you must edit the associated data source. To edit the field names in a Publisher address list, choose the Edit Publisher Address List command on the Mail Merge menu. To edit an external data source, you must once again use the word processing, spreadsheet, or database program you used originally.

Insert Field Codes in a Publication

1 Select a text frame and move the text insertion point where you want the first field code to appear.

2 On the Mail Merge menu, choose Insert Field. The Insert Fields dialog box appears.

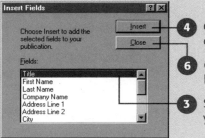

4 Click Insert to place a field code in your publication.

6 Click Close to exit the Insert Fields dialog box and return to your publication.

3 Scroll through the list box to find the field you want to insert. Click to select it.

5 To insert additional field codes, repeat steps 3 and 4.

7 In your publication, single-click the field code to select it. The entire field code will be highlighted.

8 Use Publisher's normal text tools to apply character formatting. You can also cut, copy, or paste the field code.

Merging and Previewing a Publication with a Data Source

Before you can print a mail merge document, you must substitute the address list entries for the field code placeholders. The Merge command accomplishes this task and shows you an on-screen preview of the results.

Use the Label PageWizard to set up a mail merge document. When you use the Label PageWizard, Publisher asks whether you want to set up the publication for mail merge. If you answer yes, Publisher will create the document and then walk you through the process of opening a data source and inserting field codes.

Preview a merged publication at any time. The Merge command itself is issued only once. Subsequently, you can preview your mail merge document before printing it by choosing the Show Merge Results command on the Mail Merge menu. The first entry will appear in place of the field codes, and the Preview Data dialog box will appear. Use the Preview Data dialog box to move through individual entries in the address list. Close the Preview Data dialog box when you are satisfied that the merge has been successful.

Why isn't Show Merge Results available on the Mail Merge menu? The Show Merge Results command is available only after you have connected your publication to a data source, inserted at least one field code, and issued the Merge command.

Merge and Preview a Publication with an Address List

1 On the Mail Merge menu, choose Merge. Publisher replaces the field codes with the first entry from your address list. The results are displayed in the document window, and the Preview Data dialog box appears.

2 Use the forward and backward arrows to move through the entries, or type an entry number in the text box and then press Enter.

3 When you have finished previewing the merged document, click Close to return to your publication. The displayed entry is replaced by the field code designations.

Publisher displays the total number of entries in the address list.

Cancel a Mail Merge Operation

1 On the Mail Merge menu, select Cancel Merge. Publisher displays an alert box asking if you want to cancel the merge.

2 Click Yes to disconnect the publication from the data source and to convert any field codes in the publication to normal text. Publisher will delete the double brackets and convert the words that were inside them to regular text. Click No to maintain the field codes and the connection to the data source.

Sorting and Filtering Information in an Address List

Publisher provides two powerful tools to help you manage address lists: sorting and filtering. Sorting allows you to change the order of entries in the address list. Entries typically appear in the order in which you type them. Sorting the entries alphabetically by last name makes it easier to locate the item you want. You can

Will sorting or filtering change the contents of the address list? No. Sorting does not actually change any of the entries in the address list; it merely changes the order in which entries appear on screen and print. Likewise, when a filter is applied to an address list, entries are not deleted. Entries that do not meet the selection criteria are skipped when the address list is merged with the publication.

also determine the preview and printing order of merged documents. For example, you can comply with bulk mailing regulations by sorting and then printing all zip codes sequentially. You can sort an address list using up to three different fields.

Filters allow you to use only a portion of a larger address list for the current mailing. Filters can be thought of as selection criteria. Only the entries that meet the selection criteria will be merged with the publication at preview or print time. One common filtering technique is to target specific geographic areas by using entries from a particular city, state, or zip code. You can also create specialized filters. For example, you can filter a mailing by the age or income of the recipient, provided that you created the appropriate fields in the address list. You can apply up to three different filters to each merge operation.

Change the Order in Which Entries Are Merged with a Publication

1 On the Mail Merge menu, choose Filter Or Sort. The Filtering And Sorting dialog box appears.

2 Select the Sort tab.

3 Open the drop-down list box and choose a field to sort by.

4 Select Ascending to sort entries from A through Z or from 0 through 9. Select Descending to sort entries from Z through A or from 9 through 0.

5 To use additional sort criteria, repeat steps 3 and 4 for one or two more fields.

Click here to remove the sort order. After removing the sort criteria, Publisher will arrange the entries in the order they were originally entered.

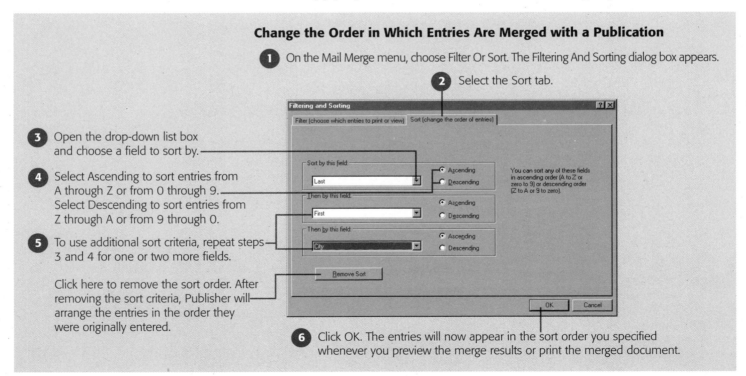

6 Click OK. The entries will now appear in the sort order you specified whenever you preview the merge results or print the merged document.

Why are the entries in my address list not sorted as I specified when I preview or print the merged document? In all likelihood, you changed the sort criteria in Publisher's address list dialog box. Changing the sort order in that dialog box affects the display of entries within the address list; it does not affect the merge operation. To sort entries during a merge operation, choose the Filter Or Sort command on the Mail Merge menu.

Why can't I view or print all the entries in my data source? Check to see if you have a filter applied to the data source. Choose the Filter Or Sort command on the Mail Merge menu and click the Remove Filter button to delete any filters. Publisher will then preview and print all the entries in the address list.

Change the Order in Which Entries Appear On Screen Within a Publisher Address List

1 On the Mail Merge menu, choose Edit Publisher Address List. The Open Address List dialog box appears.

2 Choose the file containing the address list, and then click Open. The address list dialog box appears.

3 Click the Filter Or Sort button. The Filtering And Sorting dialog box appears.

4 Select the Sort tab.

5 Open the drop-down list box and choose a field to sort by.

6 Select Ascending to sort entries from A through Z or from 0 through 9. Select Descending to sort entries from Z through A or from 9 through 0.

7 To use additional sort criteria, repeat steps 5 and 6 for one or two more fields.

8 Click OK. The entries will now appear in the sort order you specified whenever you access or edit the Publisher address list.

Use a Filter to Merge Selected Entries with a Publication

1 On the Mail Merge menu, choose Filter Or Sort. The Filtering And Sorting dialog box appears.

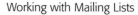

What is the difference between the And and Or choices in the Filtering And Sorting dialog box? If you choose the And operator, entries must meet both criteria to be merged with the document. If you choose the Or operator, entries can meet either criteria (but not necessarily both) to be merged with the document.

If you create a filter in which the City field is equal to Paris *and* the State field is equal to TX, Publisher will find entries for Paris, Texas.

If you create a filter in which the City field is equal to Paris *or* the State field is equal to TX, Publisher will find entries for Paris, Texas; for all cities in Texas; and for Paris, France.

Why does Publisher tell me that no entries match my filter criteria when I know there are matching entries? You have probably misspelled the phrase in the Compare To text box. Publisher requires you to spell the phrase in the text box exactly as you have spelled it in your data source. A filter will not work if you search for entries in the city of "Ausin," when your data source contains entries for the city of Austin.

Use a Filter to Merge Selected Entries with a Publication *(continued)*

2 Select the Filter tab.

3 Open the drop-down list box and choose a field that will be part of the filter criteria.

4 Choose one of the four comparison phrases: Is Equal To, Is Not Equal To, Is Less Than, or Is Greater Than.

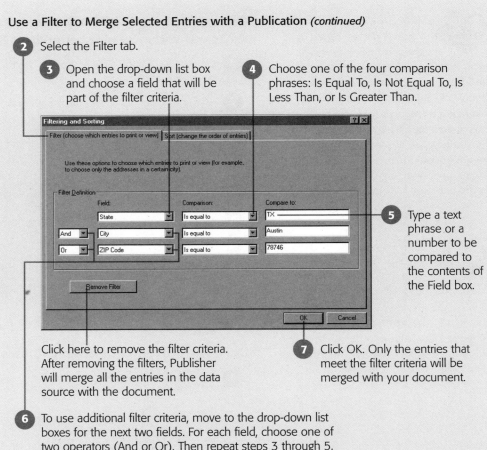

5 Type a text phrase or a number to be compared to the contents of the Field box.

Click here to remove the filter criteria. After removing the filters, Publisher will merge all the entries in the data source with the document.

7 Click OK. Only the entries that meet the filter criteria will be merged with your document.

6 To use additional filter criteria, move to the drop-down list boxes for the next two fields. For each field, choose one of two operators (And or Or). Then repeat steps 3 through 5.

In the current example, Publisher will merge entries from Austin, Texas, and from the surrounding suburbs that share the same zip code as Austin.

Why are the entries in my address list not filtered as I specified when I preview or print the merged document? If you changed the filter criteria in Publisher's address list dialog box, the display of entries within the address list is affected, but the merge operation is not. To filter entries during a merge operation, choose the Filter Or Sort command on the Mail Merge menu.

Use filters to proofread entries in an address list. You can create filters to search for problems in an address list. For example, searching for an empty zip code field will find incomplete addresses. If you included a date field, you can search for and delete old records.

Take advantage of Publisher's special printing functions for mail merge documents. Publisher's Print Merge command helps you generate mail merge documents more efficiently. For example, you can specify where on a sheet of labels Publisher should begin printing. If you've already used two rows of labels, you can begin printing at the third row. You can even print a test of the document to be sure that the mail merge is working properly.

For more information about printing mail merge documents, see Chapter 14.

Use a Filter to Locate and Display Specific Entries in a Publisher Address List On Screen

1 On the Mail Merge menu, choose Edit Publisher Address List. The Open Address List dialog box appears.

2 Choose the file containing the address list, and then click Open. The address list dialog box appears.

3 Click the Filter Or Sort button. The Filtering And Sorting Dialog box appears.

4 Select the Filter tab.

5 Open the drop-down list box and choose a field that will be part of the filter criteria.

6 Choose one of the four comparison phrases: Is Equal To, Is Not Equal To, Is Less Than, or Is Greater Than.

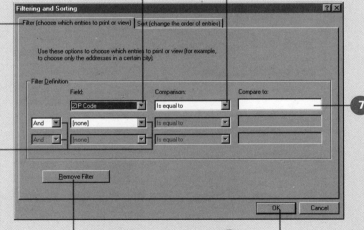

7 Type a text phrase or a number to be compared to the contents of the Field box.

Click here to remove the filter criteria. After removing the filters, Publisher will display all the entries in the address list.

9 Click OK. Only the entries that meet the filter criteria will appear in the dialog box when you scroll through the address list.

8 To use additional filter criteria, move to the drop-down list boxes for the next two fields. For each field, choose one of two operators (And or Or). Then repeat steps 5 through 7.

In the current example, Publisher will display any entry that is missing a zip code.

PageWizards can create
complete documents. The
flyer shown here includes
WordArt effects and a picture.

This logo—complete with a picture and
graphical accents—was generated using a
partial-page PageWizard design assistant.

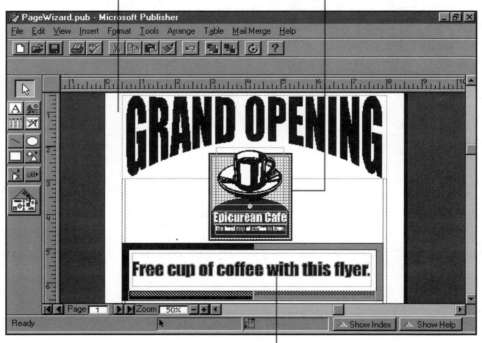

This preformatted headline was inserted
from Publisher's standard Design Gallery.

PageWizards, Design Gallery, and Custom Templates

Microsoft Publisher 97 offers PageWizards and the Design Gallery to help a novice designer overcome the biggest obstacle at the start of any project—a blank page. PageWizard design assistants are miniprograms that ask you for project information and then create a design based on your answers. Publisher's Design Gallery contains a wide variety of fully formatted objects. These objects can add a professional touch to your documents instantly.

Once you've created a document, you can reuse it easily by saving it as a template. Templates allow you to build new publications on the solid foundation of an existing design.

PageWizards

You can use a PageWizard design assistant to create a complete document or a single design element within a larger publication. To create a full publication, access PageWizards from the Startup dialog box. Publisher offers the many PageWizards listed below:

- Banner
- Brochure
- Business Card
- Business Form (14 types)

Choose the printer before you start the PageWizard. PageWizards assume that you will use the default printer already designated in Microsoft Windows 95 Control Panel. If you create a publication using a PageWizard and then change printers in the Print Setup dialog box (accessed from the File menu), your publication might not print correctly. If you want to change to a different printer, be sure to do so before you start the PageWizard.

For more information about how to change the default printer, see Chapter 14.

- @ Calendar
- @ Card & Invitation
- @ Envelope
- @ Flyer
- @ Label (8 types)
- @ Letterhead
- @ Newsletter
- @ Postcard

- @ Resume
- @ Sign
- @ Specialty (for a publication such as a menu, catalog, gift tag, poster, certificate, event ticket, recipe card, itinerary, phone ad, punch card, or price tag)
- @ Web Site

You can also use a PageWizard design assistant to create any of the following partial-page objects. You add partial-page elements to a publication by clicking the PageWizards tool on the main toolbar, located on the left side of the screen.

- @ Ad
- @ Calendar
- @ Coupon
- @ Logo

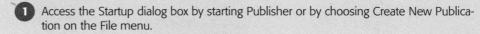

Create a Whole Publication

1 Access the Startup dialog box by starting Publisher or by choosing Create New Publication on the File menu.

Create a Whole Publication *(continued)*

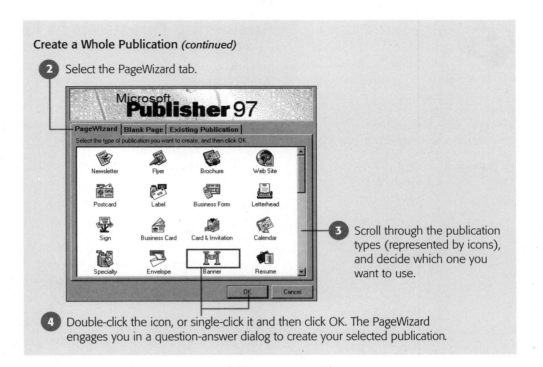

2 Select the PageWizard tab.

3 Scroll through the publication types (represented by icons), and decide which one you want to use.

4 Double-click the icon, or single-click it and then click OK. The PageWizard engages you in a question-answer dialog to create your selected publication.

Why did I get an error message when I tried to create a single design element? Designs created by a PageWizard can be very complex, with many text, picture, and WordArt objects grouped and positioned within the boundaries of the frame. If you draw a frame that can't accommodate the PageWizard design, Publisher displays an error message.

You need to draw a larger frame to accommodate the design. After the PageWizard has completed its work, you can resize the design.

If you need help creating a frame, see Chapter 2. For information about grouped objects, see Chapter 4. If you need help with resizing objects proportionally, see Chapters 4 and 9.

Create a Single Design Element

1 Click the PageWizards tool on the main toolbar. A flyout menu with four partial-page options appears.

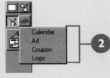

2 Select the element you want to create. The Crossbar pointer appears.

3 Draw a frame. The frame you draw determines the size of the PageWizard object.

4 The PageWizard engages you in a question-answer dialog to create your selected element.

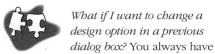

What if I want to change a design option in a previous dialog box? You always have the opportunity to move backward through the PageWizard dialog boxes to review and change your choices. Just click the backward pointing arrows to return to the previous screen or the first screen.

Answering Questions in PageWizard Dialog Boxes

PageWizard documents and partial-page elements vary dramatically in both content and complexity. This variety is reflected in the questions that the PageWizard design assistants pose as you move through the PageWizard process. The examples below illustrate how PageWizards address various design issues:

@ The Newsletter PageWizard asks you how many columns of text you want on each page.

@ The Business Form PageWizard asks whether you want to include specific items, such as tracking numbers or tax ID information, in a quote form.

@ Several PageWizards, such as the Itinerary PageWizard (found under Specialty), do not offer layout choices.

The PageWizard does not create a document or a partial-page element until you click the Create It! button. Once you do, the PageWizard gets to work. When the document is created, the PageWizard always presents one final dialog box asking if you need step-by-step help. You can respond in the following ways:

@ Choose Yes, and then click OK, to move to the document workspace with Publisher's help system activated.

@ Choose No, and then click OK, to move to the document workspace without opening Publisher's help system.

The Design Gallery

Publisher's Design Gallery contains a number of objects that can enhance a publication with a click of the main toolbar button shown below.

You can insert Design Gallery objects in a publication, or you can copy the formatting attributes to objects already in your publication. Best of all, you can customize the Design Gallery by adding your own creations to it.

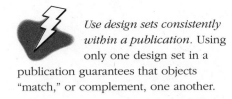

Use design sets consistently within a publication. Using only one design set in a publication guarantees that objects "match," or complement, one another.

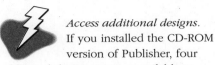

Access additional designs. If you installed the CD-ROM version of Publisher, four additional design sets are available to you. These designs are also categorized as Classic Designs, Jazzy Designs, Modern Designs, and Plain Designs, but the phrase "CD Deluxe" distinguishes them from the standard design sets.

The Design Gallery includes four standard design sets:

- Classic Designs
- Jazzy Designs
- Modern Designs
- Plain Designs

The standard design sets include 12 categories:

- Attention Getters
- Headlines
- Mail Permits (only available with the Plain Designs set)
- Ornaments
- Pull Quotes
- Reply Forms
- Sidebars
- Table Of Contents
- Titles
- Web Email Buttons
- Web Page Buttons
- Web Page Dividers

Insert a Design Gallery Object in a Publication

1 Click the Design Gallery tool, or choose Design Gallery on the Tools menu. The Design Gallery dialog box appears.

The advantage of dragging a sketch into a publication. If you drag a thumbnail sketch from the Design Gallery into your publication, the Design Gallery window won't close. You can continue to browse through the Design Gallery and insert additional items. When you've finished browsing and dragging, click the Close button to return to your publication.

Insert a Design Gallery Object in a Publication *(continued)*

The title bar always lists the current design set, such as Classic Designs, shown here.

3 Scroll through the thumbnail sketches, and select the design element you want.

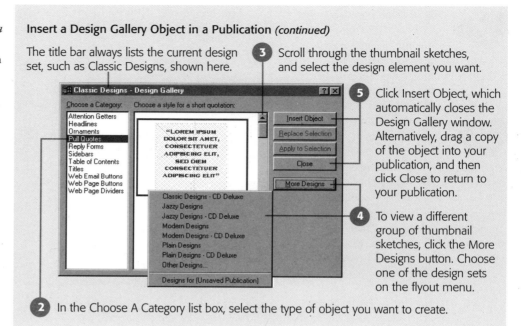

5 Click Insert Object, which automatically closes the Design Gallery window. Alternatively, drag a copy of the object into your publication, and then click Close to return to your publication.

4 To view a different group of thumbnail sketches, click the More Designs button. Choose one of the design sets on the flyout menu.

2 In the Choose A Category list box, select the type of object you want to create.

Replace a Selected Object with an Object from the Design Gallery

1 Select the object you want to replace.

2 Click the Design Gallery tool, or choose Design Gallery on the Tools menu. The Design Gallery dialog box appears.

3 In the Choose A Category list box, select the type of object you want to create.

4 Scroll through the thumbnail sketches, and select the design element you want.

5 To view a different group of thumbnail sketches, click the More Designs button. Choose one of the design sets on the flyout menu.

6 Click Replace Selection to delete the selected object and insert the Design Gallery object in its place. The Design Gallery dialog box closes automatically.

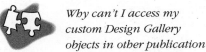

Use the Format Painter to copy attributes. If you've already inserted a Design Gallery object in your document, you can use the Format Painter to copy its attributes to other objects in the document. Using the Format Painter allows you to choose which formats you copy. For example, you can select a drawn object in order to copy its fill color and border to another object.

Select the individual object within the Design Gallery element whose formats you want to copy. Click the Format Painter tool on the standard toolbar. Position the pointer over the object that you want to reformat. When the pointer changes into the Paintbrush pointer, click the object.

Why can't I access my custom Design Gallery objects in other publication files? The custom objects you add to the Design Gallery are only available in the current publication.

Copy Formatting Attributes from a Design Gallery Object to a Selected Object

1 Select the object you want to reformat.

2 Click the Design Gallery tool, or choose Design Gallery on the Tools menu. The Design Gallery dialog box appears.

3 In the Choose A Category list box, select the type of object whose formatting you want to copy.

4 Scroll through the thumbnail sketches, and select the design element you want. You must select a design element that consists of a single object. Publisher can't copy the formatting attributes of grouped objects.

5 To view a different group of thumbnail sketches, click the More Designs button. Choose one of the design sets on the flyout menu.

6 Click Apply To Selection to copy the formatting attributes from the Design Gallery object to the selected object in your publication. Publisher will change the appearance of the selected object but will not alter its size or content.

7 Click Close to return to your publication.

Customizing the Design Gallery

You can customize the Design Gallery by creating your own objects or by importing objects into it. Publisher doesn't normally allow you to add an object to one of the standard or deluxe design sets from within your Publisher document. However, you can easily add items to new design sets created for the current document.

When you add a custom object to the Design Gallery, Publisher saves it with the current publication only. You can use it over and over again in the current publication. If you want to have access to the same custom object in more than one publication, you must either copy the object from document to document or import the design set from the publication where it is saved. Once you've added a custom object to the Design Gallery, you can add items to its category or create additional categories.

Can I add more than one object at a time to the Design Gallery? Yes, you can perform a multiple selection and add several objects to the Design Gallery simultaneously. However, the multiple selection is not added to the Design Gallery as a series of individual objects; instead it is added to the Design Gallery as a single grouped object.

 How to modify Publisher's design sets. Publisher will not allow you to add a custom object to its own design sets. Nor can you easily delete an object from these design sets. You can circumvent these restrictions by removing the read-only attribute from the file containing the design set you want to modify. Then open the file and follow the steps in this section. All the original design set files are located in the Microsoft Publisher\PageWiz folder. They are named as follows:

- @ Classic.pub
- @ Modern.pub
- @ Class_cd.pub
- @ Modrn_cd.pub
- @ Jazzy.pub
- @ Plain.pub
- @ Jazzy_cd.pub
- @ Plain_cd.pub

Add the First Custom Object to the Design Gallery

1 Select the object you want to add to the Design Gallery.

2 Click the Design Gallery tool, or choose Design Gallery on the Tools menu. The Design Gallery dialog box appears.

3 Click the More Designs button, and choose Add Selection To Design Gallery on the flyout menu. Publisher displays an alert box and asks if you would like to create a new design set.

4 Click Yes. The Adding An Object dialog box appears.

5 Type an object name.

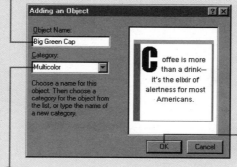

7 Click OK. The Create New Category dialog box appears.

6 Type a category name.

8 Type a description for the new category, and then click OK.

9 Save the publication to permanently associate the Design Gallery addition with the publication.

Add a Subsequent Custom Object to the Design Gallery

1 Select the object you want to add to the Design Gallery.

2 Click the Design Gallery tool on the main toolbar, or choose Design Gallery on the Tools menu. The Design Gallery dialog box appears.

Add objects quickly to the Design Gallery. You can quickly add objects to the Design Gallery by choosing Add Selection To Design Gallery on the Tools menu. If you use the Tools menu instead of the Design Gallery tool on the toolbar, you'll go directly to the Adding An Object dialog box.

Why can't I see my custom design objects in the Design Gallery? When you first open the Design Gallery, Publisher displays one of the four standard design sets. The name of the current design set is always displayed in the title bar. If the title bar of the Design Gallery dialog box doesn't contain the name of the current publication, click the More Designs button and then choose Designs For [Publication Filename] on the flyout menu. Once you've switched to the design set for the current publication, the categories you created will appear in the list box and your custom design objects will be visible in the preview window.

Add a Subsequent Custom Object to the Design Gallery *(continued)*

3 If the title bar of the Design Gallery dialog box doesn't contain the name of the current publication, click the More Designs button. Choose Designs For [Publication Filename] on the flyout menu.

4 Click More Designs, and then choose Add Selection To Design Gallery on the flyout menu. The Adding An Object dialog box appears.

5 Type an object name.

6 Select a category from the drop-down list box, or type a completely new category name.

7 Click OK.

8 If you are creating a new category, type a description in the Create New Category dialog box that appears, and then click OK.

9 Save the publication to permanently associate the Design Gallery addition with the publication.

Import Design Gallery Objects from Other Publications

1 Open the publication to which you want to add custom Design Gallery objects.

2 Click the Design Gallery tool on the main toolbar, or choose Design Gallery on the Tools menu. The Design Gallery dialog box appears.

3 Click the More Designs button, and then choose Other Designs on the flyout menu. The Other Designs dialog box appears.

4 Locate the file containing the custom objects you want to copy.

5 Highlight the file name. Use the Preview area to confirm that you've selected the correct file.

6 Click OK. All the custom categories and custom objects will be copied to the Design Gallery associated with the current publication.

Managing the Design Gallery

You can enhance the effectiveness of the Design Gallery by deleting or renaming categories and objects, or by creating categories when the contents no longer suit your purposes.

Use the shortcut menu to modify the Design Gallery. You can delete, rename, and create categories directly from the Design Gallery dialog box. In the Choose A Category list box, right-click the category you want to modify. On the shortcut menu that appears, choose the appropriate command.

Delete, Rename, or Create Categories in the Design Gallery

1 Open the publication that contains the category you want to modify.

2 Click the Design Gallery tool on the main toolbar, or choose Design Gallery on the Tools menu. The Design Gallery dialog box appears.

3 If the title bar of the Design Gallery dialog box doesn't contain the name of the current publication, click the More Designs button. Choose Designs For [Publication Filename] on the flyout menu.

4 Click More Designs, and then choose Edit Categories on the flyout menu. The Edit Categories dialog box appears.

5 If you want to delete or rename a category, select it.

6 Do one of the following:

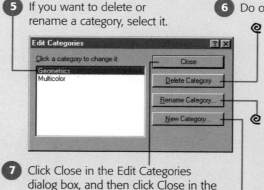

  Click here to delete the selected category. In the confirmation dialog box that appears, click Yes to delete the category, or click No to return to the Edit Categories dialog box without making any changes.

  Click here to rename the selected category. In the Rename Category dialog box that appears, type a new name and a new description. Click OK to rename the category.

  Click here to create a new category. In the Create New Category dialog box that appears, type a name and a description. Click OK to create the category.

7 Click Close in the Edit Categories dialog box, and then click Close in the Design Gallery dialog box to return to your publication.

8 Save the publication to make the changes permanent.

Delete or Rename Objects in the Design Gallery

1 Open the publication that contains the category from which you want to delete or rename an object.

2 Click the Design Gallery tool, or choose Design Gallery on the Tools menu. The Design Gallery dialog box appears.

3 If the title bar of the Design Gallery dialog box doesn't contain the name of the current publication, click the More Designs button. Choose Designs For [Publication Filename] on the flyout menu.

4 Select the category containing the object you want to delete or rename.

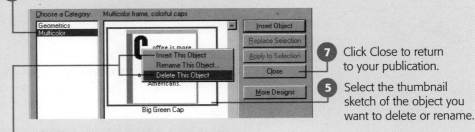

7 Click Close to return to your publication.

5 Select the thumbnail sketch of the object you want to delete or rename.

6 Click the right mouse button. On the shortcut menu that appears, do one of the following:

- Select Delete This Object. (Alternatively, you can press the Delete key without clicking the right mouse button.) In the confirmation dialog box that appears, click Yes to delete the object, or click No to return to the Design Gallery dialog box without deleting the object.

- Select Rename This Object. In the Rename Object dialog box that appears, type a new name and then click OK, or click Cancel to return to the Design Gallery dialog box without renaming the object.

8 Save the publication to make the changes to the Design Gallery permanent.

Learn by example. By taking apart a group of objects created by a PageWizard design assistant or inserted from the Design Gallery, you can learn quite a lot about design, such as how to combine text, table, picture, and WordArt elements. After you've dismantled the design, you can simply discard it because it can be re-created easily.

For information about the structure and layout of documents, see Chapters 3 and 4.

What to Consider When Modifying PageWizard and Design Gallery Objects

Using a PageWizard design assistant or inserting an object from the Design Gallery can jump-start your design process. However, you will probably need to modify your document's layout by using Publisher's standard text, table, picture, and WordArt tools. Before you start changing your design or importing text and pictures, identify all the elements in the layout and analyze whether the design is suitable for your purposes.

Layout Issues

The underlying structure of a document can make it easier or harder to modify a design. The following reminders might help you modify designs more efficiently:

- In the Page Setup dialog box, note which publication layout, paper size, and orientation options have been selected. For example, if the Normal layout option has been selected, the actual page size of the publication will vary depending on the size of the paper installed in your printer.

- Check which layout guides, if any, have been created for the publication. Layout guides can help you move and create objects with greater precision. If you intend to make major modifications to the publication (changing the number of columns, for example), you should modify the layout guides first.

- Go to the background to discover which elements will repeat on every page of the document. Remember that you can't edit elements that have been placed on the background until you move from the foreground to the background.

Object Attributes

Click each object in the layout, and note whether it is a text object, a table object, a picture object, a WordArt object, or a drawn object. Identifying an element properly can help you edit it more efficiently. Consider the following before you attempt to modify an object:

For more information about Publisher's toolbars, see Chapter 1.

Preserve text formatting in PageWizard documents and Design Gallery objects. Before you type or import copy, define type styles using the sample text contained in the publication or object. First highlight the text. Then highlight the contents of the Style text box located on the Format tool-bar. Replace the existing style name by typing a new style name, and then press Enter. In the Create Style By Example dialog box that appears, click OK.

For more information about creating a text style by example, formatting text, and linking text frames, see Chapter 5.

@ Identify each element by the formatting options that appear on the Format toolbar. For example, if you identify a text design as a WordArt element, you'll know that you must double-click it to enter new copy.

@ Determine whether a particular design element is composed of one object with complex formatting or of multiple objects. It is much easier to edit a single text frame with attributes for border, object color, and shadow than it is to edit a group consisting of a text frame, a tinted rectangle, and several lines.

Type Styles

PageWizards and Design Gallery objects do not contain defined type styles; instead, they contain preformatted text frames. Preformatted text frames affect copy in the following ways:

@ If you type your copy, Publisher preserves the formatting attributes of the PageWizard or Design Gallery object.

@ If you import a word processing file and the copy contains type styles, Publisher attempts to replace the formatting attributes of the PageWizard or Design Gallery object with the formatting attributes of the imported type styles.

Fonts

PageWizards and the Design Gallery use standard TrueType fonts that ship with either Windows 95 or Publisher. You should change the selected font if any statement below is true:

@ The font does not complement other text objects in your document.

@ The font does not appeal to you aesthetically.

@ You've deleted fonts from your system, and the PageWizard or Design Gallery object uses a font that is no longer installed on your computer.

Text Frames

When you import text into a preformatted document, the text flows through all the connected text frames. Always check the text flow in your publication in two ways:

@ Locate all the connected text frames in the publication by clicking the Frame Jump buttons that appear at the upper left or lower right corner of a selected text frame.

@ If you want more control over the text flow process, disconnect the text frames before you import the text. Then reconnect the frames as needed to handle text overflow.

Object Organization

Both PageWizard design assistants and the Design Gallery organize complex designs by grouping objects. You can work with groups in the following ways:

@ You can resize and reposition all the elements in a group simultaneously without ungrouping them.

@ If you want to change the size, the position, or the stacking order of an individual element within the group, you must first ungroup the objects.

@ You can change the content and formatting of an individual element within a grouped object without ungrouping it. Simply click on the individual object to subselect it.

Templates

A template is like a standard Publisher document except for one important difference: when you open a template file, Publisher makes a copy of the template for your use and leaves the original template file undisturbed. Publisher's template feature is a powerful tool that allows you to save your custom designs for later use.

Any publication that you design or modify can be saved as a template. For example, if you want to use a customized letterhead repeatedly, save it as a template. Then, whenever you write a letter, you can start with a clean document

Why can't I find a Templates tab in the Startup dialog box or a Template subfolder on my hard disk? If you are installing Publisher for the first time, no templates exist. Publisher will automatically create a Templates tab in the Startup dialog box and a Template folder the first time you save a publication as a template.

If you are upgrading from Publisher version 3, the old templates will be available from the Templates tab in the Startup dialog box.

Where should I store my template? Don't worry about the Save In drop-down list box or the files list box. When Publisher saves a document as a template, it always stores the file in the Template subfolder.

(equivalent to a fresh piece of stationery) that already contains your logo, your company address, and predefined type styles for the body of the letter.

Save a Publication as a Template

1. Choose Save As on the File menu. The Save As dialog box appears.

2. In the File Name text box, type a meaningful name for the document that doesn't duplicate the name of an existing template. For example, *Letterhead* could identify your company stationery. (Don't type a file extension; the extension *.pub* will be added automatically.)

3. Turn on the Template check box at the bottom of the dialog box.

4. Click Save. Now when you look through the list of available templates, your letterhead template appears in the list in alphabetical order.

Printing Your Project in Black and White or in Color

For a complete description of Control Panel, refer to the Windows 95 online help system.

PageWizards and the default printer. PageWizard design assistants make decisions about page size, orientation, and font availability depending on the capabilities of the default printer. Make sure you choose the correct printer as the default printer *before* you use a PageWizard.

Setting Up the Printer

The Microsoft Windows 95 Control Panel settings allow you to configure your computer hardware. By adjusting Control Panel settings for your printer and monitor, you can improve overall printing performance and influence the final appearance of your publication.

Identifying the Default Printer

When you begin a new publication, Microsoft Publisher 97 assumes that you want to use the printer designated as the default printer in Windows 95 Control Panel. You can select the printer you would like to use as the default.

Select the Default Printer

 1 On the Windows 95 Start menu, choose Settings. On the cascading menu, choose Printers.

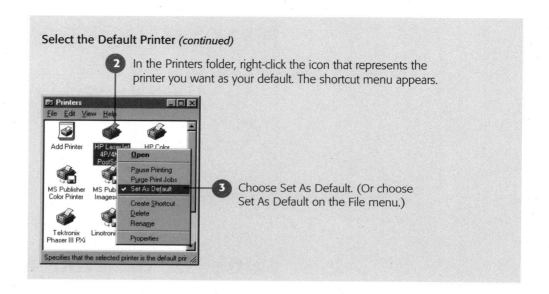

Select the Default Printer *(continued)*

2 In the Printers folder, right-click the icon that represents the printer you want as your default. The shortcut menu appears.

3 Choose Set As Default. (Or choose Set As Default on the File menu.)

Selecting Spool Options and Controlling the Print Queue

In a process known as spooling, Publisher routes your document to the print queue (the lineup of print jobs) instead of sending it directly to the printer. Spooling lets you continue to work while your document prints. The file is spooled to the print queue at high speed, and as soon as the entire file is in the print queue, you can resume work. Windows 95 provides configuration options for spooling that affect the speed and quality of the print job. You select options in the Spool Settings dialog box.

Once you've chosen configuration options, generating a standard document is a simple procedure. Even after you send a document to the print queue, you can cancel printing, pause printing, or rearrange the order in which files will print.

How to interrupt the print job. While information is being spooled to the printer, a dialog box that contains a Cancel button appears. When you click Cancel, Publisher stops sending information to the printer. However, any pages that have already been sent to the printer and stored in its memory will print.

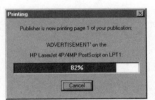

Select Spool Options

1 Open the Printers folder.

2 Right-click the icon that represents the printer you want to configure. On the flyout menu, select Properties. The printer Properties dialog box appears.

3 Select the Details tab.

4 At the bottom of the Details tab, click the Spool Settings button. The Spool Settings dialog box appears.

5 Select the settings you want.

This option speeds up spooling. But because the entire file must be spooled to the hard disk, multipage documents require substantial amounts of free disk space.

This option turns spooling on.

This option requires less free disk space but might cause a multipage document to take longer to print.

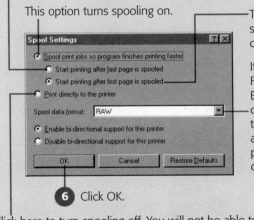

If your printer supports the Spool Data Format option, choose either RAW or EMF. The RAW data format ensures compatibility with your printer but might take longer to print. The EMF data format accepts generic metafile data and can print faster, but it might not be totally compatible with your printer.

6 Click OK.

Click here to turn spooling off. You will not be able to return to work until the entire file has been sent to the printer.

Control the Print Queue

1 Double-click the printer icon that appears on the taskbar during printing. (Or double-click the printer icon in the Printers folder.) The Print Queue window appears.

2 On the Document menu, select Pause Printing or Cancel Printing.

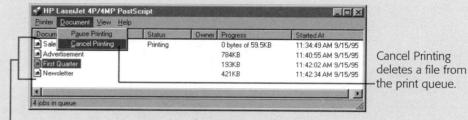

Cancel Printing deletes a file from the print queue.

The print queue lists files in the order in which they will print. To change the order, select a file and drag it to a new position in the list.

Printing a Document Using Default Settings

The preset (or default) options in the Print dialog box include generating one copy of each page in your publication, collating the pages, and inserting crop marks. These options work well for standard documents. They can be used to generate printouts quickly and efficiently.

Print a Document with the Default Settings

1 Choose Print on the File menu. The Print dialog box appears.

2 Click OK.

Overriding Defaults: Controlling the Current Print Job

In some cases, the default options won't suit your needs. The Print dialog box (shown on the opposite page), which appears when you select the Print command on the File menu, allows you to control the printing process in a number of ways.

How to bypass the Print dialog box. To bypass the Print dialog box, click the Print button on the Standard toolbar.

You can access the Print dialog box by pressing Ctrl-P.

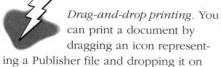

Drag-and-drop printing. You can print a document by dragging an icon representing a Publisher file and dropping it on top of the icon for your printer. Windows 95 will open Publisher in order to print the file.

Choose Printer Options for the Current Print Job

1 On the File menu, select Print. The Print dialog box appears.

2 Change the settings as appropriate.

The name of the current default printer is selected and displayed the first time you open the dialog box. Open the drop-down list box to select a different printer that is installed on your system.

Click here to access the printer Properties dialog box.

Turn on this check box to save the printed version of your document to disk, instead of sending it directly to a printer.

If you decide to print a section of a larger publication or a single page, enter the starting and ending page numbers in the From and To text boxes, respectively.

Click here to access two printing options. If you are printing a publication for which the page size is larger than the paper size, the Tile Printing Options button appears. If you are printing a publication for which the page size is smaller than the paper size, the Page Options button appears.

Enter the number of copies you want to print.

Turn on this check box to collate copies. Publisher prints each copy of your publication in the correct page order. You can speed up printing by turning collation off. When this check box is turned off, Publisher prints every page 1, then every page 2, and so on.

For more information about Tile Printing Options and Page Options, see pages 284 through 286.

To print blank boxes rather than artwork, turn on Do Not Print Pictures. This speeds up printing considerably. (The Picture Display command on the View menu influences the appearance of the document on screen *and* at print time. The Do Not Print Pictures check box in the Print dialog box affects the printed output only.)

Turn on this check box to insert guides that help you trim a publication to the final size. Publisher requires at least 0.5 inch of free space on the page to add crop marks. Publisher also prints the name of the publication, the page number, a date/time stamp, and (in the case of spot-color separations) registration marks along the edge of the paper.

3 Click OK to begin printing.

Is there any difference between accessing the printer Properties dialog box from the Windows 95 Printers folder and accessing the printer Properties dialog box from within Publisher? Yes, there is an important difference. If you use the Properties button in Publisher's Print or Print Setup dialog box to access the printer Properties dialog box, the changes you make will apply only to the current document. If you use the Windows 95 Printers folder to access the printer Properties dialog box, the changes you make will apply permanently to the printer for all applications and all print jobs. Using the Printers folder also displays additional tabs in the dialog box.

Changing Basic Printer Characteristics

Whereas Publisher's Print dialog box offers options that control the current printing job, the Print Setup and printer Properties dialog boxes offer options for changing the printer characteristics. Use the Print Setup dialog box, accessed from the File menu, to choose the current printer as well as the paper tray, size, and orientation.

The printer Properties dialog box can be accessed by clicking the Properties button in the Print or Print Setup dialog box, or by right-clicking a printer icon in the Printers folder and choosing Properties on the shortcut menu. Certain hardware configuration options are only available in the printer Properties dialog box. The options might vary dramatically depending on the capabilities of your printer. Several basic options that are probably available to you are of particular use to desktop publishers, including the ability to create custom paper sizes, determine nonprinting paper margins, and change the resolution of the printout.

Select the Printer and Paper Options

1 On the File menu, choose Print Setup. The Print Setup dialog box appears.

2 Select the options you want.

When to use the Manual Feed paper option. Specify Manual Feed if you want to feed envelopes, small cards, or heavier stocks through your printer. Feeding thick or smaller than standard paper by hand can help you avoid paper jams.

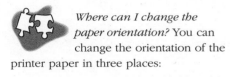

Where can I change the paper orientation? You can change the orientation of the printer paper in three places:

- The printer Properties dialog box, accessed from the Printers folder: sets the default orientation for the printer.

- The Print Setup dialog box, accessed from the File menu: sets the orientation for the current document. The orientation you choose in the Print Setup dialog box is automatically reflected in the Page Setup dialog box and is saved along with the publication.

- The Page Setup dialog box, accessed from the File menu: sets the orientation for the current document. The orientation you choose in the Page Setup dialog box is automatically reflected in the Print Setup dialog box and is saved along with the publication.

Select the Printer and Paper Options *(continued)*

Open the Size drop-down list box to choose one of the standard paper sizes.

Open this drop-down list box to choose a printer from the list of currently installed printers.

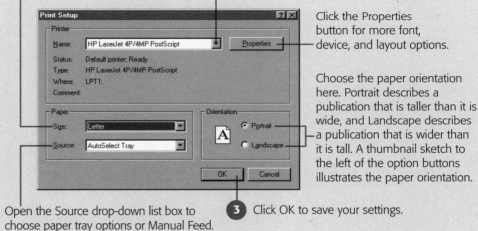
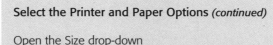

Click the Properties button for more font, device, and layout options.

Choose the paper orientation here. Portrait describes a publication that is taller than it is wide, and Landscape describes a publication that is wider than it is tall. A thumbnail sketch to the left of the option buttons illustrates the paper orientation.

Open the Source drop-down list box to choose paper tray options or Manual Feed.

3 Click OK to save your settings.

Customizing the Paper Size

You can give your designs an aesthetic boost by using special paper stock, such as note paper, folded cards, and postcards. Many stationery stores, office supply stores, and mail order companies carry specialty papers that will work with a desktop laser printer. To print on these nonstandard papers, you must define a custom paper size.

Select an Atypical Paper Size for Your Document

1 In the Print or Print Setup dialog box, click the Properties button. The printer Properties dialog box appears.

Why can't I select a custom-sized paper in Publisher?
When you want to use custom-sized paper for a Publisher document, open the Print Setup dialog box, click the Properties button, and then select the custom paper in the printer Properties dialog box. If you attempt to select a custom-sized paper directly from the drop-down list of paper sizes available in the Print Setup dialog box, Publisher defaults your selection to a different size.

Select an Atypical Paper Size for Your Document *(continued)*

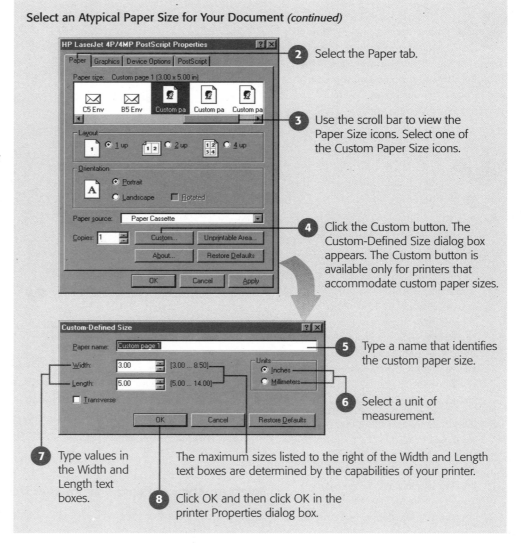

2 Select the Paper tab.

3 Use the scroll bar to view the Paper Size icons. Select one of the Custom Paper Size icons.

4 Click the Custom button. The Custom-Defined Size dialog box appears. The Custom button is available only for printers that accommodate custom paper sizes.

5 Type a name that identifies the custom paper size.

6 Select a unit of measurement.

7 Type values in the Width and Length text boxes.

The maximum sizes listed to the right of the Width and Length text boxes are determined by the capabilities of your printer.

8 Click OK and then click OK in the printer Properties dialog box.

Accommodating Nonprinting Margins

Most printers are alike in one important way: they reserve a portion of the page for gripping the paper and feeding it through the printing mechanism. This portion of the page cannot contain any printed image or text. Whenever you plan a publication, be sure you set page margins that are at least as wide as your printer's nonprinting margins.

 How can I determine nonprinting margins for my older printer? Older printers typically do not supply Windows 95 with information about nonprinting margins. You can still determine the size of the nonprinting margins empirically by creating a new publication. In the Print Setup dialog box, select the printer and the largest paper size your printer can accommodate. In the Page Setup dialog box, choose the Normal option (indicating that the page size matches the paper size). Using the Box tool, draw a rectangle that covers the entire page. With the rectangle selected, choose Fill Color on the Format menu, and then choose a color or gray tint in the Colors dialog box that appears. Don't choose the Clear or White options. Print the page. The unshaded areas around the edge constitute the nonprinting margins.

Determine the Standard Nonprinting Margins for Your Printer

1 In the Print or Print Setup dialog box, click the Properties button. The printer Properties dialog box appears.

2 Select the Paper tab.

3 Click the Unprintable Area button.

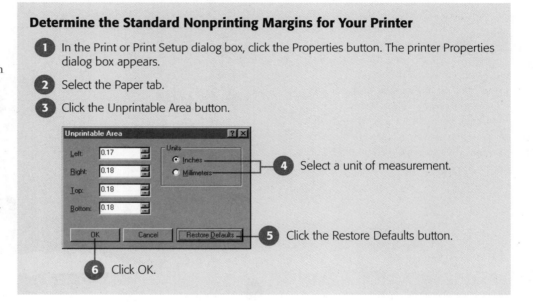

4 Select a unit of measurement.

5 Click the Restore Defaults button.

6 Click OK.

Adjusting the Print Quality of Documents

Many printers allow you to change the resolution settings. Lowering the resolution results in shorter printing time—a useful feature if you need to print your document many times, as when you are experimenting with a design or proofreading text. Depending on the capabilities of your printer, you might also have access to a resolution setting called halftoning, which affects the appearance of scanned pictures.

How is resolution measured? Printer resolution is measured in dots per inch (dpi). Halftone resolution is measured in lines per inch (lpi), also known as line-screen frequency or simply as screen frequency.

Create special effects with halftone settings. You can transform a photographic image into a textured illustration by using unusual halftone settings. In the following example, a line-screen frequency of 25 and a screen angle value of 30 degrees convert a conventional photograph of a small boy into an abstracted illustration with a noticeably large dot pattern.

Why aren't the tiling options available in the Print dialog box? Tiling is available only when you use the Special Size option in the Page Setup dialog box *and* the printer's paper size is smaller than the document's page size.

Specify the Resolution Settings

1 In the Print or Print Setup dialog box, click the Properties button. The printer Properties dialog box appears.

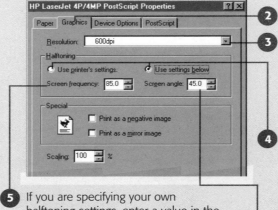

2 Select the Graphics tab.

3 Open the Resolution drop-down list box and choose the appropriate resolution or quality setting. Choose lower dpi values for faster printing; choose higher dpi values for quality output.

4 Use the printer's default halftoning settings or your own specifications. The default, or "factory," settings are designed to provide the best combination of picture resolution with a wide range of gray tones.

5 If you are specifying your own halftoning settings, enter a value in the Screen Frequency text box. Higher values increase the apparent resolution of a picture but decrease the number of gray tones. Lower values decrease the resolution of scanned pictures but increase the number of gray tones.

6 If you are specifying your own halftoning settings, enter a value in the Screen Angle text box. The default setting of 45 degrees minimizes the regular dot pattern in the halftone screen, producing smooth tonal transitions in photgraphic images.

7 Click OK.

Printing Atypically Sized Publications

It doesn't matter to Publisher how big a banner or a poster might be. An oversized document is still considered a single page. If the paper size is smaller than the document page size, Publisher prints the publication page across several sheets of paper in a process known as tiling.

When you print a small publication, such as a business card or a label, on a larger sheet of paper, Publisher lets you choose how the page will fit on the paper. You can opt to center the publication page on the paper, or to print multiple copies of the publication on a single sheet of paper.

For more information about the Page Setup command, see page 32 in Chapter 3.

For more information about changing the position of a ruler's zero point, see pages 53 through 54 in Chapter 4.

Print only a single tile of your poster or banner. You don't have to reprint an entire banner or poster to check a section of your design—to correct a spelling mistake, for example. Instead, select the Print One Tile From Ruler Origin item in the Poster and Banner Printing Options dialog box. (Because Publisher treats the entire poster or banner as a single-page document, you can't use the Print Range area in the Print dialog box.)

Before you use this option, however, you must change the zero points of both the horizontal and the vertical rulers in your publication so that they align with the upper-left corner of the tile you want to print.

Print a Poster or a Banner

1 On the File menu, choose the Page Setup command and confirm that the Special Size layout option is selected.

2 On the File menu, select the Print command. The Print dialog box appears.

3 Click the Tile Printing Options button. The Poster And Banner Printing Options dialog box appears.

4 Select Print Entire Page.

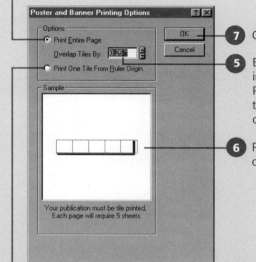

7 Click OK to return to the Print dialog box.

5 Enter a value from 0 through 6.25 inches in the Overlap Tiles By text box. By default, Publisher overlaps the image by 0.25 inch to avoid any white gaps between sections of the poster or the banner.

6 Preview the layout of the poster or the banner in the Sample area.

Select this option to print a single section, or tile, of the poster or the banner.

Why isn't the Page Options button available in the Print dialog box? Page options that allow you to print more than one copy of a publication on a single sheet of paper are available only when you use the Special Size or Label option in the Page Setup dialog box *and* the printer's paper size is large enough to accommodate more than one copy of the document's page size.

For more information about nonprinting margins, see page 283.

The trouble with 0-value margins. Although Publisher allows you to enter a value of 0 in the Side Margin and Top Margin text boxes, you would rarely want to do so. Setting these margins at 0 places a portion of the page into the printer's nonprinting margin. When you print the publication, part of your design might be cut off.

Print a Small Publication

1 On the File menu, choose the Page Setup command and confirm that the Special Size layout option is selected.

2 On the File menu, select the Print command. The Print dialog box appears.

3 Click the Page Options button. The Page Options dialog box appears.

4 Specify how you want the document to be printed on the page.

Select this option to print one copy of the publication centered on the paper.

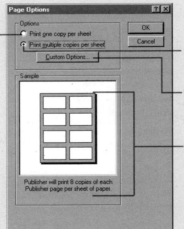

Select this option to print multiple copies of the publication on a single sheet of paper.

Click the Custom Options button to display the Custom Options - Small Publications dialog box and modify the default arrangement of copies on the paper.

Publisher always shows (and lists) the number of copies that will fit on a single sheet of paper.

Enter new values in the margin and gap text boxes. The minimum value you can enter is 0. The maximum value is determined by the paper size and the page size.

Turn on this check box to have Publisher automatically calculate the spacing between copies.

5 Click OK in the Custom Options - Small Publications and the Page Options dialog boxes, or click Cancel in both dialog boxes to return to the Print dialog box.

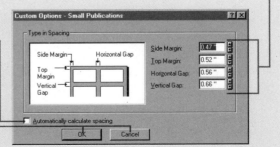

Why are the pages for my folded document printed out of order? When Publisher prints the pages for a folded publication, they will appear to be out of order. Don't worry. This odd-looking arrangement, called the imposition, ensures that the pages will appear in the correct order when you fold the sheets in half along the spine of the book.

 Why does Publisher insert blank pages when I print my book? The book layout works only when the number of pages in your document is a multiple of 4 (4, 8, 12, and so on). If the number of pages is not a multiple of 4, you will have "blanks" at the end. If you want to insert blank pages in specific locations, use the Page command on the Insert menu.

Printing Folded Publications

The Special Fold option in the Page Setup dialog box prints documents that are ready to be folded into a book or pamphlet.

Print a Book or a Booklet

1 On the File menu, choose the Page Setup command and confirm that the Special Fold layout (which includes Book Fold) is selected.

2 Go to the last page in the document and verify that the total number of pages is a multiple of 4. In your book, each sheet of paper will contain four pages (two on each side).

3 On the File menu, select the Print command. The Print dialog box appears.

4 In the Print Range area, select an appropriate option:

- Print the entire book: select All. Publisher figures out the imposition for the entire book and then automatically prints two pages on each sheet of paper.

- Print only a portion of the book: select Pages and enter page numbers in the From and To text boxes.

- Print a single selected page: select Current Page.

5 Click OK.

6 If you are printing only a portion of the book, a confirmation dialog box appears. Click Yes to print the selected pages as a separate booklet. Publisher recalculates the imposition for the selected pages so that the first page in the range becomes a right-hand page. Click No to print the selected pages as part of the entire book. Publisher preserves the imposition for the entire book by printing the selected pages along with the appropriate facing page in each spread.

Arranging the Pages of a Book by Hand

Most laser printers print on only one side of the paper, but you can still create a book using Publisher, your laser printer, and a copy machine. Look at the following illustration of an eight-page book, which will help you understand how a book or magazine is constructed. You perform two basic operations when assembling a book:

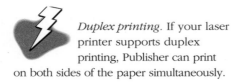 *Duplex printing.* If your laser printer supports duplex printing, Publisher can print on both sides of the paper simultaneously.

 Why can't I find the Print Merge command on the File menu? If the Print Merge command is not available, it means that you haven't properly set up the publication for mail merge. Connect the publication to a data source and insert at least one field code in the publication. The Print Merge command should now be available.

 For information about Publisher's mail merge components (address lists, data sources, and field codes), see Chapter 12.

@ Use a copy machine to make double-sided pages.

@ Bind the book by folding, assembling, and stapling the pages.

The first page of your book must be a right-hand (recto) page, and the last must be a left-hand (verso) page.

When Publisher prints the pages in a book, it starts from the outside and works toward the center two facing pages, also called the center spread. When you assemble your book, you also work toward the center.

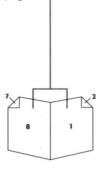

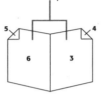

For an eight-page publication, copy the sheet containing pages 8 and 1 onto the back of the sheet containing pages 2 and 7.

Then copy the sheet containing pages 6 and 3 onto the back of the sheet containing pages 4 and 5.

Printing Mail Merge Documents

When you print a mail merge document, Publisher prints the results of the Merge operation, meaning that each copy of the publication contains an entry from the address list. The Print Merge command offers specialized options that can help you test whether the mail merge is working properly. In addition, several of Publisher's standard print options have new significance when you are printing a mail merge publication.

Print a Merged Document

1 On the File menu, choose Print Merge. The Print Merge dialog box appears.

Page layout options for mail merge labels. In the Page Setup dialog box (available from the File menu), Publisher offers over 60 page layouts for Avery labels—the standard brand for sheets of multiple labels. Each layout is identified by an Avery product number.

If you are not using Avery labels, you can still choose an appropriate layout based on the label size and the description of the layout given in the lower left corner of the dialog box.

Print a Merged Document *(continued)*

2 Select All Entries to print all the entries in your data source, or enter a range of entries to be printed. These print options reflect any filter or sort criteria you applied to the data source.

Open this drop-down list box to specify where on a sheet of labels Publisher should begin printing. For example, if you've already used two rows of labels from a sheet of labels, you can begin printing at row 3. If you are not printing labels, this option will be unavailable.

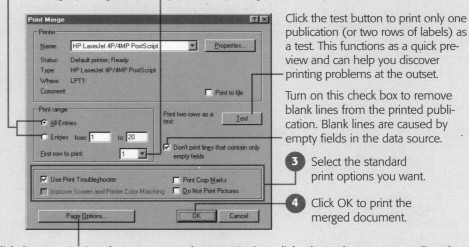

Click the test button to print only one publication (or two rows of labels) as a test. This functions as a quick preview and can help you discover printing problems at the outset.

Turn on this check box to remove blank lines from the printed publication. Blank lines are caused by empty fields in the data source.

3 Select the standard print options you want.

4 Click OK to print the merged document.

Click the Page Options button to open the Page Options dialog box, where you can adjust the placement of labels on the page. This is an especially useful tool when working with non-standard sheets of labels.

Printing Full-Color Documents

Publisher can print full-color documents on any Windows 95–compatible color printer. Digital color printers are typically limited to resolutions of 300 or 600 dpi, though you might find printers that offer slightly higher resolutions of 360 or 720 dpi. You can print a color document to a color printer attached to your computer or to a remote color printer at a service bureau.

Can I generate full-color separations with Publisher?
No, Publisher cannot create full-color separations. If you plan to reproduce your publication at a commercial printer, the service bureau or printing company can add the color images or full-color tints that you specify. For example, you can design your entire publication in black and white, using gray-scale photographs for sizing and positioning purposes. You would then ask the printer to substitute color tints and color halftone images at press time.

For information about sending files to a service bureau or commercial printer, see pages 301 through 307.

For more information about colors, tints, shades, patterns, and gradients, see Chapter 8.

Full-color documents can contain any number of colors. The colors can be imported as part of a picture file or an OLE object, or they can be created in Publisher.

Picking Colors for Full-Color Output

Publisher provides a three-tiered palette system that ranges from quick-pick color options to the full spectrum of computer-generated colors. The quick-pick palette offers you 30 standard colors and 5 gray shades. The Colors dialog box provides a basic palette of 72 colors and 12 gray shades as well as the option to customize a color. In the Colors dialog box, you can mix colors numerically by entering values into text boxes. Entering specific values allows you to match object colors precisely. You can either identify a color using the hue, saturation, and luminescence (HSL) system or specify a color using red, green, and blue (RGB) values. The RGB color model matches the color system used by your monitor, which produces the full spectrum of colors by mixing red, green, and blue primaries.

You can display the quick-pick palette from different locations in Publisher. For example, the palette appears whenever you open the Color drop-down list box in the Border, Character, Fancy First Letter, and Fill Patterns and Shading dialog boxes.

Choose a Color from the Quick-Pick Palette

1. Select the object to which you want to apply a color.
2. Click the Object Color button on the Format toolbar to access the quick-pick palette.
3. Select a color by clicking the color swatch. As soon as you select a color, it is applied to the object and you automatically return to your document.

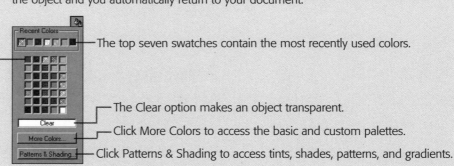

The top seven swatches contain the most recently used colors.

The Clear option makes an object transparent.

Click More Colors to access the basic and custom palettes.

Click Patterns & Shading to access tints, shades, patterns, and gradients.

Why can't I activate the option to mark colors that will not print well on my printer? This option is offered only for color printers, and even then it is available only if the printer supports the Image Color Matching (ICM) system. You must also turn on the Improve Screen And Printer Color Matching check box in the Options dialog box (available from the Tools menu).

 For more information about the Windows 95 Image Color Matching system, see pages 293 through 296.

Choose a Color from the Basic Palette

1 Select the object to which you want to apply a color.

2 Open the Format menu and choose Fill Color. (Or click the More Colors button on the quick-pick palette.) The Colors dialog box appears.

3 Select the Basic Colors option.

Colors in a particular column work well together in a design.

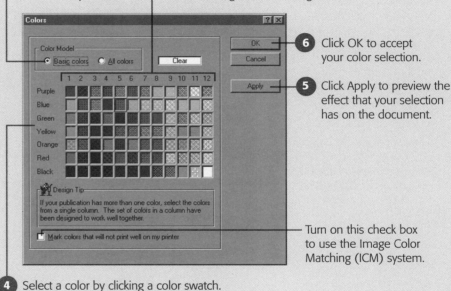

6 Click OK to accept your color selection.

5 Click Apply to preview the effect that your selection has on the document.

Turn on this check box to use the Image Color Matching (ICM) system.

4 Select a color by clicking a color swatch.

Specify a Custom Color in the Colors Dialog Box

1 Select the object to which you want to apply a color.

2 Open the Format menu and choose Fill Color. (Or click the More Colors button on the quick-pick palette.) The Colors dialog box appears.

Specify a Custom Color in the Colors Dialog Box *(continued)*

3 Select the All Colors option to display the custom palette. You can access any of 16.7 million colors in the custom palette.

4 Click in this box to place the crossbar at your chosen hue and saturation. Move the crossbar left and right to pick a hue. Move the crossbar up and down to pick a saturation (also called intensity). Colors are at full intensity at the top of the box and are grayer toward the bottom of the box.

Publisher previews the color you choose as accurately as possible. Pixels will be dithered to create the color if necessary.

Whenever it is impossible to apply a dithered color to an object, Publisher uses this solid color instead. Solid colors are typically applied to pattern fills and the outlines of WordArt letters.

7 Click OK to accept the new color.

6 Click Apply to preview the effect that your selection has on the document.

5 Move this arrow to pick the luminescence, or lightness, of the color. The luminescence is a value on a black-to-white scale.

Colors

Color Model
○ Basic colors ● All colors

OK
Cancel
Apply

Hue: 179   Red: 73
Sat: 62   Green: 212
Lum: 56   Blue: 210

Color   Solid

☐ Mark colors that will not print well on my printer

Turn on this check box to use the Image Color Matching system.

Instead of picking colors visually, enter a value from 0 through 359 in the Hue text box. In the Saturation text box, enter a value from 0 (pure gray) through 100 (full saturation). In the Luminescence text box, enter a value from 0 (black) through 100 (white).

Instead of picking colors visually, enter a value from 0 (no color) through 255 (maximum color) in each of the Red, Green, and Blue text boxes. As you increase the intensity of the color, you also make the color lighter. Entering a value of 255 in each of the three text boxes, for example, produces pure white.

See accurate colors on screen. The number of colors that you see on your computer monitor will vary depending on the video mode you are using. The standard VGA resolution, for example, can produce only 16 colors. All other colors are *simulated* with a process known as dithering. Dithered colors are not accurate. If your document contains only flat color (meaning solid colors, tints, and shades), a 256-color video mode should be sufficient. But for the most accurate view of the colors in your document (and especially in imported pictures), your monitor and video card should be capable of displaying 16.7 million colors. This video mode is often referred to as true color, or 24-bit color.

On-Screen Color and Printer Color Compatibility

The colors you see and choose on screen might not be the colors that appear in the final printout. Computer monitors and color printers use different—and not entirely compatible—color systems. The colors you see on your computer monitor are created using the RGB color model. However, images produced by a color printer rely on the CMYK color model. Translating RGB values to CMYK values can result in color shifts. The following table compares treatment of color by monitors and printers.

Comparison of Color Technologies		
Characteristic	**Computer Monitor**	**Color Printer**
Color primaries	Red, green, and blue (RGB) phosphors.	Cyan, magenta, yellow, and black (CMYK, where K stands for black) inks.
Color properties	Phosphors emit light.	Inks reflect light.
Color mixing	Is additive. Colors get lighter as you increase intensity. Full intensity of all three primaries is white.	Is subtractive. Colors get darker as you increase intensity. Full intensity of all four colors is black.
Number of available colors	The RGB color system can produce a wide color spectrum of up to 16.7 million colors. The RGB color system can simulate CMYK printing.	Color printers vary dramatically in resolution and subsequently in the number of colors they can produce. Color printers can produce only a small subset of the RGB spectrum.

Image Color Matching

Windows 95 provides an effective color matching mechanism called Image Color Matching (ICM). You don't need to understand exactly how ICM works in order to use it, but an overview of its functionality is useful here. The ICM engine reads special files called ICC (International Color Consortium) device profiles. These profiles contain information about how a particular device, such as a monitor or printer, defines colors. The ICM engine then translates from one device profile to another. ICM provides two important services:

- It allows you to see an accurate screen preview of the final printed colors.
- It alerts you to colors that will not print well on the chosen output device.

Publisher can take advantage of ICM only if all of the following are true:

- You have properly identified your monitor in the Display Properties dialog box. (Double-click the Display icon in Control Panel.)
- Your printer supports ICM, and you have turned on the feature in the printer Properties dialog box.
- You have turned on ICM in Publisher.

Windows 95 ships with several color printer drivers that include ICC profiles. You must install the appropriate printer driver, and then you must turn on ICM for the printer. The exact structure of the printer Properties dialog box will change depending on the printer, but in general you can follow these steps.

Turn On the ICM Feature in the Printer Properties Dialog Box

1 On the Windows 95 Start menu, choose Settings. On the cascading menu, choose the Printers folder.

2 In the Printers folder, right-click the icon for your printer, and then choose Properties on the shortcut menu.

3 In the printer Properties dialog box, select the Graphics tab.

4 Select the Use Image Color Matching option.

5 Click the Choose Image Color Matching Method button. The Image Color Matching dialog box appears.

Have your printer perform color matching calculations. You can increase your system's speed by using the printer's processor, rather than your computer's processor, to perform the calculations for color matching. This technique will work only if you have a PostScript Level 2 color printer. PostScript Level 2 printers can use color dictionaries to map screen colors to printer colors. To take advantage of this feature, choose Perform Image Color Matching On The Printer to download a color dictionary to the printer with each job, or choose Print Using Printer Calibration to use a color dictionary that has already been downloaded to the printer. Though this method of color matching will free up your system resources, it may result in less accurate color matching.

Turn On the ICM Feature in the Printer Properties Dialog Box *(continued)*

6 Select a color matching method. Be aware that color matching on the host (the computer that sends the document to the printer) can slow down system performance.

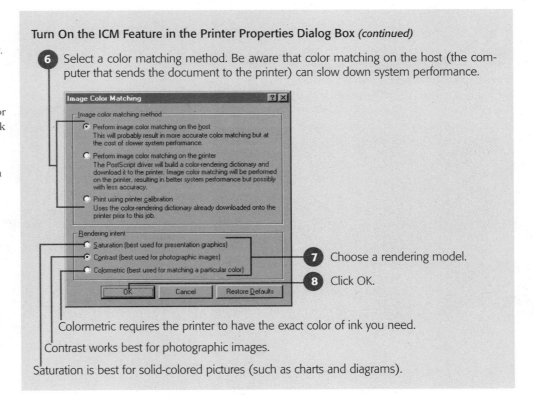

7 Choose a rendering model.

8 Click OK.

Colormetric requires the printer to have the exact color of ink you need.

Contrast works best for photographic images.

Saturation is best for solid-colored pictures (such as charts and diagrams).

Turn On ICM in Publisher

1 Open the Tools menu and choose Options. The Options dialog box appears.

2 Select the General tab.

3 Turn on the Improve Screen And Printer Color Matching check box.

4 Click OK. If the current printer does not have an ICC profile, or if the printer has not been configured to use ICM, an alert box will appear. Return to the preceding procedure and configure ICM in the printer Properties dialog box. Then return to step 1.

What colors print well?
Most of the basic colors on Publisher's palette (as displayed in the Colors dialog box) are very bright. These colors are difficult to reproduce on desktop printers. Use the custom palette to specify a color that will reproduce well on your printer.

Turn On ICM in Publisher *(continued)*

5 Select an object.

6 On the Format menu, choose Fill Color. The Colors dialog box appears.

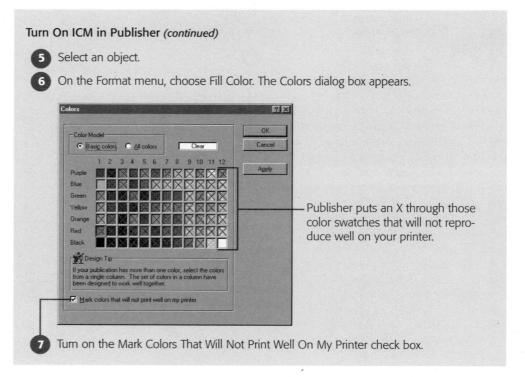

Publisher puts an X through those color swatches that will not reproduce well on your printer.

7 Turn on the Mark Colors That Will Not Print Well On My Printer check box.

For more information about setting up an outside printer, see pages 302 through 304.

Printing Spot-Color Documents

Publisher can prepare color separations to be used on a high-resolution commercial offset printing press, with these restrictions:

- Color separations are limited to spot colors. You cannot generate full-color (also known as four-color or process color) separations from Publisher.

- The maximum number of colors in a document is three: black, Spot Color 1, and Spot Color 2.

- To access Publisher's spot-color functions, you must set up your document to print on a commercial printing press.

Can I print a spot color to my local desktop printer?

Desktop printing devices generate either black-and-white or full-color output. If you print a spot-color document to a local desktop printer (in order to generate a proof of the publication), Publisher will simulate the spot color (and all of its tints) using either shades of gray or a mixture of cyan, magenta, yellow, and black inks. In order to print the actual spot color, you must generate separations and have your publication produced on a commercial offset printing press.

For more information about printing spot-color proofs, see pages 299 through 300.

When you set up a document for spot-color output, you must tell Publisher which color or colors you want to use. After you've set up the spot color (or colors) for a document, your fill choices are limited to tints, patterns, or gradients of the spot colors and of black.

Use a spot color to highlight text, drawn objects, and frames. The following logo illustrates how spot color can enhance a design.

Recolor imported artwork or WordArt elements with a spot color.

Create variation by using tints within a design, such as the 10 percent tint on the background shown here.

Choose a Spot Color (or Colors) for Output on a Commercial Printing Press

1 Open the File menu and choose Outside Print Setup. The Outside Print Setup dialog box appears.

What can I do if the color I want to use doesn't appear in the Spot Color drop-down list box? Choose the closest match from the 30 available colors. Think of these colors as placeholders. They give you a screen preview that approximates the final printed output. You will pick the ink color that will actually be used on press from a swatch book supplied by your commercial printer. The printing industry standard for colors is the Pantone Matching System (PMS).

How knockouts work. Turning off Overprint Black Objects creates a knockout in the second color. A knockout occurs when black objects print against a white background, even if "holes" must be cut into (or knocked out of) the second color. You should seek the advice of your commercial printer before you turn off this check box. Knockouts are prone to misregistration on press; ugly white gaps can appear when the black printing plate and the second-color printing plate are misaligned.

Choose a Spot Color (or Colors) for Output on a Commercial Printing Press *(continued)*

2 Select the Spot Color option.

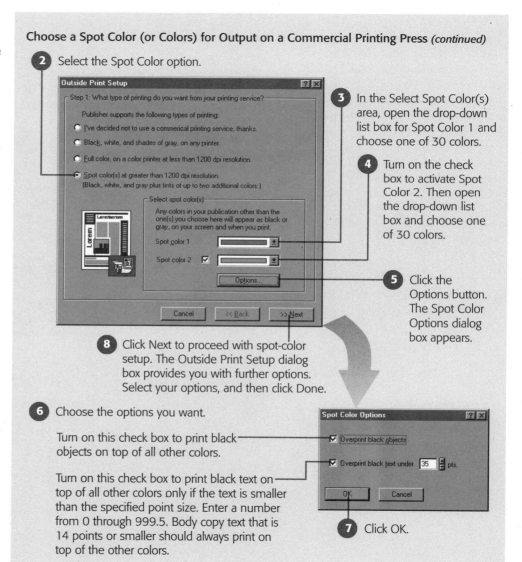

3 In the Select Spot Color(s) area, open the drop-down list box for Spot Color 1 and choose one of 30 colors.

4 Turn on the check box to activate Spot Color 2. Then open the drop-down list box and choose one of 30 colors.

5 Click the Options button. The Spot Color Options dialog box appears.

8 Click Next to proceed with spot-color setup. The Outside Print Setup dialog box provides you with further options. Select your options, and then click Done.

6 Choose the options you want.

Turn on this check box to print black objects on top of all other colors.

Turn on this check box to print black text on top of all other colors only if the text is smaller than the specified point size. Enter a number from 0 through 999.5. Body copy text that is 14 points or smaller should always print on top of the other colors.

7 Click OK.

Why can't I access the Colors dialog box? When you work in a spot-color document, Publisher doesn't allow you to create new colors. You can only work with tints, patterns, and gradients of black and the spot colors contained in your document.

Why can't I choose a shade for one of the spot colors? Publisher only allows you to pick shades of colors when the custom palette is available to you. Shades look like colors with black added to them, but technically shades are new colors. You can't add new colors to a spot-color document—you can work only with tints of black, Spot Color 1, and Spot Color 2.

Can I print spot-color separations using Encapsulated PostScript files? No. Publisher can't access any color information stored inside the EPS file. When generating spot-color separations from a document that contains EPS files, Publisher places all of the image data in the EPS file on the black printout.

For more information about importing picture files, see pages 182 through 185 in Chapter 9.

Format an Object with a Spot Color

1 Select the object to which you want to apply a color.

2 Click the Object Color button on the Format toolbar to access the spot-color palette.

3 Select a color by clicking the color swatch. You can select black or one of 10 black tints; Spot Color 1 or one of 10 tints created from Spot Color 1; Spot Color 2 or one of 10 tints created from Spot Color 2; or white.

4 As soon as you select a color, it is applied to the object and you are returned to your document.

Printing Spot-Color Proofs

A desktop printer can't accommodate a spot-color document. Desktop printers either print in black and white or in full color, so you'll have to send your documents to a commercial printing press for final printing. You can, however, print a proof of a spot-color document on your desktop printer. You can print two kinds of proofs, seen in the following illustrations:

A composite proof prints black, Spot Color 1, and Spot Color 2 on a single sheet of paper. This proof allows you to check how elements on the page register with one another. Notice that Publisher converts colors to shades of gray on a composite printout.

A separated proof prints black, Spot Color 1, and Spot Color 2 on different sheets of paper. This proof shows the structure of the separation—including surprinting and knockouts. Notice that Publisher prints the true tint percentage of each color. A 100 percent tint of a light yellow, for example, prints as solid black.

Preparing imported pictures for spot-color output. When you work in a spot-color document, you can print in only two or three colors. If you import color artwork into the document, Publisher automatically converts the colors to black and tints of black. You can add color to the picture, but you are limited to tints of the spot color you specified in the Outside Print Setup dialog boxes. Use the Recolor Picture command on the Format menu to change the colors into tints of black or tints of the spot color.

Print a Proof of Your Spot-Color Document

1 On the File menu, choose Outside Print Setup and confirm that you are printing a spot-color document.

2 On the File menu, select the Print Proof command. The Print Proof dialog box appears.

3 In the Print Range area, select All or Current Page. Notice that you can't print a specified number of pages.

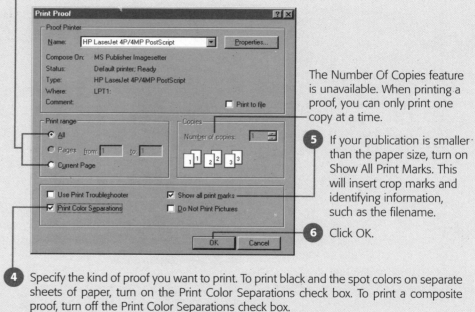

The Number Of Copies feature is unavailable. When printing a proof, you can only print one copy at a time.

5 If your publication is smaller than the paper size, turn on Show All Print Marks. This will insert crop marks and identifying information, such as the filename.

6 Click OK.

4 Specify the kind of proof you want to print. To print black and the spot colors on separate sheets of paper, turn on the Print Color Separations check box. To print a composite proof, turn off the Print Color Separations check box.

Printing on Colored Paper

Even if you own a black-and-white printer, you can easily add color to your publications by printing on colored paper. Laser-compatible papers come in a wide variety of colors. Many specialty papers are available in multicolor designs. If you design your document to be printed on one of these papers, you might

How do I choose a special paper with the right orientation? Be sure to select a special paper design that is compatible with the orientation of your document. For example, if you try to use a vertical paper design for a document with a horizontal orientation, Publisher simply rotates the paper—it does not resize your layout to fit the paper.

 Why don't the special paper designs print along with the rest of my publication? The Special Paper designs are screen previews only; Publisher does not print them. If you want these designs to appear in your publications, you need to buy the preprinted papers from PaperDirect at 1-800-272-7377.

 Why is the Special Paper command on the View menu grayed out? Your publication is set up to be printed by an outside service bureau or commercial printer. The Special Paper command is available only if you are printing to a local printer (a desktop printer connected to your computer).

find it helpful to see a screen preview of it. Publisher provides screen previews of over 30 popular papers for letterheads, brochures, postcards, and business cards. The papers are all available from PaperDirect, a paper manufacturer.

Turn the Display of Special Papers On and Off

1 On the View menu, choose Special Paper. The Special Paper dialog box appears.

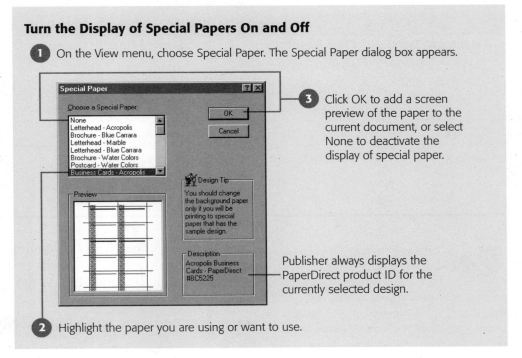

3 Click OK to add a screen preview of the paper to the current document, or select None to deactivate the display of special paper.

Publisher always displays the PaperDirect product ID for the currently selected design.

2 Highlight the paper you are using or want to use.

Preparing Documents for a Service Bureau or a Commercial Printer

Publisher provides a special feature to help you prepare your publication for high-resolution output at a service bureau or on a commercial printing press. There is no longer a strict division of labor between a service bureau and a commercial printer, so you'll need to research the services of the company you're considering using.

The following table summarizes the types of documents that can be created for an outside printer, and provides information to help you decide whether to take the document to a service bureau or a commercial printer for output.

Description of Output from Outside Printers			
Document Type	**Final Resolution**	**Service Bureau Output**	**Commercial Printer Output**
Black-and-white	600 dpi through 2540 dpi	Paper as final output. Reproduction-quality paper for making printing plates. Film for making printing plates.	Film for making printing plates. Note that some printers do not produce film; they require that you first send the file to a service bureau for film output.
Full-color	300 dpi through 600 dpi	Paper as final output.	Not applicable.
Spot-color	1200 dpi through 2540 dpi	Reproduction-quality paper for making printing plates. Film for making printing plates.	Film for making printing plates. Note that some printers do not produce film; they require that you first send the file to a service bureau for film output.

Publisher's outside printer drivers. When you install Publisher, two generic printers are added to your system: MS Publisher Color Printer and MS Publisher Imagesetter. These are generic PostScript drivers that prepare a document properly for high-resolution or full-color output.

If you want to print to an outside printer, you must set up the document—including choosing colors—*before* you design your publication. To do so, follow the steps in the three Outside Print Setup dialog boxes.

Prepare Your Document for an Outside Printer

 On the File menu, choose Outside Print Setup. The first Outside Print Setup dialog box appears.

For more information about choosing Spot Color 1 and Spot Color 2, see pages 296 through 298.

Restricting your color choices to black and white. When you print a black-and-white document to a local printer, you can work with Publisher's full-color palette. At print time, the color information is converted to shades of gray.

When you send a document to an outside printer, however, adding color to the document can cause time-consuming and costly printing problems. Publisher helps you avoid these printing headaches by restricting your color choices to black, white, and shades of gray when you indicate that you are creating a black-and-white document for outside printing. The Colors dialog box is not available to you, and the palette accessed from the Object Color button contains only black and tints of black.

Prepare Your Document for an Outside Printer *(continued)*

To return your document to local printing mode, select this option.

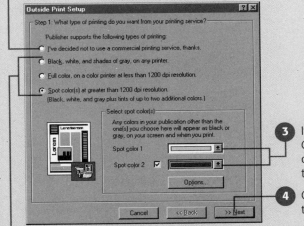

3 If you choose the Spot Color option, select one or two spot colors from the drop-down list boxes.

4 Click Next to proceed to the second dialog box.

2 Choose one of the three color options: black-and-white, full-color, or spot-color printing.

5 In the second Outside Print Setup dialog box, select either Publisher's generic outside printer driver or a specific driver that has been recommended or supplied by your service bureau or commercial printer. You can access a modified Print Setup dialog box to choose a specific printer by clicking the button in the dialog box.

6 Click Next. The third Outside Print Setup dialog box appears.

What is the Outside Printing Checklist? This checklist explains how to do the following:

@ Describe the project using terminology the service bureau or commercial printer will understand.

@ Get an accurate quote of the project's cost.

You can't read the Outside Printing Checklist on screen. You must click the button and print a copy to paper.

Two printers for each publication. When you set up a document for outside printing, Publisher maintains two different printers for each publication. The first printer is the device you specified in the Outside Print Setup dialog box. The second printer is your local printer, which is maintained normally to print proofs of black-and-white, full-color, and spot-color documents.

Prepare Your Document for an Outside Printer *(continued)*

7 Indicate the printing options you want.

Turn on this check box to include crop marks, registration marks, and identifying information such as the color name, page range, publication name, and date/time stamp.

Turn on this check box to have Publisher choose a special paper size, called Extra, which is large enough to accommodate printer marks.

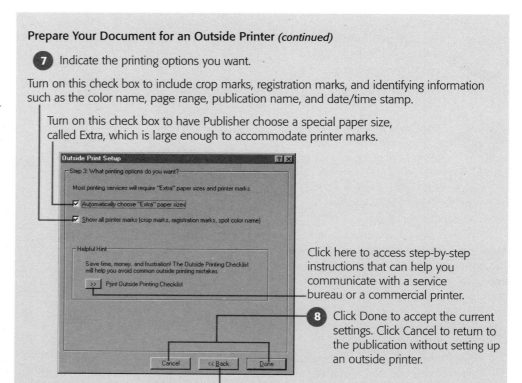

Click here to access step-by-step instructions that can help you communicate with a service bureau or a commercial printer.

8 Click Done to accept the current settings. Click Cancel to return to the publication without setting up an outside printer.

Click Back to return to a previous screen to review or change settings.

Sending a Publication to an Outside Printer

Once you've set up a document for outside printing, you have the following three output options, which are available from the File menu:

@ You can use your local printer to generate a proof of the document.

@ You can create a PostScript printer file using an outside printer driver.

@ You can use the Save As command to create a copy of the document to send to the outside printer.

There are advantages and disadvantages to each method, and your choice might be limited by the capabilities of the outside printer.

Printing on a non-PostScript printer. The Outside Print Setup dialog box uses a generic PostScript driver by default. If you will print your document to a non-PostScript printer, you must install a driver for that specific printer and then choose it in the Outside Print Setup dialog box.

How do I install a new printer driver? Double-click the Add Printer icon in the Windows 95 Printers folder to install a new printer driver on your system.

The Print To File check box. The Print To File check box, in the Print To Outside Printer dialog box, lets you print your publications on printers that are not physically connected to your computer. You can use it to print your publication using any off-site printer. For example, you might want to create a publication at home but print it at the office, where you have a high-resolution or color printer.

Sending a PostScript File to an Outside Printer

When you set up your document to print to an outside printer, Publisher chooses a generic PostScript printer driver for the current document. PostScript files are compatible with high-resolution, professional-quality output devices at service bureaus and commercial printers. Because PostScript output is not device-specific, the same PostScript file can print on any PostScript printer.

When you create a PostScript print file, you are translating Publisher's native file format into a format that contains all the information needed to print the file, including all the font information and all the commands necessary to operate the PostScript printer. Publisher assumes that the outside printer is not connected to your computer and therefore always stores the print file on disk.

Create a PostScript Print File

1 On the File menu, choose Print To Outside Printer. The Print To Outside Printer dialog box appears.

2 Select the appropriate options.

Indicate the pages you want to print.

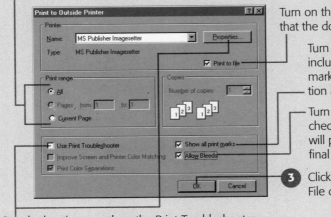

Turn on this check box to be sure that the document will print to a file.

Turn on this check box to include crop marks, registration marks, and identifying information about the file.

Turn on the Allow Bleeds check box if a tint or image will print off the edge of the final trimmed page.

3 Click OK. The Print To File dialog box appears.

Standard options—such as the Print Troubleshooter, paper size, and layout options—remain available.

Transporting large files to an outside printer. A 3.5-inch floppy disk can hold 1.44 megabytes of information. If your file is too large to fit on a floppy disk, you can transport the file using one of the following methods:

- Use a third-party compression utility, such as Pkzip or WinZip, which reduces the size of the file. You must make sure that the service bureau or commercial printer has the same version of the utility to decompress the file.

- If your system contains a Syquest, Bernoulli, Zip, or Jaz drive, use high-capacity removable media. Confirm that the outside printer can read the format.

- If your computer is equipped with a modem and the outside printer accepts files via modem, use standard telecommunications software to transfer the files over the phone line.

- Use the Windows 95 Backup utility to copy the file to several disks. The outside printer must be able to use Backup to restore the file from floppy disk to the computer system from which the publication will ultimately be printed.

Create a PostScript Print File *(continued)*

4. In the File Name text box, type an output filename that clearly identifies the publication, including an extension (for example, .prn) that identifies the file as a printer-ready document.

5. In the Folders list box, choose an appropriate location on your hard disk for the printer file.

6. Click OK.

7. After Publisher has created the file, it will ask if you want to print a final proof and Infosheet. Click Yes to print these documents, or click No to return to the publication.

8. When the file has been successfully printed to your hard disk, use Windows Explorer to transfer the PRN file to a floppy disk (or other removable media), which you will take to the outside printer.

Print a Publication Using a Printer Not Connected to Your Computer

1. Copy, restore, or decompress the print file from the floppy disk (or other removable media) to the Windows folder on the hard disk of the computer system that is attached to the printer you want to use.

2. On the Windows 95 Start menu, select Programs. On the cascading menu, select MS-DOS Prompt.

3. Use the MS-DOS Copy command to transfer the print file to the printer. Type the following command as it appears below, including spacing and punctuation, but substitute the name of your file for *filename*.

```
copy filename.prn lpt1: /b
```

Be sure to type the correct parallel port information for the computer system you are using. For example, the printer might be attached to the first parallel port (LPT1:) or to a second one (LPT2:). If the printer is attached to a serial port (such as COM1:), you must reroute the printer to a parallel port before copying the file. Also, be sure to add the /b parameter to the command line. The /b ensures that the entire file is printed, even if it contains more than one page.

See the Windows 95 online help system for details about ports.

Should I use TrueType fonts or PostScript fonts? Most Publisher users take advantage of the free TrueType fonts that ship with Publisher. Be sure to alert your service bureau or your commercial printer to the fact that you use TrueType fonts *before* you send your files for output. Many service bureaus and commercial printers have an established collection of PostScript fonts and don't like to deal with TrueType fonts. In the long run, it might be less trouble for you to purchase PostScript fonts so that your system duplicates at least a portion of the service bureau's or commercial printer's font library.

For more information about OLE objects, see Chapter 10.

Sending a Publisher Document to an Outside Printer

You can send the original Publisher document to an outside printer, but only if the service bureau or commercial printer uses the current version of Publisher. Before you send a Publisher document, confirm that the outside printer has a copy of Microsoft Publisher 97. Older versions of Publisher will not be able to open or print Publisher 97 files.

Sending a Publisher document to the outside printer has one major advantage over sending a PostScript file: if the service bureau or commercial printer encounters a printing problem, it can open the file and fix it. The major disadvantage is that Publisher documents are "live" in the sense that they can contain links to other objects or services on your computer system. For example, a Publisher document doesn't contain fonts; it contains instructions that refer to fonts installed on your system. Likewise, OLE objects point to other applications that might or might not be installed on the outside printer's computer system. Discrepancies between your computer system and the outside printer's computer system can create printing problems.

Font Issues

Be sure that the outside printer has the fonts you are using in your design. If it does not, its output device will likely substitute different fonts at print time. When you use a standard Windows 95 font such as Arial or Times New Roman, the substitution might be nearly impossible to detect. When you use a decorative or unusual font, however, the substituted font will look very different and will probably not be acceptable.

OLE Object Issues

If your publication contains OLE objects, the outside printer must have the source applications installed on its computer system in order to make any last-minute content changes to the OLE objects before printing. If the source program is not available, the outside printer will be able to display the OLE object on screen and print it but no changes can be made to the OLE object.

Recognizing the font types in your publication. Publisher allows you to mix and match font formats within a single publication. You can guarantee high-quality print-outs—and avoid printing problems—by using only scalable TrueType or Post-Script fonts in your designs. You can recognize different font types by the icons in the Font drop-down list box in the Character dialog box (available from the Format menu when a text object is selected).

The Printer symbol indicates either a printer-resident font or PostScript font.

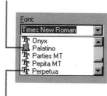

The Double-T icon indicates a TrueType font.

For a more complete discussion of bitmapped and vector (scalable) formats, see pages 179 through 180 in Chapter 9.

Preparing a Print Information Sheet

You should include an information sheet as part of the package you send to a service bureau or commercial printer. Publisher can automatically generate an information sheet. Open the document you want to send to the outside printer. (The document must be open for Publisher to generate an information sheet.) Then open the File menu and select Print InfoSheet.

The InfoSheet is printed to the default printer. It includes valuable information that you and the outside printer can use to troubleshoot problems. For example, the InfoSheet lists all the fonts contained in a publication. You can use the list to confirm that the outside printer has the correct fonts to print your publication.

Using Appropriate Fonts in Your Documents

The appearance of the printed text in your publications is largely determined by the quality of the fonts you have available. A basic understanding of font technology can help you print more efficiently, improve the quality of your publications, and avoid common printing problems.

Scalable Font Formats

Desktop publishers rely on scalable fonts (fonts that can be scaled to produce characters in varying sizes) in two formats: TrueType and PostScript. TrueType fonts are directly supported by Windows 95. When you install Publisher, you also install numerous TrueType fonts. TrueType fonts are fully scalable and provide accurate screen previews of the printed page.

PostScript fonts are supported by the PostScript printer language, which is why many service bureaus and commercial printers prefer that you use them. PostScript fonts are fully scalable. To see an accurate screen preview of a PostScript font, or to print a PostScript font to a non-PostScript printer, you must use a type manager utility, such as Adobe Type Manager.

Printer-Resident Fonts

Resident fonts are built into your desktop printer's read-only memory (ROM) or stored on a cartridge that plugs into the printer. Some printers, such as dot-matrix

Limitations of bitmapped resident fonts. Printer-resident bitmapped fonts (the fonts most commonly found in dot-matrix printers) cannot be rotated or printed as reverse white type against a black background. If you are having trouble printing text upside down (as required by the Side Fold Card and Tent Card layouts), or reversing type in a normal text frame, convert all the problematic objects to WordArt. WordArt is sent to the printer as a picture—not as text.

Why does the text in my screen display look so different from the printout? Publisher always attempts to give you a WYSIWYG (What You See Is What You Get) screen display. If the text on screen looks very different from the text that prints, you are probably using a printer-resident font for which you do not have screen equivalents. To solve this problem, use TrueType fonts, or if you are using PostScript fonts, install a type manager utility such as Adobe Type Manager, which generates accurate screen previews.

For more information about Publisher's help system, see Chapter 1.

printers or very old laser printers, use a bitmapped format for their resident fonts. Other printers, notably laser and PostScript printers, use a scalable font format for resident fonts. Which resident fonts Windows 95 makes available to you depends on the type of printer you installed. Printer-resident fonts print more quickly than fonts stored on the host computer.

Pinpointing Printing Problems: The Print Troubleshooter

The Print Troubleshooter is part of Publisher's online help system. It pinpoints the cause of many common printing problems and suggests solutions to them. The Print Troubleshooter can help you investigate problems with printing text, pictures, patterns, and gradients. It also deals with basic printer problems such as insufficient printer memory, insufficient disk space for spooling, and printer configuration. You can access the Print Troubleshooter via the Print command on the File menu. Once your publication has been printed, the Print Troubleshooter appears automatically. You can also type *Print Troubleshooter* in the help index at any time.

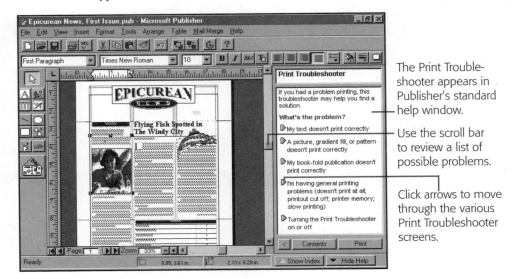

The Print Trouble-shooter appears in Publisher's standard help window.

Use the scroll bar to review a list of possible problems.

Click arrows to move through the various Print Troubleshooter screens.

Printer Memory Problems and Solutions

A laser printer's performance is highly dependent on the amount of memory it has. Older laser printers might not contain sufficient memory to print an entire page of text and graphics. Newer laser printers use sophisticated compression techniques to maximize memory. You can encounter memory problems if you've created a complex document with a wide variety of fonts or large bitmapped pictures. Memory problems are usually easy to identify. The printer might print half the page on one sheet of paper and the other half on a second sheet of paper, or it might print nothing at all.

If you do run into printing problems because of a memory shortage, try one or more of the following fixes:

- Reduce the number of fonts in your publication.

- Substitute printer-resident fonts or cartridge fonts, which don't require printer memory, for fonts that must be downloaded to the printer.

- Substitute WordArt, which prints as a picture, for downloaded fonts.

- Lower the resolution of scanned or bitmapped pictures. (Refer to Chapter 9 for the recommended resolutions for scanned pictures.)

- Lower the resolution of the printout. A page of graphics at 150 dpi requires only half as much printer memory as the same page printed at 300 dpi. But be warned: the print quality will be noticeably poorer.

- Use the Print Range option to print one page of a long document at a time.

- To proofread your text alone, turn on the Do Not Print Pictures check box in the Print dialog box. Only the text of your publication will print.

- If memory problems persist, consider adding more memory to your printer. (Refer to your printer's manual for specific instructions.)

PART 2

Design Projects

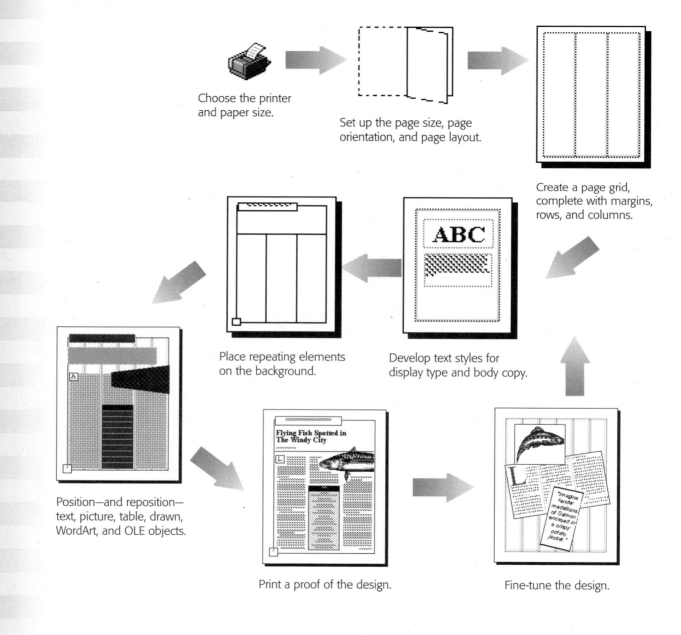

Choose the printer and paper size.

Set up the page size, page orientation, and page layout.

Create a page grid, complete with margins, rows, and columns.

Place repeating elements on the background.

Develop text styles for display type and body copy.

Position—and reposition—text, picture, table, drawn, WordArt, and OLE objects.

Print a proof of the design.

Fine-tune the design.

Flying Fish Spotted in The Windy City

"Imagine tender medallions of Salmon encased in a crispy potato jacket."

An Overview of the Design Process

There is no denying that the design process begins with inspiration. But there are certain concrete tasks—shown in the diagram on the facing page—that are common to all design projects. As you develop your own layouts, you'll discover that the design process is iterative. The only way to develop the right combination of words, pictures, and graphics elements is to experiment with variations of a layout.

Where can I find step-by-step instructions to help me re-create the design projects?
This chapter and Chapters 16 through 28 contain discussions of design theory as well as general instructions for each design project. For example, each project chapter begins with the directive to set up the publication's page size and layout guides but does not give specific instructions regarding Publisher's Page Setup and Layout Guides dialog boxes. If you want step-by-step instructions for using Publisher's tools and dialog boxes, you must refer to the appropriate chapters in Part 1, "Publisher 97 Fundamentals."

Getting Started: Project Preliminaries

There is always a correlation between a publication's purpose and the methods used to produce it. Before you begin your project, ask yourself these basic questions:

- Who is the intended audience of this publication?
- What are the purpose and the expected life span of this publication?
- What is a reasonable production budget?
- What is the delivery method for this project?

Taking the time to consider and answer these questions can help you make important decisions about your project. On a practical level, you should use this information to determine the type and cost of the following:

- Printing method
- Publication size
- Paper selection
- Choice of artwork

Planning a Publication

Three sample projects are described in the following tables. As you examine them, try to see the relationship between the project profile and the production plan.

Sample Project Number 1: Flyer for One-Day Sale		
Project Profile	Intended Audience	Local customers with easy access to the store
	Life Span and Purpose	1 week, to alert customers to savings and encourage them to visit the store
	Budget	Inexpensive
	Delivery	Store handouts, direct mail
Production Plan	Printer	Desktop laser
	Document Size	Standard, 8.5-by-11-inch letter-size document, folded to fit a standard Number 10 envelope
	Paper	Laser-compatible paper
	Artwork	Black-and-white clip art

Sample Project Number 2: Marketing Media Kit		
Project Profile	Intended Audience	Potential customers
	Life Span and Purpose	1 year, to provide information about the company's staff, products, and services
	Budget	Expensive
	Delivery	Personal sales calls, direct mail
Production Plan	Printer	Outside printer
	Document Size	Nonstandard, 7-by-10-inch document, mailed in a custom 7.5-by-10.5-inch envelope
	Paper	High-quality, coated paper
	Artwork	Spot-color artwork

Sample Project Number 3: Web Site		
Project Profile	Intended Audience	Potential customers, existing customers
	Life Span and Purpose	3 months, to deliver information about new products, provide customer support, and elicit customer feedback
	Budget	Moderate
	Delivery	Electronic delivery via the World Wide Web
Production Plan	Printer	Not applicable
	Document Size	Standard VGA screen
	Paper	Not applicable
	Artwork	Color bitmapped images

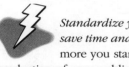

Standardize your project to save time and money. The more you standardize the production of your publication, the cheaper it will be to produce. Begin by trying to design your publication to fit on standard-size paper and in a standard-size envelope. When you vary the size of the publication, make sure that you are adhering to the requirements of printing and mailing equipment. Consult with your service bureau or commercial printer to find a document size that avoids paper waste, unnecessary handling, and extra trimming (all of which increase the cost of the job). And confirm that your publication size (meaning the envelope size, not just the page size) meets postal requirements for automated, or machinable, handling.

Printer Selection

The printer you choose will influence the design and production of your project. It's wise to consider the following printing and design issues before you begin planning a project:

- Available paper sizes. Microsoft Publisher 97 uses the current paper size when determining the imposition of pages for specially sized and folded publications. If you intend to print two-page spreads on 11-by-17-inch paper, you must confirm that the currently selected printer can handle that paper size.

- Resident fonts. The hardware-based fonts accessible to you vary from printer to printer. Only TrueType fonts will be available regardless of the printer you select.

- Document color. If you are printing to a local printer connected to your computer, Publisher gives you access to the full spectrum of computer-generated colors. The Outside Print Setup dialog box, however, restricts the number of colors to match the capabilities of your chosen output device. As an example, setting up a document for a high-resolution black-and-white printer limits your color choices to black, white, and shades of gray.

Choose an appropriate "page" size for Web publications. When you are working on electronic documents, you can choose between standard and custom screen sizes instead of page sizes. Just as with a paper-based publication, however, your choice of screen size can dramatically affect the success of your project. If your primary interest is compatibility with the widest number of computer systems, choose the Standard VGA page width. If you choose the Wide or Custom option, you run the risk of generating a Web document that is wider than your reader's screen.

For more information about selecting a printer, setting the paper size and other printer options, and managing fonts, see Chapter 14.

For more information about setting up pages, see Chapters 3 and 4. For more information about layout guides, see Chapter 4.

Page Size and Orientation

You have a lot of options when choosing how to set up your page. The decisions you make will affect the number of pages in the document, the amount of paper needed to print it, and the amount of time spent trimming and folding it. If you're mailing the publication, these decisions will also affect the cost of the envelopes (especially for an atypically sized document) and the postage.

The Book Fold layout restricts the number of pages in a publication because it requires the total number of pages to be a multiple of 4. Commercial printers often require your publications to be in multiples of 4, 8, or 16 pages.

Small publications might require extra production time (or money) to trim excess paper. This is especially time consuming if you are trimming paper manually.

Custom sizes might increase the cost of your publication, especially if you decide to mail it in envelopes. Try to design publications for less expensive standard envelope sizes, such as Number 10 (4 1/8-by-9 1/2 inches).

Grids

The key to a well-designed publication is an underlying structure, or grid, that helps you size, position, and align elements consistently. Form usually follows function, so before you set up the grid, think about the number and the type of elements you will add to your document.

Use grids when designing a Web site. When you are designing a World Wide Web publication, be sure to structure the page using a grid. Grids can prevent you from overlapping objects—a condition that causes Publisher to create graphic regions.

Use mail merge and the Page Options dialog box instead of a page grid for labels. You can set up standard page guides to mimic the layout of a sheet of labels. But doing so requires you to enter text for each label manually. Instead, set up a single label and use mail merge field codes. When Publisher prints the document, it will substitute the appropriate names and addresses for the field codes. Best of all, you can use the Page Options dialog box (accessed from the Print Dialog box) to specify how the names and addresses are to be printed on each sheet of labels.

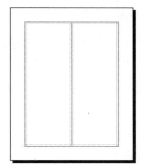

For more information about Web documents, see Chapter 11. For more information about mail merge, see Chapter 12.

The long text lines of books and technical reports are easier to read in a one-column or two-column format. Text-heavy publications do not need the flexibility of a multicolumn format.

Increasing the top page margin provides extra space for a running head—a common element in catalogs and directories.

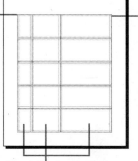

Consistent row height on each page of a document allows readers to find information quickly.

Specially sized column widths offer the layout flexibility needed by publications such as product catalogs. The columns accommodate differently sized elements, such as ID numbers, photographs, and product descriptions.

Newsletters that incorporate pictures of varying sizes and shapes require a more flexible grid composed of several columns of the same width. In general, the grid or guides should be based on the smallest common denominator that can accommodate the various elements in your layout. If your publication contains pictures of different widths, such as 1/2 and 1/3 page widths, use a six-column grid. The smallest common denominator of 1/2 and 1/3 is 1/6.

A six-column grid lets you size artwork and text frames at a number of different column measures: 1/6, 1/3, 1/2, and 2/3 page widths.

Type Choices

The power of your message depends in large part on the fonts you choose. Once you understand the basic categories and characteristics of type, you can choose fonts with confidence and combine fonts to add visual interest to your documents.

Fonts are divided into three categories:

Goudy Old Style

Serif fonts employ small lines or curves (serifs) at the ends of each stroke of a character.

Century Gothic

Sans-serif fonts are fonts without serifs. Note the straighter lines.

Lucida Handwriting

Script fonts resemble cursive handwriting.

Save type designs as text styles. Once you've developed a type design, save it as a defined text style. This allows you to use the style repeatedly, which saves you time and ensures consistency throughout a document.

For more information about text styles, see Chapter 5.

When you create your text designs, categorize text elements according to their purpose, as either display type or body copy.

EPICUREAN NEWS

Flying Fish Spotted in The Windy City

By Elizabeth Jarmen

Let's face it, Chicago is famous for stockyards, not fisheries. But times are changing. People are eating fish instead of red meat. Seafood is an important part of a heart-healthy diet because it is low in cholesterol and fat.

We're proud that the freshest fish in Chicago can be found at Epicurean Delights. The arrival of aquaculture, or fish farming as it is known among

Trout is wonderful when grilled whole over a mesquite flavored barbecue. The firm white flesh can also be filleted and boned, and then poached in white wine.

The really exciting news, however, is the introduction of Epicurean Delights' Flying Fish Service. Fish is ordered by telephone and shipped by air to arrive the next day. It's the next best thing to catching it yourself! The quick turnaround time allows us to

fresh herbs, such as savory and anise. Imagine tender medallions of salmon encased in a crispy potato jacket. Anticipate just how succulent fresh grouper can be when it is steamed in a parchment envelope with aromatic vegetables.

These recipes are particularly easy to try because they are available as prepared, ready-to-cook dishes from the Epicurean Delights kitchen. You just pop the fish into the oven,

Display type refers to text that organizes or decorates a publication.

Body copy, or body text, refers to the running text of a story. Body copy is most often organized into sequential paragraphs; it can flow from column to column and from page to page.

Headlines, subheads, fancy first letters, jump heads, pull quotes, and logos are all examples of display type.

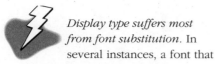

Display type suffers most from font substitution. In several instances, a font that you specify for your document might be replaced with a different font. This unintentional substitution can happen when you send a PUB file to a service bureau or commercial printer for output, or when a reader opens a Web document. In both cases, if the requested font is not installed on the system, a standard font is substituted. Although such a substitution might not be detectable for standard body copy fonts, it is quite noticeable for display typefaces. Use one of these techniques to avoid font substitution:

- Use only standard fonts such as Times New Roman or Arial in your designs.
- Contact your service bureau or commercial printer to be sure they have the fonts you need installed.
- Use WordArt (which will be generated as a graphic region) to employ unusual display fonts.

Display Type

Fonts have distinct personalities. They can be formal or casual; they can project an aggressive corporate image or an avant-garde attitude. Sans-serif fonts are widely used for display type because their simple outlines are suited to bold messages. However, at large point sizes (30 points or more), serif fonts work equally well in headlines. The following popular display fonts range from bold but legible type to letterforms that are purely decorative. Some decorative typefaces, such as Cooper Black or Snap ITC, are not legible at small sizes.

Cooper Black

Cooper Black adds weight to your words—quite literally—with very heavy strokes.

Eras Medium ITC

Eras Medium ITC gives your text an ultramodern look.

COPPERPLATE GOTHIC LIGHT

Copperplate Gothic Light looks like a traditional engraver's typeface and adds a formal note to a design.

Snap ITC

Snap ITC exaggerates and distorts letterforms for a playful effect.

Body Copy

When you choose a font for body copy, consider legibility first. Documents with hard-to-read type can lower comprehension. Because readers score higher on comprehension tests in which the text is set in serif fonts, designers frequently use serif fonts for body copy. You don't need to completely avoid sans-serif fonts for body copy, but you should use them with discretion. Restrict your use of sans-serif type to short or moderately short text blocks, such as pull quotes, captions, or catalog entries.

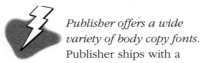

Publisher offers a wide variety of body copy fonts. Publisher ships with a number of fonts that are particularly well suited for body copy. In addition to the serif fonts listed below, the sans-serif fonts below provide enough stroke variation to make reading them a pleasure. The amount of variation among these fonts is especially dramatic when you consider that they are all technically the same size—11 points.

Baskerville Old Face

Book Antiqua

Calisto MT

Century Schoolbook

Eras Medium ITC

Footlight MT Light

Garamond

Lucida Bright

Lucida Sans

Maiandra GD

Perpetua

Let's face it. Chicago is famous for stockyards, not fisheries. But times are changing. People are eating fish instead of red meat. Seafood is an important part of a heart-healthy diet because it is low in cholesterol and fat.

Garamond, 12 point

The decorative flourishes, or serifs, at the ends of a font's vertical and horizontal lines help readers group words together. The thin and thick strokes vary more than the strokes of sans-serif fonts. This visual variety among letters can prevent fatigue when someone is reading a long text passage.

Let's face it. Chicago is famous for stockyards, not fisheries. But times are changing. People are eating fish instead of red meat. Seafood is an important part of a heart-healthy diet because it is low in cholesterol and fat.

Lucida Sans, 11 point

The more recent sans-serif fonts vary the letter thickness to make the text more legible.

Font Structure

Understanding the basic structure of a letter design can help you select an appropriate font. The following illustrations explain the way a letter is structured.

Book Antiqua — Ascenders and descenders are the portions of a lowercase letter that rise above or drop below the main body (x-height) of the letter.

A font's x-height refers to the proportional height of the lowercase letter x in that font. The letter x is the standard because it has no ascenders or descenders. A font with a large x-height has lowercase letters almost as tall as the capital letters. When you need type that is highly legible at small point sizes, select a typeface with a large x-height. A font with a small x-height has lowercase letters that are much shorter in relation to the capital letters. When you need to fit a large amount of text into a few pages, select a typeface with a shorter x-height.

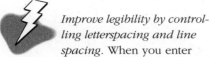

Improve legibility by controlling letterspacing and line spacing. When you enter text, Publisher uses default letter and line spacing. The letterspacing is determined by the design of the font itself. The line spacing is calculated at 120 percent of point size. These defaults work well in a wide variety of situations, but they don't work for every font at every point size. You can often improve the legibility of your designs by adjusting letter and line spacing as follows:

- Decrease letterspacing in headlines to avoid awkward white gaps that can occur between letters at large point sizes.

- Decrease default line spacing in headlines to remove the white spaces that can separate lines of the same sentence at large point sizes.

- Increase letterspacing in body copy when dealing with small point sizes or sans-serif fonts.

- Increase line spacing in body copy to improve legibility when working with highly condensed fonts, heavy sans-serif fonts, or small point sizes.

For more information about adjusting letter and line spacing, see page 324.

The width of a font is referred to as either condensed or expanded. The letters in a condensed font are narrower, so you can fit more text on a line. The letters in an expanded font are wide and widely spaced. You can usually tell whether a font is condensed or expanded by its name.

Gill Sans MT Extra Condensed Bold

Weight refers to the thickness of the strokes that form the characters themselves. A font's weight is often designated by words such as light, heavy, bold, and extra bold.

Lucida Sans Typewriter

Leading (pronounced "ledding") is the distance from the baseline of one line of text to the baseline of the next line of text. Leading is typically measured in points.

Letterspace refers to the white space between letters.

Font Combinations

Mixing and matching fonts requires a bit of knowledge and a lot of experimentation. Most designers create visual interest in a publication by choosing fonts that have contrasting yet complementary letterforms. There are no hard and fast rules where type design is concerned, but here are a few basic guidelines:

- Use no more than two font families in a document. (A font family is the set of fonts depicting different styles of a single typeface. For example, Arial, Arial Black, and Arial Narrow are all contained within the same font family.)

- Use different styles within a font family—regular, bold, italic, and bold italic—for variety and emphasis.

- Combine a serif and a sans-serif typeface for contrast.

- Look for variations on the font you're using. For example, some fonts are available in condensed or expanded widths, or in heavier or lighter weights.

Learning to use combination leading. You can make the baselines of text in a multi-column layout align across columns—a sure sign of a professionally designed publication. Just make sure that you create combinations of leading and paragraph spacing that always work out to the same total amount of space. For example, if your body copy is 10 points on 12 points of leading, design all the other elements in your publication using increments of 12-point line spacing. You could create a two-line subhead where the type is 14 points, set on 16 points of leading, with 4 points of space before (not after) the subhead. The total amount of space for the two-line subhead will be 36 points—a multiple of 12.

Publisher can automatically number pages for you. For information about this feature, see Chapter 3. For more information about the background, see Chapter 3.

Our guest chef this month is Robbin Frances—a self-proclaimed Italophile. Having spent six years roaming the kitchens of Italy, the 31-year-old chef returned to New York three years ago (recipes in tow) to open L'Accademia, one of Manhattan's most successful small restaurants.

Commitment to Quality

What keeps knowledgeable gourmets coming back to the three-star

meat from Maine complements organically grown asparagus and homemade flour-and-egg tagliatelle.

Simplicity Is Key

Frances's reliance on high-quality ingredients is part of a larger philosophy, one that can be summed up in two words: pure and simple. "Each ingredient in a dish should have integrity," she says. "I'm a believer in simplicity; letting each flavor come through in all

Times New Roman and Arial are a classic combination of serif and sans-serif fonts.

Organizing Background Elements

Consistency is an important part of any design. You can create visual consistency by including many of the following organizational elements on the background, which repeats them on every page in your publication.

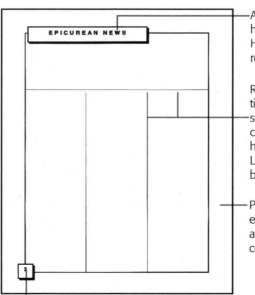

EPICUREAN NEWS

At the top of pages, running heads, or headers, clearly identify the publication. Headers can contain logos or icons that repeat on each page.

Rules (called lines in Publisher) and decorative borders can divide a page into distinct sections. Vertical lines can be used to define columns of text, and horizontal lines can highlight separate sections of a story. Use the Line tool and the Border and BorderArt dialog boxes to create these elements.

Page margins (and row and column guides) establish the basic structure of a design and add greatly to a sense of cohesiveness and continuity throughout a publication.

At the bottom of pages, running feet (or footers) usually contain a folio (or page number) to help readers locate information easily. Footers can provide volume, chapter, or date information.

Use the background for business forms. You can use the background in a number of interesting ways. For example, you can create a quick template for a pre-printed business form by scanning the form and placing the picture of the form on the background. Draw text frames on the foreground that align with the picture of the form placed on the background. Use Publisher's standard text tools to fill out the form electronically. Insert the preprinted forms into your printer. Before you print the page, turn off the background. (Choose Ignore Background on the View menu.) Publisher will print the text but not the scanned image.

Print a proof. No electronic tool can take the place of your eyes for that final reading. Print a copy of your publication to check the layout and proofread the text. Even if you are sending your publication to a service bureau or commercial printer, Publisher allows you to print proofs to a local printer.

For more information about printing options, see Chapter 14.

Placing Text and Pictures

You can move, resize, and edit text and pictures to create an integrated layout. When arranging a layout, forget that text frames are full of words and that picture frames contain images. You'll find it easier to begin your design using colored and shaded drawn objects and frames before you create actual text and pictures. This preliminary design, called a mock-up (shown below left), helps you determine approximately how much text you'll need, as well as the size, shape, and position of artwork.

Think of text frames as gray or patterned boxes.

Notice how the text and pictures follow the same overall pattern as the mock-up.

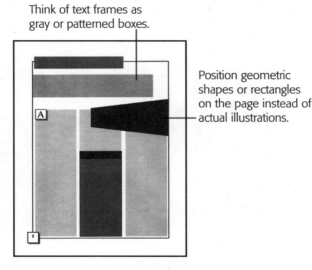

Position geometric shapes or rectangles on the page instead of actual illustrations.

The shapes and differing gray densities create a pattern for your eyes to follow.

Adjusting Text and Pictures

Designs are worked, reworked, and perfected in small increments. You should expect to try different solutions until you hit upon the right combination.

Edit text for aesthetic reasons. In most cases you will edit the text in your publications for sense—meaning that you'll change the copy to make sentences more understandable and to correct grammar and spelling mistakes. However, you should also edit the text to improve its appearance. Here are some of the common occurences that editors and designers find undesirable:

- A short line, called a widow, ending a paragraph.

- A single word, called an orphan, at the top of a page or column of continued text.

- Too many consecutive hyphens in a block of hyphenated text.

- Too much white space forming a visual pattern, called a river, in a block of justified text.

Normally, these problems are corrected by changing the text so that lines rebreak to fill out lines or lose lines.

The following checklist can help you fine-tune your documents.

- Edit the text. Sometimes the best way to fit a large story into a small text frame is to cut text lines.

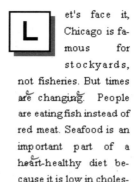

Editors look for widows (short lines that appear at the bottom of a column or paragraph) if they need to shorten the story. You can save an entire line by cutting a few words from the paragraph; that last short line disappears when the text rewraps.

- Play with the text formatting.

Let's face it. Chicago is famous for stockyards, not fisheries. But times are changing. People are eating fish instead of red meat. Seafood is an important part of a heart-healthy diet because it is low in cholesterol and fat.

Times New Roman set at 12 points on 16 points of leading

Let's face it. Chicago is famous for stockyards, not fisheries. But times are changing. People are eating fish instead of red meat. Seafood is an important part of a heart-healthy diet because it is low in cholesterol and fat.

Times New Roman set at 11.5 points on 12.5 points of leading

You can save a surprising amount of space by reducing the text point size or the leading by very small increments.

● Add supporting display type such as captions, subheads, pull quotes, or fancy first letters.

L et's face it, Chicago is famous for stockyards, not fisheries. But times are changing. People are eating fish instead of red meat. Seafood is an important part of a heart-healthy diet because it is low in cholesterol and fat.

We're proud that the freshest fish in Chicago can be found at Epicurean Delights. The arrival of aquaculture, or fish farming, as it is known among the professionals, has made trout as commonly available as beef. We found a hatchery only hours away from the heart of the city. The trout is so fresh it tastes like the fish has jumped out of the water and onto your plate!

Trout is wonderful when

curean Delights' Flying Fish Service. Fish is ordered by telephone and shipped by air to arrive the next day. It's the next best thing to catching it yourself! The quick

"Imagine tender medallions of salmon encased in a crispy potato jacket."

turnaround time allows us to offer you blue catfish from Louisiana, grouper from Florida, and Chinook salmon from Washington State

anise. Imagine ten of salmon encase potato jacket. Antic succulent fresh gr when it is steamed i envelope with aro bles. These recipes easy to try because able as prepared, dishes from the Epic kitchen. You just po the oven, microwave enjoy a delicious me later. And though w uduced, we think ou salads, such as lob relish, and shrimp onions are worthy o status. For busy pe care about the food

Display text adds texture and visual contrast to a design. Many display text blocks, such as pull quotes and Continued notices, should be added only after a layout has been roughed out.

Text colors should be functional, not merely decorative. When you create color elements in a design, do so with discretion. Too many colors will distract the reader from your message. It's best to choose colors for functional reasons, rather than purely decorative purposes. For example, you could choose to print all of the subheads in a long article in a second color. This highlights the beginning of each section and helps the reader skim a story. Functional color choices are especially important in a Web publication, where colors are used to flag hyperlinks.

● Fill boxes with colored or gray tints to highlight stories or parts of a story. Tinting is a great way to flag a sidebar (a separate but related story).

Menu

Sea Bass
Poached in a Court Bouillon

Coho Salmon
Served in a Potato Jacket

Nassau Grouper
Steamed in Parchment

Lobster Salad
With White Corn Relish

Mahi Mahi
With Mango Chutney

Maryland Crab Cakes
And Hot Pepper Mayonnaise

Tuna Enchiladas
With Tomatillo Salsa

Mesquite Barbecued Trout
And Dirty Rice

Shrimp Salad
With Green Onions

Medallions of Monk Fish
In an Anise Sauce

Choose a light tint in the Fill Patterns And Shading dialog box so that the text won't be obscured.

@ Adjust the paragraph alignment and hyphenation zone.

Let's face it. Chicago is famous for stockyards, not fisheries. But times are changing. People are eating fish instead of red meat. Seafood is an important part of a healthy diet because it is low in cholesterol and low in fat.

Let's face it. Chicago is famous for stockyards, not fisheries. But times are changing. People are eating fish instead of red meat. Seafood is an important part of a healthy diet because it is low in cholesterol and low in fat.

Let's face it. Chicago is famous for stockyards, not fisheries. But times are changing. People are eating fish instead of red meat. Seafood is an important part of a healthy diet because it is low in cholesterol and low in fat.

Increasing the hyphenation zone inserts fewer hyphens. This can lengthen a story by creating a more ragged right margin.

Decreasing the hyphenation zone inserts more hyphens and can shorten a story by tightening up loose lines.

Using justified alignment can shorten a story dramatically.

How can I find the best clip-art picture for my design? Searching through the Microsoft Clip Gallery of over 5000 images is no small task. Here are several techniques to help you find the right image in the least time:

@ If you use the Clip Gallery, narrow the search by using category and keyword descriptions.

@ If you use the Insert Picture File dialog box, look for all of the descriptive filenames. For example, you can find images of domesticated cats by looking for filenames that begin with Cat. But you can also find images of domesticated cats by looking for filenames that begin with Tabby.

@ Whether you are using the Clip Gallery or the Insert Picture File dialog box, preview the picture to confirm that it meets your requirements before you import it into your publication.

@ Combine pictures to create your own, more complex illustrations.

Choosing pictures that are executed in the same style creates a cohesive composition. Here three individual pictures are combined and overlapped to create what looks like a single drawing.

Take advantage of auto-mated checks. Publisher offers several automated functions that can help you spot potential problems in a document. The Design Checker locates common oversights such as empty text frames, text hidden in the overflow area, and covered objects. And the Check Spelling function looks for words and capitalizations it doesn't recognize.

 For more information about the Design Checker, see Chapter 4. For more information about the Check Spelling command, see Chapter 5.

 Combine irregular text wrapping and cropping. There are two ways to combine Publisher's cropping function with the irregular text wrap functions.

- First crop the picture using the normal Crop Picture tool, and then click the Wrap Text To Picture button. Publisher will maintain the crop when it creates the irregular text wrap boundary.

- Alternatively, use the Edit Irregular Wrap tool as a very flexible cropping tool. Just grab any Adjust handle and drag it toward the middle of the picture. Any portion of the picture outside the irregular text wrap boundary will be hidden and will not print.

- Recolor images to create artistic effects.

Using a very light or unusual color to tint artwork can create interesting special effects. A light gray color, for example, will produce a watermark effect, where the picture functions as a subtle background pattern.

- Crop pictures instead of resizing them.

Cropping a picture can save space, hide part of an unnecessary background in the picture, or create drama by showing only the essential part of an image.

This project teaches you how to choose and format clip art.

Party Invitation

Preparing the Publication

Microsoft Publisher 97's unique page layout options make it easy to create small cards such as invitations.

Set Up the Page

1 Choose the Side Fold Card layout. Click Yes in the confirmation dialog box to automatically produce four 4.25-by-5.5-inch pages.

2 A small page should have small margins. Set the page margins at 0.4 inch for all four sides. Make sure the page contains only 1 column and 1 row.

Use real card stock for your card projects. Instead of folding a standard letter-sized sheet of paper to create a card, try using custom-sized note cards, which are available from stationery stores and mail-order sources such as Paper Direct. These card items are produced from heavy card stock and come complete with a prescored fold line.

Follow these steps:

- In the printer Properties dialog box, select the Paper tab, and set up a custom-sized paper of 5.5 inches wide by 8.5 inches long.

- In the Page Setup dialog box, choose the Special Fold publication layout. Choose the Landscape orientation and the Book Fold layout.

Set Up the Page (continued)

3 Select the printer you will use. This project was printed on a color PostScript printer.

4 Confirm that the current paper size is 8.5-by-11-inch letter size, in Portrait orientation.

Creating the First Page

The CD version of Publisher 97 ships with over 5000 bitmapped and vector images. There is a good chance that you'll find exactly the picture you need for your project. Finding the right picture is only the first step in the design process. Even a simple design will require you to crop and format imported pictures. As you work your way through this design, notice how formatting attributes (such as Object Color and BorderArt) tie the text and picture together so that they don't appear to float on a sea of white space.

Import and Crop a Picture

1 Draw a picture frame that measures 5 inches wide by 2.5 inches high. Don't worry about exact placement now; you'll reposition the picture later in the design process.

2 Insert the picture file Beach1.wmf (found on the Publisher CD-ROM in the Clipart subfolder). Choose Change The Frame To Fit The Picture.

3 In the Scale Picture dialog box, make sure that the picture appears at 100 percent size.

4 Using the Crop Picture tool, hide unsightly black lines along the right and bottom edge of the picture, and hide approximately 2 inches of the left side of the picture.

Preserve the aspect ratio of the imported image. The original version of the Beach1.wmf image is a horizontal picture. Don't distort the picture to fit it into a vertical layout. Instead, preserve the aspect ratio when you import the picture by selecting Change The Frame To Fit The Picture in the Import Picture dialog box. Then use the Crop Picture tool to fit the picture into the layout.

Uncropped picture used for invitation

Think metaphorically and creatively when making clip-art choices. Try not to be too literal when you search for the "perfect" clip-art image. Clip-art pictures can be used as illustrations, but they can also evoke a particular mood or convey a concept. The following clip-art image depicting a joyful mood would be suitable for a party invitation, especially for a New Year's party.

Import and Crop a Picture *(continued)*

5 Using the Crop Picture tool once again, extend the top of the picture frame (increasing the size of the background). The image should now measure 2.75 inches wide by 4 inches high.

6 Move the picture frame to center it on the page, leaving 0.75 inch on each side.

Format a Picture with a Fill and a Border

1 Format the picture frame with a blue 4-point border. This project uses a bright blue color with an RGB value of 0,0,255 (a Red value of 0, a Green value of 0, and a Blue value of 255).

2 Fill the background of the picture frame with a turquoise color. Use a light turquoise with an RGB value of 175,252,253.

Add WordArt Display Type

1 Starting approximately 0.25 inch from the top of the picture, draw a WordArt frame measuring 1.5 inches wide by 0.75 inch high. Don't worry about the horizontal position; you'll adjust that momentarily.

Copy formats from one WordArt object to another. You can quickly create the second WordArt object in this exercise by using the Format Painter or the shortcut menu (accessed with the right mouse button) to copy all the formatting attributes from the first object.

Grouping objects logically makes them easier to manage. Publisher treats grouped objects as a single element, allowing you to manage and manipulate your designs more efficiently. In this exercise, for example, you grouped the display type with the picture frame *before* you aligned objects with one another. Therefore, when you subsequently center the picture frame and the decorative borders, the display type will remain in the correct position.

Add WordArt Display Type *(continued)*

2 Enter the words *BEACH PARTY* in all uppercase letters on two lines.

3 Choose the following WordArt attributes:
- Plain Text shape
- Bernard MT Condensed font
- Best Fit size
- Center alignment
- Stretch
- Blue text color

4 Click anywhere away from the WordArt frame to return to your document.

5 Draw a second WordArt frame measuring 0.25 inch wide by 0.75 inch high.

6 Type a single exclamation point.

7 Duplicate the formatting of the first WordArt element.

8 Exit WordArt.

9 Using Publisher's standard rotation tool, rotate the second WordArt frame to the right approximately 335 degrees.

10 Move the exclamation point next to the words *BEACH PARTY*.

11 Select both WordArt frames and group them.

12 Center the WordArt group horizontally.

13 Group the WordArt elements and the picture.

Why can't I see the BorderArt pattern on screen? You might need to zoom in to display small elements such as the small red dots of the BorderArt pattern. Small elements will still print, however.

Combine BorderArt patterns for unique effects. You can create interesting framing effects by mixing two or more BorderArt patterns. In this project, simple dashed and dotted patterns work well together. If you are adventurous—and especially if you create custom BorderArt designs— you can produce pattern-on-pattern motifs. Surrounding a frame with more than one border pattern requires you to place additional boxes around it.

Add BorderArt

1 Using the Box tool, draw a rectangle that exactly matches the page margins. It will measure 3.45 inches wide by 4.7 inches high. Add the Basic…Black Dots BorderArt pattern. Change the size to 8 points, and the color to basic red (an RGB value of 255,0,0). By default, the box is transparent. If you have changed the default, press Ctrl-T.

2 Using the Box tool, draw a second rectangle that measures 3.25 inches wide by 4.5 inches high. Add the Basic…Black Squares BorderArt pattern. Change the size to 14 points and the color to basic blue (an RGB value of 0,0,255). Make sure that the box is transparent.

3 Center the second rectangle horizontally and vertically.

Creating the Internal Message

Because cards—especially invitations—don't contain a large amount of text, you don't need to consider legibility first when you choose your font. An invitation is an opportunity to break out with a fun or decorative font. For this project, you should continue to use Bernard MT Condensed to provide consistency with the display type on the first page of the invitation. Bernard MT Condensed is a good choice because the heavy black letters echo the black lines in the artwork. (You'll add a variation of the artwork to this page to complete the design.) However, you'll have to compensate for the very dark letters of this font by setting the copy in a larger point size and with more line spacing than is normal.

For the text of this party invitation, see "Text for Design Projects."

Experiment with informal fonts. This invitation is a perfect opportunity to use an informal font. Publisher ships with a number of informal fonts, any one of which could work in this design. Look at the headline text formatted with Cooper Black (top), Beesknees ITC (center), and Maiandra GD Bold (bottom).

BEACH PARTY!

BEACH PARTY!

BEACH PARTY!

Choose a Font for the Text

1 Move to page 3. As with most cards, page 2 will remain blank.

2 Draw a text frame that covers the entire page from row guide to row guide and from column guide to column guide.

3 With the empty text frame selected, create a text style that has these attributes:

- ℮ Bernard MT Condensed font
- ℮ 13-point font size
- ℮ 15 points of space between lines
- ℮ 10 points of space between paragraphs
- ℮ Center alignment

4 Enter your text. The format you applied to the frame will be assigned to the text as you type.

5 Press Enter to begin a new paragraph and to insert 10 points of additional line space after the word *barbecue.* Press Enter again after the abbreviation for New York State (*NY*).

6 Adjust the rag of the copy by pressing Shift-Enter to force line breaks without starting a new paragraph. The goal is to give a pleasing, undulating shape to each text block.

Line up objects in the correct page view. Whenever you view a two-page spread, Publisher's Line Up Objects command centers objects in the middle of the spread. Before you use the Line Up Objects command, switch to single-page view. The Line Up Objects command will work perfectly.

How can I draw the objects in this project accurately? In this project (and in other projects), unusual measurements, such as a height of 1.3 inch or 1.9 inch, are given for some objects. To create these objects easily and precisely, turn off Snap To Ruler Marks on the Tools menu. As you draw the object, watch the status bar readout at the bottom of Publisher's workspace. The readout is accurate to within 1/100 inch, and it will provide instantaneous feedback as you draw or resize an object. When you've created an object with the correct dimensions, simply release the mouse button. You may also find it helpful to zoom in on the object using a magnification level of 100 percent or greater.

Add a Decorative Element

1 Make room for the decorative element by resizing the text frame. Move the top selection handle to the 2.75-inch mark on the vertical ruler.

2 Copy the picture frame, the red dotted rectangle, and the blue dashed rectangle from page 1 to page 3.

4 Resize the blue dashed rectangle to measure 2.15 inches wide by 1.7 inches high.

3 Using the Crop Picture tool (not the selection handles), reshape the picture to reveal the seashells in the lower left corner of the image. The picture should now measure 1.75 inches wide by 1.3 inches high.

The Ramsey Family invites you to a beach-side barbecue.

Sunday, July 17th
1:00 p.m.
200 Shore Road
East Hampton, NY

RSVP 516-555-2424

5 Resize the red dotted rectangle to measure 2.4 inches wide by 1.9 inches high.

6 Center the picture frame, the blue dashed rectangle, and the red dotted rectangle horizontally and vertically in relation to one another.

7 Group these three objects.

8 Center the grouped object horizontally on the page, positioning the top of the frame at the 0.75-inch mark on the vertical ruler.

Accurate folds every time. Here's a simple trick that can help you produce clean, neat folds. You must be working on a clean, hard surface, such as a desktop. Line up the top and bottom edges of the paper for the first fold. Make sure that the corners are perfectly square with one another. Run your finger along one (and only one) edge of the paper to find the true center of the paper. Begin a small crease at this point. Now run your finger across the width of the paper, letting the natural grain of the paper create the fold. The result will be a perfectly straight fold. You can repeat this process for any subsequent folds.

This technique will work with almost any paper, but it works best with high-quality paper that has a distinct grain.

Completing the Invitation

Print and Fold the Document

1 In the Print dialog box, confirm that you are printing all four pages of the invitation.

2 Print the document normally. Publisher prints page 3 upside down. Don't worry—once you've folded the paper, page 3 will appear in the correct orientation.

3 Fold the paper in half vertically so that the card measures 8.5 inches wide by 5.5 inches high.

4 Fold the card in half horizontally so that it measures 4.25 inches wide by 5.5 inches high. Once it's completely folded, the card will fit into a standard note-sized envelope.

Publisher's Outside Print Setup makes it easy to design this poster at home and then print it at a service bureau.

Large Format Poster

Setting Up the Page

This school project—a poster that celebrates Citizenship Day—is a great way to learn about Microsoft Publisher 97's outside printing functions. Your proof of this poster will be printed to a standard PostScript printer, on nine separate tiles of 8.5-by-11-inch paper. The finished poster will be printed on a single sheet of paper to a large format printer, which is typically available at a service bureau. Whenever you plan to print your file at an outside printer, find out which printer driver you should specify in the Outside Print Setup dialog box.

Set Up for Outside Printing

1 Choose full-color printing in the Outside Print Setup dialog box. When prompted, choose the appropriate printer driver. This project was created using a large format inkjet PostScript device.

2 Choose U.S. Architectural C–sized paper in the printer Properties dialog box. This will give you a large paper size of 18 by 24 inches. There is no need to use the Special Size option in the Page Setup dialog box when you have large paper installed in the printer. The Normal option will provide an 18-by-24-inch page when U.S. Architectural C–sized paper is loaded.

How can I acquire a printer driver for a large format printer? You can acquire the printer driver you need for outside (or remote) printing in several ways:

- Activate the Add New Hardware Wizard in Microsoft Windows 95 Control Panel. Windows 95 ships with a host of drivers for standard printers.

- Ask your service bureau to supply you with a copy of the necessary driver.

- Download a driver from an online service (such as the Microsoft Network) or the printer manufacturer's electronic bulletin board.

Large Format Poster

Enlarge bitmapped pictures in an image editing program. If you want to preserve the image quality of a bitmapped picture, you should not enlarge the picture within Publisher. Publisher can only stretch the picture, which increases the size of individual pixels and creates a jagged, or pixelated, effect known as aliasing.

Ideally, when enlarging a picture, you should use an image editing program to create new pixels (a process known as interpolation). Enlarging a bitmapped picture in an image editing program results in a larger file size. In this project, the original JPEG file requires 151 KB of disk space when imported into Publisher. (Publisher does not compress imported bitmapped pictures.) When enlarged to 250 percent in an image editing program, the same image requires 965 KB of disk space when imported into Publisher.

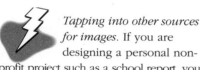

Tapping into other sources for images. If you are designing a personal non-profit project such as a school report, you can use images that you find in books and encyclopedias. Using an electronic research tool, such as Microsoft Bookshelf or the Internet, allows you to transfer information easily from the "book" to your Publisher document. One word of warning: if your project is distributed publicly, or if it is in any way a profit-making venture, you cannot copy pictures. Doing so is a violation of copyright law.

Set Up for Outside Printing *(continued)*

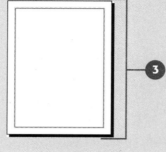

3 Create larger than normal margins of 1.25 inches on all four sides to balance the scale of the poster. Make sure the page contains only 1 column and 1 row.

Inserting and Editing the Picture

The Microsoft Clip Gallery contains a picture that is perfect for this poster—a tightly cropped photograph of the Statue of Liberty. You can use this bitmapped picture as it ships on the CD-ROM, but be aware that when inserting and enlarging bitmapped pictures within Publisher, you might end up with a jagged effect known as aliasing.

Insert a Bitmapped Picture

1 Without drawing a picture frame, insert the picture 01137.jpg from Publisher's CD.

2 Use the Scale Picture command to increase the size to 250 percent both horizontally and vertically.

Use the background to separate elements of a layout. In this design, the large blue rectangle covers almost the entire page. In addition, the white rules are placed close to where other design elements will be created). By placing the rectangle and the rules on the background, you are in effect placing them out of harm's way. Now when you return to the foreground to create and manipulate the other objects in the design, the foreground objects will be easier to select.

Why am I having trouble aligning the white rules to the white border around the rectangle? Publisher has automated tools to help you align objects to ruler marks, guides, and other objects. Because the rule surrounding the rectangle is a BorderArt attribute rather than a true object, the automated alignment options won't work. In fact, you'll achieve better results if you turn off Snap To Ruler Marks, Snap To Guides, and Snap To Objects; zoom in on the page; and align the rules by eye.

Insert a Bitmapped Picture *(continued)*

3 Use the Crop Picture tool to resize the picture to 6.5 inches wide by 9 inches high. The crown on the statue is the dramatic focus of this photograph, so trim the image from the bottom of the frame.

4 Position the top of the picture frame at the 8-inch mark on the vertical ruler. Center the picture horizontally on the page.

Adding Display Type

The title of this poster states its purpose very simply—to commemorate Citizenship Day. To make the text treatment more dramatic, the words are printed with white letters against a dark blue background.

Draw a Background for the Text

1 Move to the background, and draw a box that fills the page to all four margins.

2 Format the box with a dark blue color that is related to the blue values in the picture but is dark enough to provide contrast with white type. An RGB value of 0,25,100 works well.

3 Format the box with the Basic…Wide Outline BorderArt pattern. Size the BorderArt at 12 points. Assign a color that matches the fill color's RGB value of 0,25,100. This creates the illusion of a white rule slightly inset from the edge of the box.

4 Draw three white 5-point horizontal rules at the locations indicated.

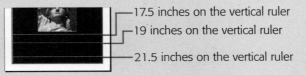

17.5 inches on the vertical ruler
19 inches on the vertical ruler
21.5 inches on the vertical ruler

5 Return to the foreground.

Printing considerations play a role when choosing a font. Both the printing method and certain technical issues must be considered when you choose a font for your project. In this project, for example, all the type will be knocked out from a blue background. You therefore want to choose a font like Calisto MT (shown below), which has thick strokes and blunt serifs that will print clearly as reverse type. This consideration is especially important when you knock out type at smaller point sizes.

CI

For the text of this poster, see "Text for Design Projects."

Enter and Format Display Type

1 Make sure you are on the foreground.

2 Draw three separate text frames that mimic the size and shape of the white outlines you created on the background in the previous procedure.

3 Make the text frames transparent.

4 Enter your text and format it as indicated.

Calisto MT font, 54-point font size, white characters, center alignment

The Barrow Street School Celebrates

Citizenship Day

September 17, 1997

Calisto MT font, bold, 120-point font size, white characters, center alignment

Calisto MT font, 38-point font size, white characters, center alignment

Adding Body Copy

Quotations are often a good source of design inspiration. Here, the inscription by Emma Lazarus that appears on the base of the Statue of Liberty is used to good effect. Because the text is so short, it works as white type against a dark background.

Enter and Format Text

1 Draw a text frame that is aligned with the top and side column guides. The bottom of the text frame should align with the top of the picture, at the 8-inch mark on the vertical ruler.

2 Format the text frame with a clear fill color.

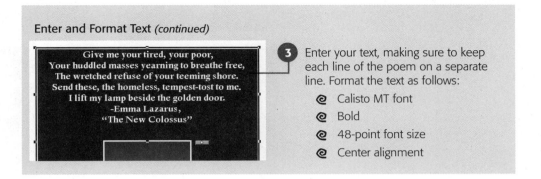

3 Enter your text, making sure to keep each line of the poem on a separate line. Format the text as follows:

- ✇ Calisto MT font
- ✇ Bold
- ✇ 48-point font size
- ✇ Center alignment

Adjusting the Design

This is a very straightforward design in which the text and the image are centered on the page. Yet, even here a few items require adjustment. Luckily, Publisher makes it easy to correct several layout problems.

The body copy text is too close to the top margin.

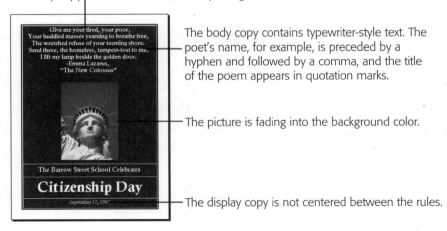

The body copy contains typewriter-style text. The poet's name, for example, is preceded by a hyphen and followed by a comma, and the title of the poem appears in quotation marks.

The picture is fading into the background color.

The display copy is not centered between the rules.

Large Format Poster

Adjust Picture Frame Borders

1 Select the picture.

2 Apply an 8-point white border to all four sides.

Proofread and Edit Punctuation

1 Delete the hyphen preceding the poet's name and replace it with an em dash.

2 Delete the comma following the poet's name and replace it with an em dash. Although this isn't grammatically correct, it serves a design function by maintaining the symmetry of the line and separating the poet's name from the rest of the copy.

3 Delete the quotation marks surrounding the poem's title and italicize the text, again for visual reasons.

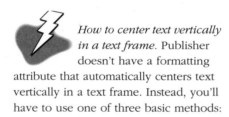

How to center text vertically in a text frame. Publisher doesn't have a formatting attribute that automatically centers text vertically in a text frame. Instead, you'll have to use one of three basic methods:

@ Resize the text frame

@ Adjust the text frame margins

@ Adjust the line spacing

Adjust Text Frame Margins

1 Select the text frame containing body copy and change the top margin to 0.5 inch.

2 Select the text frames containing the display type and change the top text frame margin to 0.2 inch. This change will align the text vertically as well as horizontally.

Producing the Poster

Before you send your poster to a service bureau, where you pay for the printout, generate a paper proof. Even when you set up a document for outside printing, Publisher maintains a local proof printer.

Print a Proof

1 Print the poster by selecting the Print Proof command.

2 Click the Tile Printing Options button.

Can I print this color poster to my black-and-white printer? Don't worry if you don't own a color printer. Publisher will print the document as black and white (and shades of gray) to your local black-and-white proofing device.

 Large bitmapped files create large publication files and larger printer files. This project takes advantage of a small, low-resolution bitmapped image from Publisher's clip-art collection. Using a higher resolution bitmap (or resizing the picture in an image editing program) would result in much larger working files. If this poster contained a 72-dpi, 24-bit picture measuring 6.5 by 9 inches, it would produce a 984 KB publication file.

Print a Proof *(continued)*

The Sample area in the Poster And Banner Printing Options dialog box shows you how the publication will be tiled across several sheets of paper.

3 Make sure Print Entire Page is selected and that the Overlap Tiles By value is at least 0.25 inch. The final proof would be printed like this.

4 Assemble the poster by trimming and taping the individual sheets of paper together.

Why don't the colors I see on screen match the final printed output? The colors you see on your computer monitor are created using the RGB color model. However, images produced by a color printer rely on the CMYK color model. Translating RGB values to CMYK values can result in color shifts.

If possible, use a printer driver that supports the Windows 95 Image Color Matching (ICM) system. If you've properly configured your system, Publisher flags those colors in the color palette that will print poorly. In addition, you should contact your service bureau. Only your service bureau can tell you how to prepare color bitmapped images for its equipment and production process.

Unless you are working with extremely high-quality images for which the color values are crucial, you should expect visually pleasing colors that are a reasonable, but not perfect, match of the monitor colors.

For more information about color systems and the Windows 95 color matching technology, see pages 293 through 296 in Chapter 14.

Transfer the Publication to the Service Bureau

1 Before you send a file to a service bureau, generate an InfoSheet. This report contains important information about your publication, such as paper size and font usage.

2 Do one of the following:

- Confirm that the service bureau has a current copy of Publisher and the fonts you've used in the document. Then copy the publication file to a floppy disk. If you've followed the instructions in this chapter, the file should require 170 KB of storage space and will easily fit on a floppy disk.

- Use the Print To Outside Printer dialog box to generate a file containing the information necessary to print the file. Once you've created the printer file, copy it to a floppy disk. The actual file size will vary depending on how you enlarged the bitmapped image and which outside printer driver you are using. But expect the file to require at least 500 KB of disk space.

3 Transport the file to the service bureau.

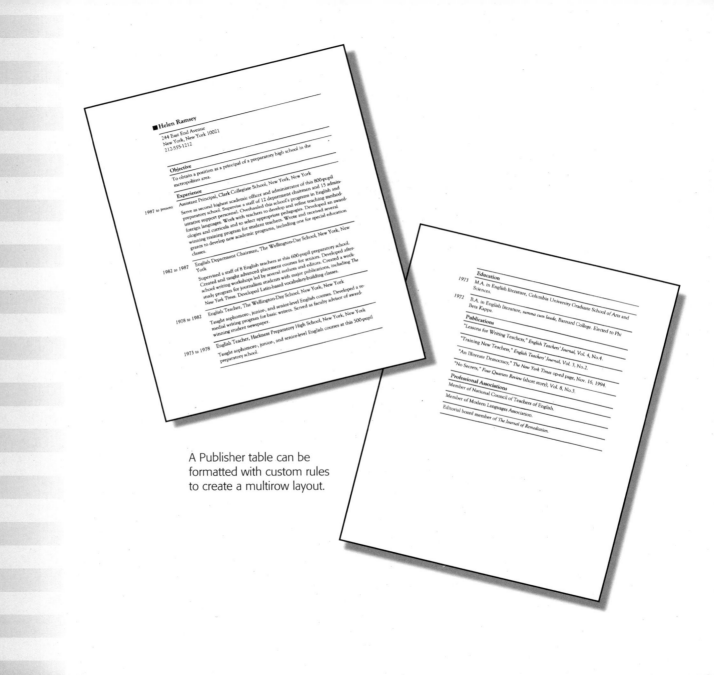

Helen Ramsey

244 East End Avenue
New York, New York 10021
212-555-1212

Objective

To obtain a position as a principal of a preparatory high school in the metropolitan area.

Experience

1987 to present — Assistant Principal, Clark Collegiate School, New York, New York

Serve as second highest academic officer and administrator of this 800-pupil preparatory school. Supervise a staff of 12 department chairmen and 15 administrative support personnel. Overhauled this school's programs in English and foreign languages. Work with teachers to develop and refine teaching methodologies and curricula and to select appropriate pedagogies. Developed several winning training program for student teachers. Wrote and received several grants to develop new academic programs, including one for special education classes.

1982 to 1987 — English Department Chairman, The Wellington-Day School, New York, New York

Supervised a staff of 8 English teachers at this 600-pupil preparatory school. Created and taught advanced placement courses for seniors. Developed afterschool writing workshops led by several authors and editors. Created a work study program for journalism students with major publications, including The New York Times. Developed Latin-based vocabulary-building classes.

1978 to 1982 — English Teacher, The Wellington-Day School, New York, New York

Taught sophomore-, junior-, and senior-level English courses. Developed a remedial writing program for basic writers. Served as faculty advisor of awardwinning student newspaper.

1973 to 1978 — English Teacher, Harkness Preparatory High School, New York, New York

Taught sophomore-, junior-, and senior-level English courses at this 500-pupil preparatory school.

Education

1973 — M.A. in English literature, Columbia University Graduate School of Arts and Sciences.

1972 — B.A. in English literature, summa cum laude, Barnard College. Elected to Phi Beta Kappa.

Publications

"Lessons for Writing Teachers," English Teachers' Journal, Vol. 4, No.4.

"Training New Teachers," English Teachers' Journal, Vol. 3, No.2.

"An Illiterate Democracy," The New York Times op-ed page, Nov. 16, 1994.

"No Secrets," Four Quarters Review (short story), Vol. 8, No.3.

Professional Associations

Member of National Council of Teachers of English.

Member of Modern Languages Association.

Editorial board member of The Journal of Remediation.

A Publisher table can be formatted with custom rules to create a multirow layout.

Résumé

The challenge of designing a résumé is to develop an uncluttered layout that is also distinctive. The hierarchy and categories of information must be clear and easily perceived. Note the use of white space, rules, and headings as organizing elements in the résumé on the facing page.

Setting Up the Page

Business documents, such as this résumé, use standard paper size and margin settings.

Select a Printer and Page Options

1 Start a new document and choose the Full Page layout on the Blank Page tab.

2 Select the printer you will use. This project was printed to a PostScript device.

3 Confirm that the current paper size is 8.5-by-11-inch letter size in Portrait orientation.

4 Use the default 1-inch margins for all four sides. Make sure the page contains only 1 row and 1 column.

Creating a Layout with the Table Tool

You'll create a more flexible layout if you use Microsoft Publisher 97's Table tool rather than the Layout Guides command to create rows and columns. The structure of a résumé, with dates in one column and descriptions in another, makes it ideally suited to a table format.

Set Up the Table Structure

1. Draw a table frame that begins at the 2.5-inch mark on the vertical ruler and that aligns with the left, right, and bottom row and column guides.

2. Set up the table with 19 rows, 2 columns, and the None table format.

3. Holding down the Shift key, move the division between the two columns to the 2.5-inch mark on the horizontal ruler.

4. Select the entire table. Confirm that the left, right, top, and bottom cell margins are 0.04 inch.

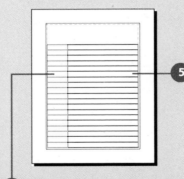

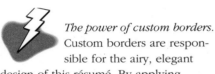

The power of custom borders. Custom borders are responsible for the airy, elegant design of this résumé. By applying borders to only the top and bottom edges of a selected range of cells, this design avoids a cramped, boxy look.

5. Select the right-hand column. Assign a 1-point border to the top, middle, and bottom sides of the column.

6. Select the left-hand column. Change the right cell margin to 0.15 inch. Increasing this margin will provide an appropriate amount of room between the date information and the text information.

Inserting and Formatting Text

The format of this résumé is actually quite simple, but it does require you to work with lots of small text objects. You can save time by creating text styles for the date, description, and category items.

The résumé text was created in a word processing program and formatted as standard paragraphs. If you insert the text directly into the table, all the copy will be placed in the first cell and the formatting attributes will be overridden. For more flexibility, place the text into a temporary text frame on Publisher's Pasteboard.

Build related styles easily. You can base a new text style on an existing text style. Simply highlight the style name you want to use as the starting point. Publisher picks up all the formatting attributes when you click the Create A New Style button. You can then make changes to create a new style.

Create Text Styles

1. Using the Text Styles dialog box, create a style named Description, and specify the following attributes:
   - Goudy Old Style font
   - 11-point font size
   - 1 space between lines
   - 6 points of space after paragraphs
   - Left alignment

2. Create a new Text Style named Date. Base this style on the Description style, but make the following changes:
   - Italic
   - 0 points of space after paragraphs
   - Right alignment

3. Create a new Text Style named Category. Base this style on the Description style, but make the following changes:
   - Bold
   - 12-point font size
   - 0 points of space after paragraphs

Removing predefined formats. When you insert a text file into a document, Publisher attempts to retain any formatting attributes, such as font, point size, and alignment, that were assigned within the word processing program. Assigning the No Style text style to the imported text deletes any associated style names and makes it easier to apply new text styles.

Note that local attributes, such as boldface or italics, are always maintained. In this example, the titles of publications remain italicized even when the Description text style is subsequently applied to the copy.

For the text of this résumé, see "Text for Design Projects."

Insert Text on the Pasteboard

1 Using your favorite word processing program, create and save a file named Resume.

2 Draw a text frame on the Pasteboard that is approximately the same size as the page.

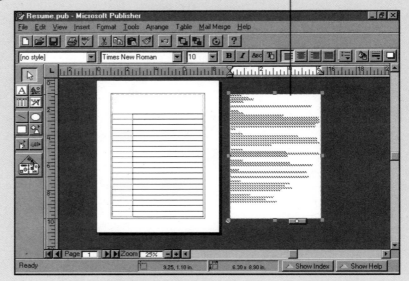

3 Insert the text file named Resume.

4 Highlight the entire story and format it with Publisher's default No Style text style.

Drag the Text to the Résumé

1 Before you move the text into the table, confirm that the Grow To Fit Text command on the Table menu is active.

2 Highlight and then drag each item to an appropriate position in the table. The table rows automatically align the date information in the left column with the related text in the right column. After you enter all the text, the table will extend past the bottom of the page margin.

Import an Excel worksheet file. You can bypass many of the procedures in this project—including the creation of the table itself—by importing an Excel worksheet file. Publisher automatically inserts an Excel worksheet as a new table.

Drag the Text to the Résumé *(continued)*

3 Highlight the entire left-hand column, and format it with the Date text style.

4 Highlight the entire right-hand column, and format it with the Description text style.

Category and Description items are positioned in the right-hand column.

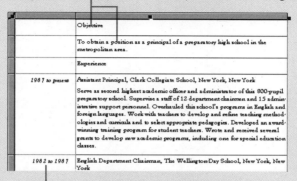

Date items are positioned in the left-hand column.

Editing the Table

Publisher's powerful tools, such as Drag-And-Drop text editing and the ability to format all the text in a column at one time, allow you to create a table quickly and easily. However, some aspects of this design must be handled manually. Specifically, you must read the table to find category items in order to assign the correct type style. In addition, you must center category headings vertically in each cell and move the portion of the table that extends past the page margins onto a second page.

How to center text vertically in a cell. Publisher can't automatically center text vertically in a cell. But you can adjust the vertical position of the text in a cell by using one of three methods:

- ✪ Increase the spacing between lines or before paragraphs

- ✪ Change the cell margins using the Table Cell Properties dialog box

- ✪ Resize the height of the entire row using the Adjust pointer

In this project, you'll adjust the spacing before paragraphs to center each category heading vertically in a cell.

Fine-Tune the Table

	Objective	
	To obtain a position as a principal of a preparatory high school metropolitan area.	
	Experience	
1987 to present	Assistant Principal, Clark Collegiate School, New York, New York	
	Serve as second highest academic officer and administrator of the preparatory school. Supervise a staff of 12 department chairmen a istrative support personnel. Overhauled this school's programs i foreign languages. Work with teachers to develop and refine tead ologies and curricula and to select appropriate pedagogies. Develo winning training program for student teachers. Wrote and receiv	

1 Scroll through the text, and assign the Category text style to categories.

2 Using the Text Style dialog box, change the Category type style by increasing the spacing before paragraphs to 2.5 points.

3 Select all the rows beginning with the category Education. Cut these rows and place them on the Clipboard using the Cut Cells command on the Edit menu. Publisher removes the text but leaves empty cells in the table.

4 Delete the empty rows from the table.

5 Insert a second page.

6 Select the Paste New Table command on the Edit menu. The following appears:

	Education	
1973	M.A. in English literature, Columbia University Graduate Scho Sciences.	
1972	B.A. in English literature, *summa cum laude*, Barnard College. El Beta Kappa.	
	Publications	
	"Lessons for Writing Teachers," *English Teachers' Journal*, Vol. 4,	
	"Training New Teachers," *English Teachers' Journal*, Vol. 3, No.2	
	"An Illiterate Democracy," The New York *Times* op-ed page. N	

Publisher retains the format of the table, including borders and text styles.

7 Align the new table with the top, left, and right page guides.

Choose a font that fits your personality and the message.
A typeface evokes a particular feeling in a reader. When you choose a typeface for your résumé, think about the characteristics of the type. Does a particular font match your personality? Is the position you are applying for professional or informal? Goudy Old Style, which is used in this project, is formal and restrained but has a very light touch. For a heavier look, you could substitute Times New Roman (top). A more formal design might take advantage of Baskerville Old Face (middle). Lucida Bright (bottom) conveys a more modern, open feeling. Experiment with possible typefaces. Remember that the most important quality of the typeface you choose is its readability.

Helen Ramsey

244 East End Avenue
New York, New York 10021
212-555-1212

Helen Ramsey

244 East End Avenue
New York, New York 10021
212-555-1212

Helen Ramsey

244 East End Avenue
New York, New York 10021
212-555-1212

Adding Name and Address Information

Even though the name and address are contained in separate text frames, they should *look* as though they are part of the table. You accomplish this by duplicating certain essential attributes of the text and table frames, such as the alignment and the 1-point rule.

Insert and Format the Name

1 Add a vertical ruler guide. Align it with the column division in the table.

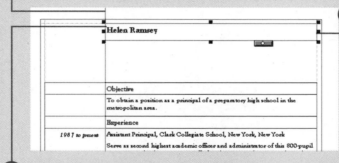

2 Draw a text frame that aligns with this ruler guide and with the top and right-hand page guides. The bottom of the text frame should align with the 1.5-inch mark on the vertical ruler.

3 Insert the name by dragging it from the text frame on the Pasteboard. The name, which identifies the subject of the résumé, is the most important piece of information in this document. Bring it to the reader's attention by making it the biggest element on the page. Format the text with the following attributes:

- @ Goudy Old Style font
- @ 14-point font size
- @ Bold
- @ Left alignment

Insert and Format the Address

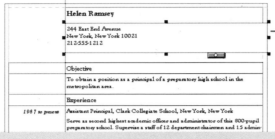

1 Draw a second text frame directly below the text frame containing the name. The bottom of the text frame should align with the 2.25-inch mark on the vertical ruler.

2 Insert the address by dragging it from the text frame on the Pasteboard. Format the text with the following attributes:

- @ Goudy Old Style font
- @ 11-point font size
- @ Left alignment

3 This is the last piece of copy from the text frame. Clean up the Pasteboard by deleting the now empty text frame.

Choosing Snap To commands saves time. Learning when to use the various Snap To options can save time and improve your accuracy. In the current project, you'll find it easier to align a ruler guide to the bottom of the text if Snap To Ruler Marks is turned off. However, it's easier to align the square bullet if Snap To Guides is turned on.

Add Decorative Elements

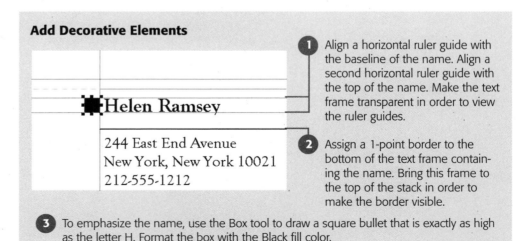

1 Align a horizontal ruler guide with the baseline of the name. Align a second horizontal ruler guide with the top of the name. Make the text frame transparent in order to view the ruler guides.

2 Assign a 1-point border to the bottom of the text frame containing the name. Bring this frame to the top of the stack in order to make the border visible.

3 To emphasize the name, use the Box tool to draw a square bullet that is exactly as high as the letter H. Format the box with the Black fill color.

Collate as you copy. If you are mailing your résumé to a long list of recipients, consider duplicating it at a service bureau. Service bureaus often offer high-quality stationery, and today's high-speed copiers can collate and even staple publications faster than you ever could by hand.

Printing the Publication

Select Print Options

1 Choose the appropriate options in the Print dialog box. Confirm that you are printing both pages, and turn off crop marks.

2 If you are printing more than one copy, consider turning off collation. Doing so will dramatically speed up the print time, although it will require you to collate by hand.

Become a Lifeguard

Put your swimming skills to the test, and possibly save a life, by signing up for lifeguard training. It's part of the Barrow Street School's afternoon program. Taught by the school's swimming coach, Jack Roth, these classes focus on the lifesaving techniques you must learn to be certified by the Red Cross. The classes will also cover basic first aid and water safety rules.

Register February 16, 1997

Junior Lifesaving: Tuesday afternoons, 3:30 to 5:30, March 5th through April 23rd. For swimmers aged 14 and under with intermediate swimming skills.

Senior Lifesaving: Thursday afternoons, 3:30 to 5:30, March 7th through April 25th. For swimmers aged 15 and older with advanced swimming skills.

WordArt can be used to create interesting rules and text effects.

Flyer

A successful flyer grabs a reader's attention with a strong image, bold head-lines, or both. Note the use of the undulating wave motif and gray shading, which break up the detail text and make the headlines stand out.

Setting Up the Page

Flyers are typically printed on one side of standard letter-sized paper. The trick to squeezing in a lot of information and keeping the text legible is to create a workable grid, which helps you maintain proportion and alignment.

Select Paper Size and Margin Options

1 Start a new document and choose the Full Page layout on the Blank Page tab.

2 Select the printer you will use. This project was printed to a PostScript device.

3 Confirm in the Page Setup dialog box that the current paper size is 8.5-by-11-inch letter size in Portrait orientation.

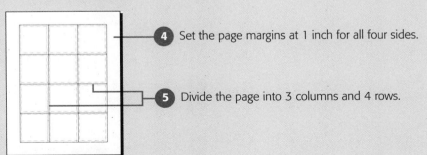

4 Set the page margins at 1 inch for all four sides.

5 Divide the page into 3 columns and 4 rows.

Repeat design motifs to create a cohesive design. In this project, the wave shape is used several times. It creates a visual pattern that holds the design together. When you create your own designs, try to develop a motif or design device that is basic enough and flexible enough to be repeated throughout a publication. As you work through this project, notice how the wave pattern, though repeated, must be modified to work with the size and placement of each text phrase or rule.

Creating the Display Type

You can make a big impact—even with a small paper size—by using large headlines. In this design, WordArt elements are used to create a bold and playful title.

The theme of water and swimming inspires the Wave 1 WordArt shape for the headline that is used as a repeating motif in this flyer. The wave shape is also used for the subhead that identifies the registration deadline and for the rules that divide categories of information.

Create the Main Headline

1 Draw a WordArt frame that spans the width of the page. If Snap To Guides is turned on, it should be easy to align the frame with the top of the page and with the guides for the first row.

2 Enter the headline text.

3 Assign the following attributes:
- Wave 1 shape
- Impact font
- Best Fit size
- Center alignment

4 Click the Stretch button so that the text fills the entire WordArt frame.

5 Make the wave effect more dramatic by increasing the Slider in the Special Effects dialog box to 100 percent.

6 Add a drop shadow within WordArt to make the text look like it is floating above the page. Assign a shadow color of Silver.

7 Click outside the WordArt frame to return to the flyer.

Use the status bar to size your WordArt frame. Instead of using the rulers to size the WordArt frame, read the status bar at the bottom of the work area as you draw the frame. When the status bar indicates that the height of the frame is 1 inch, release the mouse button.

Adjust the Special Effects Slider. The degree to which you can apply a special effect to text—and maintain legibility—depends on the number of letters in a phrase and the size of the element.

Create the Subhead

1 Draw a WordArt frame that spans the center and right-hand columns. The top of the WordArt frame should align with the top guide of the third row. The WordArt frame itself should be 1 inch high.

2 Enter the text on one line.

3 Assign the following attributes:

- Wave 1 shape
- Impact font
- Best Fit size
- Center alignment

4 Click the Stretch button so that the text fills the entire WordArt frame.

5 Make the wave effect more dramatic by increasing the Slider in the Special Effects dialog box to 85 percent.

6 Click outside the WordArt frame to return to the flyer.

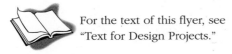

For the text of this flyer, see "Text for Design Projects."

Entering and Formatting Text

The headline and subhead take advantage of the bold shape of the Impact font. Impact is a wonderful display font, but it is difficult to read when used for body copy. Lucida Bright is an easy to read serif font. The large x-height and open letterforms give this typeface a casual feeling appropriate for a school flyer.

Type and Format Body Copy

1 Draw a text frame that spans the center and right-hand columns and includes rows 2, 3, and 4.

2 Set the text frame margins to 0 for all four sides.

3 Enter the text as three separate paragraphs. Duplicate the boldface formatting, but don't add any extra lines between paragraphs.

4 Highlight the entire story and assign these attributes:

- Lucida Bright font
- 10.5-point font size
- Right alignment

Put your swimming skills to the test, and possibly save a life, by signing up for lifeguard training. It's part of the Barrow Street School's afternoon program. Taught by the school's swimming coach, Jack Roth, these classes focus on the lifesaving techniques you must learn to be certified by the Red Cross. The classes will also cover basic first aid and water safety rules.

Junior Lifesaving: Tuesday afternoons, 3:30 to 5:30 March 5th through April 23rd. For swimmers aged 14 and under with intermediate swimming skills

Senior Lifesaving: Thursday afternoons, 3:30 to 5:30 March 7th through April 25th. For swimmers aged 15 and

5 Adjust the line spacing. Set the text on 15 points of leading, and add 10 points after each paragraph.

6 Make the text frame transparent to reveal the WordArt subhead you created earlier.

7 Send the text frame to the back in order to force a text wrap around the WordArt frame. The text will not flow properly, but you should wait to adjust it until all the elements (including the picture and the decorative rules) are in place.

Inserting, Resizing, and Recoloring Artwork

The Microsoft Clip Gallery offers a wide variety of images, including two similar images of a diver. You can use the solid black version of the diver image (Diver1.wmf), or you can import the color version of the diver (Diver2.wmf) and convert it to shades of gray. The second approach gives you a more visually interesting picture, but the flyer is still easy to produce on a black-and-white desktop laser printer.

 Changing the frame to fit the picture. You drew a picture frame based on your layout grid. But the picture of the diver has slightly different proportions than the frame you drew. You should always change the shape of the frame to preserve the aspect ratio of the picture. In this case, Publisher will reduce the height of the picture frame slightly.

 Converting colors to shades of gray. If you send color artwork to a black-and-white printer, the printer driver converts the colors to black, white, and shades of gray. You have more control over the process if you intentionally select a gray shade using the Recolor Picture command. In this sample design, for example, choose a midtone gray color as the darkest value in the picture.

Insert the Picture

1 Draw a picture frame that spans rows 2, 3, and 4 in the left-hand column.

2 Insert the picture Diver2.wmf from the Publisher CD-ROM clip-art library.

3 The image of the diver within the picture frame doesn't quite fill the layout space. Resize the diver so that the image fills rows 2, 3, and 4. You should maintain the aspect ratio. This means that the picture frame will extend past the first column guide to the 3.25-inch mark on the horizontal ruler.

4 Send the picture to the bottom of the stack to turn off text wrap.

5 Use the Recolor Picture command to convert the colors in this picture to shades of gray. Choose Gray from the standard palette.

Use Snap To Objects. Alignment of objects is a key to creating integrated page designs. You can align new elements with objects that already exist on the page by turning on Snap To Objects.

Adding Decorative Rules

Although Publisher provides many decorative rules in the form of BorderArt designs, this project uses custom rules that repeat the wave motif. You create these rules in WordArt. Publisher makes it easy to accomplish the repeating motif by allowing you to copy formats from one object to another.

Create a WordArt Rule

1 Draw a WordArt frame that spans the center and right columns. The bottom of the new WordArt frame should align with the top of the WordArt frame for the subhead and should measure 0.5 inch high.

2 Using the Insert Symbol button, insert eight em dashes (—) without spaces between them.

3 Assign the following attributes to the em dashes:
- ◎ Wave 1 shape
- ◎ Impact font
- ◎ Best Fit size

4 Click the Stretch button so that the text fills the WordArt frame.

5 Adjust the Slider in the Special Effects dialog box to 100 percent.

6 Assign a color of Silver.

7 Click outside the WordArt frame to return to the flyer.

Create a Second WordArt Rule

1 Draw a WordArt frame that spans the right column. The WordArt frame should measure 0.33 inch high, and the top should be positioned below the text at the bottom of the page (at approximately 8.63 inches on the vertical ruler).

2 Using the Insert Symbol button, insert four em dashes without spaces between them.

3 Click anywhere outside the WordArt frame to return to the flyer.

4 Select the WordArt rule you created previously. Then click the Format Painter icon on the Format toolbar. The Format Painter pointer appears.

5 Click the second WordArt rule to assign all of the formatting attributes from the first rule.

6 Double-click the new rule to edit the WordArt attributes. Adjust the Slider in the Special Effects dialog box to 40 percent.

7 Click outside the WordArt frame to return to the flyer.

Adjusting Line Breaks

If you align text with the right margin, you will add energy to a design and catch the reader's attention with the unexpected rag that results on the left side of the text block. Right-aligned copy is sometimes more challenging to read, especially if the copy contains hyphenated words. You can control the undulating edge of the text block and make this text easier to read by adjusting the line breaks.

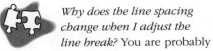

Why does the line spacing change when I adjust the line break? You are probably pressing Enter, which creates a new paragraph. Instead, press Shift-Enter to break a line without starting a new paragraph.

Adjust the Rag

1 Zoom in on the text.

2 Place the text insertion point immediately after the word *classes* on the fourth line.

3 Insert a line break by pressing Shift-Enter.

4 Repeat steps 2 and 3 wherever you think it is appropriate to break a line. (Refer to the illustration at the beginning of the chapter for suggested line breaks.)

PostScript makes it easy to resize existing designs. If you are printing to a PostScript device, you can easily resize a publication at print time. In the printer Properties dialog box, select the Graphics tab, then enter a percentage in the Scaling text box. In this example, the flyer was printed at 2/3 actual size in order to produce an advertisement for the school paper.

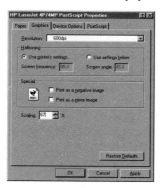

Completing the Publication

Print the Flyer

1 In the Print dialog box, turn off crop marks.

2 Specify the number of copies you want to print.

3 Print the document normally.

THE TEA ROOM

Tea ■ *Desserts* ■ *Teaware*

245 Madison Avenue
NYC
212.555.0001
www.tea_room.com

Pouchong Green, Assam, Ceylon, Darjeeling, Keemun, Lapsang/Souchong, English Breakfast, Irish Breakfast, Lady Londonderry, Prince of Wales, Russian Caravan, Earl Grey, Jasmine, Chrysanthemum, Formosa/Oolong, Gunpowder, Chamomile, Rose Hips, Iron Goddess, Vanilla, and dozens more rare and exotic teas.

A clip-art image and an elegant typeface combine
to create a company logo for this advertisement.

Phone Book Advertisement

By designing ad copy in Microsoft Publisher 97, you can avoid both the cost of an outside designer and the typesetting fee charged by the publication in which your ad will appear. When you design an advertisement, think about how you can use clip-art images (or custom shapes) to draw attention to it and reinforce your message. Is the critical information easy to find? Do readers know how to contact you?

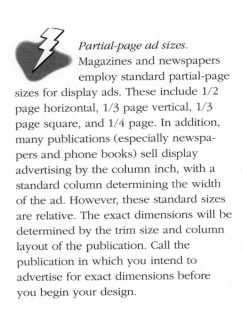

Partial-page ad sizes. Magazines and newspapers employ standard partial-page sizes for display ads. These include 1/2 page horizontal, 1/3 page vertical, 1/3 page square, and 1/4 page. In addition, many publications (especially newspapers and phone books) sell display advertising by the column inch, with a standard column determining the width of the ad. However, these standard sizes are relative. The exact dimensions will be determined by the trim size and column layout of the publication. Call the publication in which you intend to advertise for exact dimensions before you begin your design.

Setting Up the Page

The size of an advertisement designed to be run in a phone book, magazine, or newspaper is determined by the standard ad sizes of the publication. In this project, the ad is formatted for a partial page measuring 4 inches wide by 2.5 inches high.

Because the ad will ultimately be printed on a page larger than the Publisher document, use the page size of the Publisher document to represent the boundaries of the completed ad. To define the ad's boundaries, draw a box that spans the entire page edge to edge, not margin to margin.

Select Page Layout Options

1 Select the printer you will use. This project was printed to a PostScript device.

2 Confirm that the current paper size is 8.5 by 11 inches in Portrait orientation.

How can I adjust the row and column guides? You must go to the background to adjust the position of the row and column guides.

For more information about custom row and column guides, see pages 58 through 59 in Chapter 4.

How should I determine the page margins? This ad will be printed on a sheet of paper that is larger than the dimensions of the ad. You can therefore make the page margins as large or as small as you want and not be in danger of placing objects in the nonprinting margin. Setting a margin of 0 for this project creates a 0.1-inch safety area between the pink margin guides and the blue column guides. For designs in which the page size and the paper size are identical, the page margins must be large enough to prevent you from placing text and pictures in the nonprinting area of the paper.

Select Page Layout Options *(continued)*

3 Create a Special Size publication layout. The page should measure 4 inches wide by 2.5 inches high.

4 Set the page margins to 0 for all four sides.

5 Create 2 columns and 2 rows.

6 Modify the column division by moving the guide to the 2.38-inch mark on the vertical ruler.

7 Move the row division to the 1.13-inch mark on the vertical ruler.

Create the Ad Border

1 Draw a box measuring 4 inches wide by 2.5 inches high. Position the box directly over the page edges.

2 Format the box with a 4-point BorderArt rule using the Basic…Wide Midline pattern.

3 Confirm that the box is transparent.

Change the mood of a design by changing the artwork.

You can dramatically change the appearance of a design and the effect it has on the reader by substituting artwork rendered in a different style. Compare the teacup used in this project with the more photorealistic and abstract teacups shown below.

Importing the Clip Art

Publisher's clip-art collection contains multiple versions of many kinds of images. Because you have a choice of styles, you can usually find an image that evokes the right mood for your design project.

Import Clip Art

1 Starting at the column guide in the upper left corner, draw a picture frame measuring 1.3 inches wide. The frame should span row 1.

2 Insert the picture file Teacup.wmf, found on the Publisher CD. Choose Change The Frame To Fit The Picture.

3 Align the picture frame with the top and left margins once again.

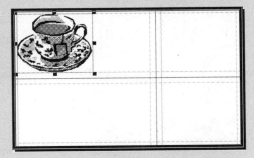

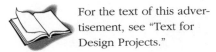

For the text of this advertisement, see "Text for Design Projects."

Creating the Ad Copy

The most important information in a partial-page display ad is the company name, address, and phone number. This copy should be set in a typeface that is easy to read. The body copy should make your points (or, in this case, a single point) very clearly. Keep the copy simple, and choose a typeface that complements your company's image and message. Here, Garamond provides the perfect understated elegance.

Type and Format the Company Name and Address

1 Create a text frame in the intersection of row 2 and column 1.

2 Type the company name, address, phone number, and other contact information, such as the World Wide Web address.

3 Format the text as indicated below:

Garamond font, bold, 14-point font size, left alignment

Garamond font, italic, 10-point font size, left alignment

Garamond font, bold, 9-point font size, left alignment

Choose a different font to change the look of an ad. To a large extent, the font you choose determines the feel of a design. Garamond, the font used in this exercise, is an elegant, rather formal font. Using a less traditional font, such as Matisse ITC (shown below), gives the design a more cutting edge look. Notice how the clip art and BorderArt have been changed to work with the new font.

Create the Body Copy

1 Draw a text frame that fills column 2 and rows 1 and 2.

2 Enter the copy, which is a list of the exotic teas offered by the Tea Room.

Easy-to-read formats make ads scannable. Remember that most people are in a rush when they are flipping through the phone book. You can communicate more effectively by designing text formats that can be read quickly. Bulleted lists, for example, highlight each piece of information on a separate line. When creating a bulleted list, you might need to edit your text by alphabetizing the list or changing the punctuation.

Rare and exotic teas:
- *Assam*
- *Ceylon*
- *Chamomile*
- *Chrysanthemum*
- *Darjeeling*
- *Earl Grey*
- *English Breakfast*
- *Formosa/Oolong*
- *Gunpowder*
- *Irish Breakfast*
- *Iron Goddess*
- *Jasmine*
- *Keemun*
- *Lady Londonderry*
- *Lapsang/Souchong*
- *Pouchong Green*
- *Prince of Wales*
- *Rose Hips*
- *Russian Caravan*
- *Vanilla*

Create the Body Copy *(continued)*

3 Format the text as follows:
- Garamond font
- Italic
- 10-point font size

4 Change the left margin of the text frame to 0.14 inch so that the text extends to the bottom of the frame.

Fine-Tuning the Design

A quick proof reveals several shortcomings to this design:

- The text block containing the list of teas isn't visually anchored along the left margin.

- Too much white space appears between the teacup and the company name.

- The white space beneath the address is awkward.

- The subhead identifying the company contains too many commas to be effective as display copy.

Making minor changes to the layout will organize the elements and make the ad easier to read.

Add a Rule Next to the Body Copy

1 Select the text frame containing the body copy.

2 Create a 1-point custom rule that runs along the left edge of the text frame only.

Is it okay to extend the text frame past the row guide that separates rows 1 and 2?

Publisher's guides always maintain a gutter (or separation) of 0.2 inch between rows and columns. In this design, that gutter is simply too much white space. Even when you extend the text frame past the guide for row 2, you are still taking advantage of the guide's alignment help. You are merely aligning the text frame with the guide for row 1.

Resize the Text Frame Containing the Display Type

1 Select the text frame containing the company name and address.

2 Using the top center selection handle, enlarge the text frame until it aligns with the bottom of the picture frame.

Add White Space Between the Company Name and the Address

1 Select the text that contains the words *Tea, Desserts, Teaware.*

2 Add 25 points of line spacing after this paragraph. This will force the address information to the bottom of the text frame.

Add Bullets to the Display Copy

1 Place the text insertion cursor after the word *Tea,* and remove the comma.

2 With no text highlighted, open the Insert menu, and choose Symbol.

3 Choose Monotype Sorts from the font drop-down list box, and select a square black bullet.

4 Select the bullet, and remove italic formatting. Make sure there is a space before and after the bullet.

5 Place a copy of the bullet between the words *Desserts* and *Teaware,* replacing the comma that is currently there.

Printing crop marks. Notice that when you print the page, the crop marks align with the edges (or borders) of your advertisement. These crop marks will help the phone book publisher trim and position the ad on the final publication page.

Use reproduction-quality paper to generate camera-ready art. In order to generate printouts that are suitable for reproduction, you must print on special paper (called Repro paper) that provides a high-contrast white background for black text and black-and-white illustrations. This paper is available from stationery stores and mail-order companies.

Printing the Advertisement

If you are working with a high-resolution printer, with 600-dpi resolution or higher, you can produce either proofs or camera-ready printouts on your laser printer.

Choosing Print Options

1 Turn on Print Crop Marks in the Print dialog box.

2 Select one of the following options in the Page Options dialog box:

- ❷ Print One Copy Per Sheet, to center a single copy of the ad on the paper

- ❷ Print Multiple Copies Per Sheet, to generate more than one copy of the ad with the least amount of paper waste

3 Print the document normally.

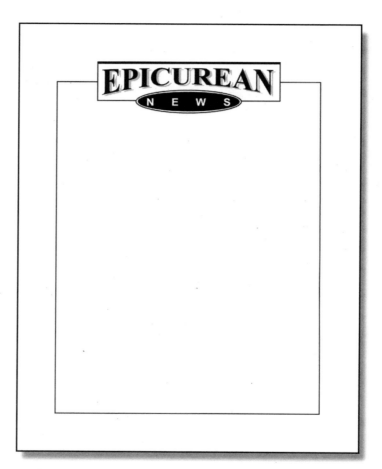

WordArt and drawn shapes work together to create a cohesive design.

Logo

Typically appearing on stationery, on business cards, and on newsletters, a logo serves as an organization's signature. The logo design should reflect the organization's overall image—for example, innovative, traditional, or playful.

Setting Up the Page

Set up Publisher's row and column guides as a drawing grid. Once you've established the grid, drawing objects precisely is simply a matter of counting units.

What if the blue guides don't match my grid specifications? Normally, when you use Publisher's row and column guides, you align objects with the light blue guidelines. Row and column guides are divided by a space (called a gutter), which in this case will throw off the grid measurement. Instead of aligning objects to the blue guidelines, use the pink guidelines. Pink guidelines fall precisely on the measurements and divisions you specify in the Layout Guides dialog box.

Select Printer and Margin Settings

1. Start a new document, and choose the Full Page layout on the Blank Page tab.

2. Select the printer you will use. This project was printed on a PostScript device.

3. Confirm that the current paper size is 8.5 by 11 inches, in Portrait orientation.

4. Set the page margins at 1 inch for all four sides. Divide the page into 13 columns and 18 rows to create a 0.5-inch grid. The math is simple: an 8.5-by-11-inch sheet with 1-inch margins contains an area of 6.5 by 9 inches, or 13/2 by 18/2 inches.

Make the working environment simpler to use. You will find it much easier to create the logo if you zoom in to a 100 percent view of the page. You will also get more use out of the ruler if you move the zero points so that they coincide with the upper left corner of the grid.

Can I use normal text instead of WordArt to create logos? You can use normal text to create a company logo. But be aware that WordArt gives you more design flexibility than normal text. In this project, for example, you'll use the Best Fit font size, which allows you to resize text as you resize the WordArt frame. You can also take advantage of special alignment features, such as letter justification, to make text phrases align with one another. These formatting options are useful for logo designs, even when you are creating a simple logo.

Creating the Main Logo Element

The design assigns different values to the two words in the logo. The word *Epicurean,* which echoes the name of the store, is the most important element and should be more prominent than the supporting word *News*.

You can enhance WordArt designs, such as this logo, by formatting the WordArt frame. Specifying larger margins, for example, opens up the design by putting space between the borders and the letters; the white space surrounding the word sets off boldface type nicely. When you add a border, be sure to choose a width that doesn't compete with your text.

Shape Text with WordArt

1 Starting at the upper left corner of the grid, draw a WordArt frame that measures 4.5 inches wide by 1 inch high. Use the pink 0.5-inch grid to make it precisely 9 squares wide by 2 squares high.

2 Type *EPICUREAN* in uppercase letters in the text box.

3 Assign the following attributes to the text:
- Deflate Bottom shape
- Times New Roman font
- Bold
- Best Fit size
- Center alignment

4 Click the Stretch button so that the text fills the entire WordArt frame.

5 In the Special Effects dialog box, change the Slider value to 40 percent, which will flatten the curve in *Epicurean*.

6 Click the Shadow button and choose the drop shadow (second from the left). Assign a shadow color of silver.

7 Click outside the WordArt frame to return to the document.

Why can't I access the WordArt frame formatting options? You can only format the WordArt frame if you select the object with a single click. Double-clicking the WordArt frame activates the WordArt toolbar, which allows you to format the text within the frame.

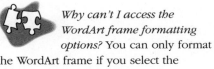

Attention to small details can make a design look more professional. In the adjacent procedure, specifying larger margins provides necessary breathing room between a border and the actual letters. The type is easier to read with the white space around it.

Format the WordArt Frame

1 Select the WordArt frame.

2 Fill the WordArt frame with a solid white color. This trick shows you whether the WordArt frame is stacked on top of or beneath the other drawn objects and text that you will add to your design.

3 Create a custom border of 1.5 points for the left, right, and bottom sides. Apply a 4-point border to the top of the frame.

4 Open the Object Frame Properties dialog box and add a margin of 0.1 inch to all four sides of the frame.

Creating the Secondary Logo Element

Look for complementary relationships between the elements on the page. The curved bottom of the word *Epicurean,* for example, suggests an oval shape that can be used as the background for the secondary text phrase.

To create decorative borders around nonrectangular objects (such as the border around the oval in the final logo design), you can stack objects with different colors and fill patterns.

Controlling the stacking order. If you use the Send To Back command (or the Send To Back button on the Standard toolbar), Publisher moves the selected object to the bottom of the stack. You have more control over the stacking order if you use the Send Farther and Bring Closer commands. These commands move objects backward or forward in the stack one level at a time. In the adjacent procedure, the Send Farther command moves the white oval behind the black oval; it is still *on top* of the primary WordArt element.

Why can I only resize the oval in 0.25-inch increments? You have Snap To Guides turned on. When you make very fine adjustments (such as the 0.1-inch enlargement in this example), you must turn Snap To Guides off. For added precision, you should zoom in to a 200 percent (or larger) magnification and refer to the status bar readout.

Draw an Oval and Create a Fancy Border

1 Draw an oval that is 2.5 inches wide (5 grid squares) and 0.5 inch high (1 grid square).

2 Fill the oval with solid black.

3 Copy the black oval, and then paste the duplicate back into the document.

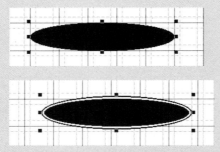

4 Format the duplicate oval with a solid white color and a black border of 1.5 points.

5 Select both oval shapes. Using the Line Up Objects command, stack and center the two ovals.

6 Select only the top white oval, and send it behind the black oval using the Send Farther command. The white oval is still selected even though it is hidden behind the black oval.

7 Holding down the Ctrl key, use a corner selection handle to increase both the width and height of the white oval from the center out by 0.1 inch.

8 Select both the white and black ovals and group them.

9 Move the combined ovals up under the curve of *Epicurean.* The bottom rule of the *Epicurean* WordArt frame should bisect the ovals.

Draw an Oval and Create a Fancy Border *(continued)*

10 Select the ovals and the WordArt frame.

11 Use the Line Up Objects command to horizontally center the ovals with the WordArt frame.

Add WordArt Text

1 Draw a WordArt frame that spans the width of the interior black oval (approximately 1.5 inches wide by 0.25 inch high). Don't worry about precise measurements, because Best Fit will resize WordArt text.

2 Type *NEWS* in uppercase letters in the text box.

3 Assign the following text attributes:

- Plain Text shape
- Arial font
- Bold
- Best Fit size

4 Choose the Letter Justify alignment option. This spaces all the letters evenly across the WordArt frame by adding extra space between the characters.

5 Change the text color to white.

7 Use the selection handles to resize the *NEWS* WordArt frame to approximately 2 inches wide by 0.20 inch high.

6 Click outside the WordArt frame to return to your logo.

8 Center the word *NEWS* in the black oval by selecting both the oval group and the WordArt frame and using the Line Up Objects command.

Why the Best Fit option is best. The Best Fit option allows you to resize WordArt text as a picture. In the current example, you can resize the word *NEWS* using the selection handles of the WordArt frame.

How do I get rid of the white boundary line around the WordArt? Don't worry about the white boundary line surrounding the *NEWS* WordArt object. It's the object boundary, which only appears on screen. It disappears when you turn on Hide Boundaries And Guides, or when you print the logo.

Use Best Fit when you know you'll have to resize your design. When you design a logo, remember that it will probably be used in a variety of publications and will need to be resized according to the layout requirements of each publication. A logo designed in WordArt can take advantage of the Best Fit option, which resizes a logo's text to fill out the WordArt frame. To maintain the aspect ratio, resize the WordArt object using a corner selection handle and the Shift key. Best Fit automatically resizes the text and re-creates the WordArt effect for the newly sized frame. In the following example, the WordArt logo has been reduced to 3 by 0.88 inch. The 3-by-0.88 inch logo has the same aspect ratio as the original 4.5-by-1.30 inch logo. You can also enlarge a WordArt element created with the Best Fit option without degrading its quality.

Positioning the Logo on the Page

Now you need to move the logo to the top of the newsletter page so that it serves as your header or banner. To avoid changing the position of the individual logo elements, you need to group the elements and move the logo as a single object. To anchor the logo on the page, add a page border.

Group the Logo Elements

1 Choose Select All on the Edit menu.

2 Click the Group button.

Center the Logo on the Page

1 With the logo still selected, choose Line Up Objects on the Arrange menu.

2 Select the following options:
- ❷ Centers, in the Left To Right area
- ❷ Top Edges, in the Top To Bottom area

3 Turn on Align Along Margins.

Publisher positions the grouped object at the top of the page and centers it between the left and right margins.

Look for relationships between elements in a logo design. As you develop your own logos, try to find structural relationships between the elements in each design. Here, for example, a repeating pattern is created when the top rule of the page border bisects the *Epicurean* WordArt frame. This page rule mimics the bottom rule of the *Epicurean* Wordart frame, which bisects the oval containing the word *News*.

Draw a Page Border

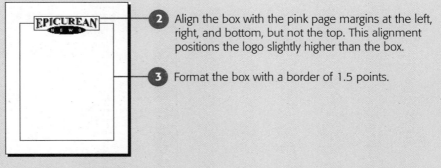

1 Draw a box that measures 6.5 inches wide by 8.5 inches high.

2 Align the box with the pink page margins at the left, right, and bottom, but not the top. This alignment positions the logo slightly higher than the box.

3 Format the box with a border of 1.5 points.

4 Send the box to the back of the stack. The top edge of the box around the page is partially hidden behind the logo.

Completing the Logo

Save the logo before you print it. You will use it again in another project.

Print the Logo

1 Choose Print on the File menu.

2 Turn off Print Crop Marks.

3 Print the document.

EPICUREAN
N E W S

Robbin Frances Cooks Food with a Philosophy

Our guest chef this month is Robbin Frances—a self-proclaimed Italophile. Having spent six years roaming the kitchens of Italy, the 31-year-old chef returned to New York three years ago (recipes in tow) to open L'Accademia, one of Manhattan's most successful small restaurants.

What keeps gourmets coming back to the three-star L'Accademia is Frances' commitment to using the freshest seasonal ingredients, many of

Robbin Frances enjoying a garden table at her restaurant L'Accademia.

which she buys from local farmers. Frances' reliance on quality ingredients is part of a philosophy that can be summed up in three words: pure and simple. "Each ingredient in a dish should have integrity," she says.

Flying Fish Spotted in The Windy City

By Elizabeth Jarmen

Let's face it, Chicago is famous for stockyards not fisheries. But times are changing. People are eating fish instead of red meat. Seafood is an important part of a heart-healthy diet, because it is low in cholesterol and fat.

We're proud that the freshest fish in Chicago can be found at Epicurean Delights. The arrival of fish farming, or Aquaculture as it is known among the professionals, has made Trout as commonly available as beef. We found a hatchery only hours away from the city. The fish is so fresh it tastes like the Trout has jumped out of the water and onto your plate!

Trout is wonderful when grilled whole over a mesquite flavored barbecue. The firm white flesh can also be filleted and boned, and then poached in white wine.

The really exciting news, however, is the introduction of Epicurean De-

lights' Flying Fish Service. Flying Fish is ordered by telephone and shipped by air to arrive the next day. It's the next best thing to catching it yourself! The quick turnaround time allows us to offer you Blue Catfish from Louisiana, Grouper from Florida, and Chinook Salmon from Washington state. We're hoping that our marine harvest inspires you to try new recipes.

Just think about Sea Bass delicately poached in a Court Bouillon of fresh herbs, such as Savory and Anise. Imagine tender medallions of Salmon encased in a crispy potato jacket. Anticipate just how succulent fresh Grouper can be when it is steamed in a parchment envelope with aromatic

(Continued on page 2)

Contents	
Herbal Update	3
Low-Calorie Gourmet	5
The Caffeine Club	6
Apple Picking Guide	7
Edible Flowers	8

Publisher gives you the tools to combine different elements, such as clip art, text, rules, headlines, and a logo, into an attractive, cohesive design.

Newsletter

Newsletters are a great promotional tool for small businesses. You can use newsletters to announce new products and special sales, and to provide other valuable information to customers. In this project, you create the first page of the *Epicurean News* and learn how to structure a multipage document.

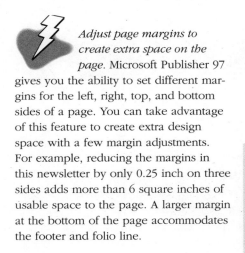

Adjust page margins to create extra space on the page. Microsoft Publisher 97 gives you the ability to set different margins for the left, right, top, and bottom sides of a page. You can take advantage of this feature to create extra design space with a few margin adjustments. For example, reducing the margins in this newsletter by only 0.25 inch on three sides adds more than 6 square inches of usable space to the page. A larger margin at the bottom of the page accommodates the footer and folio line.

Setting Up the Page

Newsletters come in all shapes and sizes. This newsletter takes advantage of the low cost and availability of standard-sized paper. The design is based on a standard three-column grid, which gives you the flexibility to size elements at three different widths: 1/3, 2/3, and full-page widths.

Select Paper and Page Options

1 Start a new document, and choose the Full Page layout on the Blank Page tab.

2 Select the printer you will use. This project was printed on a PostScript device.

3 Confirm that the current paper size is 8.5 by 11 inches, in Portrait orientation.

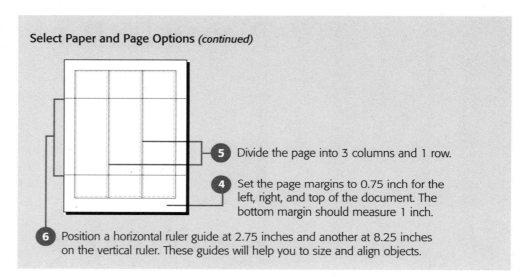

5 Divide the page into 3 columns and 1 row.

4 Set the page margins to 0.75 inch for the left, right, and top of the document. The bottom margin should measure 1 inch.

6 Position a horizontal ruler guide at 2.75 inches and another at 8.25 inches on the vertical ruler. These guides will help you to size and align objects.

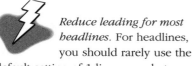

Reduce leading for most headlines. For headlines, you should rarely use the default setting of 1 line space between lines. Publisher computes 1 line space as 120 percent of point size. For a 30-point headline, Publisher creates leading of 36 points, which leaves too much white space between the lines. Notice that the Headline 1 text style you will use in the newsletter consists of 30-point letters set on 30 points of line spacing. This is called solid leading and is commonly used for headlines and other large display type.

Creating Text Styles

Newsletters typically contain many different text styles. The following table summarizes the text styles that you should create for this project. Note the visual relationship between various styles—for example, how the Headline 1 style relates to the Headline 2 style. You can minimize your work and ensure consistency by building a style from another that shares some of its attributes. Descriptive names, such as Headline 1 or First Paragraph, are used to identify the function of each text element. Only two fonts, Times New Roman and Arial, are used throughout the publication. Tone and variation are provided by bold and italic formatting.

Description of Text Styles in the Newsletter Project				
Text Style	**Character Type and Size**	**Indents and Lists**	**Line Spacing**	**Tabs**
Body Copy	Times New Roman, 10 points	First-line indent of 1 pica, justified alignment	12 points	None
Box Numbers	Arial, bold, 9 points	Center alignment	12 points	None

Text Style	Character Type and Size	Indents and Lists	Line Spacing	Tabs
Box Text	Arial, 9 points	Left alignment	12 points	None
Byline/Date/ Folio	Arial, 10 points	Left alignment	12 points	6.9 inches, right alignment
Caption	Times New Roman, italic, 8 points	Left alignment	12 points	None
First Paragraph	Times New Roman, 10 points	Left alignment	12 points	None
Headline 1	Times New Roman, bold, 30 points	Left alignment	30 points	None
Headline 2	Arial, bold italic, 12 points	Left alignment	14 points	None
Kicker	Arial, bold, 10 points, white	Center alignment	12 points	None

Creating a Template

Magazines, newspapers, and newsletters are published in cycles; any publication issued on a regular basis (daily, weekly, monthly, bimonthly, or quarterly) is called a periodical. The structure of a periodical involves two kinds of repeating elements, which together are suitable for formatting as a template:

@ Elements that repeat on every page, such as page numbers and running heads and feet, which are placed on the background of a publication.

@ Elements that appear only once in every issue, such as the logo, the date, and the table of contents. The volume number, calendar date, and words in the table of contents change from issue to issue, but the placement and style of these elements remain consistent.

Perfecting both the appearance and the placement of these elements in the template streamlines the production of subsequent issues of the publication.

How can I tell how many applications I have open at once? Whenever you have more than one Publisher application running, Windows 95 distinguishes between the different copies of the program by listing the filenames. In this example, the taskbar will display two filenames, one for the logo and one for the unsaved newsletter (called Unsaved Publication).

Copy the Logo from Another Document

1 Open the Windows 95 Start menu, and run a second Publisher application.

2 Open the publication containing the logo you created in Chapter 21.

3 Select the logo (but not the rule), and copy it to the Clipboard.

4 Close this second Publisher application. The following alert box appears:

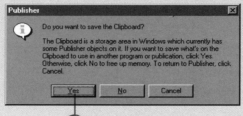

5 Click Yes to retain a copy of the logo on the Clipboard.

6 Return to the newsletter document.

7 Paste the logo onto the page.

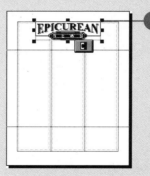

8 Using the Line Up Objects command, center the logo horizontally on the page and align it with the top margin.

A border can pull a design together. A page border provides a frame for the objects on a page. In this project, the border pulls the design together by mimicking the shapes (specifically, the line weights) of other elements on the page. The shape of the page border in *Epicurean News,* for example, intersects the midpoint of the logo in the same way that the larger WordArt frame (*Epicurean*) intersects the smaller WordArt frame (*News*) within the logo.

Use Snap To options. The date and volume text frame appears in the page margin, where there are no guides. If you temporarily turn on Snap To Objects, however, you can quickly align the text frame to the page border you created earlier. Alternatively, you can align the top of the text frame with the bottom page guide.

Create the Border on Page 1

1 Starting at the 1.25-inch mark on the vertical ruler, draw a box that aligns with the left, right, and bottom page (pink) margins.

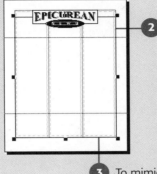

2 Format the box with a 1.5-point black border at the top, left, and right sides.

3 To mimic the design of the logo, format the box with a 4-point black border at the bottom. (You can see the difference in the line widths if you zoom in on the bottom margin.)

4 Send the box to the back, behind the logo.

Create the Date and Volume Number Box on Page 1

1 Draw a text frame so that the top edge aligns with the bottom page border. It should span all 3 columns and measure 0.25 inch high.

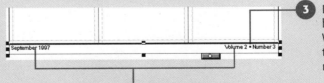

3 Insert a small square bullet (from the Wingdings font) between the volume and number information.

2 Enter the date and volume text. Insert a tab between the date and volume information.

4 Select all the copy in the text frame, and apply the Byline/Date/Folio style.

Too many borders clutter a page. By inserting border rules between rows rather than applying them to the object's frame, you avoid the common desktop publishing mistake of overformatting with too many boxes and rules. Notice that the last row of the table of contents does not have a border rule beneath it. A rule at the bottom of the table would conflict with the larger page border and clutter the page.

Create the Contents List on Page 1

1 Draw a table frame that spans the center and right columns. Align the top of the frame with the ruler guide at the 8.25-inch mark on the vertical ruler. Align the bottom of the frame with the bottom blue column guide.

2 Set up the table with 6 rows and 2 columns. For Table Format, choose Table Of Contents 3.

3 Select the entire table. In the BorderArt dialog box, apply the None border to all exterior and interior sides. While still in the BorderArt dialog box, select only the horizontal rule between rows and format it with a 1-point rule.

4 Move the division between columns 1 and 2 to the 6.5-inch mark on the horizontal ruler.

5 Select the first row, and increase the top and bottom cell margins to 0.06 inch.

6 Enter the text (as shown below) for the table of contents.

7 Format the header with the Kicker text style.

10 Mimic the logo design by superimposing a box (measuring approximately 4.4 inches wide by 0.2 inch high) over the kicker. Format the box with the clear fill color and a 2-point white border.

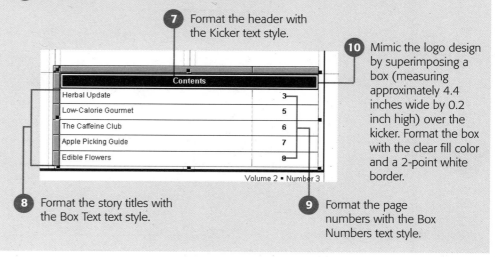

8 Format the story titles with the Box Text text style.

9 Format the page numbers with the Box Numbers text style.

Save the Newsletter as a Template

1 On the File menu, choose Save As. The Save As dialog box appears.

2 Turn on the Template check box.

3 Turn on Save Preview to save a thumbnail version of the file.

4 Enter a descriptive filename, such as Newsletter, in the File Name text box. When you click Save, the file is saved in the Template subfolder.

Create a New Publication from the Template

1 On the File menu, choose Create New Publication.

2 In the Startup dialog box, select the Templates tab.

3 Open the Newsletter template. The file that Publisher brings up is not the template but a copy of it named Unsaved Publication.

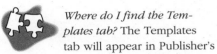 *Where do I find the Templates tab?* The Templates tab will appear in Publisher's Startup box only if you have previously saved a file as a template. If you are saving a file as a template for the first time, click the Template check box in the Save As dialog box. The Templates tab is created and is available to you.

Importing the Newsletter Text

Because Publisher automatically inserts white space, called a gutter, between column guides, the default margins of a text frame are unnecessary. Before drawing text frames, set a new default of 0 for the margins on all four sides.

Set Default Text Frame Margins

1 Select the Text tool, but don't draw a text frame.

2 In the Text Frame Properties dialog box, set all four margins to 0.

Draw Text Frames

 Draw a series of text frames. Clicking the Text tool while holding down the Ctrl key keeps the Text tool active, allowing you to draw a series of text frames without having to choose the Text tool repeatedly. When you want to return to the normal work mode, select the Pointer tool.

1 Draw a text frame that is equal in width to the left column and that measures 0.3 inch high. Align its top edge with the horizontal ruler guide at the 2.75-inch mark on the vertical ruler.

2 Draw a text frame that is equal in width to the left column. Align it with the bottom of the first text frame. The frame should be 0.55 inch high.

3 Draw a text frame that is equal in width to the left column. Align it with the bottom of the second text frame, and extend it to the end of the column.

4 Draw a text frame that spans the center and right columns. Align its top edge with the horizontal ruler guide at the 2.75-inch mark on the vertical ruler. The text frame should be 0.85 inch high.

5 Draw a text frame that spans the center and right columns. Align it with the bottom of the text frame you just drew. It should be 0.35 inch high.

6 Draw a text frame that spans the width of the center column. Align it with the text frame you just drew, and extend it to the horizontal ruler guide at the 8.25-inch mark on the vertical ruler.

7 Draw a text frame that spans the width of the right column. Align the top and bottom sides with the text frame you just drew.

If you want to re-create the newsletter as it appears in the opening illustration, you must create two files—one for each story—using your favorite word processing application. Enter the text, and follow these guidelines.

- Include the headlines, bylines, and body copy, but don't type the picture caption.

- As you create the text, press Enter after each paragraph, but don't add extra line spaces. Do not press Tab to insert paragraph indents. The Body Copy text style you created for the publication takes care of indentation.

- Type only one space after a period or a colon.

- Run the spelling checker, if available, and proofread the text before importing it.

- Save the text with filenames that will be easy to identify later, such as Chef and Fish.

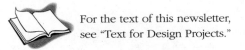

For the text of this newsletter, see "Text for Design Projects."

Import Text

1. Select the long vertical text frame in the left column.

2. Insert the text file named Chef.

3. Select the long vertical text frame in the center column.

4. Insert the text file named Fish. When prompted by Publisher to autoflow the copy, click No.

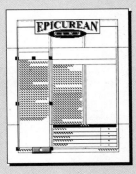

Try using intermediate magnification levels to avoid zooming. Working at the 75 percent or 66 percent magnification level can save you from constantly zooming in and out of different page views. These intermediate magnification levels provide access to a large portion of the page and still allow you to read the text.

Formatting the Lead Story

The stories on the front page of a newsletter follow a strict pecking order. The lead story always receives larger headline treatment and special formatting, such as the drop cap in this example.

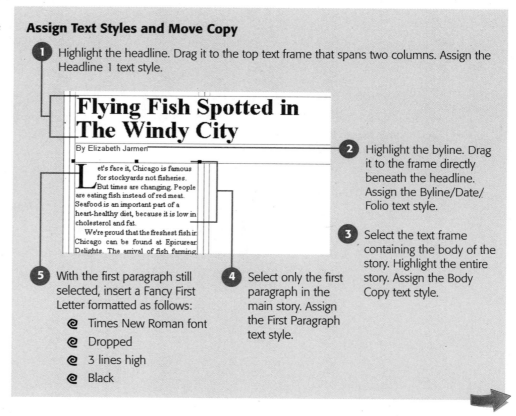

Assign Text Styles and Move Copy

1 Highlight the headline. Drag it to the top text frame that spans two columns. Assign the Headline 1 text style.

Flying Fish Spotted in The Windy City

By Elizabeth Jarmen

Let's face it, Chicago is famous for stockyards not fisheries. But times are changing. People are eating fish instead of red meat. Seafood is an important part of a heart-healthy diet, because it is low in cholesterol and fat.

We're proud that the freshest fish in Chicago can be found at Epicurean Delights. The arrival of fish farming.

2 Highlight the byline. Drag it to the frame directly beneath the headline. Assign the Byline/Date/Folio text style.

3 Select the text frame containing the body of the story. Highlight the entire story. Assign the Body Copy text style.

4 Select only the first paragraph in the main story. Assign the First Paragraph text style.

5 With the first paragraph still selected, insert a Fancy First Letter formatted as follows:
- Times New Roman font
- Dropped
- 3 lines high
- Black

6 The text frame button indicates that text is in the overflow area. Connect this text frame to the text frame in the right column by clicking the button. You'll notice that the text frame button appears again, indicating that text remains in the overflow area. You'll deal with this when you fine-tune the document later in this chapter.

Formatting the Second Lead

The type treatment for the second story on this page is more subdued: the headline is smaller, and the story does not contain a fancy first letter. However, the headline does command attention because of the kicker. Kickers precede headlines or boxed text, such as the table of contents, and help to organize a page into different sections. A kicker might identify a special story or a regular column.

Assign Text Styles and Move Copy

1 Highlight the tag line, *Guest Chef.* Drag it to the top text frame in the left column. Assign the Kicker text style.

2 Fill the text frame with black to make the white text of the Kicker text style visible.

3 Highlight the headline. Drag it to the second text frame in the left column. Assign the Headline 2 text style.

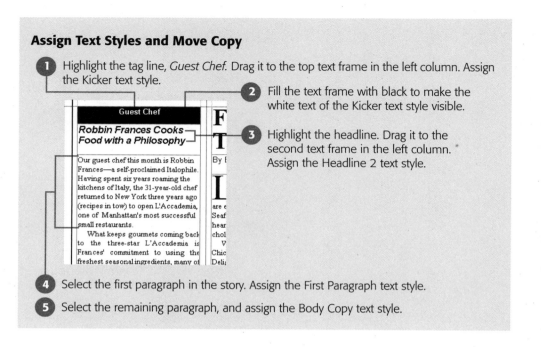

4 Select the first paragraph in the story. Assign the First Paragraph text style.

5 Select the remaining paragraph, and assign the Body Copy text style.

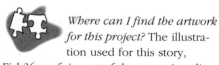

Where can I find the artwork for this project? The illustration used for this story, Fish36.wmf, is part of the extensive clip-art collection that ships with the CD-ROM version of Publisher.

Inserting and Editing Clip Art

You can add drama to an ordinary clip-art image by resizing and cropping the artwork. The ability to wrap text around the picture itself, rather than the picture frame, also makes a design more interesting.

Insert, Resize, and Crop the Fish Image

1 Draw a picture frame that spans the right column and measures 0.79 inch high.

2 Insert the clip-art image Fish36.wmf.

When to turn off text wrap. If you move the fish picture up too far, you will force the headline to wrap. You can turn the text wrap feature off by changing the stacking order of objects. In this newsletter, if you move the frame containing the headline to the front of the stack, the text will not wrap. Remember to make the text frame transparent in order to see the fish picture beneath it.

What should I do before scanning a picture? Before you create a scanned picture from within Publisher, confirm that the following are true:

- The scanner is installed properly.

- The scanner is turned on.

- The scanner is selected as the TWAIN source within Publisher.

For more information about scanners and the TWAIN interface, see pages 196 through 197 in Chapter 9.

Insert, Resize, and Crop the Fish Image *(continued)*

3 Using the Scale Picture command, resize the picture to 110 percent of its original size.

4 Move the fish up so that it nestles under the headline. Then move it left to the 4.75-inch mark on the horizontal ruler.

5 Use the Crop Picture tool to delete the fish's tail. The right edge of the picture frame should align with the black page border.

6 Click the Wrap Text To Picture button, and then click the Edit Irregular Wrap button.

7 Adjust the text wrapping boundary to fix bad line breaks.

Inserting and Editing a Photograph

Second only to importing clip art, scanning a picture is the easiest way to incorporate images into your Publisher documents. If your scanner supports the TWAIN protocol, you can acquire scanned images from within your Publisher document.

If you select the proper scanner settings, a near-perfect scanned image appears in the center of your screen. However, you'll have to make a few minor adjustments to the size and position of the photo to integrate it into the layout.

If you don't have scanning capability, select an image from the Microsoft Clip Gallery.

Determine the picture size before you scan an image. You should always scan a picture at the size at which it will be printed. The easiest way to decide on the proper size for the scanned image is to draw a dummy picture frame *before* you activate the TWAIN scanner driver. Read the status bar to get an exact size. Then delete the picture frame.

Why don't my scanning options match the options shown in the example? Scanner manufacturers often make modifications to the TWAIN interface. The actual options that you see on screen in the TWAIN window vary depending on the particular scanner installed on your system.

Scan a Photograph from Within Publisher

1 Use the Scanner Image command on the Insert menu to open a scanning utility that is TWAIN compliant.

The image was cropped and reduced during the scanning process. It was scanned at 150 dpi in gray-scale mode. This provides sufficient image data to print the image at a resolution of 75 lines per inch on a 600-dpi laser printer. The photo will require a minimum amount of editing when it is imported into Publisher.

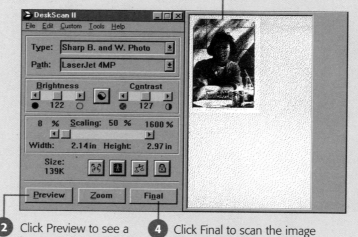

2 Click Preview to see a low-resolution version of the image.

4 Click Final to scan the image and insert it into Publisher.

3 Choose the appropriate scanner settings for image type, resolution, crop area, and size.

Why does the image look blotchy on screen? If your system is set up to run in 16-color mode, the screen image will look blotchy, or posterized. If you are working with a 256-color or better display, the image should appear normally on your screen. Regardless of how the picture looks on screen, as long as the picture itself was scanned in gray-scale mode at the proper resolution, it will print correctly.

Speed up printing times by trimming portions of a picture. Publisher's cropping function doesn't actually trim away parts of the picture—it merely hides them. Although the hidden part of the picture won't print, your printer still has to process the information, which slows down the print job. To speed up printing time, cut away unwanted portions of a photograph using your scanning or image editing software.

Position, Crop, and Format the Picture

1 Move the picture to the left column.

2 If necessary, crop the picture so that it is 1 column wide and 2.5 inches high.

3 Align the bottom of the picture with the horizontal ruler guide at the 8.25-inch mark on the vertical ruler.

4 Assign a hairline black border to the picture frame.

Fine-Tuning the Layout

Whenever you create a complex layout, you must take the time to review and adjust the various elements. At this stage of the project, there are five design problems:

@ The kicker box design is not consistent with other elements, such as the table of contents box.

@ The kicker text is not centered in its box.

@ The headline of the Guest Chef article is positioned too closely to the kicker and looks crowded.

@ The photo has no caption identifying the individual it depicts.

@ The byline for the lead story seems to float in space.

How to resize objects without changing their alignment. You can maintain the alignment of an object (relative to the page or to other objects) while you resize it by using the appropriate selection handle and pressing the appropriate key. For example, if you want to change the width of an object (such as the white border in the adjacent procedure) that is centered over another object (such as the black kicker box in the adjacent procedure), hold the Ctrl key down as you drag a center side selection handle.

Finalize the Kicker and Headline Design

1 Center the kicker text in the frame by increasing the top text frame margin to 0.08 inch.

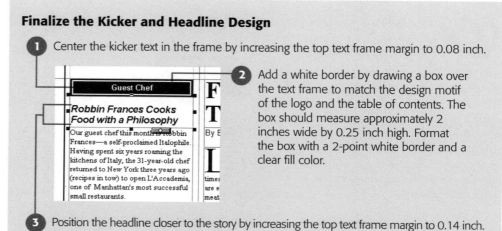

2 Add a white border by drawing a box over the text frame to match the design motif of the logo and the table of contents. The box should measure approximately 2 inches wide by 0.25 inch high. Format the box with a 2-point white border and a clear fill color.

3 Position the headline closer to the story by increasing the top text frame margin to 0.14 inch.

Add a Photo Caption

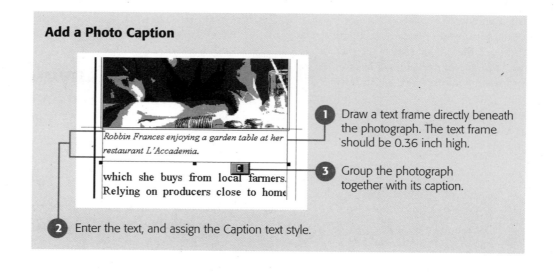

1 Draw a text frame directly beneath the photograph. The text frame should be 0.36 inch high.

3 Group the photograph together with its caption.

2 Enter the text, and assign the Caption text style.

Fix typographic problems the professional way. Professional production editors always try to fix typographic problems that occur in a complex layout, such as bad line breaks, loose lines (created when Publisher stretches a few words to fill an entire line so that columns are justified), short lines at the end of a paragraph, or widows and orphans (a single word on the last line of a paragraph or at the top of a column). You can use the same techniques they do:

- Delete a few words in a paragraph to pull up a widow.

- Add a few words to a paragraph to fill out a short or loose line.

- Decrease the spacing between characters to tighten text and improve a line break.

- Increase the spacing between characters to open up text and improve a line break.

Add a Rule to the Byline

1 Create a custom border for the byline text box. Assign a 1-point border to the top of the frame.

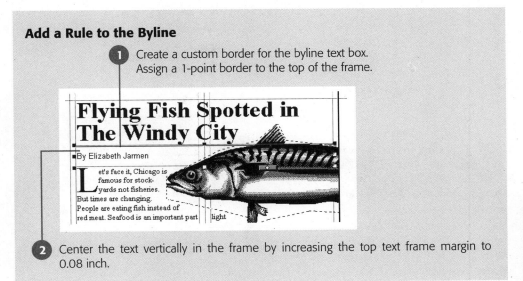

2 Center the text vertically in the frame by increasing the top text frame margin to 0.08 inch.

Fine-Tuning the Text

Once you've finalized the layout, you can turn your attention to the particulars of the text. You should always use Publisher's spelling checker and carefully proofread the document for sense. In addition, you should make adjustments so that the copy fits the layout. At this point in the project, there are several problems:

- Text remains in the overflow area of the Guest Chef article.

- Text remains in the overflow area of the Flying Fish article.

- A line breaks badly near the illustration of the fish.

How to change the formatting attributes of the Continued-On Text. Publisher always creates Continued-On Text with a default text style: Times New Roman, 8 points, italic, right alignment. In the current project, that works perfectly with the Body Copy text style, which also uses the Times New Roman font. However, if the design of your project calls for a different Continued-On Text style, change the format efficiently in the Change Style dialog box.

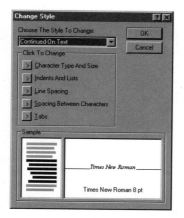

Copy Fit the Text

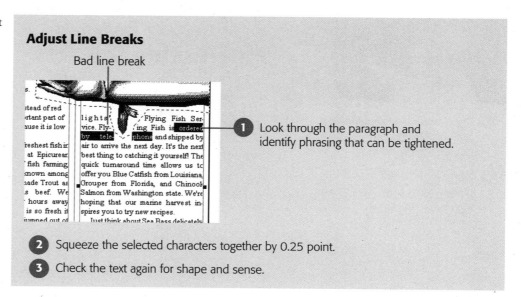

Robbin Frances enjoying a garden table at her restaurant L'Accademia.

which she buys from local farmers. Relying on producers close to home ("That means the Eastern seaboard") was a lesson she learned in Italy.

Frances' reliance on high-quality ingredients is part of a larger philoso-

1 Delete copy to shorten the story until it fits in the text frame. Here an entire sentence will be deleted.

2 Run paragraphs together if necessary.

3 Review the text for sense.

Adjust Line Breaks

Bad line break

1 Look through the paragraph and identify phrasing that can be tightened.

2 Squeeze the selected characters together by 0.25 point.

3 Check the text again for shape and sense.

Use a photocopier as a replacement for a printing press. Because this newsletter is designed to fit on a standard 8.5-by-11-inch page, it can be reproduced easily by a service bureau. So, instead of paying a premium for offset printing, you can create a large number of newsletters for pennies a copy. If you do decide to use a photocopier instead of a printing press, prepare the file in one of the following ways:

- Send the original Publisher document file to the service bureau. Many service bureaus can print directly to a photocopier from a computer network. This ensures the highest quality output.

- Print a reproduction-quality version of the newsletter on your desktop laser printer. Consult with your service bureau concerning the resolution of scanned images. You might find that reducing the half-tone resolution of your laser printer output results in cleaner, crisper photocopies.

For more information about working with an outside printer or service bureau, see Chapter 14. For more information about adjusting the printer's halftone resolution, see page 284 in Chapter 14.

Jump Text to Another Page

1 Identify stories with text in the overflow area.

> hoping that our marine harvest inspires you to try new recipes.
> Just think about Sea Bass delicately poached in a Court Bouillon of fresh herbs, such as Savory and Anise. Imagine tender medallions of Salmon encased in a crispy potato jacket. Anticipate just how succulent fresh Grouper can be when it is steamed in a parchment envelope with aromatic vegetables.

2 Use the text frame button to flow the text into another text frame on another page.

3 Use the Text Frame Properties dialog box to add automatic Continued notices to the story.

Completing the Newsletter

Print Page 1 of the Newsletter

1 Open the File menu and choose Print.

2 Select the Current Page option.

3 Turn off Print Crop Marks.

4 Click OK.

The use of a spot color is an elegant—and inexpensive—design enhancement to this catalog.

EPICUREAN DELIGHTS

Edible Flowers

Sweet Violet
A nosegay of *Viola odorata* is a gift of sweet affection. The purple blooms are, quite appropriately, a symbol of Venus. The Romans fermented crushed flowers to make a sweet wine, but modern-day cooks use crystallized blossoms as an edible decoration for desserts. Herbalists use an infusion made from flowers to cure insomnia.

Rather than offer seeds, we offer Violet seedlings instead, which can be transplanted to an outdoor site in spring. Once rooted, these perennials will return to bloom year after year. Indeed, you may find that the runners which Sweet Violets use for natural propagation invade other parts of your garden.

Seedlings (24)	#4234	2.50
Fresh flowers (1 lb.)	#4235	15.00
Plant in bloom	#4236	35.00

4

EPICUREAN DELIGHTS

Edible Flowers

Spring 1997

EPICUREAN DELIGHTS

Edible Flowers

Johnny-Jump-Up
Although these bright purple and yellow blooms look quite a lot like Pansies, Johnny Jump-Ups are totally edible. The mild flavor is slightly sweet, making Johnny Jump-Ups a perfect decoration for soft cheeses or cold fruit soups. Try combining goat cheese with Johnny Jump-Ups and watercress.

You should plant Johnny Jump-Ups in either full or partial sun at the first sign of thaw. And you can plan to enjoy both the sight and taste of the flowers in early spring. After the warm weather is over, you can still harvest these edible flowers. Simply order the potted plant instead of seeds. Our hothouse grown plants will bloom even in the dead of winter.

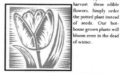

Seedlings (24)	#2234	2.50
Fresh flowers (1 lb.)	#2235	15.00
Plant in bloom	#2236	35.00

2

EPICUREAN DELIGHTS

Edible Flowers

Nasturtium
Only in recent times has Nasturtium, or *Tropaeolum minus*, been considered a purely ornamental plant. Persians nibbled Nasturtium petals as early as 400 B.C. Nasturtiums reached their peak of popularity in the kitchens of 17th century Europe. The flowers, stems, and young leaves of this plant are edible. The flavor is peppery and has a marked similarity to watercress. Indeed, Nasturtium's tangy, slightly hot taste has made it a favorite salad ingredient of Nouvelle-cuisine chefs.

Plant Nasturtium in the spring. The plants will begin to bloom in summer, but the harvest will last through fall. You can keep picked flowers fresh by floating them in a bowl of cold water.

Seedlings (24)	#3234	2.50
Fresh flowers (1 lb.)	#3235	15.00
Plant in bloom	#3236	35.00

3

Mail Order Catalog

This project meets the basic criteria of good catalog design: the page layout is uncluttered, and the critical ordering information is easy to find and scan. It is successful because the design reflects the nature of the products sold in its pages. The delicate design and the use of a spring-green spot color complement the copy about edible flowers.

Spot color choices. The spot color you choose in Publisher is used for the screen preview only. You must still designate a specific ink color for your printer. You will typically use the Pantone Matching System (PMS).

When should I use the mirrored guides option? When you create the layout guides at the beginning of a project, you should turn off Create Two Backgrounds With Mirrored Guides because you don't want to mirror an empty background. After you have added the objects you want repeated to the background, you should turn on this check box.

Setting Up the Page

This project takes advantage of Microsoft Publisher 97's spot color functions, which require you to set up the publication for outside printing.

Select Page and Printer Options

1 In the Outside Print Setup dialog box, step 1, choose the spot color option. To enhance the garden theme of the catalog, select green as Spot Color 1. Don't select a second spot color.

2 Select the MS Publisher Imagesetter as the printer for final output.

3 Select 8.5-by-11-inch paper.

4 Choose the Book Fold layout in the Page Setup dialog box.

5 Set up the page in Landscape orientation, with a trim size (page size) of 4.5 inches wide by 7.5 inches high.

6 When Publisher asks whether you want to automatically insert additional pages, click No.

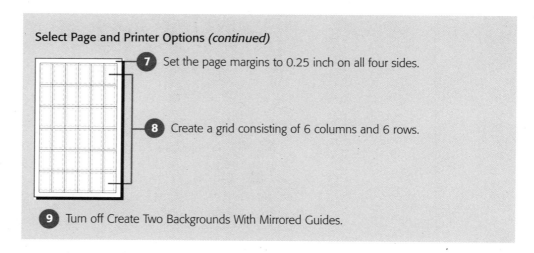

7 Set the page margins to 0.25 inch on all four sides.

8 Create a grid consisting of 6 columns and 6 rows.

9 Turn off Create Two Backgrounds With Mirrored Guides.

Use tables instead of tabs. None of the styles in this catalog contain tabs. That's because it is more efficient to use Publisher's Table tool when creating tabular information, such as the price lists that appear on each page of this catalog. Unlike tabs, tables automatically adjust row height to maintain the horizontal alignment of elements, even multiline elements.

Creating Text Styles

This document uses only two fonts: Lucida Calligraphy and Perpetua. Lucida Calligraphy serves a decorative function and is limited to display type. Perpetua serves the practical function and is used for all the body copy. Nevertheless, Perpetua's small x-height and long, delicate ascenders and descenders add the perfect typographic touch to this catalog. Use the following table to create the text styles that you will apply to the copy you type or import.

Catalog Text Styles			
Text Style	**Character Type and Size**	**Indents and Lists**	**Line Spacing**
Body Copy	Perpetua, 10.5 points	First line indent of 1 pica, justified alignment	12.5 points
Box Numbers	Perpetua, bold, 10 points	Right alignment	12.5 points
Box Text	Perpetua, bold, 10 points	Left alignment	12.5 points
First Paragraph	Perpetua, 10.5 points	Justified alignment	12.5 points
Subhead	Lucida Calligraphy, italic (default), 10 points, Spot Color 1 (green)	Left alignment	12.5 points

Use leading consistently throughout a publication. Your designs will look much more professional if you develop text styles with consistent leading. In the current project, all the text is set on 12.5 points of line spacing. Even the larger display text (such as the 16-point Lucida Calligraphy header) is set on a multiple of that leading—25 points, or exactly double the standard 12.5 points of line spacing.

Alternative font choices. The sample design in this chapter uses the Perpetua and Lucida Calligraphy fonts, but other font combinations would work equally well. You should experiment with alternative font choices, such as the Garamond and Monotype Corsiva combination and the Calisto MT and Viner Hand ITC combination shown below.

EPICUREAN DELIGHTS

Edible Flowers

EPICUREAN DELIGHTS

Edible Flowers

Creating the Repeating Elements

Publisher's background is ideal for formatting repeating elements, such as the headers and page numbers common in multipage documents. Objects placed on the background are automatically duplicated on each page.

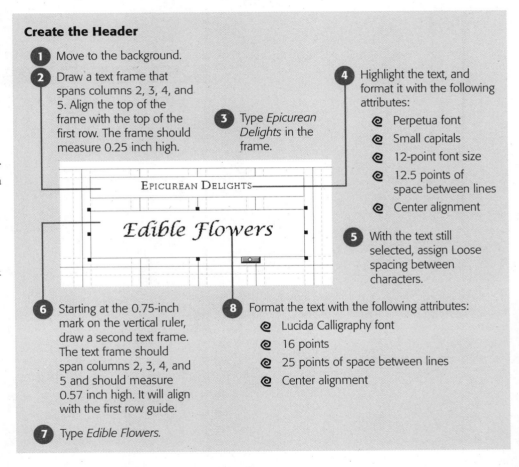

Create the Header

1 Move to the background.

2 Draw a text frame that spans columns 2, 3, 4, and 5. Align the top of the frame with the top of the first row. The frame should measure 0.25 inch high.

3 Type *Epicurean Delights* in the frame.

4 Highlight the text, and format it with the following attributes:
- Perpetua font
- Small capitals
- 12-point font size
- 12.5 points of space between lines
- Center alignment

5 With the text still selected, assign Loose spacing between characters.

6 Starting at the 0.75-inch mark on the vertical ruler, draw a second text frame. The text frame should span columns 2, 3, 4, and 5 and should measure 0.57 inch high. It will align with the first row guide.

7 Type *Edible Flowers*.

8 Format the text with the following attributes:
- Lucida Calligraphy font
- 16 points
- 25 points of space between lines
- Center alignment

Why can't I center the rule between the text lines? If you have difficulty centering the BorderArt rule between the two text boxes, turn off Snap To Guides.

Add a Decorative Rule

1 Draw a box between the two text frames.

2 Collapse the box to a single line by moving the top and bottom selection handles together until they overlap.

3 Format the collapsed box with the Vine BorderArt pattern at 15 points.

4 Center the rule between the text lines.

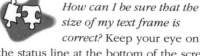

How can I be sure that the size of my text frame is correct? Keep your eye on the status line at the bottom of the screen to double-check the size of the text frame as you create it.

Insert Page Numbers as a Footer

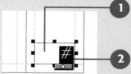

1 Draw a text frame at the bottom of the page. The frame should span the rightmost column and measure 0.25 inch high.

2 Insert a page-number mark (#).

3 Highlight the page-number mark, and format it with the following attributes:

- @ Lucida Calligraphy font
- @ 14-point font size
- @ Right alignment

When you eventually return to the foreground, Publisher will replace this symbol with the correct page number on each page.

Copy Background Elements to the Left-Hand Page

1 Switch to Full Page view.

2 In the Layout Guides dialog box, turn on Create Two Backgrounds With Mirrored Guides.

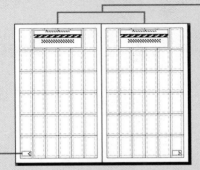

When you return to the background, you see backgrounds for left-hand and right-hand pages.

The background for the left-hand page now contains the same elements as the background for the right-hand page, except that the page-number text frame has been moved to its mirror position at the outside of the page.

3 Select the text frame containing the page-number mark on the background for the left-hand page.

4 Click the Left alignment button on the Format toolbar.

5 Return to the foreground.

Creating, Importing, and Formatting Catalog Text

Catalog copy doesn't have to be a hard sell. These sometimes historical, often whimsical descriptions of edible flowers create a mood that is supported by the delicate type treatment. Pricing information, on the other hand, should always be presented in a clear format that's easy to locate and read. Presenting the pricing information in a different format, such as a table, adds visual interest to a page.

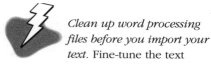

Clean up word processing files before you import your text. Fine-tune the text before you place it in your Publisher document: run the spelling checker, and proofread the copy for errors such as double words, dropped words, double spaces, and incorrect punctuation.

For the text of this catalog, see "Text for Design Projects."

Type the Text

1 In a word processing application, type the text for the body copy. Create three separate files.

2 Name the files Johnny, Nasturtium, and Violet.

Import and Format the Johnny-Jump-Up Text

> *Johnny-Jump-Up*
> Although these bright purple and yellow blooms look quite a lot like Pansies, Johnny-Jump-Ups are totally edible. The mild flavor is slightly sweet, making Johnny-Jump-Ups a perfect decoration for soft cheeses or cold fruit soups. Try combining goat cheese with Johnny-Jump-Ups and watercress.
>
> You should plant Johnny-Jump-Ups in either full or partial sun at the first sign of thaw. And you can plan to enjoy both the sight and taste of the flowers in early spring. After the warm weather is over, you can still harvest these edible flowers. Simply order the potted plant instead of seeds. Our hot-house grown plants will bloom even in the

1 Draw a text frame that spans columns 2, 3, 4, and 5. Vertically, the text frame should span rows 2, 3, 4, and 5.

2 Insert the file named Johnny.

3 Click in the first line (which happens to be an entire paragraph), and format it with the Subhead text style.

4 Click in the next paragraph, and format it with the First Paragraph text style.

5 Click in the next paragraph, and format it as Body Copy.

What can I do to adjust the placement of my fancy first letter? When creating dropped initial caps with decorative fonts, you will run into letterspacing and line spacing problems. In the adjacent procedure, for example, the bottom of the letter *J* crashes into the line of text beneath it. You can correct this problem by fine-tuning the type manually as follows:

@ Insert a line break (by pressing Shift-Enter) at the end of the third line, after the word *a*.

@ Click to place the insertion point at the beginning of the line of text that crashes into the initial cap.

@ Create a left tab stop that aligns with the indented text. Tab the line of text over to move it clear of the fancy first letter.

@ If necessary, use the Spacing Between Characters dialog box to nudge the first letter of the third line into perfect alignment.

The dropped initial cap will still appear to be cropped on screen, but it will print correctly.

Create a Fancy First Letter

1 Select the subhead.

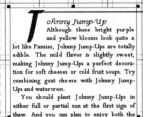

2 Create a custom fancy first letter with the following attributes:

@ Lucida Calligraphy font

@ 4 lines high

@ Combination letter position of 1 line above the paragraph and 3 dropped lines

@ Spot Color 1 (solid green)

Create the Pricing Table

1 Draw a table frame that spans columns 2, 3, 4, and 5. The frame should measure 0.75 inch high. The top of the frame should align with the top of the last row.

2 In the Create Table dialog box, create a table with 3 rows and 3 columns. Leave the Default table format selected.

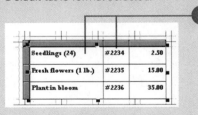

3 Using the Adjust pointer and the Shift key, widen the first column in the table until it spans columns 2 and 3 and stretches across the gutter between columns 3 and 4. Using the Shift-Adjust pointer combination, widen the second column of the table to span column 4.

4 Select the entire table. Format the top, center, and bottom sides of the table with a hairline black border.

5 Format columns 1 and 2 of the table with the Box Text style. Format column 3 with the Box Numbers style.

6 Enter the text for Johnny-Jump-Up prices.

Adding a Picture to the Catalog

In a mail order catalog, pictures are a key sales tool. People rarely buy something they have never seen, and an attractive picture can often convince someone to make an impulse purchase.

Seeing the grid. To see the the grid beneath the text frame, select the text frame and use the Object Color button (or the Ctrl-T keyboard shortcut) to make the frame transparent.

Where do I find the Spring.cgm clip-art image? The image Spring.cgm ships with the CD-ROM version of Publisher.

Import a Picture

1 Draw a square picture frame that spans columns 4, 5, and 6.

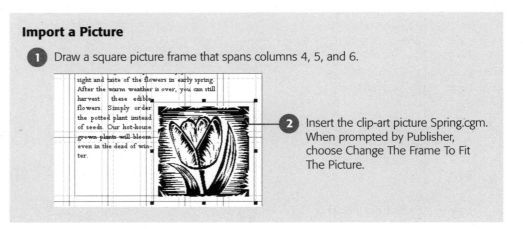

2 Insert the clip-art picture Spring.cgm. When prompted by Publisher, choose Change The Frame To Fit The Picture.

Reformat the Picture and Picture Frame

1 Recolor the picture using a 100 percent tint of the green spot color.

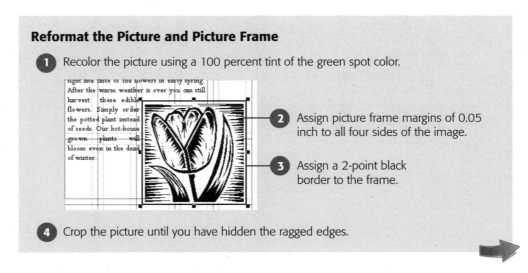

2 Assign picture frame margins of 0.05 inch to all four sides of the image.

3 Assign a 2-point black border to the frame.

4 Crop the picture until you have hidden the ragged edges.

Reformat the Picture and Picture Frame *(continued)*

5 Position the picture so that the right edge aligns with the rightmost column guide and the bottom aligns with the pink row guide near the 6-inch mark on the vertical ruler.

6 Resize the picture, holding down the Shift key to maintain the aspect ratio. The picture should span columns 4, 5, and 6.

Completing the Catalog Pages

When should I insert new pages into my design? If you wait until you have completed the layout for an entire page before inserting new pages, you can instantly duplicate the completed layout on each new page.

Insert Pages

1 Insert two pages. Be sure to add the pages *after* the current page and to select the option Duplicate All Objects on Page Number 1.

2 When Publisher asks whether you want to automatically insert the correct number of pages for a booklet, click No.

Replace the Duplicated Text with New Text

1 Move to page 2.

2 Select the large text frame containing the duplicate text about Johnny-Jump-Ups, and highlight the entire story.

Replace the Duplicated Text with New Text *(continued)*

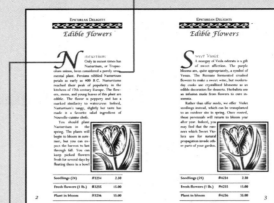

3 Insert the file named Nasturtium. The new text will replace the highlighted text.

4 When Publisher asks whether you want to use the Autoflow feature, click No.

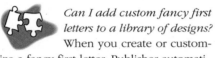
Can I add custom fancy first letters to a library of designs? When you create or customize a fancy first letter, Publisher automatically adds the design to the Gallery in the Fancy First Letter dialog box. This makes it easy for you to apply the fancy first letter format to subsequent paragraphs in the current (or other) documents.

5 Format the first line with the Subhead style and the fancy first letter you created earlier.

6 Format the first paragraph after the subhead with the First Paragraph style.

7 Format the final paragraph with the Body Copy style.

8 Move to page 3, and repeat steps 2 through 7 using the file named Violet.

Type New Table Text

1 Select the table containing the pricing information for Nasturtiums.

2 Enter the correct ID numbers.

3 Repeat steps 1 and 2 for Sweet Violets.

Creating the Cover Page

The exercises in this chapter have all stressed the importance of consistency in a publication, but every publication contains pages that are unique, such as the cover or title page. One way to minimize your workload is to copy an element from another page and then reformat it. For example, in this project, the front cover mimics the header design. Instead of creating the individual elements again, copy the header from the background. Then resize and reformat them.

Insert a Cover Page

1. Move back to page 1, and insert a new blank page *before* the current page.

2. In the alert box that appears, click OK to insert the page.

3. Toggle on Ignore Background. This command hides the header and page number on the cover. It affects only the currently displayed page.

Add and Format the Cover Text

1. Copy each object from the header design on the background to the cover page (page 1).

2. Reformat the design to match the following illustration.

Epicurean Delights is formatted at 20 points on 25 points of line spacing, and the height of the text frame is increased to 0.44 inch. The frame is stretched across the width of the page.

The decorative rule remains at a 15-point size, but it is stretched across the entire width of the page. It aligns with the top of the main text frame.

Edible Flowers fills the entire third row. The type is formatted at 32 points on 50 points of line spacing.

The text frame is filled with a hexagonal gradient. The base color is a 20 percent tint of the green spot color. The second color is a 50 percent tint of the green spot color.

Avoiding banded or striped printed proofs. If you are using a low-resolution proof printer, you may notice that printouts show the gradient fill as a series of stripes. This phenomenon is known as banding. It occurs when a printer can't produce a sufficient number of shades to create a gradual tonal transition. Banding is especially noticeable if you are filling a large object with a gradient fill, and the starting and ending colors of the fill are very similar to one another. The banding problem is typically restricted to low-resolution devices. Service bureau printers, called imagesetters, have more than enough resolution (usually 1200 to 2400 dpi) to produce gradual tonal changes.

You can minimize the banding problem by turning on error diffusion (or dithering) in the printer Properties dialog box. Not all printers support this feature, but if your printer does, use it! Error diffusion creates a random dot pattern that can minimize banding and even improve the appearance of photographic images on low-resolution printers.

Add and Format the Cover Text *(continued)*

3 Draw a text frame at the bottom of the page. The frame should span the page horizontally and measure 0.25 inch high.

4 Type *Spring 1997.*

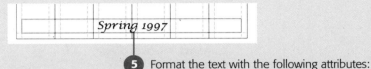

5 Format the text with the following attributes:

- Lucida Calligraphy font
- 14-point font size
- 15 points of space between lines
- Center alignment

Fine-Tuning the Layout and the Text

You should always scrutinize the layout and the text to discover and fix problem areas before you send the document to a service bureau or commercial printer. At this point in the design process, there are several problem areas:

- The picture on page 2 is not balanced with the layout on page 3.

- The initial caps on pages 3 and 4 aren't the same size as the *J* on page 2.

- In the Nasturtium story, there is text in the overflow area.

- Typewriter-style text should be replaced with typographic-style text. For example, Latin names should be italicized, and the abbreviation *B.C.* should appear in small caps.

Viewing facing pages enables you to create a balanced design. Whenever you use the Book Fold layout, use the Two-Page Spread option (found on the View menu). As you work on your design, look at it the way the reader will—as a spread rather than one page at a time. In the current project, doing so will help you rearrange the elements in the spread so that the two pages form a mirror image of each other.

Balance the Pages

1 Move to pages 2 and 3.

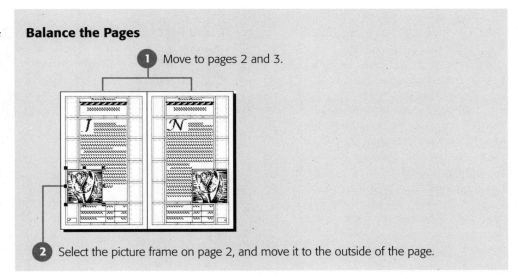

2 Select the picture frame on page 2, and move it to the outside of the page.

Adjust the Display Type

1 In the Nasturtium story, enlarge the fancy first letter by one line so that it matches the size of the *J* in the Johnny-Jump-Up story.

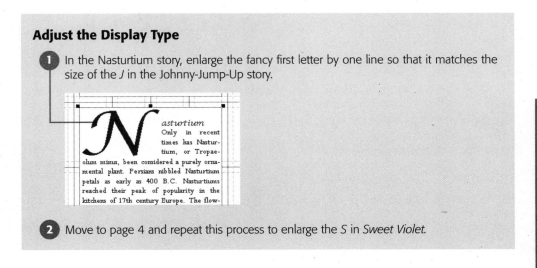

2 Move to page 4 and repeat this process to enlarge the *S* in *Sweet Violet.*

Use only true italics and boldface. You should apply italic and boldface formats only when you have the appropriate versions of a font installed on your system. *Microsoft Publisher 97 Companion* lists the versions of each font that ship with the product. The Perpetua font, used in this project, includes only normal and boldface styles. Therefore, when you apply italic formatting to Perpetua, Microsoft Windows 95 fakes the effect by slanting the normal font at an oblique angle to simulate italics. The results are less than ideal.

PostScript printers generate the most accurate proofs. Service bureaus and commercial printers generate PostScript output. You'll have an accurate reflection of your final document—including correct letterspacing and line breaks—if your local printer is also a PostScript device.

Copy Fit and Proofread the Text

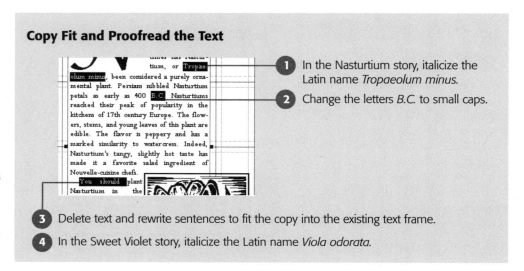

1 In the Nasturtium story, italicize the Latin name *Tropaeolum minus*.

2 Change the letters *B.C.* to small caps.

3 Delete text and rewrite sentences to fit the copy into the existing text frame.

4 In the Sweet Violet story, italicize the Latin name *Viola odorata*.

Printing a Proof and Producing the Catalog

When you print a publication created with the Book Fold layout, Publisher positions two pages of the publication on each sheet of paper. As you'll see next, this page imposition (the arrangement of pages on a larger piece of paper) guarantees that the pages will be in the correct order when you assemble the finished catalog.

Print a Proof of the Catalog to a Local Printer

1 In the Print Proof dialog box, turn on Show All Print Marks.

2 Turn off Print Color Separations.

Print a Proof of the Catalog to a Local Printer *(continued)*

 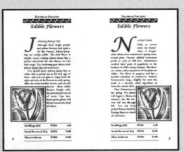

Publisher prints composite proofs. The black and green colors appear on one sheet of paper as shades of gray.

The Book Fold layout prints this catalog with pages 4 and 1 (the outside pages) on one sheet and pages 2 and 3 (the inside spread) on the second sheet.

What's a dummy? A dummy is a mock-up of the final printed, trimmed, folded, and bound publication. You can use the proofs you created on your local printer to collate, trim, and assemble a dummy catalog by hand.

Why does the file size change so dramatically when I create a PostScript printer file? When you create a PostScript printer file, Publisher must produce a file with all the information necessary to generate the printout. Images are converted to the PostScript format, and font information for nonstandard fonts (such as Lucida Calligraphy and Perpetua) is embedded in the file. As a result, the printer file can grow quite large. In this sample, the PostScript printer file requires 1.6 MB of disk space. Compare that to Publisher's format, which requires only 40 KB.

For more information about preparing files for service bureau output, see Chapter 14.

Assemble the Catalog as a Dummy

1 Photocopy pages 2 and 3 right side up onto the back of the sheet with pages 4 and 1.

2 Fold the paper down the center to form the spine of the catalog.

3 Use the crop marks as a guide to trim away the excess paper.

Transfer the Publication to the Service Bureau

1 Before you send a file to the service bureau, generate an InfoSheet. This report contains important information about your publication, such as paper size and font usage.

2 Check with the service bureau to see which of the following file formats you should generate:

- Publisher's native format. This requires the service bureau to have a current copy of Publisher and the fonts you've used in the document.
- A PostScript printer file, which you've generated using the Print To Outside Printer command.

3 Copy the publication or printer file to a floppy disk.

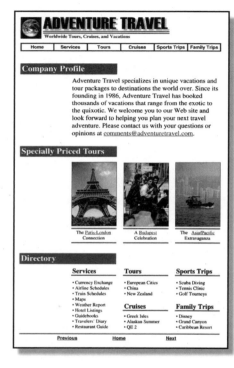

Using Publisher's special Web publishing tools, you can design complex and fully functional Web pages.

World Wide Web Site

When designing a World Wide Web site, your goal is to create a document that is easy to read on screen. This requires you to learn—and limit yourself to—the restricted formatting attributes supported by the Hypertext Markup Language (HTML), the format used on the Web.

Setting Up the Web Page

This project takes advantage of Microsoft Publisher 97's Web authoring tools, which appear when you choose the Web Page layout in the Startup dialog box.

Set Up the Web Page

1 Select the Blank Page tab in the Startup dialog box, and then choose the Web Page icon.

2 In the Web Page Setup dialog box, choose the Standard (VGA) option. Leave the page height at 10 inches.

3 Set the page margins to 0 for all four sides.

Create ruler guides for every page. To create a ruler guide that will appear on every page of a document, simply place the ruler guide on the background. You should place a ruler guide on the background only if you need to align objects consistently on different pages at the same location. In the current project, the heading of every page will be aligned with the second ruler guide.

Choose text colors that contrast with the background. Readers who will view your Web site may be using older monitors and video cards, which are capable of displaying only 16 colors. To make sure your text is legible, choose colors that contrast with the background. In the adjacent procedure, the text colors are a different hue and are much more saturated and much darker than the background.

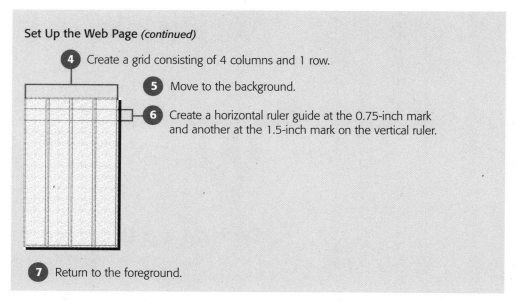

Set Up the Web Page *(continued)*

4 Create a grid consisting of 4 columns and 1 row.

5 Move to the background.

6 Create a horizontal ruler guide at the 0.75-inch mark and another at the 1.5-inch mark on the vertical ruler.

7 Return to the foreground.

Create a Custom Background and Custom Text Colors

1 In the Background And Text Colors dialog box, select the Custom tab.

2 Click the Browse button and load the texture file Fleck.gif, found in Publisher's Backgrnd subfolder.

3 Choose the following text colors from the flyout color palette:

- Body Text: navy (second row, second column)
- Hyperlink: red (sixth row, first column)
- Followed Hyperlink: teal (third row, fourth column)

Creating Text Styles

The text elements in your document will be the first thing that your readers see because text downloads so much more quickly than pictures. Therefore, it's

Why should I use a color other than black for the text in my Web document? When designing a Web document, you must distinguish between normal text, hyperlink text, and followed hyperlink text. You do this by using a different color for each type of text object. In the current project, normal text is navy, hyperlink text is red, and followed hyperlink text is teal.

Overriding the default body text color. Using Publisher's Character dialog box, you can change the color of body text on a case-by-case basis. In the current project, for example, the Web Head 1 text style is formatted as white, not navy. Employ this feature sparingly, however, because text colors in a Web document serve to distinguish between normal body copy, hypertext, and followed hypertext. You should not format normal body copy with the same color you've chosen for hypertext or followed hypertext, as it might confuse your readers.

Remember that to override the default colors for hypertext and followed hypertext you must change the colors in the Background And Text Colors dialog box.

important to structure the document by using text elements such as section headings and bulleted lists.

You should limit your text styles to the most standard fonts available: Times New Roman and Arial. In addition, you should keep the formatting simple. This will enable Publisher to convert your document to HTML without any loss of formatting.

HTML Text Styles			
Text Style	**Character Type and Size**	**Indents and Lists**	**Line Spacing**
Web Body	Times New Roman, 10 points	Left alignment	1 space
Web Head 1	Times New Roman, bold, white, 18 points	Left alignment	1 space
Web Head 2	Times New Roman, 14 points	Left alignment	1 space
Web Button	Arial, bold, 10 points	Center alignment	1 space

Creating the Repeating Elements

Like traditional desktop publishing documents, Web documents contain repeating elements, such as a running head containing the company logo. Instead of actual page numbers, however, Web documents contain page controls—buttons that move you forward or backward through a multipage document. Objects placed on the background are automatically duplicated on each page.

Import and Format a Picture

1 Go to the background. Zoom to 100 percent magnification.

2 Draw a picture frame measuring 0.6 inch wide by 0.9 inch high.

3 Insert the picture file 4055.jpg from the Publisher CD-ROM (a picture of Earth seen from space).

What is the difference between a document's background and the Background And Text Colors dialog box? The Background And Text Colors dialog box is a Web publishing tool that allows you to specify a background color or texture for all the pages in your document. Think of this dialog box as a formatting option.

The background is a standard Publisher feature that allows you to create a layout for elements (such as type, pictures, and logos) that will repeat on every page of the document. Think of the background as a layout function.

Use WordArt to incorporate unique fonts into a Web document. The logo employs a nonstandard font, Haettenschweiler. To be sure that the correct font appears on screen when a reader views this document with a Web browser, create the object as a WordArt element. Publisher automatically converts WordArt elements to pictures when it generates an HTML file.

Import and Format a Picture *(continued)*

4 Use the Crop Picture tool to eliminate the extraneous black background from the top and bottom of the picture. When you have finished, the picture should measure 0.65 inch high.

5 Align the top and left sides of the picture frame with the top and leftmost column guides on the page.

Create a WordArt Element

1 Draw a WordArt frame measuring 3.65 inches wide by 0.4 inch high. Position the frame at the 0.75-inch mark on the horizontal ruler. The top of the frame should align with the top row guide.

2 Type *ADVENTURE TRAVEL* in uppercase letters into the WordArt text box.

3 Apply the following attributes:
- Plain text shape
- Haettenschweiler font
- Best Fit size
- Navy foreground color

4 Click the Stretch button to have the text fill the entire WordArt frame.

5 In the shadow dialog box, choose the drop shadow (second option from the left). Assign a shadow color of silver.

6 Click outside the WordArt frame to return to the document.

To avoid graphic regions, create layouts with no over-lapping objects. When Publisher generates an HTML document, it converts all overlapping objects into graphic regions, which are pictures that take longer to download. As you complete each procedure in this sample project, notice how you prevent objects from overlapping: place design elements carefully, and use column guides and ruler guides.

What does a flashing red box mean? If you overlap two or more objects, Publisher warns you that these objects will be converted to a graphic region when you generate the HTML document. Resize or reposition the objects to create a layout in which objects do not overlap.

For the text of this Web site, see "Text for Design Projects."

Add Supporting Text and Rules to the Logo

1 Draw a text frame measuring 3.65 inches wide and 0.16 inch high. Position the left edge of the text frame at the 0.75-inch mark on the horizontal ruler. The bottom of the text frame should align with the ruler guide at the 0.75-inch mark on the vertical ruler.

2 Enter the text *Worldwide Tours, Cruises, and Vacations.*

3 Highlight the text, assign the Web Body style, and click the Bold button on the Format toolbar.

4 Change the top margin for the text frame to 0.

5 Draw a 2-point red rule that aligns with the left edge of the WordArt text frame and extends to the column guide at the far right side of the page. Position the rule at the 0.53-inch mark on the vertical ruler.

6 Place a duplicate of the line at the 0.58-inch mark on the vertical ruler.

Insert Page Controls in the Header

1 Draw a table frame that spans columns 1 through 4 and measures 0.25 inch high. Position the top of the table 0.88 inch below the top of the page.

2 Create 1 row and 6 columns in the table.

3 Enter the button text.

4 Format the entire table with the following attributes:
- Web Button text style
- 2-point navy border

Provide convenient controls. The page controls you create in the adjacent procedure will appear at the top and bottom of every page. Though this might seem like a duplication, it is actually a necessary convenience feature. You shouldn't force the reader to scroll back to the top of the current page simply to move to another page in the document.

Insert Page Controls as a Footer

1 Draw a text frame that spans column 1 and measures 0.25 inch high. The text frame should align with the bottom row guide.

2 Type the word *Previous*.

3 Format the word with the Web Button text style.

4 Move to column 2 and repeat steps 1 through 3, except this time enter the word *Home*.

5 Move to column 3, and repeat steps 1 through 3, except this time enter the word *Next*.

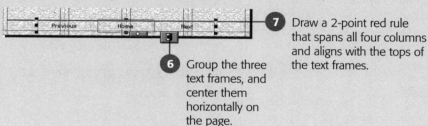

7 Draw a 2-point red rule that spans all four columns and aligns with the tops of the text frames.

6 Group the three text frames, and center them horizontally on the page.

Creating the Home Page

Like the first page of a newsletter, the first page of a Web site (referred to as the home page) should serve several functions: it should grab readers' attention with important information, and it should point them to other information in the Web site. The following design uses bold text treatments, high-quality pictures, and bulleted text to accomplish these tasks.

Create and Format Display Type

1 Move to the foreground.

Divide Web pages into screen-sized sections. Remember that your readers will be viewing this information on a computer screen. Reduce the time they spend scrolling down a page—and increase the time they spend reading a page—by dividing the page into screen-sized sections. In the adjacent procedure, for example, the headings divide the page into three sections, each approximately 3 inches high.

Turn off automatic hyphenation. HTML does not support automatic hyphenation of any kind. You should therefore select each text frame in your Web publication and disable automatic hyphenation. This guarantees that the line breaks you see in your working version of the document will match the line breaks your readers see when they view the document using a Web browser.

Create and Format Display Type *(continued)*

2 Draw a text frame that spans columns 1 and 2 and measures 0.33 inch high. Align the top of the text frame with the ruler guide at the 1.5-inch mark on the vertical ruler.

3 Format the text frame with a solid red fill color.

4 Type the text *Company Profile.*

5 Format the text with the Web Head 1 text style, and then change the top margin of the text frame to 0.

6 Paste a duplicate of the text frame at the 4-inch mark on the vertical ruler.

7 Change the copy to read *Specially Priced Tours.*

8 Paste a second duplicate of the text frame at the 7.25-inch mark on the vertical ruler.

9 Change the copy to read *Directory.*

Insert the Body Copy

1 Draw a text frame that spans columns 2, 3, and 4. The text frame should measure 2 inches high. Position the top of the text frame at the 1.9-inch mark on the vertical ruler.

2 Change all four text frame margins to 0.

3 Type the body copy, or import it from a text file.

Why am I formatting a large text block with the Web Head 2 text style? The HTML specification supports only one font size for body copy, which typically appears on screen in 10-point type. Many Web publishers circumvent this limitation by using one of the six HTML heading levels to vary the point size of body copy. In this Web site project, for example, the Web Head 2 text style uses 14-point type.

Decrease download times by decreasing the size of pictures. The pictures in this sample Web publication are less than 2 inches square. Keeping the pictures (and their respective file sizes) small will allow your readers to download this site as quickly as possible.

What will happen if I resize bitmapped pictures in Publisher? Resizing a bitmapped picture in Publisher is not normally recommended because it can degrade image quality. In this case, however, you are *decreasing* the size of the picture, which results in less image degradation than increasing the size of a bitmapped picture.

In addition, when Publisher generates the final HTML file, it will take a snapshot of the screen, automatically reducing the high resolution of these images to a resolution appropriate for monitor output.

Insert the Body Copy *(continued)*

4 Assign the Web Head 2 text style.

5 In the Hyphenate dialog box, turn off automatic hyphenation.

Import and Format the First Picture

1 Scroll down the page to the Specially Priced Tours section.

2 Starting at the 4.5-inch mark on the vertical ruler, draw a picture frame that spans column 2. The frame should measure approximately 2 inches high.

3 Insert the file 05244.jpg from Publisher's CD (a picture of Paris). When prompted, choose Change Frame To Fit The Picture. Publisher will resize the picture's height to 1.94 inches.

4 Move the picture back to the 4.5-inch mark on the vertical ruler.

5 Format the picture frame with a Hairline black border.

Import and Edit Additional Pictures

1 Paste a duplicate of the picture frame in column 3 and in column 4.

2 Select the picture frame in column 3, and insert the file 05251.jpg from Publisher's CD (a picture of street musicians).

5 Crop the left and right sides of the picture to trim it to 1.3 inches wide and 1.94 inches high.

3 Select the picture frame in column 4, and insert the file 5053.jpg from Publisher's CD (a picture reminiscent of the Hong Kong port).

4 Using the Scale Picture command, resize the picture to 75 percent of its original size.

Design efficiently by reformatting duplicate objects. You can create a layout much more quickly if you duplicate an object, reposition it on the page, and then change one or two of its attributes. In the adjacent procedure, for example, it is more efficient to insert different pictures and different text into duplicate frames than it would be to draw and format four additional frames. You'll use the same technique when you create a series of lists in the next procedure.

Add Labels to the Photographs

1 Starting at the 6.5-inch mark on the vertical ruler, draw a text frame that spans column 2 and measures 0.45 inch high.

2 Enter the text *The Paris-London Connection.*

3 Format the text with the following attributes:
- Web Body text style
- Center alignment

4 In the Hyphenate dialog box, turn off automatic hyphenation.

5 Format the text frame with a 2-point red border at the top and bottom.

6 Position a duplicate of this object in column 3.

7 Replace the text with *A Budapest Celebration.*

8 Position a duplicate of this object in column 4.

9 Replace the text with *The Asia/Pacific Extravaganza.*

Create a Bulleted List

1 Scroll down the page to the Directory section.

2 Starting at the 7.63-inch mark on the vertical ruler, draw a text frame that spans column 2 and measures 0.3 inch high.

3 Type the word *Services.*

4 Assign the following attributes:
- Web Head 2 text style
- Bold
- 2-point red border to the bottom of the frame

5 Create a second text frame directly beneath the Services text frame at the 8-inch mark on the vertical ruler. It should measure 1.6 inches high.

Why should I use the Insert Symbol dialog box to insert a bullet instead of creating an automatic bulleted list in the Indents And Lists dialog box? When Publisher converts a bulleted list created from the Indents And Lists dialog box into HTML code, it ignores any choices you've made concerning the bullet type and the indents surrounding the bullet. This lack of control can create awkward white spaces at the beginning of each line and bad line breaks. Using the Insert Symbol dialog box allows you to choose the bullet and to control (using space characters) the position of the bullet relative to the text.

Why must I draw separate text frames for each item in the Directory section? Normally, you could create a complex element like the series of bulleted lists shown here by formatting a single text frame with multiple columns. However, when you are designing a Web document, the multicolumn option in the Text Frame Properties dialog box is not available because HTML does not support multicolumn text. HTML requires you to draw a separate text frame for each column of text.

Create a Bulleted List *(continued)*

6 Enter the list copy for Services.

7 Assign the Web Body text style.

8 Using the Insert Symbol dialog box, insert a bullet from the Times New Roman font at the beginning of the first item in the list. Add a space after the bullet.

9 Copy the bullet and the space to the beginning of each remaining item in the list.

10 Use the following illustration to create and position the remaining text frames.

@ Draw four text frames for the subheads measuring 1 column wide by 0.3 inch high.

@ Draw four text frames for the bulleted lists measuring 1 column wide by 0.6 inch high.

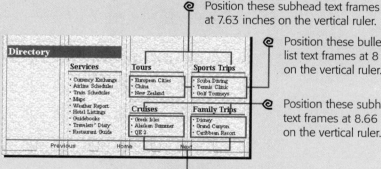

@ Position these subhead text frames at 7.63 inches on the vertical ruler.

@ Position these bulleted list text frames at 8 inches on the vertical ruler.

@ Position these subhead text frames at 8.66 inches on the vertical ruler.

@ Position these bulleted list text frames at 8.99 inches on the vertical ruler.

11 Enter the subhead and list copy for Tours, Cruises, Sports Trips, and Family Trips.

12 Copy the formatting from the Services subhead (including text style, boldface, and red border), and apply it to each subhead item.

13 Select each bulleted list item and apply the Web Body text style.

How can I publish a long text document on the Web without jumping it from page to page? If you want people to read a long text document on screen, edit it into smaller units. Look for logical breaks in the text. For example, the places where you would normally insert a subhead to introduce a new topic will also provide perfect page breaks for a Web document. Instead of using Continued On or Continued From notices, connect the text blocks in your document by creating hypertext links between the pages. You can do this overtly by inserting Go-To buttons, or you can do it subtly by associating hypertext links with specific words within the body of the text.

Creating a Second Web Page

In a traditional newsletter, you routinely jump stories from page to page because it's easy for readers to turn the page. In a Web document, however, it's important for each page to be a self-contained unit. The second page for this sample Web document contains short text blocks that are easy to read on screen.

Insert a Second Page

1. In the Insert Page dialog box, insert a blank page after the current page.

Duplicate Objects from Page 1

1. Move to page 1.
2. Select the three headings and the three pictures.
3. Ctrl-drag duplicates of these objects onto the Pasteboard.

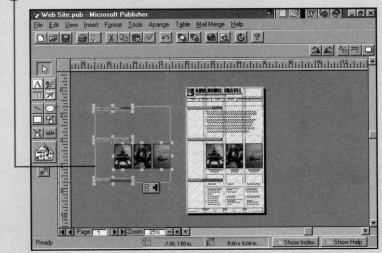

Duplicate Objects from Page 1 *(continued)*

4 Move to page 2.

5 Position the objects on the page as indicated in the following illustration.

Place this heading at the 1.5-inch mark on the vertical ruler, spanning columns 1 and 2.

Place this heading at the 4.13-inch mark on the vertical ruler, spanning columns 1 and 2.

Place this heading at the 6.75-inch mark on the vertical ruler, spanning columns 1 and 2.

Place the Paris picture at the 2-inch mark on the vertical ruler, in column 2.

Place the Budapest picture at the 4.63-inch mark on the vertical ruler, in column 2.

Place the Asia/Pacific picture at the 7.25-inch mark on the vertical ruler, in column 2.

Why am I having trouble aligning the special Adjust handle on the slanted rectangle with the 4.75-inch mark on the horizontal ruler? When you drag the Adjust handle to a new position (to change the shape of the rectangle), the cursor position does not appear on the horizontal ruler. You should pull a ruler guide out from the vertical ruler before you move the Adjust handle. Position the ruler guide at the 4.75-inch mark on the horizontal ruler. Make sure that Snap To Guides is turned on. Now when you move the Adjust handle, it will snap into perfect alignment with the ruler guide. After you have changed the shape of the slanted rectangle, remove the ruler guide by dragging it off the page and back to the vertical ruler.

Modify the Display Copy

1 Zoom in on the first heading.

2 Resize the text frame containing the heading to span columns 1, 2, and 3.

3 Highlight the existing text, and replace it with *The Paris-London Connection*.

4 Draw a slanted rectangle (found in the second row, second column of the Custom Shapes flyout menu) that spans column 4 and measures 0.33 inch high.

5 Move the special Adjust handle to the 4.75-inch mark on the horizontal ruler.

Will I create a graphic region when I position the text frame for Reservations *over the slanted rectangle?* Yes, when you follow the steps in the adjacent procedure, you will create a graphic region. Normally, you want to avoid creating graphic regions because pictures take longer to download than text. However, in this case the elements occupy an extremely small area. Converting the elements to a picture won't seriously increase the download time for this page.

Insert Web designs from Publisher's Design Gallery. You can quickly assemble a Web page design by choosing objects from Publisher's Design Gallery. Three new categories—Web Email Buttons, Web Page Buttons, and Web Page Dividers—have been added to the Gallery. These design elements can punch up a Web page with shapes, bitmapped images, tints, and borders. The two sample designs printed below are both from the Web Page Buttons category of the Classic Designs CD Deluxe collection.

Modify the Display Copy *(continued)*

6 Apply a solid navy fill color.

7 Draw a text frame measuring 0.8 inch wide by 0.2 inch high.

8 Set all four text frame margins to 0.

9 Enter the word *Reservations.*

10 Format the word with the following attributes:

- ❧ Web Body text style
- ❧ White
- ❧ Center alignment

11 Center the text frame over the slanted blue rectangle, and group the two objects together.

12 Scroll down to the second heading and repeat steps 2 through 11, except enter the text *A Budapest Celebration* in the text frame.

13 Scroll down to the third heading and repeat steps 2 through 11, except enter the text *The Asia/Pacific Extravaganza* in the text frame.

Create and Format Text

1 Move to the 2-inch mark on the vertical ruler. Draw a text frame that spans columns 3 and 4. The text frame should measure 1.94 inches high (which makes the text frame exactly as tall as the picture in column 2).

2 Type or import the text for The Paris-London Connection.

3 Format the text with the Web Body text style.

4 In the Hyphenate dialog box, turn off automatic hyphenation for this story.

5 Move to the 4.63-inch mark on the vertical ruler, and repeat steps 1 through 4, except insert the text for A Budapest Celebration.

6 Move to the 7.25-inch mark on the vertical ruler, and repeat steps 1 through 4, except insert the text for The Asia/Pacific Extravaganza.

Creating Hyperlink Connections Between Pages

You've created a two-page Web document, complete with text and picture objects. But the Web document isn't truly complete until you add interactivity in the form of hyperlinks. As you'll see in the following exercise, Publisher's hyperlinks can be applied to selected text, to pictures, and to selected areas of the page.

Add Hyperlinks to the Background

1 Move to the background.

2 Scroll or zoom to the table object at the top of the page.

3 Using the Picture Hot Spot tool, draw a frame that mimics the shape and size of the first cell in the table, which contains the word *Home*.

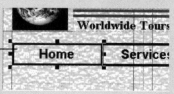

4 Create a hyperlink to the first page in your Web site.

When to use a picture hot spot. You should use a picture hot spot when you want to assign a hyperlink to a *portion* of a picture. In the adjacent procedure, your readers will move to the home page only when they click the first cell of the table. If you were completing this entire Web site, you would assign different destinations to the hyperlinks for the other cells in the table. Note that the table object will be converted to a graphic region when you generate the HTML file because the picture hot spot object overlaps the table object.

Add Hyperlinks to the Background *(continued)*

5 Move to the bottom of the page.

6 Highlight the word *Previous.*

7 Insert a hyperlink to the previous page in your Web site. Publisher changes the color of the text to red, indicating that this is now a hypertext link.

8 Highlight the word *Home.*

9 Insert a hyperlink to the first page in your Web site. Publisher changes the color of the text to red, indicating that this is now a hypertext link.

10 Highlight the word *Next.*

11 Insert a hyperlink to the next page in your Web site. Publisher changes the color of the text to red, indicating that this is now a hypertext link.

Why does Publisher force me to highlight a text phrase before I can insert a hyperlink? Publisher allows you to associate a hypertext link with a single word or phrase within a longer text block. Because of this feature, Publisher requires you to specify exactly which word or words within a text frame should be associated with the hyperlink. In the adjacent procedure, for example, you created a hypertext link for a specific email address rather than for the entire text frame.

Add Hypertext Links to Page 1

1 Move to page 1.

2 Highlight the phrase *comments@adventuretravel.com.*

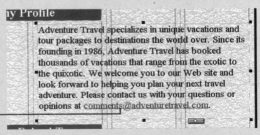

3 Insert a hyperlink to the email address listed in the text: *comments@adventuretravel.com.* Publisher changes the color of the text to red, indicating that this is now a hypertext link.

Look for hyperlink opportunities. Inserting hyperlinks in a Web document delivers tangible benefits to your reader. You can make your Web site easier to explore by providing links to other pages in the HTML document at convenient locations. You can even direct your readers to useful information by inserting hyperlinks that point to other sites on the World Wide Web. Even in this small sample project you'll find at least three more opportunities to insert hyperlinks:

@ Each bulleted item in the Directory listing should move the reader to the page containing the specified information.

@ The Reservations buttons on page 2 should move the reader to a page containing information about how to reserve a trip.

@ The text referring to specific airlines (such as TransBritain Airlines or Hungarian National Airlines) should point to the home pages of those companies.

Add Hypertext Links to Page 1 *(continued)*

4 Locate the label reading *The Paris-London Connection,* and highlight the words *Paris-London.*

5 Insert a hypertext link to page 2 of your Web site.

6 Repeat steps 4 and 5 for the word *Budapest* in column 3.

7 Repeat steps 4 and 5 for the words *Asia/Pacific* in column 4.

Insert Hyperlinks to Pictures

1 Select the Paris picture in column 2.

2 Insert a hyperlink that points to page 2 of your Web site.

3 Repeat steps 1 and 2 for the Budapest picture in column 3.

4 Repeat steps 1 and 2 for the Asia/Pacific picture in column 4.

Previewing and Producing the Web Site

Before publishing your document to the Web, use Publisher's preview feature to see how the document will be displayed by a Web browser application. Using a Web browser also lets you check the hyperlinks in the document.

Preview the Web Site and Test Hyperlinks

1 On the File menu, choose the Preview Web Site command.

Will the line breaks change when I read my document using a Web browser? Yes, lines might rebreak when your Web browser displays the text. But the variation should not change the layout significantly.

Proofread and fine-tune your Web site. You should use all of Publisher's standard tools to check your Web site for errors or inconsistencies. Run the spelling checker and the Design Checker to have Publisher alert you to potential problems. You can even print out a paper copy of the Web site to proofread the text.

Use the Web Publishing Wizard to automatically post your documents to the World Wide Web. The Microsoft Web Publishing Wizard, activated when you choose the Publish To Web command on the File menu, walks you through the process of posting an HTML document to the Web. The Web Publishing Wizard allows you to choose or create a profile for your Internet Service Provider.

For more information about the Web Publishing Wizard, see pages 240 through 242 in Chapter 11.

Preview the Web Site and Test Hyperlinks *(continued)*

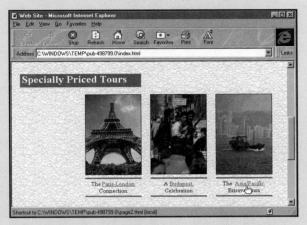

2 Check that the text formatting in the Web browser matches the text formatting you created.

3 Position the pointer over a hyperlink. The hand pointer will appear. Click the hyperlink to activate it.

4 When you are satisfied that the document appears as it should, and that the hyperlinks work as they should, close your Web browser application.

Generate an HTML File

1 In the Web Site Properties dialog box, check that you are using the home page filename and the filename extension required by your Internet Service Provider (ISP).

2 On the File menu, choose Publish Web Site To Folder.

3 In the Select A Folder list box, specify or create a folder.

4 Click OK. Publisher converts the publication file to the HTML specification. Publisher converts all imported pictures and graphic regions to the GIF format at a resolution that is appropriate for on-screen viewing.

5 Contact your ISP for more information about posting your HTML document to its server.

Combining objects such as WordArt, imported clip art, and drawn shapes helps to create a professional-looking logo.

Letterhead

Professional-looking letterhead can help a small business make a big impression. It's easy to create—a logo and a few rules frame standard-sized paper nicely.

Setting Up the Page

You set up permanent row and column guides for this document as you would for any standard business document. You can also set up temporary ruler guides to help you create the logo.

Select Printer and Page Options

1 Start a new publication, and choose the Full Page layout on the Blank Page tab.

2 Select the printer you will use. This project was printed to a PostScript device.

3 Confirm that the current paper size is 8.5 by 11 inches in Portrait orientation.

4 Set the page margins at 1 inch for all four sides. The number of rows and columns should remain at one.

6 Pull a ruler guide out from the vertical ruler to the 4.25-inch mark on the horizontal ruler.

5 Pull a ruler guide down from the horizontal ruler to the 2-inch mark on the vertical ruler.

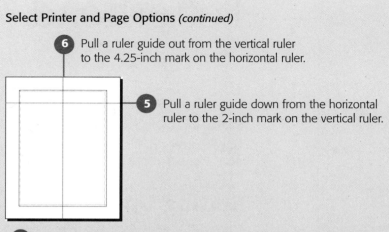

7 Move the zero points of the rulers to align with the intersection of the ruler guides.

Why should I draw an element from the center out? Drawing an element from the center out ensures that it is centered. For each object, start from the intersection of the ruler guides and hold down the Ctrl and Shift keys as you draw.

Vary rule weights to create visual rhythm. You can add interest to a logo design by varying the line weights. In the following illustration, which uses 3-point, 1.5-point, and 6-point rules, the interplay of thick and thin lines creates a visual rhythm. The logo in this letterhead project also makes use of different line weights for the rules and circles.

Creating the Main Logo Element

Draw the Background Shapes

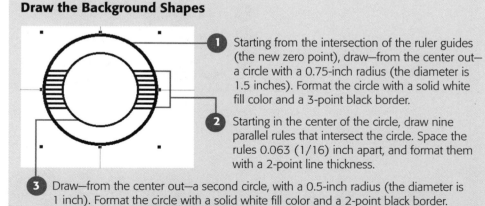

1 Starting from the intersection of the ruler guides (the new zero point), draw—from the center out— a circle with a 0.75-inch radius (the diameter is 1.5 inches). Format the circle with a solid white fill color and a 3-point black border.

2 Starting in the center of the circle, draw nine parallel rules that intersect the circle. Space the rules 0.063 (1/16) inch apart, and format them with a 2-point line thickness.

3 Draw—from the center out—a second circle, with a 0.5-inch radius (the diameter is 1 inch). Format the circle with a solid white fill color and a 2-point black border.

4 Group these elements together.

Create logos quickly with clip art. You can often create a logo quite easily by combining an appropriate piece of clip art with the name of your company. Even when you are simply placing clip art next to text, look for a special visual relationship between the two. In the following logo design, the banner is positioned very close to (and flies high above) the most important word in the company name, *Trophy*.

Combine multiple WordArt elements. Microsoft Publisher 97 offers several WordArt shapes that can wrap text around a circle or curve. You could create a version of this logo using the Circle or Button shape. But you have much more control over how the words in this logo wrap around a circle if you create two separate WordArt elements—using the Arch Up and Arch Down shapes.

Create the Main WordArt Element

1 Draw a WordArt frame that is 1.25 inches wide by 1.25 inches high.

2 Type the word *TROPHY* in uppercase letters in the text box.

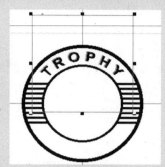

3 Assign the following attributes to the text:
- Arch Up (Pour) shape
- Arial font
- Bold
- 12-point font size
- Center alignment

4 In the Spacing Between Characters dialog box, choose the Very Loose (150 percent) option.

5 In the Special Effects dialog box, change the Arc Angle value to 105 degrees, which will flatten the curve to match the circular background shapes.

6 In the Shadow dialog box, choose the three-dimensional shadow (third option from the right). Assign a shadow color of silver.

7 Click outside the WordArt frame to return to the document.

8 If necessary, reposition the WordArt frame to center it on the upper band of the circular background.

Crop WordArt to avoid text wrapping problems. When you finish assembling the WordArt elements, notice that the WordArt frames extend past the circle. If you place the logo on top of a text frame, you'll have text wrapping problems. You can avoid these problems by using the Crop Picture tool to hide some of the white space in the WordArt frames. You will distort the effect if you resize the WordArt frames.

Create the Second WordArt Element

1 Copy the *TROPHY* WordArt element and paste a duplicate in the publication.

2 Double-click the duplicate to activate WordArt.

3 Change the text to read *SPORTING GOODS* (in uppercase letters).

4 Change the formatting to Arch Down (Pour) and 8-point font size. Leave the following options unchanged: Arial font, bold, center alignment, and three-dimensional silver shadow.

5 In the Spacing Between Characters dialog box, choose the Loose (120 percent) option.

6 In the Special Effects dialog box, change the Arc Angle to 120 degrees.

7 Click outside the WordArt frame to return to your document.

8 If necessary, reposition the WordArt frame to center it on the lower band of the circular background.

Adding a Picture to the Logo

Publisher ships with a large clip-art collection, but sometimes you'll need to edit the art to make it work in your design.

Edit Clip Art with Microsoft Draw

1 Draw a picture frame measuring approximately 0.65 inch wide by 1 inch high.

Add your own soft shadow to the logo. *You can create an interesting variation of this design by adding a shadow to make the design three-dimensional. Instead of using an automatic shadow, which can't be customized, create a photorealistic shadow using the Circle tool and a gradient fill.*

Simply draw a circle that approximates the size of the logo. Fill the circle with a gradient that changes from gray in the center to white at the edge. For the effect to work, you can't have a border around the circle because you need the white edge to blend with the paper color. As you can see in the following illustrations, the shadow effect is much softer and more realistic. You can even flatten the circle into an ellipse to simulate a shadow cast by a light source that is to the left of and in front of the logo.

Edit Clip Art with Microsoft Draw *(continued)*

2 With the picture frame selected, insert a Microsoft Drawing object by using the Insert Object dialog box.

3 Import the picture Trophy5.wmf from the Publisher CD-ROM clip-art collection into the Microsoft Drawing application window.

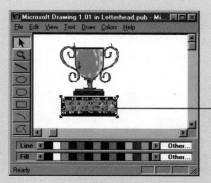

4 Delete the large base of the trophy, leaving only the cup.

5 Exit and return to Publisher. When prompted to save the image in the current document, click Yes.

6 Reposition and scale the trophy to 66 percent of its original size to fill the inner circle of the logo.

7 Use the Recolor Object command to change the trophy's color from gold to gray. Choose black as the color.

8 Select all the elements on the page and group them together.

Adding and Formatting the Address Information

It usually makes sense to use a small, compact font for presenting address and telephone information, especially when the information contains many numbers, such as a toll-free telephone number, a fax number, or a zip code. Small type is often hard to read, but you can make it more legible by subtly adjusting formatting attributes, such as letterspacing.

Add the Address

1 Draw a text frame 0.25 inch high that spans the page from the left margin to the right margin. Align the text frame with the bottom page margin guide.

2 Type the following text on one line:

15 Old Country Road Richardson TX 75081 214-555-1313

3 Format the text with the following attributes:

- ◎ Arial font
- ◎ Bold
- ◎ 9.5-point font size
- ◎ Left alignment

4 Using the indents and tabs ruler, insert a center-aligned tab in the middle of the page.

5 Insert a right-aligned tab at the far right of the text frame.

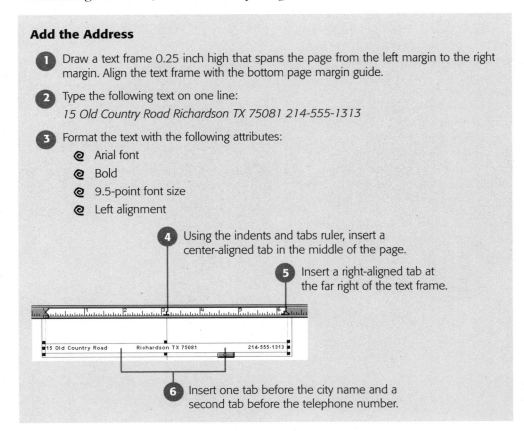

6 Insert one tab before the city name and a second tab before the telephone number.

Create a flexible letterhead design. A good stationery design must accommodate letters of all lengths, including those longer than one page. To create a design for the subsequent pages of the stationery, pick a prominent design motif from the logo or another first-page feature and repeat it on the background. These elements will repeat on every page of a letter.

Why does a pound sign appear on the page in place of a page number? The pound sign (#) appears when you are working on the background. It represents Publisher's ability to automatically number all the pages in the document. When you are working on the foreground, and when you print the document, Publisher replaces the pound sign with the number of the current page.

Insert Decorative Lines

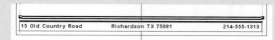

1. Immediately above the address line, draw three rules that span the width of the page. Position the rules 0.063 (1/16) inch apart.

2. Assign a 2-point line thickness to the rules.

3. Select the rules and the address line and group them.

Create Repeating Elements

1. Select the group containing the address line and the decorative rules.

2. Copy it to the Clipboard.

3. Move to the background.

4. Paste the objects.

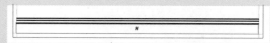

5. Select the text frame and replace the address line with a page number symbol. Center the page number in the middle of the page.

6. Return to the foreground.

7. Select the Ignore Background command for the first page.

8. Insert a second page.

Letterhead

Use the logo in other publications. After you've developed a strong company logo, use it consistently in any number of projects—letterhead, business forms, sale flyers, shopping bags, and even T-shirts—to increase awareness of your business in the community. It's an inexpensive and very effective method of advertising.

Create Text Styles for the Letterhead

1 Using the Text Styles dialog box, create a text style named Greeting for the address area of the letter. Specify the following attributes:

- Arial font
- 10-point font size
- 15 points of space between lines
- Left alignment

2 Create a second text style, named Body, for the text area. Base the Body text style on the Greeting text style, but make the following attribute change:

- 10 points of space after paragraphs

Completing the Stationery

Print a proof of the design. Then clean up the document for use as a template by returning the zero points to their default positions on the rulers and by creating ruler guides that will help you accurately position text frames on the page.

Print a Proof of the Design

1 Open the File menu and choose Print.

2 Turn off the Print Crop Marks and Collate check boxes.

3 Click OK.

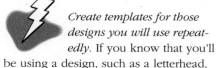

Insert ruler guides on the background to help position text frames. When you create ruler guides on the background, they appear on every page of a document. They are also out of harm's way because as long as you are working on the foreground, you can't select and move them inadvertently. Align the text frame on the first page with the top and bottom ruler guides. Align the text frame on subsequent pages with the top column guide and the bottom ruler guide. The position of the text will be consistent no matter how many letters you write.

Create templates for those designs you will use repeatedly. If you know that you'll be using a design, such as a letterhead, many times, make the file easier to access by saving it as a template.

Delete and Insert Ruler Guides

1 Return the zero points on the ruler to their default positions.

2 Use the Arrange menu to clear all the ruler guides from the page.

3 Move to the background.

4 Create a horizontal ruler guide at the 3-inch mark and another at the 9.25-inch mark on the vertical ruler.

Save the File as a Template

1 In the Save As dialog box, turn on the Template check box.

2 Type an appropriate filename, such as *Letterhead,* in the text box.

3 Click Save.

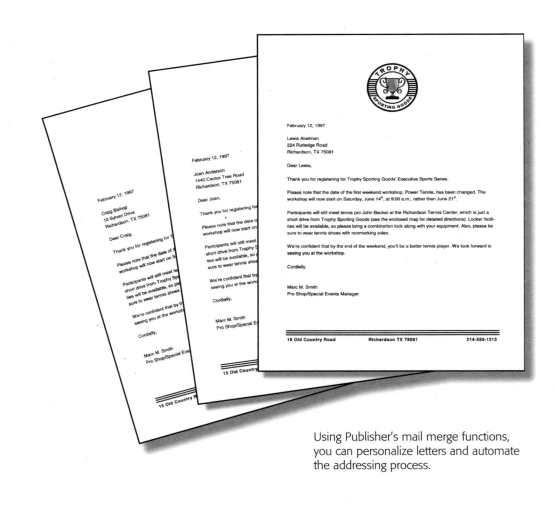

February 12, 1997

Lewis Abelman
224 Rutledge Road
Richardson, TX 75081

Dear Lewis,

Thank you for registering for Trophy Sporting Goods' Executive Sports Series.

Please note that the date of the first weekend workshop, Power Tennis, has been changed. The workshop will now start on Saturday, June 14th, at 9:00 a.m., rather than June 21st.

Participants will still meet tennis pro John Becker at the Richardson Tennis Center, which is just a short drive from Trophy Sporting Goods (see the enclosed map for detailed directions). Locker facilities will be available, so please bring a combination lock along with your equipment. Also, please be sure to wear tennis shoes with nonmarking soles.

We're confident that by the end of the weekend, you'll be a better tennis player. We look forward to seeing you at the workshop.

Cordially,

Marc M. Smith
Pro Shop/Special Events Manager

15 Old Country Road   Richardson TX 75081   214-555-1313

Using Publisher's mail merge functions, you can personalize letters and automate the addressing process.

Mail Merge Letter

After you've designed your stationery, use Microsoft Publisher 97's mail merge functions to generate business correspondence efficiently.

Setting Up the Page

As you'll see in this project, using a custom template can simplify setting up a document.

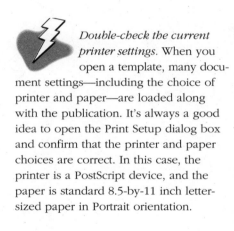

Double-check the current printer settings. When you open a template, many document settings—including the choice of printer and paper—are loaded along with the publication. It's always a good idea to open the Print Setup dialog box and confirm that the printer and paper choices are correct. In this case, the printer is a PostScript device, and the paper is standard 8.5-by-11 inch letter-sized paper in Portrait orientation.

Open a Template

1 On the File menu, select Create New Publication.

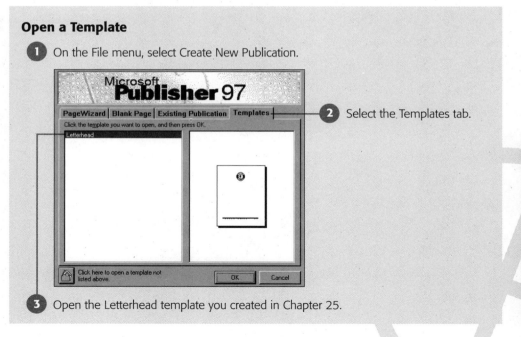

2 Select the Templates tab.

3 Open the Letterhead template you created in Chapter 25.

Creating the Address List

Setting up a basic address list in Publisher is as easy as filling in the blanks because the address list already contains fields for general information, such as names, addresses, and phone numbers. You can make the address list even more powerful by creating custom fields for data that relates specifically to your business.

For the text of this mail merge project, see "Text for Design Projects."

Can I leave fields blank in the address list? Yes, it is perfectly okay to leave blank fields in the address list. The blank fields will not appear in your publication when you merge it with the address list. If you find the blank fields distracting, however, you can always delete them by clicking the Customize button in the address list dialog box.

Enter General Information in the Address List

1 On the Mail Merge menu, choose Create Publisher Address List.

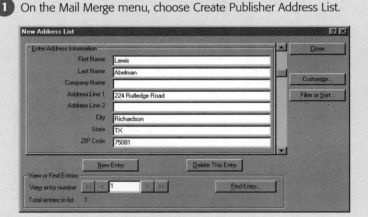

2 Enter the names and addresses for the address list.

3 When you have finished entering the names and addresses, save the address list to a file named Trophy.mdb.

Customize the Address List

1 On the Mail Merge menu, choose Edit Publisher Address List.

2 Open Trophy.mdb, and then click the Customize button.

Is it okay to misspell words when entering data in the address list? No, you must be sure that you have spelled the information you enter into the address list correctly and consistently. Publisher's spelling checker does not work within dialog boxes—only within the actual publication file. In addition, when you create filters for your data, Publisher looks for exact matches. For example, a filter will not find all the addresses in Austin if you have misspelled some of the entries as *Aussin*.

Customize the Address List *(continued)*

3 In the Customize Address List dialog box, delete the following fields:
- Title
- Country
- E-mail Address

4 Highlight Work Phone, the last item on the list.

5 Add a field called Registration after the Work Phone field.

6 Return to the Trophy dialog box, and add either *Power Tennis* or *Fly Tying* to the Registration field to identify the class in which people are enrolled.

7 Click Close to save your changes and return to the document.

Creating the Letter

Because you created text styles and saved them as part of the Letterhead template, generating this letter is basically a matter of inserting the text. Notice that you are typing dummy text, such as *First* and *Last* (designating a person's given name and surname). Later in this lesson, you'll replace this text with live field codes that link the letter to the address list.

Type and Format Text

1 Draw a text frame that spans the width of the page from column guide to column guide. The top of the text frame should align with the ruler guide at the 3-inch mark on the vertical ruler. The bottom of the text frame should align with the ruler guide at the 9.25-inch mark on the vertical ruler.

2 Type or import the text of the letter.

3 Assign text styles as indicated in the illustration on the next page.

What text formats should I assign to the letter? If you completed the Letterhead template in Chapter 25, you should have two predefined text styles available to you. If you did not complete the project in Chapter 25, create two text styles as follows:

- Greeting: Arial font, 10-point font size, 15 points of space between lines, left alignment

- Body: Arial font, 10-point font size, 15 points of space between lines, 10 points of space after paragraphs, left alignment

Use typographic-style characters instead of typewriter-style characters. You can make your documents—even a simple letter—look much more professional by replacing typewriter-style characters with typographic-style characters. In this letter, for example, the days of the month—June 14th and June 21st—are followed by superscript characters. You must use the Character dialog box to apply the Superscript (or Subscript) attribute to selected text.

Type and Format Text *(continued)*

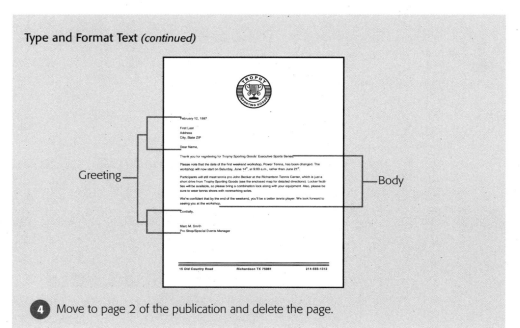

Greeting — Body

4 Move to page 2 of the publication and delete the page.

Inserting Field Codes into the Letter

Before you can take advantage of an address list, you must associate the current document with a data source. Once the connection has been made, you can insert field codes that point to specific information in the address list.

Open a Data Source and Insert Field Codes

1 On the Mail Merge menu, choose Open Data Source.

2 Locate and select the file Trophy.mdb that you created earlier. When you click Open, the Insert Fields dialog box will appear.

3 Use the following table to replace dummy text in your document with live field codes that point to the address list.

Text to Be Replaced by Field Codes	
Highlight This Text	**Insert This Field Code**
First	First Name
Last	Last Name
Address	Address Line 1
City	City
State	State
ZIP	ZIP Code
Name	First Name

4 When you have finished entering field codes, click the Close button. Your publication should resemble the following illustration.

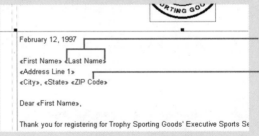

Within the working view of a publication, field codes are identified with surrounding double brackets.

Field codes can be formatted with Publisher's full range of character and paragraph formats. Here the Greeting text style was maintained when the field code replaced the original text.

Filtering and Sorting the Address List

Publisher allows you to manipulate an address list in two important ways. You can apply a filter, which uses the selection criteria you specify to create a subset of information from the address list. In this project, for example, you will use a filter to select only the address list entries of those people who have registered for the Power Tennis weekend class.

Mail Merge Letter

Use filters to find information in an address list. If you create an address list within Publisher (rather than connecting the publication to a data source created with another application), you can use filters to find information. In this letter project, for example, you can apply a filter to see how many people have registered for the Fly Tying class. Simply apply a filter in which the Registration field is equal to Fly Tying. After you've viewed the results of the search, which show that only four people have registered for this course, remove the filter by selecting the [none] option from the Field drop-down list box.

You can also sort an address list to determine the order in which entries will be viewed or printed. Although you can sort on any field in the address list, you will probably most often sort on the ZIP Code field so that you can presort a mailing to qualify for reduced postal rates.

You can't filter or sort an address list until you have merged it with the current publication.

Merge the Address List and the Publication

1. On the Mail Merge menu, choose Merge. The Preview Data dialog box appears, and the first entry in the address list appears in place of the field codes.

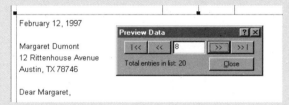

2. Use the controls in the Preview Data dialog box to see how each entry in the address list will appear when printed.

3. When you have finished viewing the entries, click Close. The field entries once again appear on screen.

Filter and Sort the Address List

1. On the Filter tab in the Filtering And Sorting dialog box, apply a filter with the following selection criteria:

   @ For Field, choose Registration.

   @ For Comparison, choose Is Equal To.

   @ For Compare To, type *Power Tennis.*

2. On the Sort tab in the Filtering And Sorting dialog box, create an ascending sort order based on the ZIP Code field.

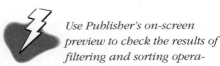

Use Publisher's on-screen preview to check the results of filtering and sorting operations. If you have applied filtering or sorting criteria to an address list, you can see the results on screen by selecting the Show Merge Results command on the Mail Merge menu. The Preview Data dialog box appears. Only those entries from the address list that meet your selection criteria appear on screen, replacing the field codes in your text.

In this mail merge project, for example, only eight entries from the address list meet the selection criteria (for Power Tennis registration) that you specified earlier.

Printing a Merged Document

Before you print the multiple copies that constitute a merged document, you should test the results of your filtering and sorting criteria by using special mail merge options that appear in the Print Merge dialog box.

Print a Test of the Merged Document

1 On the File menu, choose Print Merge.

2 In the Print Merge dialog box, click the Test button to print a single instance of the mail merge letter.

Print the Merged Document

1 On the File menu, choose Print Merge.

2 Turn off the Crop Marks check box.

3 Choose one of the following options:

  @ Select All Entries to print a copy of the publication for each entry in the address list that meets the selection criteria.

  @ Select Entries to print a copy of the publication for the subset of entries that meet the selection criteria. Enter numbers in the From and To text boxes.

4 Click OK. Publisher prints multiple copies of the document. Each copy contains a different entry from the address list.

Microsoft Publisher 97's ability to format a table with tints and custom borders helps you create this order form.

Business Form

Awell-designed business form is clear and easy to read. A user should be able to figure out exactly what information is needed and have enough room to enter text legibly. When you plan the layout for a business form, consider using the Table tool to ensure consistent alignment of rules and text. You should also remember that effects such as shading can enhance the appearance and readability of the form.

What should I do if I haven't completed the project in Chapter 25? The following procedures assume that you have already designed the letterhead in Chapter 25. You can still complete this project by making a few simple adjustments. When asked to start a publication based on the Letterhead template, start a new blank publication instead. All of the page layout options you'll need are listed in the instructions. When you are asked to use the Trophy Sporting Goods logo, substitute a piece of clip art instead.

Setting Up the Page

You can jump-start the design process by basing a new publication on an existing publication. For example, you can derive this purchase order form from the letterhead design created in Chapter 25. Even though you base this publication on an existing document, you'll still have to adjust the parameters for the project, including the column guides.

Revise the Letterhead Page Format

1 Start a new publication based on the Letterhead template you created in Chapter 25.

2 Leave the basic document attributes in place:

- ✿ 8.5-by-11-inch paper
- ✿ Portrait orientation
- ✿ Full page layout

Determine the number of columns or rows that you need. You should always base the number of column and row guides on the width and height of the smallest element in your layout. In this business form project, for example, the narrowest text block is 1/8 page wide. Therefore, you should divide the page into 8 vertical sections—or columns.

Check the group status before you move objects. Before you move the logo, check the Group button to be sure that all the elements of the logo are grouped—the two pieces pictured on the Group button should be locked together. If the elements aren't grouped, you run the risk of misaligning objects in the logo when you move it.

Revise the Letterhead Page Format *(continued)*

3 Clear all ruler guides.

4 Change the number of column guides to 8. Leave the number of rows at 1.

5 Forms typically require only one page, so delete page 2 of the document and all elements from the background.

Creating the Header

Typically, the top portion of a business form contains the company logo, the title of the form, and contact information, such as an address and telephone number. Notice that in this project the logo is placed on the left side of the form to free up space for the address and the purchase order number. This design sets off the purchase order number from the rest of the header so that it is easy to find.

Move the Logo Design Elements

1 Move the logo so that the exterior circle aligns with the leftmost column guide and the top row guide.

Why is the logo so difficult to position? Publisher might be attempting to align the object edges with row and column guides. In this purchase order project, the logo object contains a lot of white space near the edge to accommodate the Arch Up and Arch Down WordArt elements. You will find it easier to position the logo if you turn off Snap To Guides and Snap To Ruler Marks. Alternatively, you can use the Crop Picture tool to hide the extra white space in the WordArt elements.

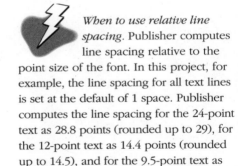

When to use relative line spacing. Publisher computes line spacing relative to the point size of the font. In this project, for example, the line spacing for all text lines is set at the default of 1 space. Publisher computes the line spacing for the 24-point text as 28.8 points (rounded up to 29), for the 12-point text as 14.4 points (rounded up to 14.5), and for the 9.5-point text as 11.4 points (rounded up to 11.5).

Use relative line spacing so that you can mix font sizes in a single text frame without worrying about the descenders on one line of text crashing into the ascenders on the next line.

Move the Logo Design Elements *(continued)*

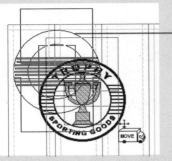

Publisher always shows you a gray outline of the elements in a group to help you position objects precisely.

2 Select the group of three rules at the bottom of the page, and move them to the 2.75-inch mark on the vertical ruler.

Insert the Address and Phone Information

1 Delete the address text box at the bottom of the page.

2 Draw a text frame that spans columns 3, 4, 5, and 6 and measures 1.5 inches high. Align the top of the text frame with the top row guide.

3 Enter the text in the illustration, and format the text as indicated below.

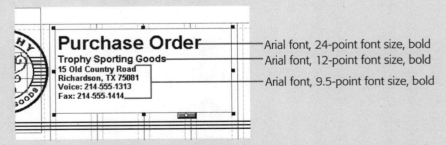

Arial font, 24-point font size, bold
Arial font, 12-point font size, bold
Arial font, 9.5-point font size, bold

4 Draw a second text frame that spans columns 7 and 8 and measures 0.35 inch high. Align the text frame with the top row guide.

Insert the Address and Phone Information *(continued)*

5 Enter a purchase order number, such as *#10065-325-0009*. Format it with the following attributes:

- Arial font
- 12-point font size
- Bold

6 Select all the elements and group them.

Creating the Vendor and General Information Items

When you create a form for actual orders, think about who will rely on it for information. For example, if all orders require approval, you need to include a place for a supervisor's signature. If you offer different types of contracts, you must include a section in which you can specify instructions, such as the Terms line in this form.

You can produce the vendor section of the form more quickly by duplicating individual frames and groups of frames and then moving them to the proper positions.

Create the Vendor Information Area

1 Pull down a horizontal ruler guide. Position it at the 4.5-inch mark on the vertical ruler.

2 Draw a text frame that spans columns 1, 2, 3, and 4 and measures 0.25 inch high. The bottom of the text frame should align with the horizontal ruler guide.

3 Type the word *Fax:* in the text box.

Sometimes Snap To Objects provides the best alignment. If you are having trouble aligning a duplicate text frame with the frame below it, turn on Snap To Objects. This command enables you to quickly snap each frame into the proper alignment.

Consider design alternatives. In this purchase order project, you create the vendor and general information items using standard text frames. However, you could create these elements using a table instead. Using Publisher's ability to apply custom borders to table cells, you could create a single table that looks exactly like the group of six text frames in the adjacent procedure.

Create the Vendor Information Area *(continued)*

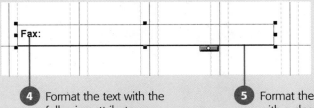

4 Format the text with the following attributes:

- ❷ Arial font
- ❷ 8-point font size
- ❷ Bold

5 Format the text frame with a clear fill color and a 1-point border at the bottom of the frame.

6 Duplicate this text frame five times. Move each duplicate up so that the bottom of the copied frame aligns with the top of the previous frame.

7 Enter labels for address and phone information as shown here.

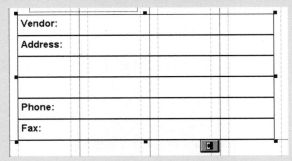

8 Select these six text frames and group them together.

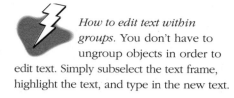

How to edit text within groups. You don't have to ungroup objects in order to edit text. Simply subselect the text frame, highlight the text, and type in the new text.

Create the Order Information Area

1 Select the group of text frames you just created, and copy it to the Clipboard.

2 Paste a duplicate of the group into the document, and position it so that it spans columns 5, 6, 7, and 8. The bottom of the group should align with the horizontal ruler guide at the 4.5-inch mark on the vertical ruler.

3 Enter the labels shown here.

| Date: |
| Resale Number: |
| Terms: |
| Ship Via: |
| Ordered By: |
| Authorized By: |

Creating the Order Table

You can easily create custom forms such as this one thanks to Publisher's ability to format an individual cell or a range of cells within a table.

Draw and Format the Table

1 Starting at the 4.75-inch mark on the vertical ruler, draw a table frame that spans all 8 columns and aligns with the bottom column guide.

2 In the Create Table dialog box, specify 16 rows, 5 columns, and the Checkbook Register table format.

3 Select the entire table. In the BorderArt dialog box, select the Line Border tab and assign a 1-point rule to the grid.

Draw and Format the Table *(continued)*

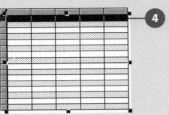

4 Select the top row, and format it with the following attributes:

- ✆ Arial font
- ✆ 10-point font size
- ✆ Bold
- ✆ Center alignment

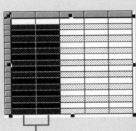

5 Select a range of cells comprising all the rows in columns 1 and 2 except the first row. Format them with the following attributes:

- ✆ Arial font
- ✆ 10-point font size
- ✆ Left alignment

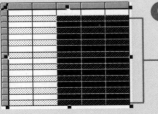

6 Select a range of cells comprising all the rows in columns 3, 4, and 5 except the first row. Format them with the following attributes:

- ✆ Arial font
- ✆ 10-point font size
- ✆ Right alignment

7 Holding down the Shift key, use the Adjust pointer to resize the columns of the table in relation to the underlying grid as indicated on the next page.

Column guides versus page guides. Publisher distinguishes between column guides, which are blue, and page guides, which are pink. Whenever you use the layout guides as a grid, align objects to the pink guides instead of the blue guides.

How do I align the numbers in the table along the decimal point? Publisher's table tools don't offer decimal alignment, but you can create this effect by choosing right alignment and then entering all numbers in a consistent format. For example, you might enter each number with a decimal point and two trailing zeros: *$00.00.*

Draw and Format the Table *(continued)*

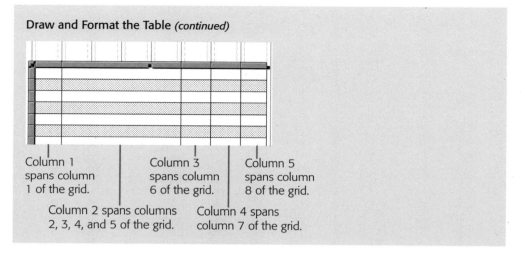

Column 1 spans column 1 of the grid.

Column 2 spans columns 2, 3, 4, and 5 of the grid.

Column 3 spans column 6 of the grid.

Column 4 spans column 7 of the grid.

Column 5 spans column 8 of the grid.

Enter the Table Labels

1 Using the illustration at the beginning of the chapter as a guide, enter the text labels into the first row of the table.

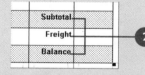

2 Create summary labels in the bottom 3 cells of column 4 of the table.

3 Format these labels as boldface.

Hide Unneeded Cells and Customize the Table Border

1 Select the bottom three rows in columns 1, 2, and 3 of the table.

Can I delete the cells I won't be using in the table? If you want to maintain the alignment of text in the table, don't delete the cells at the bottom of columns 1, 2, and 3. Instead, make this section of the table invisible by changing the formatting attributes. Doing so won't change the structure of the table, but it will make the cells invisible on the printout, producing the illusion that the cells have been deleted from the table.

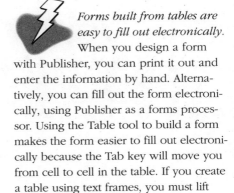

Forms built from tables are easy to fill out electronically. When you design a form with Publisher, you can print it out and enter the information by hand. Alternatively, you can fill out the form electronically, using Publisher as a forms processor. Using the Table tool to build a form makes the form easier to fill out electronically because the Tab key will move you from cell to cell in the table. If you create a table using text frames, you must lift your hands from the keyboard and use the mouse to select the next text frame.

Hide Unneeded Cells and Customize the Table Border *(continued)*

2 Fill the selected cells with a solid white color.

3 In the BorderArt dialog box, select the Line Border tab. Select the left edge, the bottom edge, and the interior vertical and horizontal dividers (but not the top or right edges), and format them with no rule. The selected section looks like the following illustration.

			Subtotal	
			Freight	
			Balance	

Though dotted cell boundaries appear on screen, they will not print.

Completing the Purchase Order

Save this file as a template so that you can use the form over and over again.

Save the File as a Template

1 In the Save As dialog box, turn on the Template check box.

2 Type an appropriate filename, such as *Purchase Order,* in the text box.

Print the Document

1 Open the File menu and choose Print.

2 Turn off the Print Crop Marks check box.

3 Enter the number of copies you want to print. Click OK.

Putting Power

You've avoided the sand trap and kept the ball out of the rough, but you're still giving up far too many strokes on the green. Trophy Sporting Goods' golf pro Emil Davis teaches you ten power tips designed to help you sink the ball into that little four-inch hole.

Videotapes of each session provide you with important feedback on your technique. The videotape is yours to keep after the weekend is over.

Only those with intermediate skills should register for this course. Participants are also required to bring their own equipment. Equipment rentals can be arranged through the Pro Shop at Trophy Sporting Goods.

When: August 8th and 9th
9:00 a.m. - 5:00 p.m.
Where: West Hills Country Club
Price: $500

Fly Tying

Imagine how proud you'll feel when you catch that trophy-winning fish with a fly you tied yourself! Under the guidance of master fly fisherman William Cruthers, you can learn the basics of the classic, and painstaking, art of tying flies.

By the end of the weekend, participants will have learned to tie at least a dozen different types of flies suitable for a variety of fishing conditions and species.

A list of required materials will be provided one week prior to class. Supplies may be purchased at Trophy Sporting Goods.

When: September 29th and 30th
10:00 a.m. - 4:30 p.m.
Where: Trophy Sporting Goods Pro Shop
Price: $800 plus materials

Reservations

Because we know how valuable your time is, we guarantee that by the end of class you'll see a significant improvement in your game or your skills—or your money back!

Space is limited, so reserve your spot for these special events today.

Stop by our store
Trophy Sporting Goods
15 Old Country Road
or call
214-555-1313
(ask for Brad Parker)

Ask for information about upcoming events on:
Tennis
Wilderness Camping
Squash

We accept American Express, Visa, MasterCard, and Diners Club. We also accept personal checks, with the proper identification.

15 Old Country Road
Richardson TX 75081

The Executive Sports Series

The Executive Sports Series

You can design and fold a brochure so that it functions as a self-mailing promotional piece.

Three-Fold Brochure

Using Microsoft Publisher 97 and a laser printer, you can produce a three-fold brochure entirely on the desktop. This self-mailing brochure is ideal as an inexpensive sales tool. You can avoid the cost of outside printing services—and the address area on the outside of the brochure eliminates the cost of envelopes!

Setting Up the Page

The layout of a three-fold brochure is determined by the two folds. It's important that you divide the page into three equal sections, called panels. You accomplish this by using a combination of page guides and ruler guides.

Set Up the Page

1. Start a new document, and choose the Full Page layout on the Blank Page tab.

2. Select the printer you will use. This project was printed by a PostScript device.

3. Confirm that the current paper size is 8.5 by 11 inches in Landscape orientation.

Can I really divide an 11-inch page into three equal sections? No. There is no easy way to divide a standard 11-inch page into three equal sections. Do the math, and the result will be the infinite fraction of 3.6666666 inches. If you inspect the current page guides very carefully, you'll find a fudge factor of about 1/16 inch on two of the panels. But this discrepancy will be hidden in the fold area between panels, so you don't need to worry about it.

Set Up the Page *(continued)*

4 Set the page margins at 0.3 inch for all four sides.

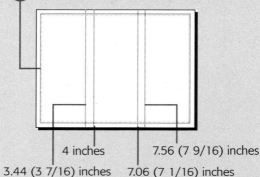

4 inches

7.56 (7 9/16) inches

3.44 (3 7/16) inches

7.06 (7 1/16) inches

5 Go to the Background. The ruler guides you create here appear on every page of the publication.

6 Pull out four vertical ruler guides. Position them at the horizontal ruler marks indicated in the illustration above.

Creating Text Styles

The table on the facing page specifies the text attributes of all the text in this project. Notice how indents are used in place of text frame margins to add white space around the text. Also notice how the spacing before and after each paragraph works to affect the flow of copy. For example, the Body Copy style includes 7.5 points of spacing after each paragraph. This formatting effectively separates each paragraph by one and a half line spaces because the line spacing is set at 15 points of leading. In contrast, the Hanging Indent style retains the 15 points of leading but doesn't add any additional space either before or after paragraphs, in order to keep the text blocks closer together.

Text Attributes for the Three-Fold Brochure				
Text Style	**Character Type and Size**	**Indents and Lists**	**Line Spacing**	**Tabs**
Body Copy	Times New Roman, 10 points	Left alignment, left indent 0.1 inch, right indent 0.1 inch	15 points, 7.5 points after paragraphs	None
Hanging Indent	Arial, 8.5 points	Left indent 0.75 inch, first line indent −0.45 inch, right indent 0	15 points	0.75 inch, left alignment
Head	Arial, 18 points, bold	Center alignment, left indent 0, first line indent 0, right indent 0	30 points	None
Subhead	Arial, 12 points, bold	Left alignment, left indent 0.1 inch, right indent 0.1 inch	15 points, 7.5 points before paragraphs, 15 points after paragraphs	None

Creating the Front Cover

The front cover sets the mood and establishes the design motif for the entire document. Publisher's Recolor Picture command makes it easy to integrate clip art into a layout. The sophisticated three-dimensional boxes are created using a custom border.

Draw the Backdrop

1. Move to the foreground.

2. Draw a box that fills the right panel of the page and is 3.04 inches wide by 7.7 inches high. The box should align with the ruler guide at the left, the column guide at the right, and the row guides at the top and bottom.

Draw the Backdrop *(continued)*

3 Format the box with a 40 percent black tint and a 1-point black border.

4 Draw a second box that measures approximately 2.84 inches wide by 7.5 inches high. Format it with the clear fill color and a 2-point white border.

5 Center the white rule on the gray box to create a 0.1-inch in-line border treatment.

Consider color options when creating your design. The Recolor Picture command enables you to modify the color of a picture so that you can better integrate the image into your design. In this project, the Recolor Picture command allows you to create a more subtle effect by printing a light gray picture on a dark gray background.

Insert and Edit a Picture

1 Draw a picture frame that is 2.46 inches wide by 4 inches high. The picture frame should be centered horizontally within the white rule you created earlier, and the bottom of the frame should align with the bottom of the white rule.

2 Insert the Fishing.cgm image from the Publisher CD-ROM clip-art library.

3 Recolor the picture using a 20 percent black tint.

4 Use the Send Farther command to place the picture behind the white rule.

Create three-dimensional effects. The panel design in this project combines light and dark borders around frames to create three-dimensional effects. When the dark rules are placed on the top and left sides (and the light rules are placed on the bottom and right sides), the frame—or button—appears to be depressed. When the light rules are placed on the top and left sides (and the dark rules are placed on the bottom and right sides), the frame appears to be raised.

Add the Title

1 Draw a text frame measuring 2.4 inches wide by 1.75 inches high.

2 Position the text frame inside the white-ruled box. The text frame should be centered horizontally within the white rule, and the top of the frame should align with the 0.75-inch mark on the vertical ruler.

3 Type the following text on three lines: *The Executive Sports Series.*

4 Format the text with the Head text style.

5 Change the top text frame margin to 0.15 inch to center the type in the frame vertically.

The
Executive Sports
Series

6 Create a recessed three-dimensional effect using the Line Border tab in the BorderArt dialog box. Format the top and left sides with a 4-point rule of 60 percent tint of black. Format the bottom and right sides with a 4-point rule of 20 percent tint of black.

Creating the Second Panel

You can save time by editing a duplicate of the design you just created.

Replace and Edit the Picture

1 Copy all the objects from the right column to the Clipboard.

2 Paste duplicates into the publication, and position them in the far left panel.

3 Select the picture, and replace it with Golfswng.wmf from Publisher's CD-ROM clip-art library.

Replace and Edit the Picture *(continued)*

4 Resize the picture so that the figure of the golfer is approximately the same size as the figure of the fly fisherman. Use the Scale Picture command to resize the picture to 120 percent of its original size.

5 Move the picture until it is approximately 0.13 (1/8) inch from the left and bottom edges of the white rule.

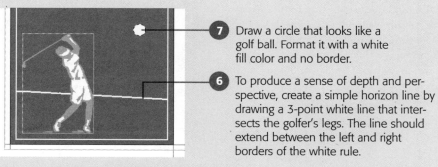

7 Draw a circle that looks like a golf ball. Format it with a white fill color and no border.

6 To produce a sense of depth and perspective, create a simple horizon line by drawing a 3-point white line that intersects the golfer's legs. The line should extend between the left and right borders of the white rule.

8 Select the golfer, the line, and the circle, and group them.

9 Use the Send Farther command to place the golfer group behind the white-ruled box.

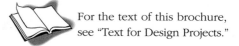 For the text of this brochure, see "Text for Design Projects."

Insert Text

1 Resize the text frame that you copied from the first panel by dragging the bottom selection handle to the 5.5-inch mark on the vertical ruler.

2 Replace the text with the text that introduces the Executive Sports Series. Don't include any extra white space between paragraphs; space will be inserted automatically when you apply text styles.

Insert Text *(continued)*

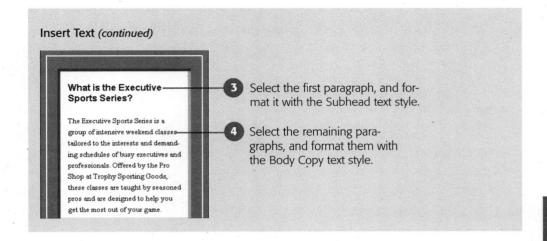

What is the Executive Sports Series?

The Executive Sports Series is a group of intensive weekend classes tailored to the interests and demanding schedules of busy executives and professionals. Offered by the Pro Shop at Trophy Sporting Goods, these classes are taught by seasoned pros and are designed to help you get the most out of your game.

3 Select the first paragraph, and format it with the Subhead text style.

4 Select the remaining paragraphs, and format them with the Body Copy text style.

Creating the Return Address

Creating the return address is as simple as copying the logo from the Letterhead template you created in Chapter 25.

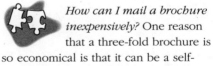

How can I mail a brochure inexpensively? One reason that a three-fold brochure is so economical is that it can be a self-mailer, meaning that you can seal it with a sticker or tape and mail it without using—or paying for—an envelope.

Import the Logo

1 Open a second copy of Publisher, and create a new document using the Letterhead template.

2 Select the logo (making sure that all the logo elements are grouped together), and copy it to the Clipboard.

3 Exit the second copy of Publisher. Click Yes when asked whether you want to save the Clipboard.

4 Paste a copy of the logo into the brochure.

Crop WordArt to avoid text wrap problems. The WordArt frames in the Trophy Sporting Goods logo must be large to accommodate the WordArt special effect (Arch Up and Arch Down shapes). When you rotate and position the logo in this project, the WordArt frames may interfere with other text elements in the brochure, causing text wrapping problems. You can avoid these problems by using the Crop Picture tool to hide some of the white space in the WordArt frames. Don't resize the WordArt frames; that will distort the effect.

Use Publisher's mail merge feature to address the brochures. You can address these brochures using Publisher's mail merge feature. Simply create a text frame where a mailing label would normally be positioned, then insert field codes from the Trophy.mdb address list you created in Chapter 26. When you print the document, Publisher will print multiple copies of the brochure. Each copy will contain a different entry from the address list.

Add Address Information

1 Directly beneath the logo, draw a text frame measuring 1.5 inches wide by 0.4 inch high.

2 Enter the following text on two lines: *15 Old Country Road Richardson TX 75081.*

3 Format the text with the following attributes:
- Arial font
- 9-point font size
- Bold
- Center alignment

4 Draw three 2-point rules beneath the text frame. Leave 0.06 (1/16) inch of space between the rules.

5 Group these objects together.

6 Rotate the group 270 degrees, and position it in the upper right-hand corner of the center panel.

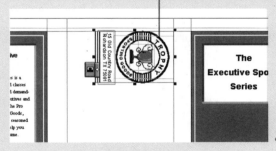

Creating the Interior of the Brochure

The interior of the brochure repeats the framework used in the panels you just created. Once again, you can create the interior most efficiently by first duplicating and then editing existing objects.

Edit the Panel Design

1. Select the backdrop, white rule, and text frame (but not the picture group) in the left panel, and copy them to the Clipboard.

2. Insert a new page.

3. Paste the objects to the new page. Publisher will position the objects in the left panel and will automatically select them (as a multiple selection), so they should move as a single unit.

4. Select the text frame and resize it so that the bottom of the text frame aligns with the 7.75-inch mark on the vertical ruler and the top of the text frame aligns with the 1.75-inch mark on the vertical ruler.

5. Select all of the text in the frame and delete it.

6. Create a new text frame that is exactly the width of the current text frame and that measures 0.75 inch high. The top of the text frame should align with the 0.75-inch mark on the vertical ruler.

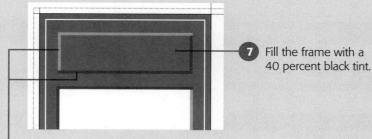

7. Fill the frame with a 40 percent black tint.

8. On the Line Border tab in the BorderArt dialog box, format the top and left sides with a 4-point, 20 percent black rule. Format the right and bottom sides with a 4-point, 60 percent black rule. This creates a raised three-dimensional effect.

Edit the Panel Design *(continued)*

⑨ Format the text frame with the Head text style, and change the color of the text from black to white.

⑩ Group all the elements in the left panel.

⑪ Copy the group, and paste duplicates into the center and right panels.

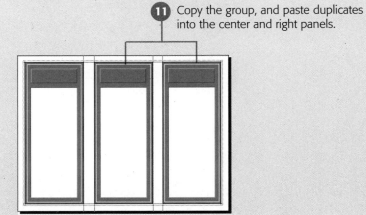

Insert Text

① Select the top text frame in the left panel, and type the words *Putting Power.*

② Select the bottom text frame in the left panel, and either type or import the Putting Power copy.

Insert Text *(continued)*

Putting Power

You've avoided the sand trap and kept the ball out of the rough, but you're still giving up far too many strokes on the green. Trophy Sporting Goods' golf pro Emil Davis teaches you ten power tips designed

3 Apply the Body Copy text style to the first three paragraphs.

4 Apply the Hanging Indent text style to the remaining text.

5 Select the top text frame in the center panel, and type the words *Fly Tying*.

6 Repeat steps 2 and 3 in the center panel, using the Fly Tying copy.

7 Select the top text frame in the right panel, and type the word *Reservations*.

8 Repeat steps 2 and 3 in the right panel, using the Reservations copy. Apply the Body Copy text style to all the Reservations copy.

Fine-Tuning the Text

No matter how scrupulous you are when you create a text style, you will always have to fine-tune the text. Take the time now to refine the text of the three stories inside the brochure.

Precision folds complete a quality brochure. Crooked, sloppy folds can ruin the appearance of a folded brochure. Use one of these methods to guarantee crisp, straight creases in your three-fold brochure:

- Purchase special prescored paper from stationery stores or paper companies (such as Paper Direct). To fold your brochures, you simply follow an existing crease in the paper.

- Create a guide (also called a template) to help you fold the brochures manually. Draw a table frame that completely covers an 8.5-by-11 inch page in Landscape orientation. Divide the table into 3 columns and 1 row. Format the table grid with a 1-point rule. When printed, this document will show you the exact location of each fold.

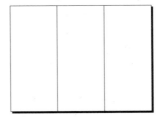

Adjust the Putting Power and Fly Tying Panels

When:	August 8th and 9th
	9:00 a.m. - 5:00 p.m.
Where:	West Hills Country Club
Price:	$500

1 Apply boldface to the first word in each paragraph of the Hanging Indent style.

2 Replace the space after the colon with a tab so that the text on the first line aligns with the indented text.

3 Remove the comma after the date information, and insert a line break for a better rag.

4 Click in the first paragraph in this section, and add 15 points of space before the paragraph.

Adjust the Reservations Panel

1 Highlight the entire story and change the alignment to Center.

2 Select the double hyphen (--) in the first paragraph and replace it with a true em dash (—).

3 Select the store name, address, and phone number, and reformat them as 12-point, boldface text.

4 Select the phrase containing the name Brad Parker, and reformat it as italic text.

5 Turn off automatic hyphenation for this story.

6 Adjust the line breaks using the Shift-Enter key combination. See the illustration at the beginning of the chapter for a guide.

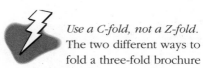

Use a C-fold, not a Z-fold. The two different ways to fold a three-fold brochure are referred to by the shape that the edge of the paper makes. A Z-fold (below left) is an accordion fold, which is unsuitable for a self-mailer because the left and right edges of the folded document are open. A C-fold (below right) is the correct choice for a self-mailer because the second fold encloses the first fold so that only one edge has to be sealed for mailing.

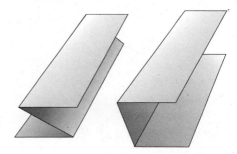

Printing and Folding the Brochure

Print the Brochure

1 Open the File menu and choose Print.

2 Turn off Print Crop Marks. Click OK.

Copy and Fold the Brochure

1 Copy page 2 of the publication on the back of page 1.

2 Fold each panel of the publication in a C-fold so that the brochure can be taped shut.

Text for Design Projects

Most of the text that you will need to complete the design projects in Part 2 appears below. If text is legible in the illustrations and procedures of a chapter, it is not always repeated here. For line spacing, indentation, and other formatting, refer to the chapters.

Chapter 16 Party Invitation

The Ramsey Family invites you to a beach-side barbecue.
Sunday, July 17th
1:00 p.m.
200 Shore Road
East Hampton, NY
RSVP 516-555-2424

Chapter 17 Large Format Poster

Give me your tired, your poor,
Your huddled masses yearning to breathe free,
The wretched refuse of your teeming shore.
Send these, the homeless, tempest-tost to me.
I lift my lamp beside the golden door.
-Emma Lazarus,
"The New Colossus"

The Barrow Street School Celebrates
Citizenship Day
September 17, 1997

Chapter 18 Résumé

Helen Ramsey
244 East End Avenue
New York, New York 10021
212-555-1212

Objective: To obtain a position as a principal of a preparatory high school in the metropolitan area.

Experience
1987 to present
Assistant Principal, Clark Collegiate School, New York, New York
Serve as second highest academic officer and administrator of this 800-pupil preparatory school. Supervise a staff of 12 department chairmen and 15 administrative support personnel. Overhauled this school's programs in English and foreign languages. Work with teachers to develop and refine teaching methodologies and curricula and to select appropriate pedagogies. Developed an award-winning training program for student teachers. Wrote and received several grants to develop new academic programs, including one for special education classes.

1982 to 1987
English Department Chairman, The Wellington-Day School, New York, New York
Supervised a staff of 8 English teachers at this 600-pupil

preparatory school. Created and taught advanced placement courses for seniors. Developed after-school writing workshops led by several authors and editors. Created a work-study program for journalism students with major publications, including *The New York Times*. Developed Latin-based vocabulary-building classes.

1978 to 1982
English Teacher, The Wellington-Day School, New York, New York
Taught sophomore-, junior-, and senior-level English courses. Developed a remedial writing program for basic writers. Served as faculty advisor of award-winning student newspaper.

1973 to 1978
English Teacher, Harkness Preparatory High School, New York, New York
Taught sophomore-, junior-, and senior-level English courses at this 500-pupil preparatory school.

Education
1973 M.A. in English literature, Columbia University Graduate School of Arts and Sciences.

1972 B.A. in English literature, *summa cum laude,* Barnard College. Elected to Phi Beta Kappa.

Publications
"Lessons for Writing Teachers," *English Teachers' Journal,* Vol. 4, No. 4.
"Training New Teachers," *English Teachers' Journal,* Vol. 3, No. 2.
"An Illiterate Democracy," *The New York Times* op-ed page, Nov. 16, 1994.
"No Secrets," *Four Quarters Review* (short story), Vol. 8, No. 3.

Professional Associations
Member of National Council of Teachers of English.
Member of Modern Languages Association.
Editorial board member of *The Journal of Remediation.*

Chapter 19 Flyer

Put your swimming skills to the test, and possibly save a life, by signing up for lifeguard training. It's part of the Barrow Street School's afternoon program. Taught by the school's swimming coach, Jack Roth, these classes focus on the lifesaving techniques you must learn to be certified by the Red Cross. The classes will also cover basic first aid and water safety rules.

Junior Lifesaving: Tuesday afternoons, 3:30 to 5:30, March 5th through April 23rd.
For swimmers aged 14 and under with intermediate swimming skills.

Senior Lifesaving: Thursday afternoons, 3:30 to 5:30, March 7th through April 25th. For swimmers aged 15 and older with advanced swimming skills.

Chapter 20 Phone Book Advertisement

THE TEA ROOM
Tea, Desserts, Teaware
245 Madison Avenue
NYC
212.555.0001
www.tea_room.com

Pouchong Green, Assam, Ceylon, Darjeeling, Keemun, Lapsang/Souchong, English Breakfast, Irish Breakfast, Lady Londonderry, Prince of Wales, Russian Caravan, Earl Grey, Jasmine, Chrysanthemum, Formosa/Oolong, Gunpowder, Chamomile, Rose Hips, Iron Goddess, Vanilla, and dozens more rare and exotic teas.

Chapter 21 Logo

See illustrations in chapter.

Chapter 22 Newsletter

Flying Fish Spotted in The Windy City

By Elizabeth Jarmen

Let's face it, Chicago is famous for stockyards not fisheries. But times are changing. People are eating fish instead of red meat. Seafood is an important part of a heart-healthy diet, because it is low in cholesterol and fat.

We're proud that the freshest fish in Chicago can be found at Epicurean Delights. The arrival of fish farming, or Aquaculture as it is known among the professionals, has made Trout as commonly available as beef. We found a hatchery only hours away from the city. The fish is so fresh it tastes like the Trout has jumped out of the water and onto your plate!

Trout is wonderful when grilled whole over a mesquite flavored barbecue. The firm white flesh can also be filleted and boned, and then poached in white wine.

The really exciting news, however, is the introduction of Epicurean Delights' Flying Fish Service. Flying Fish is ordered by telephone and shipped by air to arrive the next day. It's the next best thing to catching it yourself! The quick turnaround time allows us to offer you Blue Catfish from Louisiana, Grouper from Florida, and Chinook Salmon from Washington state. We're hoping that our marine harvest inspires you to try new recipes.

Just think about Sea Bass delicately poached in a Court Bouillon of fresh herbs, such as Savory and Anise. Imagine tender medallions of Salmon encased in a crispy potato jacket. Anticipate just how succulent fresh Grouper can be when it is steamed in a parchment envelope with aromatic vegetables.

These recipes are particularly easy to try because they are available as prepared, ready-to-cook dishes from the Epicurean Delights kitchen. You just pop the fish into the oven, microwave, or skillet and enjoy a delicious meal ten minutes later. And though we may be prejudiced, we think our cold seafood salads, such as Lobster with Corn Relish and Shrimp with Green Onions are worthy of main course status. For busy people who care about the food they eat, fish is the ultimate high-quality fast food.

Guest Chef

Robbin Frances Cooks Food with a Philosophy

Our guest chef this month is Robbin Frances—a self-proclaimed Italophile. Having spent six years roaming the kitchens of Italy, the 31-year-old chef returned to New York three years ago (recipes in tow) to open L'Accademia, one of Manhattan's most successful small restaurants.

What keeps gourmets coming back to the three-star L'Accademia is Frances' commitment to using the freshest seasonal ingredients, many of which she buys from local farmers. Relying on producers close to home ("That means the Eastern seaboard") was a lesson she learned in Italy.

Frances' reliance on high-quality ingredients is part of a larger philosophy, one that can be summed up in three words: pure and simple. "Each ingredient in a dish should have integrity," she says. "I believe in simplicity, letting each flavor come through in all its vibrancy."

Chapter 23 Mail Order Catalog

Johnny-Jump-Up

Although these bright purple and yellow blooms look quite a lot like Pansies, Johnny-Jump-Ups are totally edible. The mild flavor is slightly sweet, making Johnny-Jump-Ups a perfect decoration for soft cheeses or cold fruit soups. Try combining goat cheese with Johnny-Jump-Ups and watercress.

You should plant Johnny-Jump-Ups in either full or partial sun at the first sign of thaw. And you can plan to enjoy both the sight and taste of the flowers in early spring. After the warm weather is over, you can still harvest these edible flowers. Simply order the potted plant instead of seeds. Our hot-house grown plants will bloom even in the dead of winter.

Nasturtium

Only in recent times has Nasturtium, or Tropaeolum minus, been considered a purely ornamental plant. Persians nibbled Nasturtium petals as early as 400 B.C. Nasturtiums reached their peak of popularity in the kitchens of 17th century Europe. The flowers, stems, and young leaves of this plant are edible. The flavor is peppery and has a marked similarity to watercress. Indeed, Nasturtium's tangy, slightly hot taste has made it a favorite salad ingredient of Nouvelle-cuisine chefs.

You should plant Nasturtium in the spring. The plants will begin to bloom in summer, but you can expect the harvest to last through fall. You can keep picked flowers fresh for several days by floating them in a bowl of water in the refrigerator.

Sweet Violet

A nosegay of Viola odorata is a gift of sweet affection. The purple blooms are, quite appropriately, a symbol of Venus. The Romans fermented crushed flowers to make a sweet wine, but modern-day cooks use crystallized blossoms as an edible decoration for desserts. Herbalists use an infusion made from flowers to cure insomnia.

Rather than offer seeds, we offer Violet seedlings instead, which can be transplanted to an outdoor site in spring. Once rooted, these perennials will return to bloom year after year. Indeed, you may find that the runners which Sweet Violets use for natural propagation invade other parts of your garden.

Johnny-Jump-Up Pricing Table Text

Seedlings (24)	#2234	2.50
Fresh flowers (1 lb.)	#2235	15.00
Plant in bloom	#2236	35.00

Nasturtium Pricing Table Text

Seedlings (24)	#3234	2.50
Fresh flowers (1 lb.)	#3235	15.00
Plant in bloom	#3236	35.00

Sweet Violet Pricing Table Text

Seedlings (24)	#4234	2.50
Fresh flowers (1 lb.)	#4235	15.00
Plant in bloom	#4236	35.00

Chapter 24 World Wide Web Site

Web Button Text

Home
Services
Tours
Cruises
Sports Trips
Family Trips

Company Profile

Adventure Travel specializes in unique vacations and tour packages to destinations the world over. Since its founding in 1986, Adventure Travel has booked thousands of vacations that range from the exotic to the quixotic. We welcome you to our Web site and look forward to helping you plan your next travel adventure. Please contact us with your questions or opinions at comments@adventuretravel.com.

The Paris-London Connection

TransBriton Airlines (800-555-0000) is offering a bonus for people who book a round-trip, 21-day, advance-purchase ticket to London. You will get a free round-trip ticket from London to Paris on the Eurostar Channel Tunnel train and a free car rental for one week. Round-trip fares from the East Coast start at $700; from the West Coast fares start at $900. This offer expires December 1, 1997.

A Budapest Celebration

Hungarian National Airlines (800-555-0004) invites you to celebrate Hungary's 1100th national anniversary. The airline is offering a one-week package to Budapest for $1100 per person, including round-trip airfare from New York, 6 nights and 7 days (including breakfast) at one of several four-star hotels, free sightseeing tours, one dinner at a four-star restaurant, and other attractions. This offer expires November 15, 1997.

The Asia/Pacific Extravaganza

The Golden Unicorn Hotel Corporation (800-555-0009) has several exciting packages for its chain of four-star hotels. Sample nightly rates are $250 in Hong Kong, $150 in Manila, $175 in Singapore, and $140 in Jakarta. All rates include continental breakfast, use of health and racquet club, late check-out, and free accommodations for children under the age of 12. This offer expires May 30, 1997.

Directory

Services
- Currency Exchange
- Airline Schedules
- Train Schedules
- Maps
- Weather Report
- Hotel Listings
- Guidebooks
- Travelers' Diary
- Restaurant Guide

Tours
- European Cities
- China
- New Zealand

Cruises
- Greek Isles
- Alaskan Summer
- QE 2

Sports Trips
- Scuba Diving
- Tennis Clinic
- Golf Tourneys

Family Trips
- Disney
- Grand Canyon
- Caribbean Resort

Chapter 25 Letterhead

See illustrations in chapter.

Chapter 26 Mail Merge Letter

Address List

First	Last	Address	City	State	ZIP
Lewis	Abelman	224 Rutledge Road	Richardson	TX	75081
Joan	Anderson	1440 Cactus Tree Road	Richardson	TX	75081
Craig	Bishop	10 Sylvan Drive	Richardson	TX	75081
Jim	Brown	19 Kings Point Road	San Marcos	TX	78667
Roscoe	Chandler	1850 Ingersoll Way	Richardson	TX	75081
Sandra	Clark	2246 Boulevard East	Austin	TX	78746
Ken	Diamond	159 Mulholland Drive	San Marcos	TX	78667
Margaret	Dumont	12 Rittenhouse Avenue	Austin	TX	78746
Joe	Ehrlich	1625 Mesa Street	Richardson	TX	75081
Howard	Friedman	200 Ocean Circle	San Marcos	TX	78667
Amy	Harte	36 Fortuna Avenue	Richardson	TX	75081
Dave	Howard	289 Olean Street	Austin	TX	78727
Steven	Jackson	153 Palm Court	Richardson	TX	75081
Charles	Jones	19 Emerson Circle	Richardson	TX	75081
Jackie	Prescott	1536 Windsor Circle	Richardson	TX	75081
Scott	Resnick	619 Albemarle Road	Richardson	TX	75081
Edward	Stern	18 Hollingswood Drive	Austin	TX	78727
Bob	Taylor	4239 Cardinal Street	Austin	TX	78746
Judy	Williams	7 Summer Street	Austin	TX	78746
Steve	Young	114 Franklin Avenue	San Marcos	TX	78667

Letter Text

February 12, 1997

First Last
Address
City, State ZIP

Dear Name,

Thank you for registering for Trophy Sporting Goods' Executive Sports Series.

Please note that the date of the first weekend workshop, Power Tennis, has been changed. The workshop will now start on Saturday, June 14th, at 9:00 a.m., rather than June 21st.

Participants will still meet tennis pro John Becker at the Richardson Tennis Center, which is just a short drive from Trophy Sporting Goods (see the enclosed map for detailed directions). Locker facilities will be available, so please bring a combination lock along with your equipment. Also, please be sure to wear tennis shoes with nonmarking soles.

We're confident that by the end of the weekend, you'll be a better tennis player. We look forward to seeing you at the workshop.

Cordially,

Marc M. Smith
Pro Shop/Special Events Manager

Registration

Power Tennis

Lewis	Abelman
Joan	Anderson
Craig	Bishop
Joe	Ehrlich
Howard	Friedman
Steven	Jackson
Charles	Jones
Edward	Stern

Fly Tying

Jim	Brown
Ken	Diamond
Dave	Howard
Steve	Young

Chapter 27 Business Form

See illustrations in chapter.

Chapter 28 Three-Fold Brochure

What is the Executive Sports Series?

The Executive Sports Series is a group of intensive weekend classes tailored to the interests and demanding schedules of busy executives and professionals. Offered by the Pro Shop at Trophy Sporting Goods, these classes are taught by seasoned pros and are designed to help you get the most out of your game.

Because enrollment is limited to eight people per class, you'll receive individualized instruction that focuses on the nuances of your sport and the skills you want to build. And because classes are held on weekends, they won't conflict with your business obligations.

Fly Tying

Imagine how proud you'll feel when you catch that trophy-winning fish with a fly you tied yourself! Under the guidance of master fly fisherman William Cruthers, you can learn the basics of the classic, and painstaking, art of tying flies.

By the end of the weekend, participants will have learned to tie at least a dozen different types of flies suitable for a variety of fishing conditions and species.

A list of required materials will be provided one week prior to class. Supplies may be purchased at Trophy Sporting Goods.

When: September 29th and 30th, 10:00 a.m. - 4:30 p.m.

Where: Trophy Sporting Goods Pro Shop

Price: $300 plus materials

Putting Power

You've avoided the sand trap and kept the ball out of the rough, but you're still giving up far too many strokes on the green. Trophy Sporting Goods' golf pro Emil Davis teaches you ten power tips designed to help you sink the ball into that little four-inch hole.

Videotapes of each session provide you with important feedback on your technique. The videotape is yours to keep after the weekend is over.

Only those with intermediate skills should register for this course. Participants are also required to bring their own equipment. Equipment rentals can be arranged through the Pro Shop at Trophy Sporting Goods.

When: August 8th and 9th, 9:00 a.m. - 5:00 p.m.

Where: West Hills Country Club

Price: $500

Reservations

Because we know how valuable your time is, we guarantee that by the end of class you'll see a significant improvement in your game or your skills--or your money back!

Space is limited, so reserve your spot for these special events today.

Stop by our store

Trophy Sporting Goods
15 Old Country Road

or call

214-555-1313
(ask for Brad Parker)

Ask for information about upcoming events on:

Tennis

Wilderness Camping

Squash

We accept American Express, Visa, MasterCard, and Diners Club. We also accept personal checks, with the proper identification.

Glossary of Desktop Publishing Terms

Aliasing   In computer graphics, the effect produced when display resolution is too coarse to minimize the jagged, or stair-step, appearance of certain design elements, such as diagonal lines, curves, and circles. Aliasing is most noticeable when the individual pixels forming an image are large enough to be perceived, in which case the image is said to be pixelated.

alignment   The placement of type relative to the margins. Also, the placement of an element relative to the margins or to another element. See also *center alignment; justified; left alignment; rag; right alignment.*

antialiasing   The use of intermediate shades or colors in gray-scale or color bitmapped images that trick the eye into seeing smooth lines.

ascender   That portion of a lowercase letter that rises above the main body (x-height) of the letter, such as the long strokes of *b, d,* and *h*. See also *descender.*

ASCII files   Plain text files that do not contain any formatting codes. ASCII files are used to exchange information among applications and operating systems that would otherwise generate incompatible file formats.

aspect ratio   The ratio of width to height of an image. For example, an aspect ratio of 2:1 indicates that the width equals twice the height. The aspect ratio is an important factor in maintaining the correct proportions of a graphic when it is printed, resized, or incorporated into another document.

attribute   A formatting characteristic of an object. An attribute can indicate style, color, or position. For example, boldface is a type attribute.

Bad break   A line break that creates an awkward hyphenation (for example, a hyphenated compound word that is broken). Also, a line break that is visually jarring (for example, a page that begins with the second half of a hyphenated word).

bad rag   A visually jarring shape of a text block created by very irregular line breaks in ragged-right text.

banner   A large publication tiled across several pages. Also, the masthead logo of a newspaper or other periodical. See also *masthead; tiling.*

baseline In the printing and display of characters, an imaginary horizontal line on which the base of each character (excluding descenders) is aligned.

bit Short for binary digit. The smallest unit of data handled by a computer.

bitmapped graphic A computer graphic that is stored as a collection of bits in memory locations; one or more bits correspond to a pixel on the screen. Bitmapped graphics are typical of paint programs, which treat images as collections of dots rather than as defined shapes. Note that fonts can be bitmapped. See also *vector graphic*.

blank A computer term sometimes used to describe the character entered by pressing the Spacebar. In desktop publishing, also refers to empty pages added to a publication in order to produce a correctly folded book. For example, if a book has seven pages, Publisher automatically adds an eighth blank page to produce an eight-page book.

bleed A portion of a printed image that extends beyond the trim edge of the page. A bleed either extends smoothly across two facing pages (because the image extends beyond the "trim" on the inside page edge) or prints to the very edge of the page (because the image extends beyond the trim on the outside page edge).

BMP (Windows Bitmap format) A standard file format in which pictures are stored as a collection of pixels or bits. BMP files typically contain 2, 16, 256, or a full range of colors (16 million).

body copy The main text of a story, excluding ancillary text such as headlines, pull quotes, and captions. Also called body text or running text.

boldface A type style that makes the text to which it is applied appear darker and heavier than the text would typically appear. **This sentence is printed in boldface.**

border A boundary edge that can print around text, graphics, or an entire page.

bullet A small shape, such as a dot or a box, used to set off a block of text or each item in a list.

byline The text line that credits the author of an article.

Callout A label that identifies an element in an illustration.

camera-ready Describes completed pages (containing text, photographs, and art) in a form that the printer can photograph for making printing plates.

cap height The height of a capital letter in a particular font and size.

carriage return The action that occurs when the Enter key is pressed. Also, an older term referring to typewriters and the return of the carriage to the left margin.

center alignment The alignment of characters or an object in the middle of a line, a page, or another defined area; in effect, the placement of an element or text block an equal distance from each margin or border.

center spread   The two-page layout appearing in the center of a multipage document.

CGM (Computer Graphics Metafile format)   A standard file format that uses a set of drawing instructions, or vector information, to describe a picture graphic. CGM files are supported by many illustration and desktop publishing programs, including Publisher. See also *vector graphic*.

character   An individual letter or symbol, either printing (for example, a period) or nonprinting (for example, a space).

clip art   A collection—either in a book or on a disk—of proprietary or public-domain photographs, diagrams, maps, drawings, and other graphics that can be "clipped" from the collection and incorporated into other documents.

Clipboard   A special memory resource maintained by an operating system such as Microsoft Windows 95. The Clipboard temporarily stores a copy of the last information that was copied or cut. A paste operation passes data from the Clipboard to the current location.

color primaries   In both paper-based printing and computer graphics, a group of colors that are mixed to produce all other colors. In computer graphics, which rely on the additive color method, the primaries are red, green, and blue. In paper-based printing, which uses a subtractive color method, the primary colors are cyan, magenta, yellow, and black.

color separation   A process whereby the elements in a layout are divided into their color components. Typically, separations are either spot-color or four-color. For a spot-color separation, all elements that will print with black ink are placed on one piece of paper (or film), and all elements that will print with a spot color are placed on a separate piece of paper (or film). Publisher can generate spot-color separations for up to two spot colors plus black; it does not produce four-color separations. For a four-color (or process) separation, all colors in a document are divided into percentages of the process colors: cyan, yellow, magenta, and black. When these four colors are overlapped, they produce a wide variety of color combinations.

column rules   Thin, usually hairline, lines separating two columns of text.

composite   A printout of a color-separated page that combines all colors onto one piece of paper. On a black-and-white printer, a spot color is converted to shades of gray.

condensed font   A font style that reduces the width of each character and then sets the characters closer together than their normal spacing would allow. See also *expanded font*.

continued notice   A line of text indicating the page on which an article continues. Also, the carryover line on a page that identifies the article being continued. See also *jump head*.

copy   Text used in a printed document.

copy fitting   The process of fitting a story to a layout. Methods include editing the content, changing the text attributes, and modifying the document design.

copyright   Ownership of a work by the writer, artist, or publisher. A copyright symbol (©) is also a character in the extended alphabet.

crop   In preparing a graphic or a photograph, to cut off or hide part of the image.

crop marks   Intersecting lines that mark where paper will be trimmed to form pages in the final document.

Descender

Descender   That portion of a lowercase letter that falls below the baseline, such as the long strokes of *g* or *y*. See also *ascender*.

dingbat   A small graphical element used for decorative purposes in a document. Some fonts, such as TrueType Wingdings, consist entirely of dingbats. See also *symbol font*.

discretionary hyphen   See *optional hyphen*.

display type   Headings and titles in documents, formatted to stand out from other text on the page. Sans-serif typefaces, such as Arial and Helvetica, often work well for display type.

dither   A process in which small dots of two or more colors are juxtaposed to create the optical illusion of a new color. For example, intermingling yellow and blue dots produces the illusion of green. Dithering is often employed when a computer-generated image contains 256 or fewer colors. It is also a common printing technique, referred to as mezzotinting (for an irregular dither pattern) or halftoning (for a regular dither pattern). See also *halftone*.

dot-matrix printer   Any printer that produces characters made up of dots and that uses a wire-pin print head.

dots per inch (dpi)   A measure of screen and printer resolution expressed as the number of dots that a device can display or print per inch.

downloadable font   An individual font that can be installed in a desktop publishing system. The font information must be sent (or downloaded) from the computer system to the printer's memory before a document can be printed. Also called a soft font.

drop cap   An enlarged initial letter that drops below the baseline in the first line of body text. Publisher refers to a drop cap as a fancy first letter.

drop shadow   A special effect that places a black or gray duplicate of a selected object behind it and offsets it slightly, creating a shadow.

DRW (Micrografx Draw format)   A standard file format that is common to several Micrografx graphics programs, including Micrografx Designer and Micrografx Draw. DRW files typically store information as a series of drawing instructions but can also contain bitmapped information.

dummy   Placeholder text occupying a space in a layout. Also refers to a mock-up of the final bound publication.

duplex printing   The ability to print both sides of a piece of paper in one pass. This is a hardware function found in certain models of laser printers.

Ellipsis A set of three dots (...) usually indicating an omission. An ellipsis in printed text indicates the omission of one or more words.

em dash A punctuation mark (—) generally used to signify a change or an interruption in the train of thought expressed in a sentence or to set off an explanatory comment. In Publisher, if the Automatically Use Smart Quotes option is active, an em dash is automatically inserted whenever you type two consecutive hyphens.

en dash A punctuation mark (–) used to indicate a range of dates or numbers (for example, 1980–90) or to separate the elements of a compound adjective, one part of which is hyphenated or consists of two words (for example, pre–Civil War).

EPS (Encapsulated PostScript format) A file format that contains vector information (a series of drawing instructions). An EPS image prints with smooth rather than jagged edges but can be viewed on screen only as a low-resolution bitmapped image. An EPS file can be created in a graphics program that produces PostScript code. An EPS image does not print on non-PostScript printers.

expanded font A font style that increases the width of each character and then sets the characters farther apart than their normal spacing would allow. See also *condensed font*.

extended characters Characters in the typesetter's alphabet other than the characters found on the keyboard. They include accented foreign-language letters and copyright symbols.

Fancy first letter A drop cap or an initial cap.

fill In computer graphics, to paint the inside of an enclosed figure, such as a circle, with a color or a pattern. The portion of the shape that can be colored or patterned is the fill area.

flush Aligned or even with, as in flush left or flush right text.

flush left Aligned along the left margin.

flush right Aligned along the right margin.

folio A printed page number.

font Traditionally, all the characters available in a particular typeface (design) and size. A font is used for on-screen display and for printed output. Often used interchangeably with *typeface*.

footer One or more identifying lines printed at the bottom of a page. A footer might be printed on the first page, all pages, every even page, or every odd page, and it might be centered or aligned with the left or the right margin. It can include the folio, the date, the name of the author, or the title of a document.

format The overall appearance of a publication, including page size, binding method, page layout, and design elements such as margins, number of columns, headline treatment, and so on. Also, in desktop publishing, to format text or a graphic element means to change the appearance, or specifications, of the selected object.

formatting The elements of a style that determine the appearance of text, a graphic, or a page in a publication. For example, when you format text, you apply character and paragraph styles to the copy. When you format a graphic, you apply attributes such as a drop shadow, fill pattern, line weight, and color. When you format a page, you apply global attributes such as page size, page orientation, and page margins.

four-color separation See *color separation*.

FPO (For Position Only) A low-resolution copy of artwork placed in a document to indicate the position of the actual art that will be stripped in by the printer.

frame In Publisher, a space or box in which you place text or a graphic image and to which you can assign formatting attributes, such as a drop shadow and a border.

Graphic A representation of an object, such as a graph, a chart, an illustration, or a picture, on a two-dimensional surface.

gray scale A progressive series of shades ranging from black through white. Gray scales are used in computer graphics to add detail to images. The number of shades of gray depends on the number of bits used to describe the color of each pixel (dot) in the image. For example, 2 bits per pixel produces 4 unique shades of gray; 6 bits per pixel produces 64 distinct shades on a gray scale; and 8 bits produces 256 shades of gray. The way in which gray-scale images are represented on screen and on paper var-

ies with the capabilities of your monitor and printer as well as with the functions of the application program.

greek text In traditional design, randomly generated text—and even nonsense words—used as dummy type in the early stages of the design process. In computer graphics, greek text also refers to the screen display of type that is too small to be drawn properly. Instead of displaying fully formed letters, the graphics application presents a screen display of symbols or gray lines.

grid The division of a page into regular rectangular areas to aid in arranging, measuring, and aligning text and picture elements.

gutter The space between two rows or columns. Also, the margin between two facing pages. Also called an alley.

Hairline rule A very thin line. In desktop publishing, the thickness of a hairline rule varies depending on the resolution (measured in dots per inch) of the printer.

halftone The printed reproduction of a photograph or other illustration as a set of tiny, evenly spaced spots of variable diameter that, when printed, look like shades of gray. Many printers used in desktop publishing, notably laser printers and digital imagesetters, are able to print halftone images. Color halftones employ the same technique as black-and-white halftones, except that spots of four primary colors (cyan, magenta, yellow, and black) are printed over one another to simulate a full-color spectrum. See also *dither*.

hanging indent   A paragraph style in which the first line extends to the left of subsequent lines.

hard return   A line break, created when you press the Enter key, that signals the end of a paragraph.

header   One or more identifying lines printed at the top of a page that might include the title, author, chapter, issue date, and folio. A specific computer-related use refers to a descriptive section of an EPS file. Because an EPS picture cannot be viewed on screen at high resolution, a low-resolution, bitmapped representation of the image (in TIFF format) is usually stored in the portion of a file called a header. If the EPS header does not contain a bitmapped image, the EPS file appears on screen as a simple box with an identifying filename.

headline   The title of a story.

hue   In computer graphics, one of three components used to specify color. In the HSL (Hue, Saturation, Luminescence) color model, hue refers to the pure color. Hues are arranged around a circle, each degree on the circle identifying a unique color. For example, 0 is red, 120 is green, and 240 is blue. See also *saturation; luminescence.*

hyphenation   Breaking a word with a hyphen after a syllable and continuing the word on the next line. Used to create fully justified text or to produce a more visually appealing rag.

Image Color Matching (ICM)   The color management system in Microsoft Windows 95.

imposition   The arrangement of several pages on a larger sheet of paper in the proper order for printing and binding.

indent   Moving a line of type to the right to indicate the beginning of a new paragraph. Alternatively, adjusting the position of the left and right text margins. See also *hanging indent.*

initial cap   A first letter set in an enlarged and sometimes decorative font for graphical emphasis.

ink-jet printer   A nonimpact printer that fires tiny drops of ink at the paper.

inside margin   The space between the binding edge of the page and the text or other design element. See also *outside margin.*

italics   A type style in which the characters are evenly slanted toward the right. Italics are commonly used for emphasis, foreign-language words and phrases, titles of works, technical terms, display type, and captions. *This sentence is printed in italics.*

JPEG (Joint Photographic Experts Group format)   A bitmapped file format used to store photographic images. JPEG offers a high degree of compression.

jump head   A design element used to identify a story continued from another, usually earlier, page in a multipage publication. When a story flows from page to page, especially on noncontiguous pages, it is said to jump from one page to another.

jump line   See *continued notice*.

justified   Type that is flush—that is, aligns along both the right and left margins. Desktop publishing applications justify text by inserting extra space between the words and characters in each line. Some applications allow you to justify text vertically to create columns of equal length.

Kerning   The process of adjusting the space between a pair of letters. Typically, kerning is applied to make the spacing around letters more balanced to increase legibility. Letter pairs that usually need kerning include *AV, WA,* and *YO.*

kicker   A phrase preceding a headline that provides identifying information about the story.

knockout   A printing technique in which underlying colors are removed from a printing plate to ensure that overlying colors print as brightly as possible. For example, a red circle positioned over a blue rectangle would turn purple when printed if the underlying blue ink were not removed prior to printing. Knockouts are the opposite of surprinted, or overprinted, images.

Landscape orientation   The horizontal orientation of a page in which the width of the page is greater than its height. See also *portrait orientation*.

laser printer   An electrophotographic printer that is based on the technology used by photocopiers. A focused laser beam and a rotating mirror are used to draw an image of the desired page on a photosensitive drum. Laser printers typically have a resolution of 300 or 600 dpi.

layout   The arrangement of text and graphics on a page.

leader   A row of dots, hyphens, or other characters used to lead the eye across a printed page to related information (for example, to connect chapter titles with page numbers in a table of contents). Also, a rule that moves the eye from a label to the part of the illustration it describes.

leading   The distance between lines of type, measured from the baseline (bottom) of one line to the baseline of the next; derived from the traditional typesetting practice of inserting thin bars of lead between lines of metal type.

left alignment   The alignment of characters or an object with the left margin or the left boundary of a defined area.

letterspacing   The amount of space between letters. Adjusting letterspacing can make type more legible, create artistic effects, or fit more words on a line. Publisher refers to letterspacing as Spacing Between Characters. Also known as tracking.

line spacing   See *leading*.

line weight   The thickness of a rule, measured in points.

Linotronic   The brand name of a series of high-resolution, professional-quality imagesetters capable of printing at resolutions of 1200 or 2400 dpi.

logo   A design or graphic of a company, product, or publication name.

luminescence   In computer graphics, one of three components used to specify color. In the HSL (Hue, Saturation, Luminescence) color model, luminescence refers to the lightness of a color, where 0 represents black and 100 represents white. Publisher refers to darker colors (with low luminescence values) as shades and to lighter colors (with high luminescence values) as tints. See also *hue; saturation*.

Margin   The distance from the edge of the paper to the image area occupied by text and graphics.

masking   See *knockout*.

masthead   Traditionally, the listing of staff, ownership, and subscription information for a periodical. See also *banner*.

mechanical   A camera-ready pasteup of artwork. A mechanical includes type, line art, and FPO artwork. See also *camera-ready; FPO (For Position Only)*.

metafile   A graphics file format that can include bit-mapped or vector information or both. The EPS format is a metafile format.

mirrored pages   A layout effect in which the background page elements, such as the header and folio, are positioned at opposite sides on facing pages.

mock-up   The arrangement of elements on a page for the purpose of examining page layout.

moiré   A distracting pattern that results when two geometrically regular patterns (such as two sets of parallel lines or two halftone screens) are superimposed, especially at an acute angle. Usually the result of scanning a previously screened halftone.

monospace font   A font in which each character occupies a fixed amount of horizontal space regardless of its width—an *i*, for example, takes as much room as an *m*. Also called a fixed-width font. See also *proportional spacing*.

Nonbreaking hyphen   A manually inserted hyphen that identifies a compound word or a hyphenated name that you don't want broken if it falls at the end of a line. See also *optional hyphen*.

Object-oriented graphic   See *vector graphic*.

offset printing   A printing process in which ink is transferred (or offset) from a metal plate to a rubber blanket and then from the blanket to paper.

OLE (Object Linking and Embedding)   Pronounced "oh-lay," a way to transfer and share information among applications. An object (such as an image file) can be either linked or embedded in a document. Linking places a reference to the object in the document; any changes made to the object will be seen in the document. Embedding places a *copy* of the object in the document. Changes made to the original object will not be seen in the document unless the object is updated; changes made to the copied object will not affect the original.

optional hyphen A hyphen inserted manually when you press Ctrl-hyphen. An optional hyphen shows on screen and on the printed page only if it is used to break a word at the end of a line. See also *nonbreaking hyphen*.

orphan The last line of a paragraph printed alone at the top of a page or column of text. Good design practice avoids orphans. See also *widow*.

outside margin The space between the outside trim (page boundary) and the text. See also *inside margin*.

Page layout The size, orientation, number of pages, and margins for a document. See also *imposition*.

page size The dimensions of a publication's pages. In commercial printing, the size of the page after it is cut during the binding process.

pasteup Traditionally, the process of assembling mechanicals by pasting type and line art in place. In desktop publishing, traditional pasteup has largely been replaced by electronic page assembly.

PCD (Kodak Photo CD format) A standard file format that is used to store photographic images on a CD-ROM disc. PCD files store information in bitmapped form.

PCX (PC Paintbrush format) A standard file format for bitmapped pictures. PCX files typically contain 2, 16, or 256 colors or shades of gray.

pica A unit of measurement equal to 12 points, or approximately 1/6 inch. Picas are used to specify page measurements such as paragraph indents, text line length, column width, and margin size. See also *point*.

pixel Acronym for picture element. The smallest dot or display unit on a computer screen. The clarity of screen resolution depends on the number of pixels per inch on the monitor. A typical VGA monitor displays 72 pixels per inch.

plate A sheet of flexible metal (or even paper) containing areas that are receptive to ink (usually in the form of text and pictures) and areas that are not receptive to ink. Printing plates receive and then transfer ink to blankets (or directly to paper) during the printing process. The printing process requires a separate plate for each color. For example, a spot-color printing job would require two plates: one for black and one for the spot color.

point A typographical unit of measurement equal to 1/12 pica, or approximately 1/72 inch. Points are often used to indicate character height, letterspacing, and leading. See also *pica*.

portrait orientation The vertical orientation of a page in which the height of the page is greater than its width. See also *landscape orientation*.

PostScript A graphics language, developed by Adobe Systems, Inc., that is both resolution and device independent. That is, this format allows the same PostScript file to be printed to a 300-dpi laser printer, a 1270-dpi Linotronic imagesetter, or any other PostScript-compatible device.

printer font   A font that is stored in the permanent memory of the printer. Also called a resident font.

process colors   The four primary inks, which are cyan, yellow, magenta, and black (CYMK). They are used in the commercial printing process to create a wide spectrum of colors. If you want to reproduce color photographs, you must separate the colors in the picture (using either traditional photographic processes or a color separation program) into the appropriate percentages of cyan, yellow, magenta, and black.

proof   A printout used for the review and correction of a document.

proportional spacing   Letterspacing that is proportional to the width of the character. The letter *w,* for example, takes up more space than the letter *i.* See also *monospace font.*

pull quote   A quotation copied from the body of an article, often set in a larger point size than the body copy and emphasized by rules or boxes, or indented from both margins. Also called a breakout, lift out, or teaser.

Queue   A lineup of elements or files waiting to be processed. The most common queue in Windows 95 is the printing queue, which is created when multiple files are sent to the same printer.

Rag   The shape created by the uneven line breaks in text that is aligned along only one margin. See also *justified; ragged left; ragged right.*

ragged left   Text alignment that is even, or flush, with the right margin and uneven on the left. See also *right alignment.*

ragged right   Text alignment that is even, or flush, with the left margin and uneven on the right. See also *left alignment.*

recto   The right-hand page of a spread. A recto is always an odd-numbered page. See also *verso.*

registration   The alignment of two or more elements, such as two objects of different colors, so that they appear seamless. Misaligned objects are said to be out of register.

resident font   A font that is stored in the permanent memory of the printer.

resolution   The clarity of detail visible on screen or in the final printout, expressed as dots per inch (dpi). In printed material, the resolution depends on the printer's capacity. For example, laser printers typically print at 600 dpi.

right alignment   The alignment of characters or an object with the right margin or the right boundary of a defined area.

roman   Any typeface or type style in which the characters are upright. See also *italics.*

rule   A line printed above, below, or to the side of an element, either to set the item off from the remainder of the page or to improve the look of the page. The thickness of a rule is typically measured in points.

running foot See *footer.*

running head See *header.*

Sans serif Literally, "without stroke." Describes any typeface in which the characters have no serifs (the short lines or ornaments at the ends of each letter). Sans-serif typefaces are used frequently as display type.

saturation In computer graphics, one of three components used to specify color. In the HSL (Hue, Saturation, Luminescence) color model, saturation refers to the intensity of a color, where 0 is no color (a neutral gray) and 100 is pure color. See also *hue; luminescence.*

scalable font Also known as a vector, or outline, font. The term refers to any font that can be scaled to produce characters in varying sizes. All TrueType fonts are examples of scalable font technology.

scale As a verb, to enlarge or reduce a graphic object, such as a vector drawing, a bitmapped photograph, or an outline character font, while maintaining the object's original aspect ratio, or proportional size. See also *aspect ratio.*

scanner An input device that uses light-sensing equipment to scan paper or other media (such as 35-mm transparencies), translating the pattern of light and dark (or color) into a digital signal—or bitmap—that can be manipulated by graphics software. See also *TWAIN.*

screen The process of creating tonal variations by printing percentages of black or another color. In traditional printing, meshlike screens were used to convert continuous tone images (such as photographs) into a regular grid of dots that could be reproduced on a printing press. When a screen of a specific frequency (that is, a certain fineness or coarseness of the dot pattern) is applied to a photograph, it creates a halftone picture. When a screen is applied to a solid color, it creates an area with an even, or flat, tint. See also *halftone.*

script A typeface that simulates handwriting.

separations See *color separation.*

serif Describes any of the short lines or ornaments at the ends of a letter. A serif typeface is usually easier to read—especially in large blocks of text—than a sans-serif typeface.

service bureau A commercial business that processes computer files on a high-resolution typesetter, such as the Linotronic, and generates camera-ready copy or film.

shading In traditional graphic arts, a particular color variation produced by mixing black with a pure color. In computer graphics, a color-mixing method that varies the intensity or brightness of a color.

shadow See *drop shadow.*

sidebar A smaller, self-contained story inside or adjacent to a larger one, usually boxed, with its own headline to set it apart from the main text.

small caps A font of uppercase letters that are smaller than the standard uppercase letters in that typeface. THIS SENTENCE IS SET IN CAPS AND SMALL CAPS.

spooling In printing, the method of storing chunks of data in memory or on disk until the printer is ready to process them.

spot color The second color used in a two-color printing job. Typically, a spot color is a flat tint of color and is specified by a number in a standard color model such as the Pantone Matching System (PMS). See also *color separation*.

spread Two facing pages in a publication.

story In Publisher, all the text in an article, whether it is contained in one text frame or a series of linked frames.

style sheet A set of instructions in some word processing applications used to apply character, paragraph, and page-layout formats to a document.

subhead A subordinate title or headline.

surprinting Literally, "overprinting." During the printing process, the superimposition of one color over another color. Small black text is typically surprinted over colors to avoid registration problems. See also *knockout; registration*.

symbol font A special typeface that replaces the characters normally accessible from the keyboard with symbols, such as the letters of the Greek alphabet or algebraic or commercial symbols. See also *dingbat*.

Template In desktop publishing, a ready-made publication design that provides formatting, such as a layout grid and type formats, and that can be reused.

text The language content of a page or document, as distinguished from the graphics elements.

text styles In Publisher, a collection of text formatting attributes, including font, point size, alignment, line spacing, and letterspacing. Text styles can be named, saved, and reused. When a text style is altered, the changes are applied to all the text in a document with that style.

TIFF (Tagged Image File Format) A standard file format commonly used for scanning, storage, and interchange of bitmapped, gray-scale, and color images.

tiling A printing function that enables you to print oversized pages in sections, or tiles. Each section is printed on a single sheet of paper. See also *banner*.

tint A percentage of black or another color used to create tonal variations. Tints mix with the paper color (usually white) to create lighter tonal values. Also called a tone. See also *color separation; halftone; screen; spot color*.

tracking See *letterspacing*.

trim size See *page size*.

TWAIN A cross-platform interface developed jointly by Aldus (now part of Adobe Systems), Caere, Eastman Kodak, Hewlett-Packard, and Logitech. Used for acquiring images captured by compatible scanners, video frame grabbers, and digital cameras.

typeface Traditionally, a specific named design (including slant and line thickness) for a set of characters. Arial and Times Roman are examples of typefaces. A typeface family contains a group of related typefaces, such as Arial, Arial Black, Arial Narrow, and Arial Rounded MT Bold. Often used interchangeably with *font*.

type size The size of printed characters, usually measured in points.

type style The overall design of a typeface or typeface family. Also refers to the obliqueness, or the slant, of a typeface—usually roman (upright) or italic (slanted).

Vector graphic An object that is created as a collection of drawn lines, rather than as a pattern of individual dots, or pixels. Mathematical descriptions determine the position, length, and direction of these lines. See also *bitmapped graphic*.

verso The left-hand page of a spread. A verso is always an even-numbered page. See also *recto*.

Weight The density of letters, traditionally described as light, regular, bold, extra bold, and so on. Also, the thickness of a rule, measured in points.

widow A single word, a portion of a word, or a few short words left on a line by themselves at the end of a paragraph. A widow is considered visually undesirable on the printed page. See also *orphan*.

WMF (Windows Metafile format) A standard file format that is common to Windows-based programs. WMF files store information as a series of drawing instructions.

WPG (WordPerfect Graphics format) A standard file format generated by WordPerfect. WPG files store information as a series of drawing instructions.

wraparound text Text that surrounds a graphic. Also called runaround text.

X-height In typography, the height of the lowercase letter *x* in a particular font. The x-height represents the height of the body of a lowercase letter, excluding ascenders (such as the top of the letter *b*) and descenders (such as the tail of the letter *g*). The bottom of the x-height is at the baseline of a character.

Index

Page numbers in italics refer to figures and tables.

boundaries
hidden, 22
text frame, *80*
toggling display of, 25
using to position objects, 22
white, around WordArt, 381
boxes
adding BorderArt to, 165
applying line borders to, 162–63
flashing red, 425
brochures, *466*
addressing with mail merge, 474
creating front cover, 469–71
creating interior, 475–77
creating return address, 473–74
creating second panel, 471–73
editing text, 477–78
folding, 478, 479
inserting picture in, 470
inserting text in, 472–73, 476
mailing, 473
page setup, 467–68
printing, 479
replacing picture, 471–72
bulleted lists, 105
in ads, 373
creating for home page, 429–30
formatting guidelines for Web
publications, *230*
bullets
adding, 374
decorative, 105, 166
designs, 167
inserting, 430
business forms
creating header, 458–60
creating order information area, 462

creating order table, 462–64
creating vendor information area,
460–61
filling out electronically, 465
inserting address/phone information,
459–60
page setup, 457–58
printing, 465
purchase order form, *456*
saving as template, 465
using background for, 323
using letterhead as template for, 457–58
using tables for, 461
buttons. *See also* commands
Border, *148*
command, 9
Find, 187
Find File, 30, 31
Group, 61
Object Color, *149*, 412
option, 9
Page Options, 286
Preview Web Site, 238
Shadow, *148*
text frame, *89*

Caching, *226*
camera-ready art, 374
captions, 400
adding to home page photos, 429
card stock, 330
catalogs. *See* mail order catalogs
cells. *See* table cells
centering
logos, 382
objects, 72, 157

rules, 408
text vertically
in cells, 354
in frames, 344
CGM Graphic Import dialog box, *174*
Character dialog box, 94, 423
character formatting, 93
basic options, 93–94
changing text, 94
kerning, 96–97
maintaining, 95
overriding, 95
shortcuts, 95
spacing, 95–97
WordArt design options, 131–33
characters. *See also* fonts; special
characters
applying shadows to individual,
172
appropriate for letters, 452
baseline of, 107
changing font, *94*
changing point size of, *94*
cropping, 200
fancy first letters, 97–99, 394
adding to design library, 414
creating, 411
placement of, 411
spacing, 95–97
spacing between. *See* letterspacing
check boxes, 9
Check Spelling command, 117
Check Spelling feature, 327
circles, drawing true, 156
clicking, 4. *See also* double-clicking;
right-clicking
compared with double-clicking, 214

About the Author

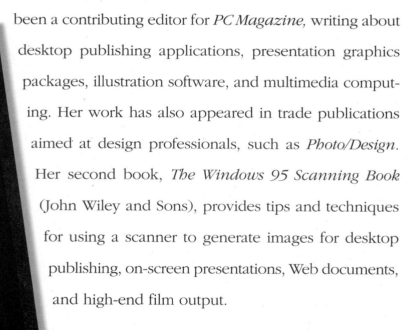

Luisa Simone is a New York–based consultant, teacher, and journalist specializing in computer graphics. For the past eight years, she has been a contributing editor for *PC Magazine,* writing about desktop publishing applications, presentation graphics packages, illustration software, and multimedia computing. Her work has also appeared in trade publications aimed at design professionals, such as *Photo/Design.* Her second book, *The Windows 95 Scanning Book* (John Wiley and Sons), provides tips and techniques for using a scanner to generate images for desktop publishing, on-screen presentations, Web documents, and high-end film output.